ohn's Croft

Pump

SunDial

N 78
B.M.80.8

E

N

H

I

85

L

L

Rocky Park Buildings

Greenhill Cottage

BM.84.7

Deer Park Oriental Buildings

93

Woodlands

Baptist Chapel
(Particular)
(Seats for 500)

Harding Villas

Weston
Villa

D I N C   S T R E E T

Methodist
Chapel

GREENHILL SCHOOL, TENBY
1896 — 1964

GREENHILL SCHOOL TENBY

1896 — 1964

An Educational and Social History

WILFRED HARRISON
M.B.E., M.A.

CARDIFF
UNIVERSITY OF WALES PRESS
1979

© UNIVERSITY OF WALES PRESS, 1979

British Library Cataloguing in Publication Data

Harrison, Wilfred
    Greenhill School Tenby, 1896-1964.
    1. Greenhill School—History
    I. Title
    373.429'63   LF1255.T

    ISBN 0-7083-0691-8

PRINTED IN WALES
BY THE CAMBRIAN NEWS (ABERYSTWYTH) LTD.

TO

VIDA, MIRANDA,

ANNA AND JOHN

CONTENTS

vii

Appendices

LIST OF MAPS AND DIAGRAMS

The maps are based upon the Ordnance Survey Maps with sanction of the Controller of Her Majesty's Stationery Office, Crown copyright reserved.

LIST OF ILLUSTRATIONS

ix

AUTHOR'S PREFACE

The older seaside town of Tenby, which was transformed into a Victorian holiday resort and further modified by changing conditions in the twentieth century, has always had a resident population of under 5,000. Together with the neighbouring parishes, it provides a manageable area for a detailed local study of the history of education. In common with various other towns in Wales, it benefited from the establishment of state-aided education and through the Welsh Intermediate Education Act 1889 and its implementation through a County Scheme. Common to all schools were certain academic requirements, matters of finance, school government, staffing, and, after 1896, inspection and examination by the Central Welsh Board. In due course, the fortunes of all were affected by a series of Education Acts and official regulations which were implemented by the Local Education Authorities down to the far-reaching re-organisation in the second half of the present century.

These events were interwoven with the political, social and economic history of the period, including the impact of two World Wars and periodic depressions, changes in agriculture and industry, a revolution in transport and striking improvements in the techniques of communications, outstanding scientific discoveries, advances in medicine and public health, the accompanying changes in human activities at work, at home and at leisure, and the arrival of the nuclear age.

Although the County Intermediate Schools (Grammar Schools after the 1944 Education Act) were bound by national legislation and by powers vested in the Local Education Authorities, their history was influenced by local circumstances, which differed from one township to another. In the course of this book, the above changes are described, where necessary, to provide a background to the story of Greenhill School, Tenby. The history of this school provides an illustration of how things worked out in practice. An account is given of local society in the late nineteenth century, of educational facilities available in the town down to that time, of townspeople who worked for the

xi

siting of an Intermediate School in Tenby, and of the difficulties they encountered before and after the school was opened.

The author writes from personal experience gained in service at Greenhill School from 1928 onwards, and with the help of official and other records and of personal reminiscences—many of them from Old Pupils—he traces the fortunes of the school during the course of three headships.

ACKNOWLEDGEMENTS

The author wishes to acknowledge the assistance of the following in providing access to various records: the Head Master (Mr. L. G. Hill) and Governors of Greenhill School, Tenby; the Tenby Borough Council; the National Library of Wales (through Mr. B. G. Owens); the Legal Division of the Welsh Office; the Legal and Architect's Departments of the Pembrokeshire County Council; the former Pembrokeshire Local Education Authority, its Director and staff; Miss Maureen Patch and the staff of the Pembrokeshire Record Office; the Tenby Museum Committee; the proprietors and staff of the *Tenby Observer;* Messrs. Lowless and Lowless, Solicitors, (through Mr. P. J. Davies); the Library of the University College of Wales, Aberystwyth, and Miss M. H. Bigwood of the same College for valuable cartographic assistance.

He also acknowledges the drawings of Terence Johns and the photographic work of Messrs. W. English, Fred Rose, Peter Davies, Michael Brace, Douglas Hardy (Five Arches Press), Eric Copland, Squibbs' Studios, and the late H. Mortimer Allen, Arthur Squibbs and Angus G. Athoe.

Many former colleagues and Greenhillians, both those mentioned in the text and many others, have contributed reminiscences and loaned or presented photographs.

Mention must be made of those who have been in close consultation with the author, who have read all or parts of the typescript and have made helpful suggestions: Mrs. Helen Bleines, Mrs. Marjorie Hugh, Miss Evelyn Ward, the late Dr. William Thomas, Sir Frederick Tymms, the Rev. O. Calvin Thomas, Dr. J. Howell Daniels, Dr. Ronald F. Walker, and Messers. Wynford Davies (former Director of Education for Pembrokeshire), W. Gwyn Thomas, and Denis Hullah, the last of whom worked with enthusiasm and infinite patience in the task of making the project known among Old Pupils.

The publication of this work has been made possible through its acceptance by the University of Wales Press Board under the Chairmanship of Sir Goronwy Daniel. The guidance of the Board and of two successive Directors and their staff, together with the skill and attention devoted to the preparation of the volume by the printers, are greatly appreciated. The generous subscriptions, which have kept down the retail price of the book, are listed separately.

Special thanks are due to Professor Emeritus Emrys G. Bowen, whose initial interest in the project led to its consideration by the Press Board. His wide experience, sound advice and practical assistance have proved invaluable both in the appraisal and presentation of the material and in the production of maps and graphs.

The preparation and writing of this book owe much to the local knowledge, criticism and inspiration provided by my wife, Vida (herself a former Greenhillian), who also assisted with the Index.

CHAPTER I

THE LOCAL BACKGROUND

'There is a fine fortress on the broad ocean
Unyielding stronghold, sea around its edge'
(Translated from the Welsh poem
'Etmic Dinbych', c.875 A.D.)

This introductory chapter is intended as a 'backcloth' to the story of educational institutions in Tenby. Accordingly, while the earlier history of the town will receive a somewhat general treatment, more detailed attention will be given to social conditions in the nineteenth century, particularly during the last decade when this Victorian holiday resort approached the zenith of its fame and attraction and when the Tenby County Intermediate School was born.

Tenby occupies a unique situation on the western shore of Carmarthen Bay. John Leland, King Henry VIII's Antiquary, noticed in the course of his itinerary c.1536-39: 'Tinbigh town stondith on a main rokke, but not veri hy, and the Severn Se so gulfeth in about hit, that at the ful se, almost the thirde part of the toune is inclosid with water.' Much of the town rests upon a peninsula of carboniferous limestone, with cliffs rising in places to some ninety feet above the sea. At the eastern extremity and joined to the rest by a narrow isthmus is the promontory known as Castle Hill, possibly the site of the original Dinbych (Little Fort) extolled in an anonymous Welsh poem in the ninth century and later mentioned in an early version of the Welsh laws. From Dinbych, through various mutations, the name 'Tenby' was derived. Therefore it seems likely that an early settlement of that name, close to the sandy cove which was destined to become the harbour, existed in the Welsh kingdom of Dyfed. Until the early nineteenth century a tidal pill enclosed the town at full tide on its westward side, thereby adding greatly to its defensive potentialities in early times. These physical features influenced the growth of Tenby—the lay-out of its fortifications, its street plan, its communications with the outside world, whether by land or water, its fortunes as

1

a port and a fishery, and in the nineteenth and twentieth centuries its development as a holiday resort.

In the late eleventh and early twelfth centuries the southern lowlands of Wales were penetrated by Norman invaders, who built castles, established lordships and brought non-Welsh elements into the area which the Elizabethan William Camden described as 'Anglia Transwalliana' (England beyond Wales). The lordship of Pembroke was established and under its successive holders—the de Clares, the Marshals and the de Valences—the little port of Tenby grew as part of their demesne. A castle was erected to protect the harbour and its approaches, and the Town Wall was constructed enclosing a 'new town', with its burgages, on the grid-iron plan. At the centre was St. Mary's Church, which was enlarged several times during its long history. The properties which closely encircled it, leaving only a narrow alley way round the fabric, remained until demolition took place in the nineteenth century. Outside the walls were founded the Magdalen and St. John's hospitals. The available evidence suggests that William de Valence, Earl of Pembroke, was responsible for the 'new town' and its fortifications. About 1290 he and his wife Joanna, granted the first charter to Tenby, relaxing feudal obligations, allowing trading privileges and a fair. Confirmation and extension of these privileges came from subsequent holders of the lordship, including King Henry IV who granted the Mayoral Charter in 1402.

Meanwhile, a grant from King Edward III allowed tolls for the building of a quay. Trade with Bristol, North Devon, the Continent and Ireland reached its peak by the fifteenth century, with imports of wine, salt and miscellaneous goods and exports of coal and coarse woollen cloth. The Tudor Merchant's House and the enlargement of St. Mary's Church and the merchants' tombs there are reminders of the prosperity of the town at this period. Also a reminder that there was insecurity during the Wars of the Roses is the Letters Patent (1457) of Jasper Tudor, Earl of Pembroke, ordering a strengthening of the Town Walls and vesting them in the inhabitants. Alongside trade fishing had flourished. About 1200 Giraldus Cambrensis, cleric, scholar and geographer and the first Rector of Tenby (albeit non-resident) had noticed the abundance of fish in the nearby waters. His observation was confirmed later by the 'Wills Mark' document dated 1627 giving bearings of a rock near which there had been formerly a

2

prolific yield of fish. Incidentally, the first to use an extended Welsh name for Tenby was the sixteenth century scholar, Humphrey Llwyd of Denbigh, who called it 'Dinbigh Ypyscot' to distinguish it from his own town—had he read Giraldus?—and from which the modern 'Dinbych-y-Pysgod (Dinbych famous for its fish) has descended.

Tradition has it that Jasper Tudor and his nephew Henry sailed from Tenby on their flight to France after the defeat of the Lancastrian forces at Tewkesbury in 1471. After Henry's return, his victory at Bosworth in 1485 and his accession, he gave rewards to his followers, among them his uncle Jasper, who was created Duke of Bedford. On the Duke's death in 1495 his estates, including the lordship of Pembroke and with it the demesne lands in Tenby, passed to the Crown. In the reign of Henry VIII this area was embodied for administrative and judicial purposes in the newly created shire of Pembroke, established under the Act of Union 1536-42. Contemporary with and in the wake of these changes came the upheaval caused by the Reformation, but Tenby appears to have produced no Protestant or Catholic martyrs. However it did produce one very notable scholar in the person of Robert Recorde who was born there c.1510. So outstanding did he become in the realm of the 'New Learning' that he has been described as 'the father of English mathematics'. During the Tudor period customs officials continued to record in the Port Books details of coastal and overseas trade, giving the names of ships and the personnel involved. Such traders must have shared the concern felt in coastal towns over the threat of Spanish invasion in 1588, the year of the Armada. Following official orders a portion of the Town Wall, near the South Gate was rebuilt. Three important documents of the reign of Elizabeth I should be mentioned. First the Charter of Incorporation 1581 confirmed previous charters and established the burgesses as 'a body corporate in deed, fact and name' and further extended their privileges. Secondly, the 1586 survey of all the Queen's lands, tenements and hereditaments within the town of Tenby provided a valuable record of all the burgages, street by street and their condition. Thirdly, in 1588 Elizabeth I granted a lease of lands to the Corporation, subject to a Crown Rent, and a Town Clerk was appointed. Further to the development of the constitution of local government was the charter of Charles I, 1631. It is a curious fact that a decline in prosperity was taking place while the responsibility of the burgesses increased, a process which was accentu-

3

ated during the Civil War (1642-48), when Tenby changed hands between opposing forces and the inhabitants suffered bombardment in 1644 and were besieged by Cromwell's forces under General Horton in 1648. Matters were made worse by an outbreak of plague in 1650-51, and a petition in the reign of Charles II bears witness to the ruin and desolation of the town. However, although trade with continental ports had long since declined, goods were still being carried in sailing coasters plying between Tenby and Bristol throughout the eighteenth century. The profitable pickling of oysters for export was terminated through overdredging in the nineteenth century.

The fear of continental invasion reappeared with Britain's entry into the Revolutionary War with France in 1793. This was underlined by the French landing at Fishguard in 1797. Instructions were given for the arming of the locals and for the disposition of cannon at strategic points. Lord Nelson visited the town during a tour of the area in 1802. With his victory at Trafalgar the immediate danger subsided. That very year, 1805, there arrived in Tenby a distinguished topographical artist, Charles Norris, who produced over 2000 pictures of the town and the neighbourhood. His *Etchings of Tenby* and the accompanying text provide a most valuable 'period picture' before far-reaching changes took place with the onset of the Regency Age. The Prince Regent led the way by popularising sea bathing at Brighton and, before long, most of the well-placed seaside resorts in southern Britain followed suit. It was realised that Tenby had the possible makings of a fashionable bathing place and by the time the *Etchings* were published a number of substantial residences had been erected in the Norton (North town), including Sion House built by John Nash (the architect of Regent Street, Buckingham Palace and of the Crescent at Bath) and the Croft House, which became the home of the Richards family who figured so prominently in the affairs of the town. However, the real impetus came from Sir William Paxton, 'nabob', banker and landowner, who made striking changes in the vicinity of the harbour, built his Public Baths there and opened them c. 1805. Paxton became involved with various undertakings of the corporation, and among them the installation of new iron water pipes to convey water from the Butts Field to the conduits in the High Street.

Mention should be made of three official documents which are informative about the affairs of Tenby in the first half of the nineteenth

4

century. The first is entitled *Reports from Commissioners on Proposed Division and Boundaries of Boroughs, Part VIII, 1832*, the year of the Great Parliamentary Reform Bill. The second document is headed *First Report of the Commissioners appointed to Inquire into the Municipal Corporations in England and Wales, 1834*. The latter reviews the ancient Charters, examines critically the constitution of the Corporation and the way in which the Mayor and Officers were appointed. The Commissioners referred in particular to disputes which had arisen concerning the administration of property in the town. Reference was also made to improvements which had taken place there since 1810. These included a new market, a water undertaking, a new slaughter house and a pound. The sequel to this Report on the national level was the Municipal Corporations Act 1835 and this Act, in turn, was the forerunner of the third of these important official documents relating to Tenby, namely the *Act for the improvement of the Borough of Tenby*, which received the Royal Assent of the young Queen Victoria on 9 May 1838. Many of the powers conferred by the Act led to measures which were subsequently recorded in the minute books of the Council. Much of the subsequent history of the town, particularly its further development as a holiday resort, hinged upon the implementation of the provisions of this Act, together with other Acts of Parliament passed in the course of the remaining part of the nineteenth century.

We are fortunate in having another vivid 'period picture' of Tenby in the mid-nineteenth century through the eyes of Mrs. Fanny Price Gwynne, a competent water-colour artist and the author of a number of guides to the locality. The second edition of her *Sketches of Tenby and its Neighbourhood: an Historical and Descriptive Guide* was published in 1852. Some of the historical material would need revision today, but her account of the contemporary scene is clear and informative. She was a witness of important local events in the 1860s. First came the railways. The South Wales Railway Company's line reached Haverfordwest in 1853 and there were four-in-hand coaches linking Tenby with the Narberth Road Station (Clunderwen). The Pembroke and Tenby Railway, built by David Davies of Llandinam was opened in 1863, extended to Whitland in 1866 and was eventually taken over by the Great Western Railway Company, which provided transport for more and more families seeking their holidays. The connection of Tenby with Bristol by sea, which had survived from the Middle Ages, declined. Fear of a continental invasion had not completely vanished with Trafalgar and Waterloo. A further scare, created by Napoleon III, in the 1860s led to the erection of a number of coastal forts, one of which was constructed on St. Catherine's Island. This remains one of the landmarks of Tenby, as does the Welsh National Memorial to Albert, the Prince Consort, unveiled on Castle Hill in 1865. From then onwards there was a series of building developments, taking in more and more of the former town fields outside the old town walls—a movement which was well advanced by the last decade of the century.

The 1890s found Tenby seething with political, religious, social and personal antagonisms which pervaded the proceedings of the Borough Council and were reflected in the local press. These conflicts involved Conservative versus Liberal, Anglican versus Non-conformist, Gladstone's Irish Home Rule Bill, the Welsh Church Disestablishment Bill, the Welsh Land Commission's Report, local government reform, state control of education and national defence, with the essential part to be played by the Navy clearly reflected close at hand in Milford Haven and at Pembroke Dock. It was against this background that Tenby County Intermediate School came into being.

In Tenby, party divisions over most of the above matters were exacerbated and complicated by the reactions of individuals and factions to local problems. There were those who sought to give the town a new image by imitating the larger and more popular resorts. The Esplanade was extended, the Duke of York's Walk was constructed about this time and the Royal Victoria Pier was officially opened in 1899. There was also the social round, ranging from the Tenby Races and the Hunt Week Ball to theatricals and important musical events at the Royal Gatehouse Assembly Room. Rugby Football was played by the Harlequins and the Swifts, subsequently merging to form Tenby United. The Cricket Club existed rather precariously. The Annual Lawn Tennis Tournament and the Flower Show at the Victoria Gardens were notable successes. The more serious minded had given their attention to the establishment of the Tenby Museum in 1878, an institution which survived various vicissitudes and which under expert guidance, was destined to become one of the best local museums in Wales. The patrons of these activities were the local gentry and businessmen who in turn became the prime movers in the efforts to establish a new school in the town. The Governing Body of the Tenby County Intermediate School first met in 1894, but did not escape the effects of the personal and political animosities of the time, as the well-known friction between such pioneers as the Conservative C. W. R. Stokes and the radical C. F. Egerton Allen indicate. The second half of the nineteenth century when peace and good will did not always prevail in the affairs of the town, saw, nevertheless, a spate of church building and restoration which should have been 'an outward and visible sign of inward and spiritual grace'. The Congregationalists, the Baptists and the Methodists all moved to new buildings. There was restoration work at St. Mary's and the Cemetery Chapel was built, while in 1893 the new Roman Catholic Church in Potter's Field was consecrated by Cardinal Vaughan.

Behind this seeming prosperity and progress there remained in the background the urgent need to deal with matters of public health. The Cottage Hospital had been opened in 1871, but the reports of the Medical Officer of Health show that scarlet fever, smallpox and diphtheria were much in evidence, sometimes reaching epidemic proportions. The Medical Officer had frequently reported on the insanitary conditions of many of the dwelling houses and the slaughter house, while urging the provision of an isolation hospital, filter beds for the water supply and a mortuary for the town. Even so, apart from the shadow cast by the Boer War, the reign of Queen Victoria, crowned by he Diamond Jubilee, went out in a blaze of glory. Senior citizens were both proud and very sure of themselves and looked forward to future progress towards bigger and better things. Local patriotism was expressed in such names as Victoria Street, Victoria Gardens, Edward Street, the Jubilee, the Jubilee Bandstand, the Royal Gatehouse, the Royal Lion and the Cobourg Hotels. At the time little attention was paid to the news from Germany, not only of the Kaiser's ambitious naval programme announced in 1878 but also of a new kind of cab, mechanically propelled, with the fantastic speed of eleven miles per hour, or even to the news from nearby Saundersfoot, where William Frost was reported to have obtained provisional protection for inventing a new flying machine. Here were the first rumblings of things to come, things that were destined to put the horse-drawn carriages, which plied sight-seers to local beauty spots, out of business and make it possible

7

for prospective holiday-makers from any British centre of population to reach Majorca or the Costa Brava quicker than they could reach Tenby in spite of the great expectations following upon the Great Western Railway's 'take over' of the Pembroke and Tenby Railway in 1896! However, for years to come the railway brought more and more visitors into the locality. Meanwhile it was an accepted sight to encounter horse manure on the rough surfaced roads, which were muddy in winter and dusty in summer, so requiring regular sprinkling by water-carts.

The atmosphere of late Victorian times remained on into the new century—the Edwardian Age—so aptly called by some historians the 'Victorian Aftermath'. Church going was still the fashion and, winter and summer, the Esplanade was the scene of a parade of people in their best clothes after morning service. In season the visitors who stayed in the hotels dressed for dinner and paraded thus on fine summer evenings as late as the nineteen-twenties. It was only in the years between the two great wars that things began to change. Visitors came in ever increasing numbers, especially from the industrial areas. More private hotels and boarding houses were established. After the Second World War 'bed and breakfast' replaced 'full board' in many houses. The volume of motor car and motor coach business increased and along with them came the private caravans. The Brixham trawlers, once a familiar sight in the harbour, were replaced by pleasure craft, whether sailing dinghies or more and bigger motor launches. New buildings and suburban housing spread greatly, absorbing more and more of the area mentioned in the 1832 Report as being 'extensive and leaving ample room for expansion'. In this way the centre of gravity of the town has shifted outside the Walls, but surprisingly the resident population has increased but little. The 1891 census in the late Victorian era recorded 4,542. In 1961, after the Second World War, the figure was 4,752 and in 1971 the total was 4,995.

At the end of all these post war changes came the re-organisation of local government. In March 1974, the Tenby Borough Council which had its roots deep in the past, held its last meeting in the Guildhall, significantly the old Croft House and former home of the Richards family, which had been acquired in 1948 as a Council Chamber and Office.

8

CHAPTER II

THE EDUCATIONAL AND SOCIAL BACKGROUND

Section 1: Early Educational Facilities and the Establishment
of Intermediate Education in Wales

The evidence for the existence of schools in Tenby in the seventeenth
century is fragmentary. There was the short lived appointment of
James Picton, Master of the School at Tenby at £40 per year, 'approved'
under the provisions of the Puritan *Act for the Propagation of the
Gospel in Wales* 1650. Also payments made for making good the wear
and tear on the windows, doors and fabric of school premises are to
be found in the St. Mary's *Churchwardens' Accounts* for the second half
of the century and a Borough Chamberlain's Account, dated 9 November 1687, records a sum of five pounds and ten shillings expended on
'Repaioringe of the Skole house.'

In the first half of the eighteenth century, the local links with the
S.P.C.K. (Society for the Promotion of Christian Knowledge), founded
in London in 1699, are of special interest. The success of this society
in the setting up of Charity Schools and in the distribution of religious
literature depended upon local patronage and organisation. The
leading benefactor in Pembrokeshire was Sir John Philipps of Picton
Castle—the fifth Baronet, known as 'the good Sir John'. Among
other prominent supporters in the area were John Pember of Prendergast,
John Philipps at Kilgetty and the Rev. John Holcombe, M.A., Rector
of Tenby from 21 March 1730 to 23 July 1770. The records of the
S.P.C.K. include references to schools at Begelly, Templeton, St.
Issell's, Penally and Tenby. Fortunately there is available, a further
source of information in the Borough of Tenby muniments, where a
well-preserved series of Chamberlains' Vouchers (1725-1750) contains
a number of authorisations for payments to be made to teachers in
Charity Schools in the town from 1730 to 1738, which was the period
immediately following the appointment of the Rev. John Holcombe as
rector. Not only was Holcombe an active member of the S.P.C.K.,
but as rector, he was closely associated with the local Corporation (he

9

served as Chamberlain 1744-45) and it seems possible that he was able to secure from that body financial support for the education of poor children, as shown by the Chamberlains' Vouchers.

Alongside the payments made to teachers in the Charity Schools was a number of Vouchers authorising the quarterly and half-yearly salaries paid to successive Masters of the Grammar School at Tenby. The first of these was 'William Weston A.B.: Master of the Public Grammer School' to be paid five pounds 'being his Quarter's Salary due at Christmas last as Master of the Said School from this Corporation. Dated 9th of January 1733-4'. Then on 11 July 1734 Robert Nash, Alderman, Chamberlain, was instructed 'to pay unto the Rev. J. Holcombe the sum of ten pounds being his halfe year's Salary due at Midsumer last for Keeping of the public Grammer School of the Town'. The Rector received similar payments for this service in 1737 and 1738-39, Others who held the appointment were Mr. Andrew Edwards, 1735-36, Mr. Philip Saunders, 1737 and Lewis Evans, 1738-49. The last named may have been the Lewis Evans who was Curate of Tenby from 1758 to 1767. It would appear from the Records that for some fifteen years the Borough Chamberlains were paying out an annual salary of £20 to the current holder of the office of Master of the Grammar School.

Unfortunately, the material at present available for the study of education in Tenby in the second half of the eighteenth century is very scanty. However, there has been preserved in excellent condition the *Borough of Tenby Order Book 1777 to 1835*, in which there are scattered some instructions for the appointment of teachers. With one exception the payments mentioned do not tally with those previously discussed and in one entry only does the term 'Grammar School' appear and that without naming the Master. The extracts speak for themselves.

Borough of Tenby the 5th of April 1777

> Ordered that Henry Davies is appointed Schoolmaster agreable to the order agreed on the 27th January last, that the said Henry Davies be forthwith admitted to the Gratuity and School Room on Teaching Four Poor Burgesses such as the Mayor and Common Council shall appoint. And to teach Reading and Writing at two shillings and sixpence a Quarter, Arithmetic at three shillings, Latin &c. & to make his Agreement for as much as the Parents and he can agree for.
> Henry Davies.   Robt. Reed Mayr (and five other signatories)

10

Apparently calculation was rated more highly than verbal communication. The inclusion of Latin in the syllabus suggests that Henry Davies was Master of the Grammar School, although the financial arrangements differ from those noted previously. The provision for contributions from parents was in line with the practice in the earlier Charity Schools in South West Wales, as shown in the records of the S.P.C.K. The next entry in the Order Book was on 30 June 1783, giving approval for one guinea a quarter to be allowed till further orders to Henry Lewis, a schoolmaster on condition of his educating two lads during such allowance. On 29 June 1784, William Llewelling, a Schoolmaster, was allowed a similar amount

'till other order, to commence from the 24th Instant and on condition of his Educating in the manner of his School two lads during such allowance, if appointed by the Mayor or some other Magistrate of this Borough.'

Unfortunately this gentleman 'blotted his copybook' and the 'other order' came on 28 May 1789:

'Whereas frequent complaints being made to us that William Llewelling the present Schoolmaster being frequently drunk and and greatly neglecting the School to the great prejudice of the Scholars. It is now unanimously agreed that the said William Llewelling be discharged from the said School the 24th Day of June next and another be appointed in his place.'

The last reference to a school in the Order Book was on the second day of January 1818. The Mayor and Common Council ordered 'That the sum of Twenty Pounds Annually be pd. to the Master of the Grammar School in this Town during pleasure on his undertaking to Educate four Boys to be recommended by the Mayor and Common Council, free of expense'.

Some mention must be made of school premises. In his *Church Book of St. Mary the Virgin* Edward Laws made reference to the proceedings of the General Sessions at the Guildhall, Tenby, 8 October 1688, when William James Cl. (i.e. Clerk in Holy Orders) was presented by a Grand Jury 'for suffering the walls of the Vicareige next adjoining the Skool to lay open for people to make a lastell, to the great annoyance of the inhabitants and prejudicale to the Skoole.' The vicarage was a miserable cottage at the angle of St. George's Street and Church Street; it was in fact one of a string of insanitary

11

and uncomfortable buildings which then clustered closely round the church, leaving only a narrow alleyway for passage round that edifice. Westwards of the vicarage stood a building which had been listed in an Elizabethan Survey of Burgage Lands in 1586 as: 'One house called Izabell's Chapel after converted into the charnell house near the Vike-ridge on the est part and the Churchyard on(e) the north . . .'. The upper floor was used as a mortuary chapel and the lower as a bone hole. Laws states that in the seventeenth century the bones were cleared and fireplaces were added so that the building could be used as a schoolhouse. Possibly this was the schoolhouse referred to in the seventeenth century *Churchwardens' Accounts*; there is a possibility that the puritan James Picton taught there and that the eighteenth century Charity Schools were housed in these premises, which later in that century were converted with the upper floor as a workhouse and the lower as a public latrine. This property was demolished along with others in the church precincts in the course of the next century.

It should be remembered however that another building (also demolished) close to the church is known to have been used as a school. This was the fifteenth century cruciform porch which was situated outside the west door of the church. One of the entries in the Church-wardens' Accounts 1661-62 reads: 'Pd. for carryinge some loose boards from the schoolehouse in the Church . . . 00: 01½'. Edward Laws quotes in full a letter dated 21 April 1892, which he received from Mr. N. J. Dunn, whose father in the early nineteenth century had built Brick House and Bank House (now Morris Bros and Barclays Bank). The letter describes this property and the western precincts of the church including 'a very fine elm tree, and large, old fashioned school with slightly ecclesiastical windows. I went there myself when young. Mr. Wright kept it, and I believe, Mr. John Hughes late Vicar of Penally kept it when curate to Dr. Roch at Tenby'. Most likely this cruciform structure was where the Masters of the Grammar School, several of whose names are known from eighteenth and nineteenth century records, did their teaching. On 11 June 1793 there was an order 'pursuant to the consent of a Vestry holden in and for the Parish of St. Mary in Tenby . . . where it was by a very great majority of the Inhabitants of the said Parish agreed, that the School house, lime house and appurtenances at the west end of the

Church be removed; for the company to assemble before prayers, and to render access to the West Door of the said Church more commodious . . . ' This was in the Corporation Order Book, but according to the evidence of Edward Laws and of W. Gwyn Thomas in his description of the church, the West Porch and with it the schoolhouse remained standing until 1831, that is one year before the appointment of a successor to Dr. Nicholas Roch, who was mentioned in Mr. N. J. Dunn's letter.

Although the schools were held within the precincts of St. Mary's Church, the payments for repairs and of salaries were made by the Borough Chamberlain on the instruction of the Mayor and Members of the Common Council. From the middle of the sixteenth century onwards the Rectory of Tenby was under the patronage of the Crown and, from the reign of Elizabeth I, much of the control of the administration of the church passed to the Tenby Corporation. How this came about has been explained by Edward Laws and by Gwyn Thomas in their respective accounts of the church.

After a lawsuit in 1718 the Corporation neglected its responsibilities, while retaining Church and Charity Lands, and the church became dilapidated. Such was the case down to the visit of the Royal Commission on Public Charities in 1833. In common with other Corporations, the Tenby Corporation had used the revenues of Charitable Bequests for purposes other than those originally intended, including use for the relief of the Poor Rate. Of over thirty charities only one is known to have been earmarked for educational purposes. By a deed dated 1730, Gethin's lands were conveyed together with a sum of £30 to five trustees towards the maintenance of a school for the children of the poor. The lands, consisting of two pieces of pasture, later known as Conduit Park and Reservoir were leased to the Corporation at £25 per annum.

It must be concluded that since the church fabric was neglected, the school quarters, whether in the former St. Isabel's Chapel until the late eighteenth century or in the West Porch, suffered the same fate. The pupils were very few in number and those who taught them, with the exception perhaps of Rector John Holcombe, were unlikely to have possessed many of the requirements quoted by Mary Clement from the *S.P.C.K. Account of Schools 1704* and *National Library of Wales M.S.S. No. 15.*

The Schoolmaster must be 'a member of the Church of England of sober life and conversation, not under, 25, a frequenter of Holy Communion, hath a good government of himself and his passions, of meek temper and humble behaviour, of a good genius for teaching, who undertakes well the grounds and principles of the Christian religion and is able to give account thereof to the minister of the parish or Ordinary on examination, who can write a good hand and who understands the grounds of arithmetic, one who keeps order in his family and is approved of by the minister of his parish ... ' Such a paragon was also expected to teach from 7 to 11 a.m. and 1 to 5 p.m. in summer, and from 8 to 11 a.m. and 1 to 4 p.m. in winter, and all for about £5 a year in most Charity Schools in Pembrokeshire. Poor Abner Nash, 'teacher of the Charity Schools' in Tenby received only £4 for teaching twelve children, while his better-off neighbour 'the Master of the Grammer School' had £20. Of course the poor clergy were ready to conduct schools so as to add to their meagre stipends.

During the course of the nineteenth century the provision of education in Tenby was influenced by movements at the national level combined with local circumstances arising from the development of the ancient borough as a holiday resort. The changes initiated by Sir William Paxton and others continued throughout the century, affecting both the physical appearance of the town and the content of its population, which statistics show to have increased more than fourfold by the eighteen-nineties. The census figures give the number of inhabitants as follows:—

Date			Population
1801	St. Mary's	In and Out-Liberties	984
1831	do.	In-Liberty	1942
	do.	Out-Liberty	186
1891	do.	In-Liberty	4542
	do.	Out-Liberty	168

The process of change involved demolitions, street widening, the building of residences, substantial and otherwise, within the medieval walls and outside them, more especially after the eighteen-fifties. In

14

consequence the Borough Council were faced increasingly with the problems of laying out streets and paving, the provision of adequate drainage, sanitation, water supply and lighting and of finding the money needed for these undertakings.

The Georgian style houses and terraces, which were erected during this period, provided either residences or holiday lodgings for 'gentlefolk', the well-to-do business people, the retired naval and army officers and clergy. In less pretentious quarters were housed the rest of the community, ranging from modest tradesmen down to the 'meaner sort', the so-called working class. The educational facilities which became available, whether through the efforts of religious bodies and individual philanthropists or through private 'adventure', reflected the strata of a snobbish society which existed on into the twentieth century. A brief reference must be made to the nineteenth century schools, some of which eventually became the main source of supply of pupils for the Tenby County Intermediate School. More details are to be found in Official Reports, school records, trade directories and local newspapers.

The Royal Commission's Report on the Borough of Tenby, 1834, included a statement that the Corporation had established no school or means of instruction for the poor and that they had refused a grant of ground to certain individuals for that purpose. However, in 1832 the Hon. W. H. Yelverton, Thomas Nicholls, Elliot Voyle and William Tuder had obtained from Sir Richard Bulkeley Philipps of Picton Castle a lease of part of the ruins of Tenby Castle for the establishment of a school on the principles of the National Society (a Church of England organisation set up in London in 1811). The premises which now form part of the Tenby Museum, are described in Part I of the much criticised *Reports of the Commissioners of Enquiry into the State of Education in Wales 1847*. Commissioner Ralph Robert Wheeler Lingen and his three assistants were in Tenby and the neighbouring parishes over the Christmas period 1846 and the beginning of January 1847. Not surprisingly, no schools in Tenby were in session at the time but some evidence was obtained from Dr. R. W. Falconer, M.D. and visits were paid on 29 and 30 December.

Sub-Commissioner Morris arrived at the School on Castle Hill on 29 December and afterwards reported: '... The school is held in two rooms, the upper for the girls and the lower, which is flagged, for

15

the boys. The rooms are commodious and the windows command fine seaviews. The spot is exposed but must be very healthy. The path approaching it runs along the edge of the cliff towards its upper end and would be considered dangerous for English (sic) children. In the boys' school there are a blackboard, cards on the walls, maps of the world, of England, three of Palestine, of the wanderings of the Israelites in the Wilderness, and a table of chronology. The writing was good. There were no prints of any kind.' The Report goes on to describe the furniture and apparatus as being in a good state of repair, mentions the numbers on the books as 66 boys and 55 girls and the use of the monitorial system in the school. Reference was also made to the Sunday school which was held there. According to a centenary note in *The Tenby and County News* of 1 June 1932, the Trustees selected as the first master of the school a gentleman who had spent the first years of his life as a slave-driver in the West Indies. 'William Thomas was his name but he was better known as "Billy Snuffy".' However, despite the unpromising character of his West Indian experience, one of his old pupils spoke of the kindness of his disposition and later remembered him as 'one of the most painstaking masters I have ever known.' Some time later the school was in charge of Mr. Russell Mathias, who continued his service when the National School moved in 1874 to Upper Park Road to the new Parochial Schools, built from designs by Mr. D. Birkett, Architect, with accommodation for 250 boys and 200 girls and managed by a Committee of Subscribers. The opening of these new premises was accompanied by the closure and absorption of the Infants School previously held in a stone building which still stands on the north side of the footway leading from Greenhill Road to the Railway Station. This school had been founded in 1836 through the benevolence of Mrs. Bird Allen. After her death one of the main benefactors was Lt-Col. Thomas Wedgwood (a grandson of Josiah I) of St. Mary's Hill.

Passing reference must be made to the Sunday schools in the town. The Blue Book of 1847 includes three in addition to the National School, already mentioned. There was the Baptist Ebenezer Sunday School, established in 1843, supported by subscriptions and collections and most likely conducted in the building now used as a fire station in the South Parade. (The Baptist Chapel is marked on that site on a map of Tenby, dated 1849.) In Lower Frog Street there was the

Tabernacle (Independent) Chapel with its own Sunday school, and at the Wesleyan Chapel in the High Street was held a Sunday school which had been founded in 1816. Subsequently this school was to develop into a day school, and, from 1881, to move into the basement of the new chapel in Warren Street, This structure, built by Mr. W. Davies of Tenby to the designs of Mr. K. W. Ladd at a cost of £3,600, was said to be capable of accommodating 400 children in its schoolrooms, which remained in use until the Tenby Council School was opened under the Pembrokeshire Local Education Authority in 1916 in new premises which bear the date 1915.

It should be noticed that in Tenby there was no school under the auspices of the British and Foreign Schools Society (a non-denominational body founded in 1810) and that the Wesleyan School filled the place which might have been taken by a British School. Government grants to voluntary societies, initiated in 1833 and subsequently extended, with accompanying inspection of proficiency in the three Rs', were continued by the provisions of W. E. Forster's Elementary Education Act 1870. It was considered that the elementary education available at the Parochial and Wesleyan Schools in Tenby made unnecessary the setting up of a Board School under the terms of the Act. In 1880 attendance at school was made compulsory up to an age not more than 13 and in 1891 schooling was made free in all public elementary schools.

A year before the opening of the Tenby County Intermediate School, the *Annual Report of the Committee of the Privy Council of Education 1895* gave the following summary for the area which would eventually provide the catchment for that school and part of which territory would be disputed with Narberth County School, not only in the late nineteenth century but during the educational re-organisation of the nineteen-sixties.

List of Schools inspected in 1894

Name of School	Accommodation Provided	Av. Attendance	Amount of Grants
Tenby Parochial	751	326	£216 9s. 7d.
Tenby Wesleyan	327	156	£130 9s. 0d.
Penally (National)	127	46	£47 15s. 0d.
New Hedges (National)	80	32	£49 4s. 6d.

Amroth (National)	101	57	£43 1s. 8d.
Pentlepoir (Board)	81	70	£64 3s. 4d.
Saundersfoot (Board)	184	117	£87 17s. 10d.
Stepaside (Board)	173	119	£95 9s. 0d.
Redberth (National)	144	63	£78 11s. 0d.
Begelly (Board)	118	62	£53 17s. 3d.
St. Florence (National)	132	45	£65 1s. 6d.
Carew (National	123	66	£58 17s. 11d.
Manorbier (National)	128	80	£68 3s. 4d.

The above institutions were intended primarily for the offspring of the poorer inhabitants of the district. For those who had the means there were the distant public schools, the grammar school at Haverfordwest and a succession of private schools in Tenby itself. Some of these sprang up in parts of the town where one would least expect to find such schools. Many of them were short-lived and most were advertised with extravagant claims tinged with snobbery. No such detail appears in *Pigot's Trade Directories* which provided lists under the heading 'Academies and Schools', giving the names of the proprietors and in some cases the locations. Thus in 1830 there were four, in 1835 three and in 1844 seven advertised.

None of the establishments in the above Pigot's litst is mentioned in the Blue Book of 1847. However, this does provide some information about the proprietors of other schools, two of them dating earlier than Pigot's Directory of 1844. There was Captain Cook, who taught in the ground-floor room of a stone-built and slated house, furnished with two desks besides his own, two tables, five benches and a clock. Most of his pupils were tradesmen's mechanics but he professed to understand the Classics, several branches of Mathematics and French—with the doubtful qualification of having been a prisoner of war in France from 1805 to 1814 during the Napoleonic War. Others noted by the the Royal Commission were Mr. Eddy—an Independent preacher, Miss Fitzsimmons—very amiable and intelligent with a superior education, and Mrs. Griffiths—who taught children from 5 years of age and who was said to have taught navigation to many captains of vessels.

Shortly after the publication of the earliest numbers of the *Tenby Observer* in 1853, the proprietors of the local private schools began to make use of its advertisement columns to extol the virtues of their establishments. A sprinkling of such notices appears throughout the rest of the century. An examination of them reveals that the survival of these schools for any length of time was exceptional. Some disappeared with the death or departure of the owner from the town, while others may have atrophied through lack of support. Nevertheless, others sprang up to take their places or new Principals replaced the old in going concerns. A list of the addresses indicates that some of the schools were on the small side:—Croft Cottage; Tenby Grammar School, Cresswell Street; Clifton Rock Grammar School; Norton Cottage; Ivy House; 2 Olive Buildings; Greenhill; St. Mary's Hill; Lower Slate House; Sherborne Cottage, South Cliff Street; St. Clare's House, Esplanade; 2 Paragon; Somerset House, Esplanade; Apsley, Victoria Street; Farnham House, South Cliff Street; Tredegar House; Myrtle House, St. Mary's Street; Clynderwen House, Victoria Street; Bellevue House; St. Andrew's, North Cliff.

A few examples of the 'Observer' advertisements will serve to illustrate the attractions offered by those who ran these schools:

'Mrs. Charles Tasker, has the honour to inform the Nobility and Gentry of Tenby and its vicinity that she purposes immediately opening an Establishment for the education of Young Ladies in Music, Singing, the Continental Languages and the usual routine of English Studies in which she will be assisted by a protestant Parisian. References to Parents of children for many years under Mrs. Tasker's care. Further particulars to be obtained of Mrs. Loder, Croft Cottage.' (5 Oct. 1855)

By 1878 Mrs. Tasker had moved:
'Educational Home for Indian and other Children, Lower Slate House, Tenby. The Musical Department under the supervision of Mr. C. H. Tasker. The Continental Languages by a Resident Foreign Governess.' (3 Jan. 1878)

In 1890 Mrs. Tasker was still advertising but by this time she was at Myrtle House, St. Mary's Street.

19

'Ivy House, Tenby.   Mrs. F. Hauptmann receives a select number
of Young Ladies to Board and Instruct in the usual course of a
solid and Polite Education.   Terms for Pupils under the age of
12 years 25 guineas per annum.   For those over that age 30
guineas per annum.   Day Pupils 8 guineas per annum.   Including
French taught by a resident Native, and German, Music, Singing
Drawing and Dancing.'   (16 July 1878)

Later the above school was moved to Norton Cottage.

GREEN HILL SCHOOL, TENBY

'Large House and Grounds, Playground, Gymnasium &c.   Thoroughly appointed.   Pupils prepared for Oxford, Cambridge and
London University Examinations.   A preparatory Class for
little Boys.   Principal: H. Goward, M.A., LL.B.'
                                                        (3 January 1878)

Henry Goward had acquired the estate known as Greenhill and had
extended the residence for the purpose advertised.   These premises,
which were eventually to become the Tenby County Intermediate
School, will be described in detail later.   In 1946, four years after his
retirement, Mr. J. T. Griffith, the second Headmaster of the Tenby
County School, wrote a reminiscence in which he referred to the private
school '... Known as Green Hill School, which flourished exceedingly...
It was one of the best known in West Wales.   It had a strong boarding
element and among its pupils were several who became great public
figures, such as Augustus John, the world famous painter, and Judge
J. Lloyd Morgan.'
    Augustus John's short stay at Greenhill is recalled in his own auto-
biography *Chiaroscuro*.   His comments on his experiences at the school
verge on the Dickensian: 'The Head Master, a noted champion of
liberty, wielded at the same time a heavy ruler ...   Every morning
the labours of the day were prefaced by a short homily by this little
man, followed by a hymn or perhaps "Scots, wha hae" and lastly the
Doxology.   Our Head, as he stood before his assembled charges,
presented a distinctive and memorable figure.   His large bespectacled
face was crowned with a lofty crest of white hair; he wore a white tie,
a frock coat and button boots.   His trousers always seemed short

without being turned up. This ardent Gladstonian was a pillar of the Congregational Tabernacle. Greenhill was an exceptional type of school, not exactly a grammar school, being unendowed, but it catered for the middle classes in the widest sense, and Latin was certainly taught, after a fashion. The Head was assisted by a Staff comprising two of his daughters and several under masters. The latter came and went with surprising frequency and seemed to belong to the pauper section of Society, being always hungry, ill-clad and down-at-heel.' John goes on to describe the permanently deafening box on the ear, which he received from the drill master, and several of his escapades including a 'backhander' which he gave to the second master, leading to Augustus' withdrawal from the school. Of his Art education he wrote: ' . . . in addition to the official task of copying lithographs of Swiss scenery in three chalks, I went further on my own and practised drawing from life. I found good models in the masters. My reading and writing both improved immensely at Greenhill but not my Arithmetic. Both my brother and I were so backward in this subject as to require a class to ourselves, the lowest of the low.' He goes on to say how they were sent to a school at Clifton before returning to a newly opened one called 'St. Catherine's' at Tenby; this establishment at the corner of Victoria Street and South Cliff Street was advertised by Mr. A. C. F. Evans, B.A., who with his staff, undertook to prepare boys for the Public Schools and the Royal Navy. Mr. Evans' references included The Right Honourable Lord Watson and the Rev. Donald Macleod, D.D., Chaplain to the Queen.

Mention must be made of Henry Goward's decision to close Greenhill School. He may have been influenced by the dwindling of numbers, owing to depression of the 1880s, and the property was offered for sale. Meanwhile Goward was deeply immersed in the religious and political issues of the day, frequently expounding his strong Liberal and Nonconformist convictions in the local press. By 1890 he had decided to depart for British Columbia, relinquishing his Presidency of the Tenby Liberal Club and receiving from his personal friends the parting gifts of a purse of money and an illuminated address. From afar 'this upright and excellent citizen' continued to express his views by writing to the local paper. For several years the Greenhill estate remained unsold for want of a buyer prepared to pay enough to satisfy the owner. The sale of the property and the circumstances which led to part of it being purchased for use as the Tenby County School will be described in due course.

It would be interesting to discover whether any records of the advertised private schools have survived and, if so, how many pupils there were, where they came from, and from what family background. What standard of education was provided in them? Some of them, such as St. Catherine's, Miss Black's and St. Andrews continued their work in the first part of the twentieth century and reports of various functions and examination successes appeared from time to time in the local press. Clearly, most of the proprietors set their sights on a particular 'class' and were closely associated with the Established Church Those schools which catered for the young ladies were intended to instruct them in the polite accomplishments, including Music, Drawing and one or more of the continental languages, which were considered appropriate for the society to which they belonged, or to which they aspired to belong. For the young gentlemen there was little offered beyond the preparatory stage. The more usual symbol of success was admission to a public school such as announced by R. J. Reynolds, a new proprietor of St. Catherine's in his advertisement: 'Recent Success: Scholarship (Foundation) at Wellington College'. Of course, Goward at Greenhill could claim that he provided what could be described as secondary education and that some of this pupils appeared in the Pass Lists of the Oxford and Cambridge Local Examinations. It seems likely that a number of these private schools took in pupils from the families of professional and business people who fell into the category mentioned in an advertisement of 2 January 1896: 'Miss Black . . . begs to inform the parents of her Pupils and others that she has taken on Bellevue House as A Middle Class School for Girls and will continue her work there after the Holidays.' For many years this last establishment, along with a few other private schools was to supply a sprinkling of girls and boys for the Tenby County School.

The Tenby County Intermediate School was opened officially on 23 September 1896. In common with other 'County Schools' in Wales it came into being through local efforts following upon the Welsh Intermediate Education Act of 12 August 1889. In 1881 there had been published the *Report of the Committee Appointed to Inquire into the Condition of Intermediate and Higher Education in Wales with Minutes of Evidence and Appendix. Presented to both Houses of Parliament by*

22

Command of Her Majesty. This Committee, under Lord Aberdare as Chairman, had been set up by Gladstone's government in 1880, and its investigations and recommendations were influenced by the following:

(a) the massive report of the *Taunton Schools Enquiry Commission* 1868, covering some 3,000 endowed schools, in twenty volumes, the last of which contained reports on Wales and Monmouth,

(b) the provisions of the Endowed Schools Act 1869 and the work of the Endowed Schools Commissioners set up under the Act,

(c) the work of the Charity Commissioners, who were entrusted with the duties of the Endowed Schools Commissioners from 1874 onwards, and who reconstructed some 800 endowments in England and Wales.

However, the Charity Commissioners were in no position to plan a system of schools, placed where they were needed and organised under an overall scheme with suitable control at the local and national level. These limitations, as far as Wales was concerned, were recognised by the Aberdate Committee who noted 'At the very best, existing educational institutions of a class above Public Elementary Schools, are not only insufficient in number but so inconveniently situated and in some cases so fettered by denominational restrictions as to be at once inadequate to meet the needs of the Principality and unsuitable for the character of the population.' One of the Committee, Lewis Morris of Carmarthen, well-known for his service to Welsh literature and to the cause of Intermediate and Higher Education in Wales, addressed a meeting at the Tenby Liberal Club in September 1888. He moved a resolution 'That this meeting, feeling strongly that adequate provision for higher education in Wales is of vital importance to the national life, respectfully urges on the government the pressing necessity for a comprehensive "Intermediate Education Bill" and urges that the time has now arrived for a Royal Charter for a Welsh University; and that the meeting instructs the Chairman to send a copy of this resolution to Lord Salisbury, to the Lord President of the Council, to the Rt. Hon. W. E. Gladstone, to the Hon. A. J. Mundella and to the Member for the Pembroke and Haverfordwest Boroughs.'

Meanwhile, in parliament, attempts had been made to carry legislation based upon the proposals of the Aberdare Committee. A short contemporary account of these events, by men involved in them, was given in *A Manual to the Intermediate Education (Wales) Act, 1889*, by Thomas Ellis (Liberal M.P. for Merioneth since 1886) and Ellis Griffith (Barrister at Law and Fellow of Downing College, Cambridge), published in November 1889. In his 'Introductory Note' to this slim volume, William Rathbone (radical M.P. for Caernarfonshire 1880 and for the Northern Division of that County 1885) stated 'It is just and proper that Wales, which has long been left in the background, should be the first part of the United Kingdom in which the importance of Intermediate Education has been recognised by a grant from the Imperial Treasury.'

In 1885 Mr. Anthony John Mundella, M.P. for Sheffield, Vice-President of the Council under Gladstone, introduced an Intermediate Education Bill for Wales, embodying the principle of a Treasury Grant. Thereafter, Welsh M.P.s pressed for further efforts and in 1888 Mr. Mundella introduced an amended Bill designed to meet their criticisms. Then in 1889 a Bill, amended yet again, was supported by Welsh Members, regardless of party. Lord Salisbury's Conservative Government 'seeking the necessity of settling this question and fulfilling promises often repeated by successive administrations, on condition of large and serious amendments, assisted energetically in carrying the Bill through both Houses of Parliament.' In order to ensure support for this measure the Welsh M.P.s had accepted the Government's alterations of it, though not entirely in agreement with them, regretting in particular the omission of a Welsh Board of Education.

The Welsh Intermediate Education Act came into operation on 1 November 1889. So far as 'consistent with the tenour thereof', it was to be construed as one with the Endowed Schools Acts 1869 to 1889. The main features of the Act were as follows:—

(a) Its purpose was 'to make further provision for the intermediate and technical education of the inhabitants of Wales and the County of Monmouth.'

(b) The kind of education to be provided was defined in Clause 17. 'The expression "Intermediate Education" means a course of education which does not consist chiefly of elementary instruction in reading, writing and arithmetic, but which includes Latin, Greek, the Welsh and English Language and Literature, modern languages, mathematics, natural applied science, or in some such studies, and generally in the

24

higher branches of knowledge, but nothing in this Act shall prevent the establishment of scholarships in higher or other elementary schools. The expression "Technical Education" includes instruction in

(i) any of the branches of science and art with respect to which grants are for the time being made by the Department of Science and Art;

(ii) the use of tools and modelling in clay, wood or other material;

(iii) commercial arithmetic, commercial geography, book-keeping and shorthand;

(iv) any other subject applicable to the purposes of agriculture, industries, trade, or commercial life and practice, which may be specified in a scheme or proposals for a scheme of a joint education committee as a form of instruction suited to the needs of the district; but it shall not include the practice of any trade, or industry, or employment'.

The second of these definitions should be compared with Clause 8 of the Technical Education Act, 30 August 1889. However, it is note-worthy that the new 'County Schools', for the first half-century of their existence, clung to the course of education prescribed in the first of the definitions in Clause 17. Not until the mid-twentieth century were the courses broadened, as for example, to include the study of Agriculture at Bush Grammar School, Pembroke, and a wider range of technical subjects, especially in the comprehensive schools. Only recently then has the full scope and intention of the Intermediate and Technical Acts of 1889 come close to realization.

(c) The initiative for implementation of the Intermediate Education Act was vested in the County Councils of Wales and Monmouth, newly elected under the Local Government Act of 1888. In each one there was to be appointed 'a joint education committee of the county council ...consisting of three persons nominated by the county council, and two persons ... well acquainted with the conditions of Wales and the wants of the people, preference being given to residents within the county for which such joint committee is to be appointed, nominated by the Lord President of Her Majesty's Privy Council.' Appropriate provision was made for the filling of vacancies and any of the Assistant Charity Commissioners was to be at liberty to attend any meeting of a joint education committee to take part in its proceedings, but without the right to vote.

Unless parliament directed otherwise, the joint education committees were to function for three years, commencing on 1 November 1889.

(d) Each county council was to make 'proper provision for enabling the committee to transact its business.' The Clerk of the County Council was to act as clerk to the joint education committee, which was to be governed by the rules affecting county council committees, but without being required to submit its acts for the approval of the county council.

(e) It was to be the duty of the joint education committee to submit to the Charity Commissioners a scheme or schemes for the intermediate and technical education of the inhabitants of their county, either alone or in conjunction with the inhabitants of any adjoining counties. Alternatively, there could be submitted to the Commissioners proposals on which schemes could be based. In either case there were procedures for modification and adoption of a scheme and for petition against it. The county committees were empowered to include in their projects not only the administration of educational endowments, which are defined in the Act, but where a county council recommended a payment out of the county rate a scheme could be prepared for the establishment of schools even where there were no endowments. The plans put forward would determine the appointment and functions of the governing body of each school and provide regulations concerning property, discipline, fees, curricula etc.

(f) There were important financial clauses in the Act:

(i) A county council could recommend their joint education committee to include in a scheme a provision for a payment out of the county rate, leviable as a separate item when collected from the ratepayers. The addition to the county rate for the purpose of defraying contributions for intermediate and technical education under the Act was not in any year to exceed one half-penny in the pound, on the aggregate amount of the rateable value of the county. The above could cover payment for any scholarship allowed for in a scheme.

(ii) There were to be government grants: 'The Commissioners of Her Majesty's Treasury shall annually out of moneys provided by Parliament pay in aid of each school aided by the county and subject to a scheme made under this Act such sums as hereinafter mentioned.' The sums paid were to depend upon the efficiency of the schools 'as ascertained by such annual inspection and report as may be required by the regulations from time to time made by the Treasury for the purpose of this section.' The aggregate amount paid in any year was not to exceed the amount payable in that year out of the county rate. It transpired that the necessary inspection was provided for when the Central Welsh Board was established in 1896.

Financial resources additional to the above were discussed by Ellis and Griffith in a Chapter headed 'The Framing of A Scheme'. They pointed out that there would be available, through the Science and Art Department at South Kensington, grants for certain subjects and in certain cases for fittings and apparatus. There would be the fees payable by parents towards the maintenance of the schools and the maximum and minimum of them would be inserted in a scheme. Lastly there would be an appeal to people to make generous contributions for the provision of handsome and suitably-fitted buildings. The joint education committees would be looking into the educational needs of the localities likely to be affected by their schemes. It was expected that there would be keen competition among towns and districts for securing new schools and that the decision would be in favour of those areas where the inhabitants proved themselves most capable of public-spirited effort.

At this stage it is convenient to return from the national to the local level and to discover how the Welsh Intermediate Education Act was put into effect in Pembrokeshire. The setting up of a joint education committee and its work in preparing a scheme for the establishment of secondary schools at various centres in the county will be noticed, but it is the main purpose here to examine the course of events leading to the foundation of the Intermediate School in Tenby. While there were problems common to all the localities concerned, there were some peculiar to Tenby and certain difficulties led to delays which caused the school there to be the next to the last of its kind in the County to be opened.

An assessment of the situation in Pembrokeshire is provided in the statistical tables in the Ellis and Griffith 'Manual', 1889. Appendix A gives the population of the county, according to the 1881 Census as 91,824. The approximate number of boys and girls to be educated in secondary schools, calculating about 20 per 1,000, was estimated as 1,850. According to Appendix B, the resources for this purpose were based on a Rateable Value of £410,520 for the Shire. From special rates there could be made available £850 . 5s. under the Welsh Inter-mediate Education Act and £1,710 . 10s. under the Technical Education Act.

Following upon the Local Government Act of 1888, the elections for the first members of the Pembrokeshire County Council were held on Wednesday 16 January 1889. Of the forty-eight Councillors elected there were thirty-six for the County Divisions and twelve for the Boroughs. Five candidates stood for the two Tenby seats, not at that time in separate wards. The two successful ones were William Henry Richards, Croft House, Esquire, (Conservative 250 votes), and Morgan Mathias Thomas, South Parade, Tenby, Solicitor, (Liberal 236 votes). The former played a leading part in the moves to secure an intermediate school for Tenby and was destined to become the first Chairman of the Local Governing Body. The latter was later appointed Returning Officer and at the ensuing by-election in August 1891 the seat was won by Captain Brook (Conservative). After sixteen Aldermen had been elected and the vacancies had been filled, the total membership of the County Council was sixty-four. The Minutes record a series of meetings of the Provisional Council in the first three months of 1889. A number of Committees was set up and Mr. Henry George Allen of Paskeston was appointed Chairman, replacing Lord Kensington, who had occupied the office during the preliminary stages. The first meeting of the fully constituted County Council was held at the Shire Hall, Haverfordwest, on Monday 1 April 1889.

It was not until the Council's meeting of 4 February 1890 that action was taken towards implementing the provisions of the Welsh Intermediate Education Act. A motion, of which notice had been given by the Rev. Lewis James at the previous Quarterly Meeting, was carried unanimously: 'That in accordance with Clause 5 of the Welsh Intermediate Education Act 1889 three members be now nominated by the County Council as County Council Members of the Joint Education Committee and the County Council recommend their Committee to insert in any Scheme in accordance with Sec. 3 Sub. Sec. 1 of the Said Act, a provision for a payment out of the County Rate to an amount not exceeding $\frac{1}{2}$d in the £ of the expenses of carrying into effect such Scheme or part thereof.' In accordance with this resolution the following gentlemen were then appointed: Mr. W. Watts Williams (of St. David's), the Rev. Lewis James (of Brynbank), Mr. Benjamin Rees (of Hendre). To these were to be added the local nominees of the Lord President of the Council, namely Mr. Henry George Allen (Chairman of the County Council) and Mr. W. S. de Winton (of Haverfordwest).

At the first meeting of the Joint Education Committee, held on Tuesday 22 April 1890, the Hon. W. Bruce of the Charity Commission was present and the Rev. Lewis James was appointed Chairman. Representatives of the Press were not admitted but the *Tenby Observer* carried a report of the proceedings, presumably from information released after the meeting. An early awareness of the new educational opportunities had been shown by the residents of the Fishguard, Pembroke and Narberth districts, from which letters were addressed to the Committee, staking claims that schools should be sited in their areas and suggesting that deputations might be received in Haverford-west. Five months were to elapse before the first public move was made in Tenby. However, the Committee decided to inform the petitioners as well as interested residents of other areas that applications would be considered and that they would be based on the following questions:

(a) For what area would the proposed school provide?

(b) What is the population of such area?

(c) What is the number of children likely to attend the proposed school and what are the grounds for this calculation?

(d) Can a good site be obtained with ample playground accommodation and at what cost (if any) and in what situation?

(e) What sum will the inhabitants of the district raise towards the building?

(f) Are there any charities used as doles or otherwise in the district which might be used as scholarships or exhibitions with the consent of the Trustees?

By December 1890 the Joint Education Committee had received applications and deputations and at their meeting on the 16th, they discussed the position of Haverfordwest Grammar School and Tasker's School and outlined a provisional Scheme whereby there would be in Pembroke Borough a school for 100 girls and 150 boys, at Tenby a school—its nature to be determined, for Narberth and Whitland a mixed school controlled jointly with the Carmarthenshire authority, at Cardigan a school controlled jointly with the Cardiganshire authority, and for Fishguard and St. David's conditional consent for a school each. It

29

should be added that by the beginning of 1891 a meeting at Milford Haven had proposed to raise a sum of £400 to build a school there and to send a deputation to the Joint Education Committee. During the following months local committees were formally constituted in the various areas and correspondence passed between them and William Davies George, Deputy Clerk of the Peace, who acted as Secretary to the Joint Education Committee. Starting with the above tentative programme, the Joint Education Committee worked out details of a Scheme which, after some modifications would be submitted to the Charity Commissioners.

The first important batch of recommendations was received by the Pembrokeshire County Council at the Quarterly Meeting of 5 May 1891. The proposals were:

(a) that schools be granted to the following, subject to certain conditions to be observed by the inhabitants.

Pembroke Dock. A Dual School for 100 to 150 boys and girls in separate departments.

Tenby, Narberth, Milford Haven. For each a Dual School for 50 to 80 boys and 30 girls.

Cardigan. A joint school for 150 between Cardiganshire and Pembrokeshire.

St. David's and Fishguard. Each to have a trial school for 40 for a period of 5 years.

(b) that the apportionment of income and financial arrangements for building be reported at the next County Council Meeting.

(c) the new schools will provide for 545 boys and girls and the old schools at Haverfordwest 250, making the total for the County 795, that is 7 per 1,000 on the population of the districts of the new schools and, including the old schools, $8\frac{1}{2}$ per 1000 on the population of the whole County. Mr. Bruce having stated that this proportion is nearly the same as that adopted in other counties of Wales.

(d) a new school should not cost less than £15 per scholar, but in one, being a select school, not less than £17. 10s., as the wealth and taste of the inhabitants demand a more ornate building.

This last reference was to Tenby where the local residents were to deny that there was a demand for a more ornate building than elsewhere, as was understood by those who were preparing the Scheme for the County. This dispute will be discussed in the course of the description of events in Tenby.

The Joint Education Committee continued their work on 14 May. After discussing the question of six free seats in the Pembroke Dock School for the children of employees of the War Office, they gave careful consideration to ways and means of increasing the grant for buildings. First calculations had been based upon the use of two years' income from the Rate allowed since the Welsh Intermediate Education Act 1889, making possible a grant of one third of £15 per head. The Committee were now advised by Mr. Bruce to think in terms of the use of three or four years' income. One year had elapsed since the Education Act and two years more would be needed for the Queen's approval of a Scheme and after that a year would be required for the building of schools. Accordingly, the whole of the income would not be needed for maintenance even in the fourth year. This opinion led the Committee to decide in favour of a basis of three years during which the income from local taxation was likely to yield £1,500 per year, or even more in the year following. They set aside £200 for technical purposes, thus leaving £1,300 which, together with interest would make a total of £4,000 at the end of three years. It was now determined to increase the grant for buildings from £5 to £7.10s. per head.

Important matters affecting efficiency and administration were then deliberated. First there was the move to set up a Central Welsh Board of Education, the function of which would be the examination and inspection of schools. Mr. Bruce pointed out the advantages of such an arrangement, said that it was hoped that the Treasury would accept the proposed examinations as sufficient for the purpose of government grants and asked that the Joint Education Committee might agree, with other counties, to contribute a percentage of a halfpenny rate. The Committee agreed to support the new Board but no amount of financial contribution was specified. Secondly, the Committee reached agreement on the constitution of the County Governing Body which would supersede the Joint Education Committee on the expiry of its term of office, and thirdly, there was some discussion about the Local Governing Bodies (School Managers) who would be in charge of School Districts. Mr. Bruce drew attention to two counties where such bodies included representatives of subscribers and donors to building funds and suggested that this might be borne in mind in Pembrokeshire.

Throughout the year the Joint Education Committee were at work, modifying and adding to their proposals affecting finance, administration, the allocation of schools and their accommodation. There were continuous negotiations and manoeuvres between the local committees, the Joint Education Committee and the Charity Commission until the Scheme, with some amendments, was the subject of a resulution at a Special Meeting of the Pembrokeshire County Council on 6 December 1892: 'That the Draft Education Scheme (prepared by the Joint Education Committee for the County of Pembroke appointed under the Welsh Intermediate Education Act) be approved and adopted and that this Council consent to appoint representatives on the Governing Bodies named therein as soon as it has received the Sanction of Her Majesty in Council.' The draft proposals were then sent for the approval of the Charity Commissioners, who in their turn circularised copies among the local committees and received their criticisms. The end product was the document which was approved by Her Majesty in Council on 30 April 1894.

This scheme was subject to the Welsh Intermediate Education Act 1889, the Local Taxation (Customs and Excise) Act 1890 and the Endowed Schools Act 1869 and Amending Acts. There were to be taken into account the Foundations of Haverfordwest Grammar School, Mary Tasker's School in the Town and County of Haverfordwest and Eastgate School in the Parish of Narberth. The endowments of these last are set out in the First Schedule of the document. Elsewhere in the text were the provisions for dealing with the foundations.

Details of the Scheme occupy thirty-three pages made up of eight Parts and six Schedules. Part I is confined to definitions of words and expressions used. Parts II and V are concerned with finance and administration at the County and District levels, while Part VI is devoted to plans for the new intermediate schools and Part VII to scholarships, bursaries and exhibitions. General provisions are contained in Part VIII. In view of the importance of this Scheme in the history of education in Pembrokeshire, some of its principal features should be noticed here.

There were to be eight County School Districts, each comprising of a group of parishes, as listed in the Second Schedule, which also

32

gives the location of the schools and the population of each catchment area:—Pembroke Dock 23,000, Tenby 8,000, Narberth 12,000, Cardigan (shared with Cardiganshire County Council) 10,000, Fishguard 6,000, Saint David's 6,000, Milford Haven 8,000, Haverfordwest—figure not given. For each school there was to be a body of School Managers (the Local Governing Body) and overall administration in the shire was to be entrusted to the County Governing Body. The constitution and functions of the governing bodies were laid down—their composition, eligibility for membership, elections, the filling of vacancies, term of office, number of meetings, the quorum, matters entrusted to them, the rules for the conduct of business.

There were special transitory provisions for the concluding phase of the work of the Pembrokeshire Joint Education Committee, which was to arrange the first elections of the new governing bodies and to manage the transference of authority to them.

As the County Governing Body was to figure prominently in administration and in negotiations during the inaugural phase and the early history of the County Schools under the Scheme, attention should be drawn to its composition and to some of its functions.

This Body was to be composed of twenty-seven members, twenty-five of them Representative Governors and two Co-optative. The Representative Governors were to be appointed: 14 by the County Council, 1 by the Council of the University College of Wales at Aberystwyth, 1 by the University College of South Wales and Monmouth shire, 8 by the School Managers (1 from each District) and 1 by certificated teachers in Public Elementary Schools.

The most important responsibility of the County Governing Body, under the Scheme, was to be the management of the Pembrokeshire Intermediate and Technical Education Fund, called the 'General Fund'. This fund was to be drawn from five sources:—

(a)   the product of a rate of one halfpenny in the £1, based upon the aggregate value of the property in the County, and to be levied by the County Council each financial year, commencing with that current with the date of the Scheme.

(b)   the Exchequer contribution, which was the residue of the sum received by the County Council under the provisions of the Local Taxation (Customs and Excise) Act 1890, after

33

deducting therefrom £200 in each of the first four years and £100 in every other year—beginning with the year 1890.

(c) the Treasury grant paid each year in aid of the schools under the Welsh Intermediate Education Act.

(d) the endowments of Mary Tasker's School Haverfordwest and of Eastgate School Narberth, as listed in the First Schedule, but not those of Haverfordwest Grammar School, noted in the same Schedule. All other endowments if any.

(e) additional donations or endowments which subject to the Scheme, may be received by the County Governing Body for the general advancement of the Intermediate or Technical Education in the County.

The above financial resources were to be drawn upon for three main purposes.

First there was to be assistance towards the provision of school premises. Out of the Exchequer contributions received in the four financial years 1890-94, the County Governing Body were to put into a separate account, called the Building Fund, the sum of £1,300 per annum to accumulate at compound interest. The County Governing Body were to pay to the Managers of each school District, except Haverfordwest, a portion of the Building Fund, provided that within three years of the date of the Scheme there would be set aside a piece of freehold land suitable for a school building and a sum of money paid into the banking account of the Managers, or guaranteed by responsible persons, not less than the amount specified in the fourth column of the Fourth Schedule.

Secondly there must be created a reserve fund. Out of the income from the General Fund, the County Governing Body were to set aside annually a sum of not more than one fifth and not less than one tenth to meet the expenses of the Scheme. These included the management of property and business, the examination and inspection of the schools by the Central Welsh Board when established, the expenses of travelling teachers, County Exhibitions, contributions to a Pension Fund. Also there was special provision in respect of temporary school premises at St. David's and Fishguard and towards the annual maintenance of Haverfordwest Grammar School.

Thirdly there was to be an allocation for the maintenance of the schools. The County Governing Body were to apportion annually among the School Managers of the Districts the residue of the income from the General Fund, according to the percentages indicated in the fifth column of the Fourth Schedule. A condition was that the School Managers should apply one fifth of the sum allotted to them for the provision of scholarships and bursaries.

Alongside their financial responsibilites, the County Governing Body were to be closely concerned with the efficiency of the schools. They had the sole power of appointment and dismissal of the Head-masters and they were linked with the School Managers through the County Council representatives of whom there were three on each local governing body. Moreover, in conjunction with the Central Welsh Board, the County Governing Body were to provide and pay for the yearly examination and inspection of all County Schools by competent examiners and inspectors unconnected with the schools. From these officials the County Governing Body was to receive written reports on the proficiency of the scholars and the condition of the schools as regards organisation, methods of instruction and discipline. From Haverfordwest copies of the reports were to be sent to the School Managers, to the Head Masters and to the Charity Commissioners.

In section 2 of this chapter an account will be given of the establish-ment of one County School, that at Tenby. This will include a description of local financial and other difficulties, the constitution of the Managers, the acquisition of premises and equipment, syllabuses of instruction and the course of events down to the official opening. Meanwhile, the story of this one particular school is best understood against the background of the plans for the County Schools which were elaborated in Part VI of the Scheme. The schools were to be Day Schools, but boarders could be admitted on the request of the Managers, Some, known as 'Dual Schools', were to have two departments, one for boys and one for girls, with separate entrances, playgrounds and classrooms, though the Managers could arrange for the boys and girls to be taught together. Each school was to be so conducted as to be eligible for the financial support already mentioned.

The School Managers were to hold office for three years and were to be eligible for re-election. One of their first tasks, in consultation with the County Governing Body, was to provide 'proper buildings planned with a view to convenient extension and for the number of day scholars specified in the second column of the Fifth Schedule and for such number of boarders, if any, if thought fit'. The buildings were to include so far as practicable chemical and physical laboratories and workshops and a kitchen and laundry and proper furnishings and fitting. The accommodation for boarders was to be provided for other than from the General Fund. Out of the income applicable to the school the Managers were to make provision for the plant and apparatus, repairs and improvements and the payment of rates and taxes. They were to be responsible for the sanitary condition of the premises. The conduct of business and the keeping of records must be according to the rules of the Scheme. Other responsibilities were the prescription of subjects of instruction and their relative prominence, the arrangement of vacations, the payments of day scholars, the number and payments of boarders if any and fixing the number of assistants and the annual amounts needed to maintain them.

The provisions for staffing the schools are of special interest. The Head Master must have taken a degree in the United Kingdom. (There was a special provision for Haverfordwest Girls' School). For appointment or dismissal there was to be a Special Committee composed of five members appointed by the County Governing Body and three by the Local Governing Body. The post of Head Master was to be advertised and appointment was to be made by a special meeting of the County Governing Body after receiving a report from the Special Committee. Upon taking up office the Head Master must sign a declaration, which was to be entered in the Minute Book. He must not be the holder of any ecclesiastical office or any other employment; neither he nor any assistant could be a Governor of the school; he was not required to be in Holy Orders; there were rules concerning the occupation and surrender of any official residence.

The powers of the Head Master were considerable. His views and proposals were to be taken into account with regard to subjects of instruction, plant and apparatus. Subject to the Scheme, he was to have under his control the choice of books, the methods of teaching, the arrangement of classes and school hours, internal organisation and discipline and the authority to expel or to suspend scholars—though cases were to be reported to the Managers. Moreover the Head was to have the sole power of appointment and dismissal of assistant staff (except in the case of Cardigan) and, subject to the approval of the Managers, was to determine how the aggregate sum they allocated for the maintenance of Assistant Masters, school plant and apparatus was to be divided for these purposes.

The Head Master's income was to be the yearly stipend of £120 (except in the case of Haverfordwest Girls' School) plus the capitation payment for each scholar in the school, calculated on a scale fixed from time to time by the Managers, but in any event not less than £1 and not more than £3 for each scholar.

The Tuition Fees were to be fxed from time to time by the Managers, at the rate of not less than £3 and not more than £6 per scholar (except at Cardigan). Where there were two or more children of the same parents attending school at the same time a reduction could be made in respect of such children after the first but no fee must be less than the amount of the capitation payment to the Head Master. The payments of boarders, apart from tuition fees were not to exceed £30 per head. All tuition fees were payable in advance, either to the Head Master or to such person as the School Managers might from time to time determine.

Conditions were laid down for the admission of pupils. Except by special permission of the Local Governing Body, no scholar could be admitted under the age of 10 years (9 at Cardigan and at Haverfordwest Girls) and none could remain in school after the age of 17, or the end of the term that such age would be attained. In special cases permission could be given for a scholar to remain in school until the age of 18. For five years from the date of the Scheme this age limit could be stretched to 19, upon written recommendation from the Head Master. The school was to be open to all children of good character and sufficient health, either residing with their parents or in lodgings licensed by the School Managers, or boarding under approved conditions. Applications for admission were to be made to the Head Master or to some approved person. A pupil would be admitted either after passing an examination, equivalent to the Fifth Standard, under the direction of the School Managers, or if a scholar in a public elementary school after reaching the Fifth Standard. (Fourth Standard in the case of Haverfordwest Girls' School and in Cardigan). Provided there would be room available, those found fit and subject to the provisions of the Scheme, would be admitted according to the date of their application.

The remainder of Part VI of the Scheme is taken up with the subjects in which instruction should and could be given according to the provisions of the Welsh Intermediate Education Act.

37

Part VII of the Scheme gives details of scholarships, bursaries and exhibitions and sets out the regulations and conditions to which they were to be subject.

The School Managers must maintain scholarships, to be called County Scholarships, not less in number than ten per cent and not more than twenty per cent of the scholars in the school during the last term of the preceding year. The scholarships were to be tenable for one year but could be renewed from year to year by the School Managers on the written recommendation of the Head Master. Not less than half of the whole number of County Scholarships must be awarded, with total exemption from tuition fees, to children who on their admission to a County School, had spent not less than three years in a Public Elementary School. The remainder of these scholarships were to carry exemption from one half of the tuition fees and were to be awarded to scholars already in the school, except in cases where the Head Master made adverse reports concerning character and conduct. All Scholarships were to be subject to the regulations of the County Governing Body. After deducting the value of these awards the Local Governors could apply the residue to augmenting the value of the County Scholarships and to the maintenance of County School Bursaries, consisting of payments which would assist needy scholars to meet the expense of travelling to and from school, the cost of books and stationery and other incidentals. The number of pupils receiving such assistance would depend upon the funds available and upon the judgement of the Managers.

The County Exhibitions, each of a yearly value of not less than £10 and tenable for not more than three years at any University, University College or other institution of university, professional, or technical education were to be awarded by the County Governing Body on the result of such examination as they would think fit. Those eligible were to be boys and girls either with not less than two years' attendance in a County School or holders of Scholarships under the Scheme.

This analysis of the Scheme for Intermediate Education in Pembroke-shire, approved by Her Majesty in Council in 1894, is to be concluded with a note of the Fourth and Fifth Schedules which summarise the particulars of the proposed County Schools, including type, accommodation and finance.

Particulars of Schools, Grants from Building and General Fund to each District, and Building Fund Subscriptions

1. District and Site of School	2. School	3. Grant from Building Fund	4. Building Fund Subscript- ions	5. Annual Grant Percentage of residue of General Fund
		£ s.	£	
Pembroke Dock	Dual	1,515 0	735	31·5
Tenby	,,	707 0	525	10·95
Narberth	,,	808 0	600	16·43
Cardigan	,,	656 10	487	13·69
Fishguard	Mixed	404 0	300	8·21
St. David's	,,	404 0	300	8·21
Milford Haven	Dual	707 0	525	10·95
Haverfordwest	Girls★	—	—	+

★ The existing buildings of Mary Tasker's School to be used for this School

+ A fixed annual sum of £250 in addition to the endowment of Mary Tasker's School.

× As an example, the Local Governors' Minutes of 22 August 1896 include a note of Maintenance Grant received:— £514. 15s. 8d. of which one fifth, £102. 17s. 6d, was the sum to be applied in Scholarships.

School Accommodation

1. Name of County School	2. Accommodation for Day Scholars		
	Boys		Girls
Pembroke Dock	90		60
Tenby	40		30
Narberth	50		30
Cardigan	80		50
Fishguard		40	
St. David's		40	
Milford Haven.................	40		30
Haverfordwest	—		—

The first meetings of the Local Governing Bodies, the School Managers, were held in August 1894. A preliminary meeting of the County Governing Body took place on 31 August and the fully constituted Body met on 14 September, with the Rev. Lewis James as Chairman and Mr. W. Davies George as Clerk. The subsequent efforts of the Local Governors with the support of the County Governing Body and with the approval of the Charity Commission led to the opening of the County Schools as follows: Haverfordwest Girls (September 1894), Narberth (15 January 1895), Fishguard (17 January 1895), Pembroke Dock (21 January, 1895), St. David's (29 April 1895), Tenby (23 September 1896), Milford Haven (30 September 1896). It should be remarked that the Schools at Narberth, Pembroke Dock and St. David's were inaugurated in temporary premises and moved into new quarters in September 1898.

The School at Cardigan, of which the catchment area lay either side of the River Teifi, was supported jointly by the Pembrokeshire and Cardiganshire authorities, having been brought into existence in 1896.

In 1897 all these schools were inspected 'in compliance with the Treasury Regulations.' The Inspectors' Report revealed that at the time of their visitation there were on the attendance roll 494 pupils, of whom 290 were boys and 204 were girls. Of these pupils, 272 came from urban and 222 from rural parishes, 45 were under 12 years of age, 260 were between 12 and 15, 95 were between 15 and 16, and 94 over 16. The permanent staffs comprised 7 Head Masters, 1 Head Mistress, 10 Assistant Masters and 12 Assistant Mistresses—a proportion of 1 member of staff to 17 pupils.

The County Schools were now launched on their respective careers. Many years were to elapse before they were able to acquire the resources needed to develop their potential under the Scheme.

In due course, modifications of the Scheme became necessary, following upon the Board of Education Act 1899 and the Balfour Education Act 1902. Draft amendments, which were published in 1903, were altered by a Scheme of the Board of Education of 15 July 1904, which in its turn was replaced by the scheme 'Approved by His Majesty in Council, 14 May 1912'. The local application of these changes will be taken into account in the story of the County School at Tenby.

Section 2: The Establishment of the County Intermediate School in Tenby

It was not until September 1890 that the first public move was made towards support for the establishment of an intermediate school in Tenby. Mr. C. F. Egerton Allen, Cambridge graduate, barrister, former member of the Legislative Council of the Governor General of India and later Liberal M.P. for the Pembroke and Haverfordwest Boroughs (1892-95), joined with other Tenby residents in petitioning the Mayor, Councillor Nicholas Adamson Roch, to convene a meeting 'for the purpose of considering the advisability of aiding in the erecting of a School-house in South Pembrokeshire under the Intermediate Education Act.' As yet it was not realised that more than one secondary school would be established in the South of the County. The meeting was held in the Town Hall over the entrance to the Market in the High Street on the evening of 24 September. Among those present were local gentry, and professional and business men of the town.

The Mayor presided. He explained the main points of the Intermediate Education Act, mentioning that while current expenses of new

41

schools could be met by one halfpenny in the pound Rate in the county, by an equivalent amount in government grant and by 'scholars' fees', there was no provision for the cost of erecting school buildings for which a considerable sum would be needed. The business of the meeting was to discuss the best means of raising money in aid of building a school house in South Pembrokeshire.

In the ensuing discussion, which was given full coverage in the *Tenby Observer,* several speakers expressed the opinion that more emphasis should be placed on the needs of Tenby. Mr. C. F. Egerton Allen described in some detail the benefits of the Act, which was one removed from party dispute. 'They had to thank the Conservative Party for the Act and the Liberal Members for Wales for pressing it on the attention of the Conservative Government. To give the nation a good education was the best benefit they could confer upon it.' Referring to the problem of raising money for building purposes, Mr. Allen said that in Narberth and Pembroke promises of support had been limited by conditions that the schools should be located in Narberth and Pembroke. He hoped that such conditions would not hamper offerings in Tenby, although he admitted that the prospect of having a school there would be an incentive to contributions. This view was also favoured by John Leach, the founder of the *Tenby and County News* in 1893, who said that since the Act had to be carried out the best they could do was to try and get a school established at Tenby or, failing that, at the nearest point.

Some dissentient voices were raised in the debate. Dr. Douglas A. Reid, formerly a surgeon in the Crimean War, feared a rise in the Rates and was apprehensive about a possible appropriation of Local Charities for educational purposes, a theme to which he was to return later in a letter to the local newspaper. Sentiments, doubtless shared by many others in the town, were expressed by one, John Griffiths, who asked whether it was right that he should be expected to contribute a halfpenny Rate for the purpose of supporting 'college' children of a higher class than himself. The discussion then turned to the Technical Education Act which, as the Mayor pointed out, would give the Borough Council the opportunity of raising a Rate independent of the Intermediate Education Act.

It was then resolved unanimously 'That this meeting of the inhabitants of Tenby gratefully looks forward to the benefits ensured by the establishment of a School in South Pembrokeshire, under the provisions of the Welsh Intermediate Education Act, 1889, and desires to support the establishment by subscribing to a fund to aid in the building of a School house.' For the furtherance of this resolution and the collection of subscriptions a committee was then appointed, consisting of W. H. Richards, J.P., C. C.; Benjamin Harries; J. E. Arnett; A. H. Brookman; John Leach; J. Bancroft, H. M. Inspector of Schools; J. T. Jones; J. A. Jenkins; G. Chiles; F. C. Egerton Allen.

The *Tenby Observer* of 16 October reported on the progress of the Fund Raising Committee, which had met and had decided to ask the Tenby Borough Council to hold a special meeting and offer a site. The Committee's Chairman was W. H. Richards, Justice of the Peace for the County and the Borough, Alderman, eight times Mayor of Tenby, High Sheriff in 1878, the third of the Croft House family to figure prominently in local affairs during the course of the nineteenth century. The Chairman was to communicate with Mr. W. Davies George, Deputy Clerk of the Peace and Clerk to the Pembrokeshire Joint Education Committee, asking what steps would be necessary for the County Council to receive a deputation from Tenby to urge the claims of the town for the establishment of a school there. The local newspaper listed in full sixty promises of subscriptions, amounting to £212. 4s. 6d. should the school be placed in Tenby and £101. 8s. 6d. should it be set up elsewhere. At this time, of course, it was not known how many of the new centres of secondary education would be set up in the south of the county.

Frank B. Mason's 'Observer' columnist was eloquent in outlining the new scheme of education, in extolling its advantages and in his exposition of the claims of Tenby which he considered should be brought to the attention of the Joint Education Committee. Here is a sample of the arguments:—

'The advantages offered to all are to be paid for rateably by all—no one should feel under invidious obligation in allowing his family to partake of the benefits offered.'

'The Schools, as the title suggests, are for young people who have passed through the education of their childhood and require equipment for their work in life . . . they should be the stepping stone to Higher Education if a scholar shows ability. If the university is not desired, the education will enable him to compete in any occupation with the

43

best educated. The youth of Wales will have at their door the same education that fits the sons of those who can afford to pay the fees of an English public school, to take the prizes of the professions and the higher careers of commerce ... This education will be provided within the means of all but the very poor, and for the children of very poor parents who show ability it is hoped that scholarships and exhibitions will be provided.'

For health and convenience of approach, Tenby was to be preferred to Pembroke Dock or Narberth. Tenby was sited between the two and there were attractions for families to remain or settle in the town. This would mean that more money would be spent there. The scholars, the school establishment of teachers, and those connected with them would constitute a large additional community in the town.

And then followed an exhortation to the Local Committee: 'We trust that the Committee will go forward with the task they have undertaken and use their best endeavours to obtain for Tenby what would undoubtedly be one of the greatest benefits that could be conferred upon the place, considered from a pecuniary or educational point of view.'

Part of the above was an echo of the current notion that the new secondary schools should ape the public schools and compete with them on equal terms; part was a rhapsody compounded of idealism and material interests. According to a report in the same newspaper, similar sentiments were expressed at the Special Meeting of the Tenby Borough Council on Friday 17 October 1890. The Mayor pointed out the advantages of schools at Clifton, Cheltenham and Rugby; and Councillor J. A. Jenkins, a local auctioneer, supporting a request for the Treasury's permission for the Council to provide a suitable site for the school, said that the project would be one of the greatest boons conferred upon the town and that it would mean the spending of £7,000 or £8,000 a year there and bring in families. The Minutes of this Special Meeting record three resolutions:

    (a)   That application be made to the Treasury for leave to alienate, by way of gift, a portion of the Corporation property as a site for the School under the Welsh Intermediate Education Act.

    (b)   That a Deputation from the Town Council wait upon the Joint Education Committee at their next Meeting, in conjunction with the Deputation appointed by the Public Meeting.

(c)   That the Mayor represent the Council at such a Meeting.

The sequel to the first of the resolutions was that the Quarterly Meeting of the Town Council on 10 November received from the Lords of the Treasury a reply to the application which the Town Clerk had made on the Council's behalf. Their Lordships pointed out that 'application should be made to the Local Government Board by formal Statutory Memorial, preceded by one month's public notice,' and added 'For convenience sake your letter and its enclosure have meantime been forwarded to the Department with a copy of this reply.'

After some discussion the Council resolved '... that the Town Clerk prepare the necessary Memorial to the Local Government Board and submit it at the next Council Meeting.' However there were obstacles ahead. The adjourned Quarterly Meeting of the Borough Council, held on 25 November, was faced with a communication from Alfred D. Adrian, Assistant Secretary to the Local Government Board. He stated that the Lords Commissioners of the Treasury had forwarded to the Local Government Board the Council's application 'for consent to the alienation by way of gift of certain corporate lands as a site for a School under the Welsh Intermediate Education Act 1889'. The Board had given the matter their consideration, but in the absence of any authority in the above Act for such arrangement as proposed, they were not prepared to entertain the application as one to which they could properly accede under the Municipal Corporations Act 1882. The letter continued 'The Board are aware that the Lords of the Treasury have, on various occasions, sanctioned the alienation of corporate property for educational purposes with inadequate consideration, but they understand from their Lordships that they have of late years been increasingly unwilling to consent to such alienation at anything less than the true market value of the land to be alienated, especially in those cases where Parliament has given rating powers for the educational purposes for which such grants are required.' However, the sting was in the tail. 'This consideration is especially applicable in such a case as the present where long standing and heavy debts remain to be cleared off by the Town Council and when every effort should be made to extinguish old liabilities.'

45

The Council, apparently undaunted by the rejection of their request and by the reminder of their existing debts, approved of a draft reply which was read by the Mayor. The first paragraph of this indicated that, irrespective of their application for sanction to present a school site, the Town Council had been considering means to extinguish their debts. These proposals were outlined, and then the letter continued '. . . the Tenby Council would beg to observe that the reason why they have requested sanction to give a school site is because Parliament do not appear to have given any rating powers for the provision of school sites or for building upon them. The extent of the Rating powers as the Town Council can apprehend is for the imposition of a Rate not exceeding a halfpenny in the £1 for the annual expenses of the School. The Town Council would beg to say that they find it is the unanimous wish of the Town that they may have power to present a school site.'

Meanwhile, before the end of November, there was better news from Haverfordwest. The Tenby Council were informed that their Deputation had stated Tenby's case in a meeting of the Joint Education Committee, which was attended by Mr. Bruce, representing the Charity Commissioners. There was now a prospect of two schools in the south, one of them at Tenby and the other at Pembroke Dock. There were further developments when the Joint Education Committee met on Tuesday 16 December. In the provisional scheme then outlined, there would be a school at Tenby, though its nature was yet to be determined. At the next Quarterly Meeting of the Tenby Borough Council, on 11 February 1891, Mayor Roch informed his colleagues that, subject to official confirmation, Tenby had been selected as a centre for intermediate education. He referred to the problem of a site and a building, which he understood Mr. Bruce, Assistant Charity Commissioner, to have said would cost £1,600. The Mayor went on to suggest that, if owners and occupiers of property in the town would agree for one year to contribute 2/- in the £1 additional to the Rates which stood at 4/- in the £1, the £1,600 would be raised. However, this novel solution appears to have met with no response and no more was heard of it.

Next, Alderman W. H. Richards convened the Tenby Fund Raising Committee for 20 February at the Town Hall. It was agreed that a letter concerning the proposed school at Tenby, received by the Alderman from the Deputy Clerk to the County Council, should be laid before the Borough Council on the following Tuesday 24 February. The contents of this letter are of special interest in that they gave the first indications of the kind of school which would be set up in Tenby and the conditions under which the Joint Education Committee were prepared to frame their proposals for such an establishment. First, the School was to be a Dual School for boys and girls in separate departments; secondly, a freehold site of about two acres in extent must be provided by the locality; thirdly, buildings for not less than 50 boys and 30 girls in separate departments must be provided at a cost of not less than £17. 10s. per head, the Joint Education Committee's contribution to the cost of such buildings was to be an amount not exceeding £5 per head; fourthly, the amount raised by local contributions was to be paid into the bank by 1 January 1892 or a sufficient guarantee given for the same. The Joint Education Committee concluded by expressing the hope that a local committee would be definitely constituted to act as a means of communication between the Joint Education Committee and the locality.

The discussion which ensued in the Borough Council was largely concerned with the proposed cost of the school. It was noted that, on a basis of £17. 10s. per pupil, a building for 80 would cost £1,400, towards which the County Council would provide £5 per head amounting to £400, thus leaving £1,000 to be found locally. Towards this sum £300 had been promised by subscribers so that another £700 would be required. There was some argument over the conditions which it was known would impose upon Tenby a cost per head of £2.10s. more than in any other of the proposed centres in Pembrokeshire. On the problem of a site for the school, a remark from the Mayor revealed that at this stage St. John's Croft was under consideration as a possibility. The Council decided to refer Mr. Davies George's letter to their Estates Committee for a detailed report.

When the Tenby Fund Raising Committee (hereafter to be called the Local Committee) met on 3 April it was agreed that their Chairman, Alderman W. H. Richards, should be Secretary and the intermediary between the County Committee and themselves. Inevitably the cost per head for building a school at Tenby was the main topic discussed and it was agreed to ask the Joint Education Committee to reconsider their proposal. A letter was received from the local committee at

47

Milford Haven suggesting joint action with themselves and Pembroke in negotiations at the county level.

The proposals of the Joint Education Committee, put forward in May 1891, concerning the allocation of schools and their accommodation and the modification of financial arrangements, have been discussed already, but the Committee's intention concerning Tenby should be noted again since this became a point of dispute between the county and the local committees. The recommendation was that a new school should not cost less than £15 per scholar, 'but in one, being a select school, not less than £17.10s., as the wealth and taste of the inhabitants demand a more ornate building.' The decision of the Joint Education Committee to increase the grant for buildings from £5 to £7.10s. did nothing to allay the anxiety of the Local Committee who were being asked to provide more costly premises than would be the case in other Districts. Alderman Richards kept his Local Committee informed of the deliberations in Haverfordwest and on 20 May placed before them a letter dated 14 May from Wm. Davies George, Deputy Clerk of the Peace. This communication was to inform Local Committees of the Intermediate Education Committee's decision 'to grant a proportion of the estimated cost of building Intermediate Schools at the rate of £7 10s. per scholar, provided that the Local Committee find the remainder of the estimated cost and offer a suitable site for a building.' 'This Committee will be glad to hear that the Local Committee assents to the above terms, and when such a site can be offered for inspection, will feel pleasure in coming to Tenby to look at it and to confer with the Local Committee on the steps which should next be taken to promote their Scheme.' However, when these proposals were considered by the Local Committee it was argued that, since the Joint Education Committee still thought that the school in Tenby should be of a more ornate character than any other in the County, then a proportionately larger sum of money should be allocated for the purpose. Accordingly it was resolved to ask the Joint Education Committee for £750, drawing attention to the fact that even if this request were favourably received, the sum of £600 to be found locally would press hard on their exertions and would still be more than other Local Committees would have to raise.

The Tenby Local Committee's observations were received unsympathetically in the Joint Education Committee when they met on

9 June. Mr. Bruce remarked that the Joint Committee had been informed all along that Tenby required a more expensive school than other places; the people there seemed to want a nice building but they did not want to pay for it. The Chairman, the Rev. Lewis James, stated there was a tendency to wriggle on this question and that if Tenby wanted a school at all they could easily raise £1,000 there. The Clerk was then instructed to write to the Local Committee saying that the grant could not be increased and reminding them that they had previously accepted proposals when the total of the grant stood at £500, whereas it was now £600. Reference was to be made to the proceedings of 17 February when it was considered that the increased cost in Tenby could be met, since it was a richer community than the others. The *Tenby Observer* of 21 May 1891 pointed out that W. H. Richards had set the County Committee straight on this matter, as the Local Committee had never asked for more ornate buildings. However, the authorities in Haverfordwest remained adamant at this stage, and back in Tenby the two main problems were being faced, that of the site for the new school and that of raising enough money for the building.

The Borough Council had referred the question of the site to their Estates Committee, by which reports were prepared after meetings in March 1891. Proposals to use either St. John's Croft or land in Heywood Lane were met with a storm of protest from landowners and residents, especially in the latter area. At the request of Mr. Sackville H. Owen of St. Mary's Hill a petition was lodged before a Special Meeting of the Council on 17 April 1891.

> *To the Mayor and Corporation of the Town of Tenby*
> We, the undersigned having heard that you intend offering a site in Heywood Lane for the building of the Intermediate School, desire to express our hope that you will select some other site.
> We consider that a school in our midst would not only be a nuisance but would materially affect the value of the property in the immediate neighbourhood . . .

The eight signatories lived in the larger residences in Heywood Lane. It would be interesting to hear the reaction of these petitioners if they could return to see the developments which have now taken place in their old haunts—a nursery school, a junior school, a comprehensive school expanding to take 1,300 pupils, and housing developments including the Maudlins, Newell Hill, Leach Way, and Heywood Court on the site of the former tennis courts where Welsh Championship were played.

The problem was thrown back to the Estates Committee and, in due course, at a Quarterly Meeting on 18 November the Council resolved 'that two acres of Lower Knowle Park be given to the Joint Education Committee for a site for a school under the Welsh Inter-mediate Education Act.' A 'Local Note' in the *Tenby Observer* of 26 November 1891 referred to this decision of the Council. 'It may not be generally known even to the Tenbyite—where the Lower Knowle Park is, and therefore for their information it may be stated that it is a field lying to the north of the old road immediately behind the Pine Plantation above the Gasworks and nearly opposite the Cemetery. . . It is generally admitted that the position is well suited for the purpose.'

What imagination! It is tempting to speculate as to what inspiration the pupils would have derived from their proximity to the gasworks and the cemetery had the school been planted there.

The writer of the above 'Local Note' could not resist the opportunity of a 'dig' at the property owners and residents who had objected to the two previous sites. 'The Council, I suppose, regarded their objection as reasonable and withheld the two sites. Therefore I hope owners of property in that district will reciprocate and mark their appreciation either by a substantial contribution where such has not yet been promised—or by augmenting what they have already undertaken to give.'

While a solution to the problem of the site was being sought the Tenby Local Committee were redoubling their efforts to raise money. At their meeting on 29 September 1891 they were informed that the Joint Education Committee would not advance beyond £600 in aid of the school in Tenby, and Alderman W. H. Richards reminded them that £900 must be deposited at the London and Provincial Bank before 1 January 1892 in order that the grant could be obtained. Nearly £300 had been promised as a result of the first canvas, but the Local Committee now decided upon further action by circular letter and by an appeal through the Press. So a letter was drafted, outlining the prop-osals and the financial situation, a copy was published in the local newspaper, others were sent out to residents and personal visits were paid, soliciting subscriptions. In addition, Mr. Egerton Allen made

50

a strong appeal in a personal letter in the 'Observer'. By the end of October the total sum promised reached £347. 2 s. 0d., but replies were still awaited from landowners residing out of town but holding property in Tenby.

By December, the Joint Education Committee were ready with their proposed Scheme for Intermediate and Technical Education which would be sent later to the Charity Commissioners, as required by the 1889 Act. With the Committee's approval, the *Tenby Observer* of 17 December 1891 published details of the Scheme and underlined its implications for Tenby. The plans proposed for Tenby, based on an earlier draft drawn up for Pembroke Dock on 9 June were as follows:—

(a) The Tenby District was to include, in addition to the town, the St. Mary Out-Liberty and the parishes of Caldey, Gumfreston, St. Florence and Manorbier. (There was to be sharp criticism of this allocation).

(b) The school was to be established with the aid of the building fund, out of which the Joint Education Committee had allocated £600 to Tenby on condition that a sum not less than £800 and a suitable site would be forthcoming through voluntary effort. Income for maintenance of the school was to be assisted out of public funds. Tenby's share from the County Rate, the Treasury Grant and the Local Taxation Grant was to be £238, allocated according to the population of the District.

(c) A suitable site and buildings were to be provided, with accommodation for a Dual School for 50 boys and 30 girls in separate departments. It was to be a Day School but there was power for the School Managers to arrange for the reception of boarders, either in the Master's House or in lodgings under their control.

(d) Tuition Fees were to be not less than £5 and not more than £8 per Scholar and the Boarding Fee must not exceed £35.

(e) No scholar was to be admitted under the age of 10 years and no scholar was to remain in school after the age of 17 without consent of the Governors. No pupil was to be admitted to the school unless he had passed the Fifth Standard at a Public Elementary School or an equivalent examination prescribed by the Governing Body.

51

(f) The curriculum was to follow the pattern prescribed in the Intermediate Education Act.

    (i) There were to be rules for Religious Instruction. The Bible was to be taught in the school, the details being left to the local Governors in consultation with the Head Master. If the Head Master kept boarders, they were to be allowed to attend such places of worship and to have such reasonable facilities for Religious Instruction and from such teachers as their parents would think fit. By notice in writing addressed to the Head Master a parent could claim for a scholar exemption from religious worship or from religious instruction.

    (ii) Instruction was to be given in Reading, Writing, Arithmetic; Geography, History; English Grammar; Composition and Literature; Mathematics; Latin; at least one modern European Language; at least one branch of Natural Science, with special attention to the industries of the District; Drawing, Vocal Music; Drill and other Physical Exercise; and, for the Girls, Domestic Economy and the Laws of Health.

    (iii) Instruction could be given in any of the following:—
Greek; Welsh Grammar, Composition and Literature; Mechanics, Principles of Agriculture, Navigation, Mensuration; Shorthand; Working in Wood and Iron; and, for Girls only, Cutting Out, Laundry Work; and in other such subjects as the Managers and the County Governing Body would think fit.
Classes in Natural Science, Mechanics and other Technical subjects, in all cases, were to be associated with sufficient experimental demonstration and practical teaching.

(g) The Tenby Local Governing Body was to consist of fourteen members of whom eleven to be elected by the following:—
Subscribers of £5 and upwards for the next 5 years 2, the Borough Council 2, the Guardians of the Rural Parishes 2, the County Council 3, the Voluntary Schools 2. The remaining three members, two of them women, were to be

co-opted. The functions of the Governing Body were listed:— the receipt and application of Science and Art Grants; the maintenance of buildings; the management of Local Finance, including the fixing of Tuition Fees and the Capitation Fee due to the Head Master; the arrangements for boarders; the control of Instruction, Holidays etc. subject to the Scheme; the control of Religious Instruction; the regulation of Entrance Examinations; the power to give leave to pupils to remain in school after the prescribed age; the management of scholarships; the submission of Reports and Accounts to the County Governing Body. All members of the Governing Body were to hold office for three years and the Representatives Members need not belong to the body or class appointing them. Men and women were to be equally eligible. The County Council were to elect their representatives after the other bodies had done so, but prior to the co-opting of members.

These proposals for the school in Tenby were for the most part the same as those for schools in the other Districts involved in the Scheme for the County. There were differences in points of detail and there were to be disputes and some changes, as will be seen later. However, a knowledge of the above plans is helpful to an understanding of the work of the Local Governing Body and the establishment and functioning of the County Intermediate School in Tenby, although four years and nine months were to elapse before the first pupils were to enter its doors—and then not on the site at Knowle Park as the Council had intended, following their deliberations in 1891.

The year 1891 closed with a Special Meeting of the Borough Council on Tuesday the 29th day of December. Alderman Richards presented a Memorial from the Tenby Local Committee. The Memorial outlined events from the Public Meeting of 24 September 1890 onwards, indicated that £380 had been collected or promised, mentioned the proposals of the Joint Education Committee, added a note on the attractions of the Scheme and the strong desire which existed in the town to see its fulfilment, expressed appreciation of the Council's offer of the Lower Knowle Park site, and continued '. . . while recognising the valuable and generous aid afforded to their endeavours by the favourable consideration already shown, the Committee venture to ask for a money subscription as well,' and concluded ' . . . no endeavours of the Committee are likely to result in collecting more than £500 from individuals, and they must rely for the balance of £300 on the support of public bodies. Your Memorialists therefore humbly request that a grant of £200 be made to them.'

The following resolution, proposed by Alderman Richards and seconded by Councillor Egerton Allen (both of them prominent members of the Local Committee), was put to the Council and carried: 'That the Corporation grant £200 towards the Building Fund of the proposed Intermediate School at Tenby, such £200 to be paid out of the £400 paid by Mr. S. H. Owen on the renewal of the lease of St. Mary's Hill.'

The news of the Council's grant was given to the Local Committee on Friday 5 February 1892, along with the information that, in response to a letter from Chairman W. H. Richards, the Joint Education Committee had extended the time for collecting subscriptions to secure a school at Tenby 'until May 1st next.' The same concession had been made to Pembroke Dock. Then, against the advice of the Chairman, the Committee supported a suggestion from Egerton Allen that they should send a deputation to the Tenby Charity Trustees, asking for their financial support. Another Memorial was duly prepared and submitted; it included a reference to Section 30 of the Endowed Schools Act 1869, which provided that endowments for apprenticeship fees could be applied for, with the assent of the appropriate authority, for the advancement of education. The memorialists were of the opinion that the endowment of the William Risam Charity and part of that of the Dr. Jones Charity fell into the above category. The *Tenby Observer* of 17 March 1892 reported the text of this request and that of the Charity Trustees' reply, over the signature of Edward Laws. The Trustees had given the matter careful thought but found themselves unable to give a grant because they considered that the local charities were to be disbursed exclusively for the benefit of the poor who had a prior claim over 'an educational establishment for the well-to-do principally maintained out of rates and taxes.' However, more was to be heard of the possible use of local charities for educational purposes just over a year later.

In the meantime, during the year 1892, the Charity Commissioners gave consideration to the draft Scheme for Intermediate Education in

54

Pembrokeshire and then circularised it in letters to the local bodies concerned.

In Tenby the letter was referred to the Corporation's Estates Committee who, in turn, reported a number of objections to the Scheme at a Special Meeting of the Council on 13 December. These criticisms, which were recorded in the Council Minutes, were forwarded to the Charity Commissioners by the Town Clerk, Mr. C. W. R. Stokes, who also represented Manorbier on The County Council. A similar attack upon the Scheme was drafted on behalf of the Local Committee by Egerton Allen. A copy of this letter, addressed from Croft House and signed by W. H. Richards, survives. As the objections raised by the Council and the Local Committee were of some significance for the future of the school at Tenby, they should be noticed in some detail.

First there was criticism of the Second Schedule of the Draft Scheme concerning School Districts: 'The County has been divided into Districts contiguous to the Towns where the schools are to be placed, but the District allotted to Narberth manifestly encroaches on the District which should be allotted to Tenby. Five or six Parishes from the Pembroke Union are taken for Tenby, but not one from the Narberth Union, yet it is as convenient for the children living to the north of Tenby to come to school there, as it is for the children living to the south and west.'

'A map is sent herewith, showing the Districts as at present divided and a red line shows the suggested alterations. The Joint Education Committee appear, by providing equal accommodation, to anticipate equal attendance from the two Districts, thereby implying an equal division of population.' In objecting to this arrangement, the Borough Council proposed an amendment re-allocating the parishes:—

'*For the Tenby District* The Town and Parishes of St. Mary (Out-Liberty), Caldy, Gumfreston, Penally, St. Florence, Redberth and Manorbier from the Pembroke Union; and East Williamston, Jeffreston Reynoldton, Begelly, and St. Issell's from the Narberth Union.'

'*For the Narberth District* All the Pembrokeshire parishes of the Narberth Union, except those in the Tenby District.' (These proposals for the catchment area should be compared with the present situation affecting the Greenhill County Secondary School, Tenby, with a recent background of territorial dispute between Tenby and Narberth during the implementation of the Pembrokeshire Local Education Authority's programme of re-organisation in the third quarter of the twentieth century. It is worth noting that, over the years there has been a desire on the part of parents in Saundersfoot, Stepaside, Amroth and Begelly to send their children to the school in Tenby and that some people in the Kilgetty-Begelly area have looked upon Windberry Top as a watershed north of which children gravitated towards the secondary school in Narberth).

The Borough Council's next objection was against the Fourth Schedule of the Draft Scheme, concerned with the allocation of Annual Grants from the General Fund, according to the population of the Districts concerned. If the Council's proposed amendment concerning re-allocation of parishes were accepted, then the amount of the Annual Grant should be amended accordingly. That for Pembroke Dock, £748, should be £745; that for Tenby £238, should be £341; that for Narberth, £442, should be £342.

A further amendment proposed was a reduction of Tenby's contribution to the Building Fund from £800 to £600, to place Tenby District on an equal footing with the others: 'At Pembroke Dock, Narberth, Fishguard, St. David's and Milford Haven, the Grant from the Building Fund is equal to the Building Fund Subscription, and the distinction is uncalled for, especially when it is remembered that there are no large owners of property in Tenby as in other Districts.' (Tenby was expected to find £800 out of £1,400 and the others £600 each out of £1,200.) 'The Tenby Corporation have offered a Freehold Site and £200 in Money to the Building Fund; they are therefore justified in protesting against this extraordinary demand.'

There was criticism too of the Capitation Payments and the Fees proposed for the Tenby School, as compared with others in the County. Amendments affecting Tenby were requested in Columns 4, 5 and 6 in the Fifth Schedule:

4.	5.	6.
Annual Capitation payment to Head Master or Mistress	Tuition Fees for year	Maximum for Boarders per year

	Minimum	Maximum	Minimum	Maximum	
Scheme					
proposed	£2	£4	£5	£8	£35
Amendt.	£1	£3	£3	£6	£35

It was argued that the fees should not vary between Tenby and other schools unless a distinction could be fairly drawn against Tenby: 'The instruction to be given is the same for Tenby as for the other schools. The qualifications of the Teaching Staff are the same. The fixed stipend of the Head Master is the same. The cost of Board and Lodging is the same for Masters and Pupils. The same class of Boys and Girls will present themselves. Even if the parents at Tenby wanted to pay more for education than parents at other Schools, such a distinction should not be made, it is submitted, under the provisions of the Welsh Intermediate Education Act 1889 . . . '

In due course the protests of the Borough Council and the Tenby Local Committee won some concessions. The newly launched *Tenby and County News* (first published by John Leach on 25 October 1893), in its issue for 1 November, surveyed the course of events locally since the passing of the Intermediate Education Act. It was noted that the above mentioned protests had resulted in the fees being lowered to the same amount as in other schools, in the Tenby contribution to the Building Fund being reduced from £800 to less than £600 (£525 actually), and in an addition to the Tenby District of the parish of East Williamston and part of that of St. Issell's, thus raising the Annual Grant from £238 to £297. However, the Local Committee were still pressing for a larger Annual Grant and contending that the District should include all the parishes mentioned in their previous protest.

Here then in 1893 were some local gains affecting finance and organisation. By the end of the year too there were opened up new prospects of the purchase of suitable premises for the school. A description of this development will follow a reference to two other events of local interest, both of them relevant to the history of education in the area.

The first of these concerned the activities of the Pembrokeshire Technical Education Committee, which having already explored the possibility of securing for Pembrokeshire farmers some instruction and advice in Veterinary Science and Agriculture, embarked upon the formation of Cookery Classes. They had engaged a Miss Jones of the Cardiff School of Cookery, and a series of classes was formally inaugurated at the Royal Lion Hotel Assembly Rooms in premises recently used as a Roman Catholic School. The Mayor of Tenby, Councillor C. J. Williams, and Alderman W. H. Richards, C.C., spoke and other local worthies were present to see the beginning of classes which were time-tabled for Adults, ex-school Girls under 15 and School Girls—these last on Saturdays and Sundays.

The other event of some significance was an Official Enquiry into the Tenby Charities, held by order of the Charity Commissioners, at the Town Hall, Tenby, on Thursday 25 May and Friday 26 May. In opening the proceedings, Mr. G. S. Murray, Assistant Charity Commissioner, stated that there were some thirty charities to be investigated falling into three groups administered respectively by the Charity Trustees, the Tenby Corporation, and the Rector and Churchwardens of St. Mary's Church. Evidence was heard from those responsible. The 'Observer' of 1 June carried a long account of the information given to the Charity Commissioner as well as an editorial, condemning those who were responsible for omitting from the Welsh Intermediate Education Act adequate financial provision for the project—'hence in every county in Wales endowments of old established schools have been overhauled, charitable trusts investigated and church property attacked to provide money for the free education of people who can afford it.' Eyes were being cast on Tenby's ancient charities, the writer continued, and he went on to point out that Egerton Allen had led the attack locally by agitating against the Charity Trustees in a meeting of the St. Mary's Vestry. The Editor's fears were given some substance by Mr. Murray's remarks when concluding the Enquiry, saying that it was possible that the Charity Commissioners, in making a new Scheme would propose that some of the funds administered by the Charity Trustees might be devoted to education as well as apprenticing. As elementary education was already provided for, funds might be usefully applied to Technical Classes. At this juncture, Mr. Egerton Allen intervened to suggest the possibility of using such resources to found a scholarship for poor boys to be tenable at the Intermediate School.

However, one of the most important happenings in the history of the Tenby County School was the Local Committee's opportunity of

58

acquiring for their purpose the House and Grounds which formed part of the Greenhill Estate. A short history of this property provides a relevant background to the combination of circumstances which led to the Local Committee's option to purchase.

Apparently there was no Greenhill Estate when William Couling produced his plan of the Tenby Corporation Lands in 1811, but the area, later to become the estate, was indicated as being in the possession of Sir William Paxton an early 'developer' who realised the potentialities of Tenby as a holiday resort and built his Baths at the Laston. On the Tithe Map of 1841 the lands concerned were numbered 425 and 426 and they were listed in the accompanying Schedule of Owners and Occupiers as: House and Plantation—1 Rood 14 Perches, the Meadow— 1 Acre 1 Rood 16 Perches. Both were owned and occupied by Edmund Morgan, whose son-in-law, William Learmonth Esq., erected a stained glass window in St. Mary's Church at the east and of the Aisle of the Rood of Grace (St. Nicholas' Chapel). 'In Memory of Captain Edmund Morgan, of Greenhill, Tenby, died at Tenby, September 13th 1873.'

The above-mentioned Greenhill, the house in the plantation, had been built, probably in the 1830s, in the Georgian style which was becoming fashionable in Tenby in the first half of the nineteenth century. The outward appearance of the original structure can be appreciated by a visit to the site and by a study of the accompanying photograph. The eastern end of the House may have had a hipped roof, altered by later building operations, and it is possible that the porch was not part of the original structure. The hall, with the lower stairway, was at right-angles to a central corridor which served the rooms to the north and south of it. The principle ground-floor room in the south-west corner had one window with a view of the south and a graceful bow window in the western wall, with a flight of steps leading to the grounds, and, until 1863-1866 when the Pembroke and Tenby Railway was opened and then extended to Whitland, commanding an uninterrupted prospect across the Pill Fields and the former tidal estuary of the Ritec. The pattern of corridor and rooms was repeated on the first floor, with a range of attics under the roof. The present stairway leading to the basement may have replaced an earlier one which gave access to the kitchens.

After the death of Edmund Morgan the property passed into the hands of Ezra Roberts, a partner of David Davies of Llandinam in the construction of the Pembroke and Tenby Railway. After Ezra Roberts left the town, the estate was acquired by Henry Goward, M.A., LL.B., who converted the premises into a private school and made the first extensions by adding classrooms at the east end of the original building.

I have already given a short description of Goward's School and noted his decision to close it and to embark for British Columbia in 1890. This school was called to mind by Mr. J. T. Griffith in his reminiscence in the 1946 issue of the *Greenhillian:* 'This School occupied only the present house, part and the old buildings attached to it, consisting of the two rooms on the ground floor and the two on the first floor immediately above, with a small lean-to where the boys entrance from the grounds now is. At this time there was no Greenhill Avenue nor any building between the School and the lower part of Warren Street. I have referred to this former existence because I could not help feeling conscious during my early years, that the present School when established did enjoy a valuable good will from the Old Green Hill School, and this, I believe, survives today.'

Of special interest is the Notice of Sale which appeared in *The Tenby Observer* dated October 31, 1889:—

Freehold Residential Property
Situate in the Borough of Tenby and comprising an area of about Four Acres, known as GREENHILL. The Residence is stone built and well adapted for a Gentleman's Residence, School, or Public Institution. Mr. J. A. JENKINS is instructed to offer for Sale by Auction (unless previously disposed of by Private Treaty), the above PROPERTY, on WEDNESDAY, November 6, 1889, at the Cobourg Hotel, Tenby, at two o'clock in the Afternoon precisely.

The House standing in its own Grounds, is delightfully situated on limestone rock, near the sea and the Railway Station, with a Private Entrance from the Grounds to the latter, and containing 4 Reception rooms and 12 Bedrooms with the usual offices. Ornamental Pleasure Grounds, Tennis Lawn, and very productive Gardens with Vinery, Peach and Cucumber Houses, Conservatory &c.

The Sanitary Arrangements are perfect. Hot and cold water to Bathrooms and Gas laid throughout the House.

There is a large number of well-grown Forest Trees and Shrubs round about the Premises, also a double drive from the principal Entrance.

For cards to view and further particulars apply to the Auctioneer, Fern House, Tenby, or to the undersigned.

Chas. Wm. Rees Stokes
Solicitor, Tenby.

Fern House, Tenby, October 14, 1889.

It so happened that the Ordnance Survey, which started the series of 25 Inch to the Mile maps in 1853, had spent six years in the survey of the Counties of Pembroke, Cardigan and Carmarthen before their departure for Edinburgh in September 1888. Some seventy men had made Tenby their headquarters with an office at Belgrave House on the Esplanade. Tenby appeared on *Pembrokeshire Sheet XLI II*. On this map, the Greenhill premises described in the advertisement are shown with Goward's additions and with the glasshouses situated to the east of the main building. A double entrance-drive commences in Greenhill Road near the north-east corner of the grounds, where a Bench Mark '80.3 indicates the altitude in feet above Mean Water at Liverpool. (The 'B.M.' is now on a stone two feet from the corner just inside the Greenhill Avenue a few yards from the present entrance to the grounds). The surveyors noted the trees surrounding the school building—one wonders whether they saw the evergreen oak standing close by the gate. A playground on the south side and a square piece of ground beyond it, stretching down to Warren Street, had yet to be built over, and Greenhill Avenue had not been laid out.

Meanwhile, the sale of the Greenhill estate failed to attract a bona fide buyer with enough capital to develop it. There was a rumour that Mr. Goward had been tempted at one time with an offer of £5,000. Now he had taken his departure and the residence and grounds remained idle and neglected until 1893. On 20 and 27 April and on 4 May the property was re-advertised to be sold in three Lots at the Royal Gatehouse Assembly Rooms, Tenby, on Tuesday 16 May 1893. For the most part the details of the earlier advertisement were repeated in 'Lot 1', but there were some additions:— 'Also a piece of ground, held under an Agreement from the Corporation of Tenby for the residue unexpired for a term of 31 years, which lies between the above Premises and the Greenhill Road, at a ground rent of £5 per annum.' 'Lot 2' consisted of 'A large Freehold Garden adapted for building sites, adjoining Lot 1, having a frontage to the Greenhill Road of about 66 feet and a frontage of about 105 feet overlooking the sea and the picturesque village of Penally.' With this Lot was to be sold '. . . a piece of Freehold Building Ground adjoining and having a frontage in Harding Street of about 40 feet.' 'Lot 3' comprised: 'A large piece of Freehold Building Land adjoining the first two Lots with a frontage of about 90 feet in Warren Street and about 154 feet in Harding Street. Both these Lots are specially suitable and desirable for Building Purposes.' (As indeed they proved to be in due course.)

On 16 May, Mr. J. A. Jenkins offered the property for sale. The whole was knocked down for £3,000 to Mr. Arnott of 7 Esplanade, but as he did not complete the purchase, the Estate was re-advertised by Mr. F. B. Mason on 5 October. (Mr. Jenkins had died suddenly in August). On 11 October, a Special Meeting of the Tenby Borough Council appointed a Committee to decide what sum to bid for the premises for the purposes of an Infectious Diseases Hospital so as to fulfill a need repeatedly advocated by Dr. Griffth Lock, M.O.H. to the Tenby Urban Sanitary Authority. The news of such a possibility brought forth a memorial from over a hundred ratepayers, protesting that the conversion of Greenhill into such a hospital would be detrimental to the value of the neighbouring property and adversely affect the impression of visitors arriving at the nearby railway station. In the event, the Council resolved not to pursue the purchase, and it transpired that one of its most prominent members came forward as a prospective buyer. There had arrived on the scene Clement J. Williams, retired pin manufacturer and lithographic printer of Birmingham, with money to invest and to give lavishly. He bought Penally House in 1889, installed electric light there and in the village church, topped the poll in the Tenby Borough Council Election of 1891, was elected Mayor no less than eight times, purchased 14 The Norton and other properties in the town and became deeply interested and financially involved in many local projects of the time. His portrait, in Mayoral Robes, hangs above the stairway in the Guildhall.

The sale, which was held on Wednesday, 18 October, was described in *The Tenby Observer* and in the *Tenby and County News*. The latter reported a large and representative gathering at the Royal Gatehouse Assembly Rooms and listed the more important people present, including the Mayor (Mr. Clement J. Williams) and the Town Clerk (Mr. C. W. R. Stokes). After describing the property, Mr. Mason submitted the whole in one Lot. 'The first bid received was from Mr. Clement J. Williams and competition was maintained between that gentleman and Mr. R. Ormond of Pembroke until £2,500 was reached, when the sale was declared open, and Mr. Williams, having advanced another £50 the Property was secured by him for £2,550. There was a considerable amount of applause when it was known that the Mayor of Tenby had become the purchaser.' It was considered that Mr. Williams had secured a good bargain. 'The Observer' looked forward to immediate development 'with considerable employment for workmen now out of work.' The new owner made known his intentions of developing part of the land as the housing estate, which was named Greenhill Avenue, but he was prepared to sell the House and Grounds for use as a school.

No time was lost. The Local Committee met on the spot on Monday, 30 October. There were present W. H. Richards, Esq., (Chairman) and Messrs. C. F. E. Allen, M.P., C. W. R. Stokes, A. H. Brookman, B. Harries, J. Leach, G. Chiles, Jas Rogers (Sen), Jas. Rogers (Jun.). They looked at plans of the proposed housing development and of the premises, including the House and the additions which Goward had made for his school. The rooms were lofty, with plenty of light and air, there were lavatories and bathrooms, there was a house suitable as a Master's residence and there was a large playground. The Committee were favourably impressed. They were assured by Mr. Stokes that if the property were considered suitable there would not be much difficulty about arranging terms of purchase. The Chairman was then asked to convey to the County Committee a resolution recommending the suitability of the premises.

The Tenby Local Committee next met on 25 January 1894. They were informed that the Rev. Lewis James, Chairman of the Joint Education Committee had looked over the Greenhill property, though no further move had resulted from his visit as yet. Also the Chairman of the Local Committee, read a copy of a letter which Mr. Egerton

63

Allen had sent to the Education Department in London, suggesting alterations in the proposed scheme for the school at Tenby to meet the new conditions now that premises of a suitable character could be secured at once and at a moderate cost, viz. £1,500, this being the price at which Mr. Williams was willing to sell to the County Governing Body when it came into being.

When the County Governing Body and the Local Governing Bodies, as constituted under the Scheme for Pembrokeshire, were set up in the summer of 1894, the Tenby Borough Council appointed Alderman W. H. Richards and Mr. C. W. R. Stokes (Town Clerk) as its two representatives on the Local Governing Body on 2 July; and on 16 July the results of the elections of local governors were announced in Haverfordwest. Details were published in the *Tenby and County News* of 25 July. Then on Tuesday 7 August the County Council appointed its representatives, three on each Local Governing Body.

In Tenby the next step was a preliminary meeting of the Local Governors on 11 August at the Council Chamber 'for the purpose of co-opting 3 Governors in accordance with the provisions of the Scheme'. The election of one man and two women, as required, was duly recorded in the very first Minutes. The first Board of Governors for the Tenby County Intermediate School was now complete:

William Henry Richards Esq., Croft House, Tenby Charles William Rees Stokes, Esq., 6 Croft, Tenby	Appointed by the Town Council of Tenby
Robert Lock Esq., Lansdowne House Tenby John Rowland Rowlands, Moranedd, Tenby	Elected by Subscribers of £5 and upwards
Bernard Kendall Esq., Elm Grove, St. Florence John Lambert Broughton, Esq., The Abbey, Penally	Elected by Managers of Voluntary Schools

William George Parcell Esq., Manorbier The Rev. George Bancroft, Bethesda	Elected by the Poor Law Guardians of the District
The Rev. Thomas Evans, South Cliff St., Tenby The Rev. John Lloyd Williams, The Manse, Tenby Benjamin Harries Esq., St. Bride's, Saundersfoot	Appointed by the Pembrokeshire County Council
Clement John Williams Esq., Penally House. Mrs. Edel A. Rowe, St. Andrews School, Tenby Mrs. W. G. Parcell, Manorbier	Co-opted by the Tenby Governors

From the Foundation of the Local Governing Body to the Official Opening of the Tenby County Intermediate School

The course of events from August 1894 to September 1896 may be traced through the Minutes of the County Governing Body and those of the Local Governing Body (the Managers), through the correspondence between these two bodies and through the correspondence with the Charity Commissioners. The Minute Books provide the bare bones of the story. More details are to be found in the regular reports which appeared in the Tenby newspapers, though due allowance must be made for personal opinions, prejudices and antagonisms.

The first meeting of the fully constituted Local Governing Body was held at the Council Chamber on Thursday 23 August 1894. It was resolved that the Press should be admitted to future meetings, provided other local governors made a similar arrangement. Mr. W. H. Richards, who had been Chairman and Secretary of the Local Committee, was now elected Chairman of the Managers for the year and provision was made for an 'ad hoc' chairman to preside in the event of Mr. Richards' absence. Mr. Clement J. Williams was appointed as representative on the County Governing Body. Mr. C. W. R. Stokes was acting Clerk, and although there was talk of advertising this post, it was not filled until Mr. James Hughes was appointed at a salary of £15 a year in September 1896.

The immediate problem was Mr. Clement Williams' offer of the Greenhill property as a school for the sum of £1,500. It was noted that the Rev. Lewis James and the Local Governors had gone over the buildings and grounds which were considered suitable. It was thought that the purchase would make possible a saving of about £500. A sub-committee was then set up to report on the building and the question of financing the purchase and fitments.

The sub-committee worked swiftly. Its report was dated 25 August 1894. The premises were considered entirely suitable; on the ground floor the boys could have a large cloakroom and two large classrooms while the girls could be given two large classrooms upstairs, along with a dormitory which could be adapted as a cloakroom. There were other rooms which could be used for scholastic purposes. Furthermore there was an ample playground. Precise details and measurements had been furnished to the Rev. Lewis James, Chairman of the County Governing Body. It was noted that the House drainage could be connected with a new sewer which had been laid on the Greenhill estate by Mr. Clement Williams and that the site left nothing to be desired from the point of view of sanitation. The proposed purchase price of £1,500, which included the School and the Residence, with ample accommodation for boarders, was regarded as satisfactory. The amount of money raised locally amounted to about £525 in the school account at the London and Provincial Bank, Tenby.

In due course the plans and detailed proposals were produced before the County Governing Body in Haverfordwest on 14 September 1894, by Mr. William Husband 'the Architect of the School Managers'. The plans were approved and they were to be forwarded to the Charity Commissioners for their consideration.

The above William Husband, who figured prominently in the planning and supervision of necessary works at the school before and after its opening, was destined to see members of his family make good use of the new educational opportunities open to them. The term 'architect' in the modern sense was not then in use. In fact Mr. Husband's card described him as 'Registered Plumber, Sanitary Engineer, Hot Water Fitter etc., 8 Clareston Road, Tenby'. Born in London, he was educated at St. Stephen's School, Westminster, and then followed his father and grandfather in the trade of Master Plumber. He and his wife Helen Honor lived for a time in Dorset and then at

Barnet Grove, Lavender Hill. Remnants of his library and correspondence show him to have been a scholarly man with a natural interest in his children's education. In 1882 he was in correspondence with Mr. C. W. R. Stokes, Solicitor and Town Clerk of Tenby, who later became a Town Council representative on the Local Governing Body of the County School. Stokes had written to Husband: 'I know that a first class plumber could do well here and if you came I should give you all the work of my Clients and myself into your hands, but of course I can not give you a permanent engagement at so much per week.' Mr. Husband arrived in 1883 and his wife and family followed as soon as was convenient. This small bearded man became a familiar figure in Tenby acquiring a knowledge of its drains and finding plenty of work, including plumbing installations at St. Catherine's Fort, at Amroth and Lawrenny Castles and, notably at the new Marine Baths, opened in 1887 at South Gate House at the top of the approach to the Castle Sands, where he installed pumps and pipes for lifting salt water from the sea. By 1894 Mr. Husband was well-known not only to Stokes, but to other members of the Local Governing Body by whom he was engaged as 'architect', a circumstance which was to result in criticism from certain opponents of Stokes at a later date.

Before the end of the year William Husband's plans and specifications in respect of the Greenhill premises were returned to the County Governing Body's Building Sub-Committee by the Charity Commission, along with the observations of their Architect, J. Henry Christian, of Whitehall Place, and were then passed on to the Local Managers. Some nine months were to elapse before negotiations could be completed and necessary work of alteration and improvement could be commenced. During this period in 1895 the County Governors had to consider ways and means of purchasing the residence, which formed part of the property, and the problem of acquiring part of the grounds which had previously been leased by the Tenby Corporation to Mr. Goward during his stay at Greenhill.

When the County Governing Body met on 26 February 1895, they had been informed by Mr. Stokes of his interview with the Charity Commissioners who had told him that the County Governors must take the conveyance and raise the money to buy the House. Following this advice and the recommendations of their own Sub-Committees, the County Governing Body then resolved 'that the permission of the

Charity Commissioners be sought to borrow a sum not exceeding £800 from the Public Works Commission, or otherwise, and that the instalments of Principal and Interest on the Loan be paid out of the rent of the House.' At this stage no one of the Governors could have even guessed that their enquiry about a loan was but an early stage in a search which would last until 1899—but more of this later.

The February meeting also approved of an application to the Tenby Borough Council for the freehold of the plot of land in front of Greenhill Garden and of a piece adjoining, called the Quarry. The Town Clerk of Tenby wrote, expressing his Council's agreement 'to convey to the County Governing Body the land in front of Greenhill, let to Mr. Williams on a yearly tenancy, also the quarry adjoining, subject to the land being used for the purpose of the Intermediate School only.' The Borough Council then applied to the Local Government Board for leave to alienate the two pieces of land concerned but they received a reply rejecting the request out-of-hand: 'The Board direct me to state that their views as to transactions such as that now in question were explained in a letter which they addressed to you on 14th November 1890', wrote C. K. Dalton, Assistant Secretary to the Board, 'It would be contrary to the Board's established views to authorise the alienation of corporate lands . . . even though the proposal may be that the land should be appropriated for purposes in education.' The upshot was that the Local Managers applied for a lease of the said ground and the Borough Council agreed 'That the ground in question be let for a term of 75 years at a nominal rent of 5/- per annum to the County Governing Body.' Incidentally, this final arrangement was not made until 12 September 1895. An additional item in the Managers' expenditure would be walling off the Quarry, in the interests of safety.

Alongside these negotiations in 1895 were the exchanges of letters and the to-ings and fro-ings between the Local Managers, the County Governing Body and the Charity Commission over the plans prepared by William Husband and modified by Mr. Christian. On 13 June the Local Governors required Mr. Husband to amend the plans as stipulated; the drainage was to be carried out as Mr. Christian suggested, the ventilation of the girls' attic was to be improved by a dormer window the roof of the attics must not be raised and an undertaking was to be given not to use the attics as dormitories. The light of the boys' attic was considered sufficient, subject to the window being open. These and other improvements were thought by Husband to be unlikely to add to the cost. Further points were raised in a letter of 24 July from the Charity Commission to the County Governing Body:—

Mr. Christian, the architect, expressed the view that the plans and specifications should be approved, subject to certain changes. Certificates as to reductions or alterations should be issued by some one more responsible than the Clerk of Works, damp proof courses should be specified to all walls, timber should be specified as Baltic, seven pounds lead should be used for gutters, the fall of drains should be specified as not less than one in thirty, girders should have nine inch bearing at each end, the framing posts for partitions would be $4\frac{1}{2}$ and 3 inches at least, the air-tight covers to man holes should be set in stone curb or should have a wide iron flange.

On the understanding that these changes would be made, the purchase of the premises for the Tenby County School would be approved. The draft of the Conveyance of the premises, when approved, should be forwarded 'to this Office' and should be accompanied by a certificate as to the sufficiency of the title of the assurer of the premises. There should be a statement as to whether the school should be a day school only, or a day and boarding school.

On 10 September the County Governing Body's Building Committee reached the following agreements in respect of the above requirements:

(a) The certificate required by the Charity Commissioners should be given by William Husband, as architect of the works.

(b) The County Governing Body should give the Charity Commissioners the undertakings required by them.

(c) Mr. Stokes should give a certificate as to the sufficiency of the title of Mr. Clement Williams to the Premises.

(d) The conveyance of both the schools and the master's house should be prepared by Mr. Stokes and approved by the Clerk to the County Governors so that it would be executed and ready for completion at the next meeting of the County Governing Body.

(e) The County Governing Body should inform the Charity Commissioners that the school should be a day school with permission to take boarders.

(f)   The Building Committee, considering the purchase and completion of the Schools and the Master's House, saw that a sum of £300 above the fund in hand would be needed to complete the purchase of the Schools including alterations and additions, and that a sum of £800 would be required for the Master's House.

The Committee stated that a sum of £5,549 then stood to the credit of the Building Fund for the county and that out of this the County Governing Body were under obligation to pay £5,201, leaving a balance of £348, a share of which would be paid to the Tenby local Governors in addition to the £707 provided for in the Scheme. Also the County Governing Body would pay a sum of £35 for desks and furniture required for fitting up the school. Furthermore, the Building Committee agreed that the Local Governors should advertise for tenders for carrying out the work specified at the School and the Master's House and report to the County Governing Body on 8 October which tender they had accepted.

Mr. Stokes, who had been present for the Building Committee's discussions, placed the letter and the agreements before the Tenby County School Managers on 16 September. He proposed and the Governors agreed that advertisements for tenders, including the cost of laying out the grounds should be sent to the Press. In referring to the time for the contract, Mr. Stokes said that the work would take until Christmas and that he hoped the school would be ready for the following January. It was resolved that Mr. Husband should be the architect to superintend the carrying out of the works and to give the certificates required.

The advertisement duly appeared in the local newspapers. Those desirious of tendering could see plans and specifications at the Town Clerk's office in Crackwell Street 'any day between the hours of ten and five on and after the 20th instant.' Tenders were to be submitted not later than 5 o'clock on 1 October. When the Local Governing Body met on 2 October the terms of the contract were read to them by Mr. James Hughes, who represented Mr. Stokes. It was stated that the work on the school was to be completed by 1 January 1896 and that on the residence on 1 February. Five builders had inspected the plans and two of them had tendered, namely Alfred Richards and James Adams

£817. 10s., and Samuel Cole and Thomas Morris £845. Mr. Husband explained that filling and enclosing the quarry was included in the tenders, but not laying out the grounds. The tender of Richards and Adams was accepted. The *Tenby and County News*, in reporting on this noted that Adams had built the quay wall for the Corporation and that Richards had been foreman for building the new Roman Catholic Church. However the *Tenby Observer*, which had already criticised the County Governing Body and the Local Committee for being lethargic over the project, was now sceptical about the tenders received for the work at Greenhill. It was suggested that the persons tendering were being asked to squeeze six months' work into three and that men who wished to keep their reputation did not compete, and valuable work was being entrusted to men who would be obliged to scamp it. This attitude contrasts sharply with a 'Local Jotting' in the *Tenby and County News* of 16 October, reporting that work had commenced on 10 October and that the internal decoration was to be undertaken by Mr. George Davies 'who, like the contractors Messrs. Richards and Adams is a capable man and competent, from his practical knowledge, to go through with the work.' In the writer's opinion (i.e. John Leach), it was an advantage that the contractors were themselves working men.

On Sunday, 10 November, the Local Governors suffered a severe loss through the sudden death of William Henry Richards, J.P., C.C., who had played a prominent part in the initial stages of providing a County School for Tenby, as a generous subscriber to the local building fund, as Chairman and Secretary of the Local Committee, as a County Councillor who boasted that he never missed a meeting, as a member of the County Governing Body, and as the first Chairman of the Local Governors. 'By a cruel stroke of fate one of our most prominent and respected citizens has been removed from our midst.' began the Editorial in the 'County News' of 13 November 1895. The deceased was in his 52nd year. A head and shoulders photograph of him by Charles Smith Allen was copied by the 'County News'. He was shown as having a good head of hair with a centre parting, a flowing moustache and a small Napoleon III beard. His eyes give the impression of alertness and the twinkle in them adds to the slightly humorous expression in a smooth countenance.

Mr. Richards had completed his eighth Mayoralty on Saturday 9 November and had proposed as his successor Mr. Benjamin Harries, haberdasher and mercer at Victoria House, High Street (now part of the premises of Messrs T. P. Hughes and Son Ltd.)   On Sunday morning Alderman Richards left his home, Croft House, to take his place in the traditional Mayor's Sunday procession from the Town Hall.   He was in the process of stepping off the pavement at the top of the hill by the corner of the Royal Gatehouse Hotel, when he staggered and fell into the road.   Mr. J. Bancroft, H. M. Inspector of Schools, who was close behind, went to his assistance and with the help of bystanders removed him into the Hotel.   Dr. D. A. Reid of the Norton was called but his visit was in vain.   Mr. Richards died within a quarter of an hour of his fall; the cause of his death was subsequently announced as apoplexy. However, Leach's newspaper reported that Mr. Richards had had a cold for a few days and added that he had looked pale at the last Council Meeting and had been troubled by attacks made upon him lately 'in a section of the local press'—a reflection of the bitter antagonisms in the town's affairs which were given full coverage in the two 'weeklies'. Crowds flocked to pay their last respects at the funeral in Tenby Cemetery on Wednesday, 13 November.

There were numerous tributes to the Alderman's services and wide interests, not least for his furtherance of the cause of education.   At a meeting of the County Governing Body on 12 November, regret was expressed at the news of W. H. Richards' death, and on the 21st the Local Governors passed a resolution: 'That the Governors express their sense of the great loss they have sustained by the death of their late Chairman, Alderman W. H. Richards who took a deep interest in all the affairs of the town, and especially of this Board, and who was always a friend to the cause of education.'

The place of W. H. Richards as the Town Council's representative on the County School Local Governing Body was taken by Mr. C. F. Egerton Allen, who attended his first meeting on 2 January 1896 and made the formal declaration of acceptance, as required by Clause 27 of the Scheme. So Egerton Allen, (lawyer, radical politician, genealogist, member of the Tenby Museum Committee for over twenty years, contributor to the columns of the Tenby Observer particularly over controversies affecting the Tenby Gas Consumers Co. in 1895, an opponent of C. W. R. Stokes and other Conservatives in the town), joined the County School Managers and gradually became more and more critical of the conduct of business, being especially vehement in his attacks upon Mr. Stokes.

At the same meeting, Mr. Clement J. Williams was appointed Chairman and was subsequently re-elected to this office until 1912, so presiding over the final stages leading to the official opening of the school and the important early phase of its existence. The new Chairman had the advantage of experience in business and of public life. A member of the well-known firms of F. D. Taylor & Co. and Edelsten Williams & Co., pin manufacturers and lithographic printers, New Hall Works, Birmingham, he had retired from active business and settled at Penally House in 1889. Reference has been made to his services on the Tenby Borough Council. For a time he served on the Pembrokeshire County Council, for many years he was a Justice of the Peace of the County and of the Borough, in Queen Victoria's Diamond Jubilee Year he became High Sheriff of Pembrokeshire, in 1899 during one of his terms of office as Mayor, the completed Victoria Pier was opened by the Duchess of York, who later became Queen Mary. He appears to have had a shrewd eye for acquiring and developing property; when the South Cliff Estate was being sold in 1895, Mr. Stokes purchased on his behalf the Tenby Skating Rink known as Victoria Gardens and several other Lots; Greenhill Avenue was laid out under his direction, Clement Terrace was named after him, and, for the better housing of the poor, he built a block of workingmen's flats (later known as Harbour Court) in Bridge Street. He was lavish in his hospitality. At the opening of the newly covered Market on 1 January 1892 he presided, in his Mayoral robes, over a feast he had provided for seven hundred 'working class folk' from Tenby and Penally, when the glass-roofed structure was bedecked with flags, and steaming joints of meat were carried in there by the staff of Mrs. Hughes of the nearby Cobourg Hotel. Clement Williams presented £500 towards the cost of the Royal Victoria Pier, he built the landing slip in the harbour, later known as 'the Mayor's Slip', he was a generous supporter of the Cottage Hospital on many occasions, and, last but not least, he was a substantial subscriber to the local building fund for the Tenby County School and his good will enabled the County Governing Body to purchase the Greenhill premises on what came to be regarded as very favourable terms. He was a familiar figure in his horse-drawn carriage on the road between Tenby and Penally. A Royal Doulton plate in the possession of the Tenby Museum bears a picture of him in his yachting cap. The portrait in the Guildhall and a photograph in the Museum show him in his Mayoral robes, having lost most of his hair, with a firm resolute mouth, having the appearance of being proud without being haughty, of having dignity without conceit and, to all external appearances enjoying good food and good health.

During much of the period January to September 1896, the Governors, at District and County level, were concerned with financing the purchase and alterations of the School and Residence to the satisfaction of the Charity Commissioners, whose approval was necessary before the Conveyance could be completed. Meanwhile, the Local Managers resolved that public subscriptions should not be used towards the purchase of the House and arrangements were made for Mr. Rowlands, Treasurer of the Local Fund, to draw upon the account at the London and Provincial Bank for the interim payments to the contractors.

On 13 January the Local Governors decided to publish an up-to-date list of subscriptions both paid and promised and to appeal for further help. Mr. Stokes stated that the total cost of purchase of the property would amount to £1,620 (including 2 Years' Interest at 4%) of which £952. 8s. 6d. would be apportioned for the Schools and £666. 11s. 6d. for the Residence. It was estimated that the total cost of the schools allowing for repairs and alterations, would be £1,602. 8s. 6d. The funds available, including the Building Grant of £707, subscriptions received £512 and subscriptions promised £45 would amount to £1,264. 0s. 0d., so leaving a deficiency of £338. 8s. 6d. The cost of the House, including £200 for necessary work, would be £867. 11s. 6d., to meet which there was to be a loan of £800. 0s. 0d., leaving a further deficiency of £67. 11s. 6d. To deal with this situation, the County Governing Body, meeting in February, decided that in addition to the £800 loan already agreed for the Residence they would apply for leave to borrow £400 towards the purchase and outlay of the schools. This would leave a further £100 to be found locally for architects' fees and other incidental expenses such as laying out the grounds. It was expected that the interest on £800 would be paid by the Head Master in lieu of rent and the interest on £400 would be provided out of school income. At their next meeting the Local Managers resolved that the Capitation Fee for each scholar was to be fixed at £2, and that the salary of the Head Master would be £120 plus the Capitation Fee of £2 for each scholar in the school. The amount to be paid to the Head would depend upon the number of pupils in attendance and his rent for the residence would be dependent upon the rate of interest upon £800.

Mr. H. T. Morley, formerly Borough Surveyor of Tenby, was asked to value the whole property so that a certificate could be supplied to the Charity Commissioners. In this connection, it is clear that the county authorities regarded the Greenhill purchase as a good bargain for the meeting of 21 March passed this resolution:—

'The County Governing Body are satisfied that the money paid to Mr. Clement Williams for the School Buildings and site is not less than the value of the buildings alone and that the site may be considered to have been provided free and that the conditions of Clause 45(a) have been compiled with.' A copy of this resolution was to be forwarded to the Charity Commission. Of course, no money had as yet been paid. Mr. Williams, however, had made it known that he would be prepared to permit the school to be used at once, leaving the payment of purchase money to stand over until official sanction had been obtained.

In the course of the summer, the prospects for the Tenby School began to brighten. On 1 July, the Hon. W. W. Bruce attended a meeting of the County Governing Body in Haverfordwest, expressed his satisfaction with the draft Conveyance of the Schools and Residence and handed it back to Mr. Stokes to be re-engrossed. At the next meeting of the same body the Conveyance was signed by Mr. Clement Williams and by the County Governors present that day. The members also agreed that cheques should be payable to the Treasurer for the Tenby School as follows:—£746. 2s. 6d. (comprising £707 Building Fund Grant and £39. 2s. 6d. interest accrued thereon from April 1894) £75. 11s. 6d. being a share of the surplus Building Fund and £514.17s.8d. being Maintenance Grant, making a total of £1,336.11s.8d. These were sent to the Treasurer, J. R. Rowlands, Esq., National & Provincial Bank, Tenby, along with a letter from Mr. W. Davies George, dated 18 August 1896.

'Mr. Stokes has handed to the County Governing Body today a Conveyance of these premises, executed by the Vendor, Mr. Clement Williams, the purchase money forming the consideration with interest, amounting to £1,654. 15s. 0d., and towards this I have handed to Mr. Stokes to give you cheques amounting together to £1,336. 11s. 8d., leaving the balance £318. 3s. 9d. to be found by the local Managers, pending the raising of the sum about to be borrowed by the County Governing Body.'

On 22 August, the Local Governors received the above letter and heard a financial statement from Mr. Stokes, who also reported on the latest decisions made in Haverfordwest. Out of the Maintenance Grant, one fifth viz. £102. 19s. 6d. had to be paid towards the Scholarship Fund and the remainder would go towards the purchase and alteration of the premises. A cheque for £1,654, being purchase money, was to be drawn in favour of Mr. Clement Williams, but not before Mr. Egerton Allen had raised objections to the Local Governors' being told by the County Governors what to do and had accused Mr. Stokes of dealing with financial and other matters without authority or instruction. The acrimonious discussion which followed was reported at length in the 'Observer', but the Local Governors' Minutes discreetly recorded the fact that Mr. Allen was the only member who voted against the resolution in favour of paying the cheque to Mr. Williams and of the Governors' agreeing to find the balance needed to complete the schools and premises, pending the raising of the loan by the County Governing Body.

Copies of the Draft Conveyance of 16 December 1895 and of the Conveyance dated 18 August 1896 have been preserved in the Legal Department of the Offices of the Pembrokeshire County Council. The document recites the agreement of Clement John Williams to sell to the Governors:

'... the heraditaments herein described ... in consideration of the sum of One Thousand six hundred and twenty pounds ...
... the said Clement Williams as Beneficial Owner hereby conveys unto the Governors All that messuage or tenement with the outbuildings yard garden and pleasure grounds thereto belonging called "The Green" otherwise "Greenhill' situate in the Parish of St. Mary In-Liberty in the County of Pembroke formerly in the occupation of Ezra Roberts afterwards of Henry Goward and now vacant containing by estimation One acre and thirty-nine perches or thereabouts which said premises formed part of an Estate known as the "Greenhill Estate" and are more particularly delineated and described in the Plan drawn on these presents and thereon colored pink ...'

As the financial statement presented by Mr. Stokes on 22 August is informative, the details are worthy of note.

The business of raising a loan proved to be protracted and tiresome. To the original deficiency were added other items such as the laboratory, which came into being after the school was opened. For the sake of convenience, this part of the story will be followed through to its conclusion, by-passing furnishing, equipment, appointment of staff and the official opening, for the time being.

On 29 June 1897, some nine months after the opening, the Managers were informed by their Chairman that the amount of the loan would be £959. 2s. 6d. and that arrangements were in progress with the Yorkshire Penny Bank, Leeds, for borrowing this sum at three and a quarter per cent. On 26 October, the Clerk of the Governors was instructed to write to the County Governing Body, urging them to complete the Loan for the School, Residence and Laboratory forthwith, 'as the non-completion of the Loan is very unsatisfactory to the Governors.' In November, the Governors were informed by Mr. Davies George that money could not be advanced on the order of the Charity Commissioners but that a legal mortgage would be required. The November meeting of the County Governors agreed to negotiate a loan for those schools for which the amount required was known and to go into this matter on 1 April 1898. On hearing this the Local Governing Body resolved to give the County Governing Body notice 'that if the loan for the Tenby School is not negotiated by 1st May the Charity Commissioners will be communicated with direct on the subject'. By 24 May Mr. Davies George reported that he had been in negotiation with Messrs. Preston and Co. who had tendered for carrying out this loan. However, it proved unnecessary to proceed further with this firm as the Central Welsh Board circularised the various county authorities, pointing out that the Montgomeryshire County Council had arranged a loan for school buildings at two and three quarters per cent through the Public Works Loan Commissioners. At last, on 23 January 1898, the Local Governors received from the Clerk of the County Governing Body a letter enclosing the Draft Order of the Charity Commissioners as to the proposed loan which they sanctioned as follows:—School £520, Residence £415, interest £2. 15s. per cent repayable in thirty years from the date of advance by sixty half-yearly payments of £22. 19s. 9d

77

Liabilities

	£	s.	d.	£	s.	d.
Purchase Money of Schools and Residence	1,500					
Interest thereon at 4% from 16 Dec. 1894 to 18 August 1896, less tax.	154	15	5			
				1,654	15	5
Contractors on Schools	612	2	0			
do. on Residence	220	13	0			
				832	15	0

Schools

	£	s.	d.	£	s.	d.
Caleb Morris, Iron Gate for Schools	2	0	0			
Bonville's Court Colliery for cinders		19	5			
D. E. Thomas, Report to send Charity Commissioners on Site etc.	3	3	0			
H. T. Morley on value of do.	1	1	0			
Expenditure paid in laying out the grounds etc. by day work and other payments as per particulars rendered	17	4	5			
Wm. Husband preparing plans & specifications and superintending the works	15	15	0			
				40	2	10

House

	£	s.	d.	£	s.	d.
Wm. Husband preparing plans & specifications and superintending the works	5	5	0			
Expenditure laying out grounds & by day works as per particulars	4	15	3			
				10	0	3
				2,537	13	6

	£	s.	d.
House Expenditure yet to be incurred in repairs to Greenhouse, doing up garden, building up wall and estimated at	25	0	0
	2,562	13	6

Assets in the Hands of the Treasurer

	£	s.	d.	£	s.	d.
Received from the County Governing Body Building Fund Grant	707	0	0			
Surplus do.	75	11	6			
Interest accrued thereon	39	2	6			
Maintenance Grant received £514 15s.8d. less one fifth to be applied in Scholararships £102 17s. 6d. as per Scheme	411	18	2			
				1,233	12	2

By Subscriptions received as per Bank Book, including further donation of £25 from Mr. Clement Williams and £4 8s. 0d. received by him at Penally and interest from 18 January 1896 £4 0s. 6d.   571 13 6

   1,805 5 8

Deficiency to be made up by County Governing Body   757 7 10

   2,562 13 6

as follows: on the School £12. 15s. 8d. by the County Governing Body and £10. 14s. on the Residence by the Local Governors.

The Mortgage, *The Governing Body of the Intermediate and Technical Education Fund of the County of Pembroke to the Secretary of the Public Works Loan Commissioners,* is dated 16 May 1899. The document recites the provision under the 1894 Scheme for the raising of money by mortgage if needed, outlines the situation in respect of the Tenby School, quotes the recent Order of the Charity Commission including the terms of the loan and continues '... the Public Works Loan Commission have agreed to advance the sum of £935 on the terms stated ... ' As security, the County Governing Body are to assign to the Secretary of the above Commission and his successors 'all the said Annual Contributions payable out of the County Rate to the General Fund as defined in the said Scheme and all and every other moneys which the said Governing Body ... have power to charge for the purposes of security ... ' The half-yearly payments are to be made by the County Governing Body to the Cashiers of the Bank of England every 16th day of November and 16th day of May succeeding the date of the Mortgage.

This document was signed by twelve of the County Governing Body 'being the majority present' in the presence of William Davies George, Clerk to the said County Governing Body. It is interesting to note that the date for the final payment of any money remaining unpaid was to be 16 May 1929, over a year after the present writer had taken up duties at the County School.

The long delay between the inauguration of the Scheme for Intermediate Education in Pembrokeshire and the opening of the 'County School' in Tenby, which has been accounted for, became the subject of frequent argument in the local Press. The 'Observer' had cast doubts upon the contract for the work to be finished within three months, but in the issue of 21 November 1895 it was remarked that repairs and additions were going on apace and that there were hopes of being ready not later than the beginning of February 1896. Then in the issue of 7 May 1896 came the comment:

> 'I hear that the work at the new Intermediate School at Tenby is just completed, and, considering the amount to be done, the time occupied, I am told, is not excessive. Consequently the same incompetent person had a hand in preparing the specifications

which stipulated that the work should be finished by January 1st or the contractors were liable to a fine of £5 per week. This of course would mean ruin to them. Now I am pretty sure that the contractors were much too wide awake to imagine they could complete the job by January 1st; so there must have been a friendly arrangement all round, which is not by any means desirable in connection with public work.'

Then six weeks later, in a time of drought and a heat-wave, in the same newspaper it was remarked that the date of opening of the school was still problematical, and that there appeared to be no arrangements incidental 'to opening the schools which have been given over as completed by the contractors nearly 3 months. . .At present the school premises are empty and uninhabited.'

Leach's *Tenby and County News* of 1 July 1896, after stating 'We have more than once had to complain about the delay in opening the Schools', proceeded to set out in full the correspondence between C. W. R. Stokes, the Rev. Lewis James, William Davies George and the Charity Commission, emphasising in particular the financial difficulties encountered and maintaining that the delay was not due to the Local Governing Body.

On 23 July the 'Observer' returned to the attack: 'All through we have blamed the Local Governing Body, despite efforts to throw the blame elsewhere . . . There can be no two opinions as to who is responsible for the scandalous state of the school scheme.' The handling of the affair was described as 'a glaring piece of jobbery', perpetrated by those who pretended to carry out the scheme in the interests of the town, the inhabitants of which had subscribed about £600 towards the funds necessary. The time clause stipulating that the building should be finished in January was a farce and subterfuge to prevent any except the Governors' favourite friends from obtaining the tender. Those who fixed the job knew the contractor could complete the work in just about double the time. The Governors should be giving an account of their stewardship, the 'Observer' concluded.

The 'County News' of 29 July, in an editorial, sprang to the defence of the Governors:

'A violent and altogether unjustifiable attack upon the local governors, appearing last week in the columns of a contemporary, calls for notice at our hands. Its weight—if it can be said to

81

have any—is of course minimised by the local estimate of the writer. It is, we think, pretty generally understood by now that anything and everything that comes across the path of his desires or judgement is ipso facto "anathema" and that the business and editorial side of his concern, each sharing the one source of being, are like the Siamese Twins—the sensations of the one reflected in the other—the real motive which prompted the attack and inspired the string of vituperation against all concerned is not far to seek.'

The editor then set out to counter the various accusations made by the 'contemporary', who was, of course, Mr. Frank B. Mason, who appears to have been engaged in some contracting business himself. With regard to the allegations of jobbery and the governors' friends getting the contract, it was pointed out that the building foreman of 'this public mentor' had spent some time over the specifications, presumably with the object of tendering, but the matter had been dropped because it was too complicated. This was a case of 'sour grapes'. The reasons for the delays were re-stated. What had happened was unavoidable. If the difficulties could have been foreseen, no doubt the course originally urged by the Rev. J. Lloyd Williams would have been taken—to open the Schools in temporary premises. But it was not thought necessary, as it was then and has been all along the aim of the Local Governing Body to complete and open the Schools on the earliest possible date, and no effort on their part has been wanting to accomplish this.'

So much for the problems and arguments. Now for the staffing, equipping and details of the inauguration of the new school.

A preliminary step towards the appointment of the Head Master was taken when a committee was set up for the purpose early in 1896. Representatives of the Local Managers were C. J. Williams Esq., the Rev. J. Lloyd Williams and Egerton Allen Esq.,; for the County Governing Body the representatives were the Rev. Lewis James, the Rev. William Evans, G. B. Brewer Esq., R. Ward Esq. and Archdeacon Hilbers. On 1 July the C. G. B. agreed upon advertisements to appear in the *South Wales Daily News*, the *Western Mail*, the *Times Educational Supplement* and *The Schoolmaster*. When the County Governors met again on 18 August 1896, the Selection Committee presented their report on the applications received and recommended for consideration the names of Mr. Adams, Mr. Perman and Mr. Coffin. When a vote was taken the results were 16, 5 and 0 respectively. It was then resolved that Mr. J. W. B. Adams be appointed and that the unsuccessful candidates be allowed their second class rail return fare. The *Tenby and County News* noted the appointment of Mr. J. W. B. Adams B.A., (Hons.) of Pembroke College, Oxford 'at present tutor in Classics and Literature at Isleworth College for Teachers'. At Oxford he had been president of the College Musical Society, captain of the Cricket XI and member of the Football Team. He was backed by an impressive array of writers of Testimonials—the Master and Dean of Pembroke College Oxford, the Hon. E. L. Stanley, Professor Firth M.A., of Balliol College Oxford, P. A. Barnett Esq., of Trinity College Oxford, J. G. Bettany Esq., Christchurch Oxford, and the Rev. M. E. Browbe M.A., of Oriel College Oxford. (May be this was why one of his pupils remarked later that he brought a different atmosphere to the town of Tenby!) Adams' father was a Pembroke-shire man, was Head of Fleet Road Higher Grade School, said to be the largest of its kind in London, and was chairman of the Pembroke County Club in London. According to Visitors' Lists in the Local Press, the Adams family had holidayed in Tenby.

The new Head Master attended his first meeting of the Managers on Saturday 22 August, the day they resolved 'That the Schools be formally opened on the 23rd of September that being the day on which Her Majesty would have reigned longer than any of her predec-essors, and that it be made a day of public rejoicing.' Significantly this was the proposition of His Worship the Mayor, Mr. Benjamin Harries, seconded by Mr. Clement Williams. Thus, Mr. Adams was left with one calendar month in which to come to terms with his new post and see to details of equipment and staff appointments. Much of the equipment then bought, for example the desks, was destined to remain in use much scarred and scored by the doodling of successive generations of pupils, for nearly fifty years.

This same meeting had a heavy agenda. In addition to the Convey-ance of the premises and financial matters, already noticed, the Gov-ernors agreed that cheques should be signed by the Chairman, two of the members and the Clerk, a practice which continued until after the 1944 Education Act was implemented. A sub-committee was to arrange to advertise for a Clerk at a salary of £15 per annum.

It was resolved that eight Free Scholarships would be offered, five of them for boys and three for girls. The Head Master suggested that the Scholarship Examination should be held on 16 September and the papers marked by him. Fees were fixed at £6 per pupil. It was agreed that Mr. Adams should see to the advertisements for Scholarships, the Opening of the Schools, the Terms, the Fees and other details, the posts of Assistant Master and First Mistress. The salary of the Mistress was to be £100 and that of the Science Master £100 plus half the Science Grant, in which connection an application was made to the Science and Art Department, South Kensington, with a view to obtaining recognition as a Science and Art School. The salaries should be considered alongside the current prices in the Tenby Market where beef was from 6d. to 9d. a pound, lamb 9d. to 10d. and new potatoes 1½d. to 2d. per pound.

Staff appointments were made in time for advertisement of the school prospectus in the *Tenby Observer* on 24 September, the day following the official opening. The First Assistant Mistress was Miss M. Alice Burrell B.A. (Hons.) of London University, late Lecturer at Westfield College, London. She was appointed on 17 September. The Science Master was Mr. J. C. Kirkman, B.Sc., Kingswood Grammar School and Durham College of Science, Honours and Prizeman in Physics, Medallist of the Science and Art Department at South Kensington. He appears to have been engaged in time for the inauguration of the school, but his name first appears in the Governors' Minutes of 1 October, when a guarantee was given that he should be paid, in addition to his salary, £20 for the first year, as the Science Grant could not be obtained before about November 1897. He was to teach Science and Mathematics. There were two interesting part-time appointments. First there was Edward J. Head, Certificated Art Master, South Kensington. The Head Master recommended him to the Governors as 'well qualified and successful with pupils in the higher branches of Art teaching (Advanced Shading, Painting, Still Life etc.).' For his services no payment would be required from the Governors or the Scholars at the School, as Mr. Head would be content with half the grant earned by the Intermediate Scholars and with the appearance of his name on the advertisement as 'Visiting Art Master.' Already in 1895 he had opened classes at the Tenby Parochial School under the auspices of the Science and

Art Department, South Kensington. Many aspiring local artists were influenced by him, notably Augusta Bowen, daughter of the Station Master at Tenby, on the Pembroke and Tenby Railway. In the spring of 1896 she and Mr. Head both had pictures accepted at the Royal Academy. The other appointment was that of the visiting teacher of Music, Mr. W. Cecil Williams, A.R.C.O., who had succeeded Mr. Cyril Church as Organist and Choirmaster at St. Mary's Church, a post he was to hold for forty-seven years. Mr. Williams' name appeared in the Prospectus but not in the Governors' Minutes.

While a special sub-committee went ahead with arrangements for the official opening which was at last within reach, the September meetings of the Managers dealt with various minor appointments.

The Official Opening. Wednesday 23 September 1896.

'. . . the commencement of a new epoch in the educational history of Tenby . . .' (*Tenby and County News* 24 September 1896)
'. . . after 6 years of vicissitudes, delays and blunders, Tenby Intermediate Schools were formally declared open yesterday, Wednesday . . .' (*Tenby Observer* 24 September 1896).

Both newspapers gave very full coverage to the day's proceedings, differing in points of detail and emphasis. Both carried a picture of the Liberal Mayor, Councillor Benjamin Harries, J.P. The 'County News' added a view of the school from the main entrance, copied from a photograph by Mr. Reginald Truscott of Tenby, and a picture of the Chairman of the Governors, Clement J. Williams Esq., J.P. Both gave versions of the background story from the time of the first public meeting at the Town Hall in September 1890, both gave accounts of the procession to the school and of the ceremony there, both described the Luncheon at the Cobourg Hotel. The 'Observer' could not resist some criticism of the arrangements by which some subscribers received invitations at the eleventh hour and others none at all. He went on to state that the principal event turned out to be the sumptuous luncheon at the Chairman's expense and there the speeches were too long. On the other hand, the 'County News' was full of praise for everything and at one point got carried away in describing the new opportunities available to poorer children: 'If the poet Gray were still alive, he would have to rewrite part of his famous

"Elegy". "Chill penury" will no longer have power to "repress the noble zeal" of embryonic genius, or "freeze the genial currents of the soul" of any boy or girl with brains that are likely to lead their owner to greatness.' The writer pointed to the benefits of the scheme by which poor scholars might have a chance of receiving travelling expenses, books and stationery provided out of bursaries which would be founded if funds permitted.

This must have been a memorable year for Mayor Benjamin Harries, what with stormy scenes in the Council Chamber and the devastating October gales which played havoc with shipping and shattered the stone pier. For quiet satisfaction he would look back on 27 June, when in company with some 2,000 ladies and gentlemen, he attended, in his Mayoral robes, the Installation of Edward, Prince of Wales, as Chancellor of the University of Wales, in a colourful ceremony at Aberystwyth. Or again on a more homely scale he would recall the Public Holiday he had declared in Tenby to mark the occasion of Queen Victoria's sixtieth accession day and to celebrate the opening of the new school. On the morning of 23 September, members of the Council and Corporation officially accepted his invitation to meet at Victoria House and drink a 'Loyal Toast'. Other toasts were drunk and there were many more to follow later in the day.

Almost all the shops were closed during the day. 'From an early hour the Town wore quite a gay festive appearance, bunting being displayed both officially and privately', wrote the 'Observer' reporter. There was a profusion of flags at the Town Hall and at the Intermediate Schools in Greenhill Avenue 'an attempt had been made to render the exterior more attractive to the public gaze, an effort which was successful to a certain extent. Right across the large entrance gate, from tree to tree, a span of variously coloured flags floated gaily in the breeze, pleasantly contrasted to the autumnal tints of the trees surrounding the school premises. The grounds were in excellent condition, a great deal of trouble having been bestowed upon them. . .Inside the building, which is admirably adapted for an educational establishment lavish preparations had been made to receive the visitors'.

Punctually at 12 o'clock a procession left the Town Hall, in the High Street, for the school. Headed by the Town Crier, the Mace Bearers, and members of the Tenby Volunteer Fire Brigade, the Corporation Officials, members of the Council, the Town Clerk, the

Mayors of Tenby and Pembroke, Sir Lewis Morris, the Clergy and Ministers of the Town, walked to the School Gates where they were met by Mr. Clement Williams and his fellow Governors, Mr. J. W. B. Adams (Head Master), Mr. J. C. Kirkman (Assistant Master) and Miss M. Alice Burrell (Assistant Mistress). A notable absentee was Mr. Egerton Allen. After an exchange of greetings, the procession moved through the grounds to the rear of the school, where they were met by a number of townspeople and the choir boys of St. Mary's, who sang the National Anthem, led by Mr. W. Cecil Williams. The party then moved upstairs to the main room 'large, lofty and well-ventilated' with a carpeted platform, decorated with plants, at one end.

The Chairman of the local Governors presided, supported by the Mayor of Tenby, the Mayor of Pembroke (Alderman Walter Simon, J.P.) and other dignitaries. After some appropriate opening remarks, the Chairman called upon His Worship the Mayor of Tenby to declare the Intermediate Schools open. The Mayor referred to the need which would be supplied in the new school, to the Corporation's interest in the project over a period of six years, to the welcome presence of Sir Lewis Morris, one of the pioneers of Welsh education, to the generous support of Mr. Egerton Allen and his family and to the late Mayor, Mr. W. H. Richards who had been Chairman at the earliest meetings and who had taken the deepest interest in the school. He was pleased to note that there would be set up a W. H. Richards Scholarship, 'to perpetuate the memory of such a good public man'. The Mayor continued: 'I think the ceremony of today must appeal to all thoughtful minds when we think of the many young lives who will, from day to day, pursue their studies here to fit them to take their part— who knows?—perhaps in the history of our nation. I have great pleasure in declaring the Schools open, with earnest prayers that God may bless and prosper the work here.'

Apologies for absence were received from the Bishops of St. David's and Llandaff, Lord Kensington, the Rev. J. Lloyd Williams and Mr. G. E. Brewer.

Then came further speeches. The Rev. Lewis James, Chairman of the County Governing Body, outlined the history of the Intermediate Education movement in Pembrokeshire, with which he had been closely associated, referred to the delays affecting the Tenby School, congratulated the town upon the possession of a school so beautifully situated and so well adapted for its purpose and upon having secured the services of a Head Master, who came with excellent credentials. The Rev. William Evans then gave an earnest address upon the progress of education in Wales.

During an interval, the Tenby Male Voice Party, conducted by Mr. Richard Williams, the young Llanelli baritone lately arrived in the town, sang 'All hail the power of Jesu's name'. (Richard Williams was to have a long association with the music of the School and of the Congregational Church). There followed the presentation of certificates by Mrs. Parcell and Mrs. Rowe to the students of E. J. Head's Art Classes.

After Sir Lewis Morris had spoken upon the Arts in Wales, the proceedings concluded with the Benediction and the singing of the 'Old Hundredth'. The platform party led a tour of inspection of some fifty pictures by the Art students, before returning to the Town Hall prior to adjourning to the Cobourg Hotel for luncheon.

The Luncheon at the Cobourg Hotel was given by Mr. Clement Williams 'to commemorate the sixtieth year of the reign of Queen Victoria and also the opening of the Tenby Intermediate Schools'. There were some fifty to sixty guests for this 'superbly laid and excellently served meal, which reflected the highest credit on the culinary department of this well-known hostelry and upon Mrs. J. B. Hughes, proprietress'! The menu would have gladdened a nineteenth century gourmet and would have won a nod of approval from Hannah Glasse and Mrs. Beeton.

OYSTERS

SOUPS: Clear mock Turtle; Hare.

REMOVES: Roast Beef; Lamb; Turkey; Chickens; Tongue; Ham; Pigeon Pies; Lobsters.

SECOND SERVICE: Grouse; Partridges.

ENTREMENTS: Venetian puddings; Jellies; Whipped cream; Stewed pears; Trifle, Cream; Camembert and Cheddar Cheese.

DESSERT: Grapes; Pears; Apples; Filberts; Coffee; Liqueurs.

Mr. Clement Williams presided, with the Mayor of Tenby on his left and the Mayor of Pembroke on his right. The local newspapers reported the names of most of the guests. These included clergy and ministers, members of the Borough Council and their Officials, the educationists Sir Lewis Morris and Mr. J. Bancroft, H.M.I., representatives of the County Governing Body, the Local Governors, the Head Master and his newly appointed staff, representatives of the Press, Subscribers and friends.

If the meal verged on the gargantuan, the Toast List and the long speeches would have outlasted an oriental banquet. The toast of Her Majesty the Queen, the Prince and Princess of Wales and the Royal Family was proposed by the Chairman. Other toasts followed. They were succeeded by appropriate replies, in some cases from more than one speaker. Also there were Toasts to the Clergy and Ministers, the County Governing Body and the Local Governing Body, the Pembrokeshire County Club in London, the Tenby Intermediate School, the Mayor and Corporation, Mr. J. R. Rowlands (Treasurer of the Governors), the Visitors, the Press, the Ladies and the Chairman. Among these speeches, the one which should be mentioned in detail is the reply of Mr. J. W. B. Adams to Mr. C. R. W. Stokes' toast: 'Success to the Tenby Intermediate School'.

The Head Master said that he was greatly obliged for the manner in which the toast had been received and that a more appropriate way of celebrating Her Majesty's long and glorious reign could not well have been devised. The Queen and every member of the Royal Family took the warmest interest in the educational advancement of the people. He continued: 'I may say that I do not commence my professional work in Tenby as a stranger; as the son and grandson of Pembrokeshire men, who commenced their careers as teachers in the County, I venture to think that there is some degree of appropriateness in my appointment as Principal of the Tenby Intermediate Schools. I will say nothing of my father, who is present, but of my grandfather I will remark that his work as one of the pioneers of popular education in Pembrokeshire is still held in high esteem by many Pembrokeshire people; and I earnestly trust that in the future the result of my labours here may bear some degree of similar appreciation and success.' Mr. Adams expressed his pleasure at the kind way in which he had been received and the encouragement given to him during the preliminary organisation. 'It has been said: "Happy is the nation that has no history". In the Tenby Schools we have as yet no brilliant list of successes to rejoice over but at the same time no discouraging list of failures to deplore. If with present material we lay a solid foundation for future success during the first year of work, we are certain in future to secure a long roll of successes. Our history has to be made, and speaking on behalf of my colleagues, Miss Burrell and Mr. Kirkman, who come among us with high academic distinction, I may say it will be our earnest and constant endeavour to make the history of the Tenby Intermediate Schools of such a character as will redound to the credit and honour of the Town.' He spoke of discouragements which would have to be faced and went on to say that no educational system was yet perfect and that the keenest critics did little or nothing to help in the solution of difficulties as they arose. The line of action would be a united effort for the intellectual and physical development of every scholar. 'Gallant little Wales should utilise to the utmost the present advantage over England in having an organised system of intermediate education, and we wish Tenby to take a high place in the competition. By eliminating every shade of faction and party, and by heartily uniting to assist in the development and success of the Tenby Intermediate School, we may hope with full confidence to make this institution one of the best of its kind, not only in Pembrokeshire, but throughout the Principality.' Mr. Adams' lofty peroration was followed by loud cheers from the assembled company.

After the remaining speeches, the meeting was rounded off with the singing of the National Anthem.

After all the rhetoric of the formal occasion, it seems appropriate to conclude the account of the official opening by noticing the names of the first winners of the County Scholarships. There is no report of these names having been mentioned by the speakers at the ceremonies on 23 September, but they were published in the two newspapers on the 24th. Twenty-one pupils from the Primary Schools in the parishes of Tenby, Penally and St. Issells sat at the County Schools on Wednesday, 16 September, for the nine scholarships to the value of £6 each, five for boys and four for girls. Mr. Adams conducted the examination and members of the Governing Body who attended were Messrs. J. R. Rowlands, C. F. E. Allen, William Parcell and James Hughes (Clerk).

The successful candidates were as follows:—

Babb, Leonard John William, Victoria Street, Tenby.
Davies, Benjamin Pugh, Trewern Saundersfoot.
Morley, Bertie, 31 The Norton, Tenby.
Murray, Thomas Charles, Griffithston, Saundersfoot.
Parrott, Arthur William, Tudor Square Tenby.
Husband, Eleanor Elizabeth, 8 Clareston Road, Tenby.
Morris, Alice, Upper Frog Street, Tenby
Nicholls, Margaret Gwendoline, Westgate House, Tenby.
Sweet, Florence Ethel, Penally.

These boys and girls were part of the material with which Mr. Adams hoped to lay a foundation for future success during the first year of work in the school.

Chapter III

THE EARLY HISTORY OF TENBY COUNTY
INTERMEDIATE SCHOOL

'There will always be hewers of wood and drawers of water'
(J. W. B. Adams).

Section 1: The Early Years

The Tenby Corporation Guide for 1903, compiled by Douglas A.
Reid, M.D., Medical Officer of Health for the Borough and former
surgeon in the Crimea, contains a photograph of the County School,
specially taken by R. J. Truscott. This was the front view of the
premises when the first pupils were registered on 24 September 1896.
In the foreground an elongated central grass plot, with three lofty elms,
was encircled by a carriage drive. The Head Master's residence,
clearly distinguishable from the school portion, was linked with it by
communicating doors upstairs and down. The school itself, a two storey
structure with tall sash windows, consisted of four large classrooms
two of which overlooked the Boys' playground at the rear while the
other two looked over Greenhill Road, the lower of the latter being used
as a laboratory 'so called'. Old Pupils still remember the labels
'B Room' opposite the Laboratory, 'C Room' above 'B', 'D Room'
above the Lab. The girls entered the grounds through a gateway
down Greenhill Road and the boys through a back gate in Greenhill
Avenue. According to J. T. Griffith, a later Headmaster, a single storey
lean-to at the east end served as the boys' cloakroom, while the girls'
cloakroom consisted of a narrow strip alongside the upstairs corridor
later incorporated into the classroom which overlooked St. John's
Croft.

During that first term the classrooms were heated by coal fires in
black barred grates with cobbles purchased from the Tenby Gas
Consumers' Company (at 15/6 per ton!) while artificial light, when
required, was supplied by gas-jets fed with gas from the same company.
When Professor E. D. Jones came to inspect the Laboratory in February
1897, he suggested that the 'present' gas burners should be replaced by

single light incandescent burners, as the 'present' ones were unsuitable for Art Classes 'by reason of two shadows cast'. The Governors took no immediate action.

The late Mr. and Mrs. Robert Thomas, formerly of St. Julian Street, and the late Mr. Reginald Farley, dentist in Tudor Square, who were among the first generation of pupils, recalled that during the earliest days the desks had not arrived and that chairs and tables had been obtained temporarily from Mr. Edward Grabbam, Ironmonger, in the High Street. As there was no bell, pupils were summoned to class with a whistle. Prayers were held in one of the upper classrooms. In October the Chairman reported to the Governors that at least sixty pupils must be provided for and that additional furniture must be acquired.

Then there was the problem of setting up the Science Laboratory. On 14 December the Governors received a report of their sub-committee and resolved 'That the recommendation of the Committee be adopted and that the tender of Mr. W. H. Husband for fitting up the large room at £52 be accepted and that Mr. Kirkman be instructed to obtain the necessary chemical apparatus and material set out in a list by him at a cost not exceeding £75.' As late as October 1898 the Science and Art Department, South Kensington, were pressing the Governors to acquire additional apparatus. Mr. Spencer, Science Master in succession to Mr. Kirkman, eventually supplied the information for the necessary order. Mr. J. T. Griffith, who was appointed Science Master in 1903, described the early Lab., in his reminiscence in the 1946 Jubilee issue of *The Greenhillian*: 'The Science Laboratory as it was then (mis)called was the present Chemistry Laboratory, but its only equipment was a demonstration bench . . . in front of the fireplace, with a tip-up trestle bench on the west side, and that bench under the present large windows. A raised dais in three stages served to hold the long desks for classroom purposes.' (The demonstration bench and three stage dais were later moved into the Science Lecture Room when the premises were extended.)

The above details are mentioned to show that the school began with the barest of necessities and that, even allowing for inflation over the past eighty years, the costs were ridiculously low compared with present expenditure, say, on a single item of laboratory equipment. Whereas Mrs. Clement Williams, wife of the Chairman of the Governors, made a gift of £25 towards the cost of the Laboratory, Mr. Egerton Allen, always a persistent critic of his fellow Managers in their handling of finance, voted against the expenditure on the Lab., against the purchase of two clocks at £2. 10s. 0d. each and against the recommendation of Mrs. Parcell and Mrs. Rowe to purchase a Mornington and Weston piano from Cowtan's in Tudor Square at a cost of £25. Incidentally, that piano was still in use in 1928.

According to the earliest Admission Register, there were admitted in the Session 1896-1897, 38 boys including 14 from Tenby Wesleyan School, 6 from Tenby National Parochial School, 1 from New Hedges National Parochial, 4 from Saundersfoot Board School, 1 each from Begelly and Pentlepoir Board Schools, 1 from Warren, and 1 from Narberth County School. The other boys came from private Schools, among them Miss Hitchings' of Tenby 1, Hoylake School 1, St. Oswald's Ellesmere, Salop 1, and Mr. Ellis of Haverfordwest 1. Written into the Register and then deleted were the names of four boys who had failed to obtain a Scholarship: one 'who could not read or write properly', one 'not up to Standard V of an Elementary School', and another 'not sufficiently prepared'.

During that first year 36 girls were registered:— 10 from Tenby Wesleyan, 2 from Tenby National Parochial, 3 from St. Florence National Parochial, 1 each from St. Clears and Pentlepoir Board Schools, 1 each from Narberth and Pembroke Dock County Schools. Admission of girls from Private Schools included 2 from a Private School in Manchester, 1 from Bath, 3 from Miss Kinnelly of Pembroke and 3 from Miss Black's School at Tenby.

Some statistics were given in the Report of the first Central Welsh Board Inspection, signed by Owen Owen, Chief Inspector, on 23 October 1897, following a visit to the school by temporary Inspector, Mr. Headlam, on 29 June. He noted that there were then on the roll 36 boys and 35 girls. Of these pupils 2 were boarders and 6 resided in approved lodgings; 66 came from within the School District and 5 from without; 53 were from urban and 18 from rural parishes. 'A majority were children of tradesmen and workmen.' Mr. Headlam did not report the proportion of children of farmers, professional people and ministers of religion. However, the ages of the pupils were noted:— 11 under twelve, 33 twelve to fourteen, 13 fifteen to sixteen and 14 over sixteen. The various types of school from which they came were given; so were the Fees and 8 holders of Scholarships to the total value of £48. The school was arranged in four Forms, namely IV (the highest), III, II, I, with a staff consisting of the Head Master, two Assistant Masters, an Assistant Mistress and two visiting teachers. Old Greenhillians remembered that Mr. Kirkman taught Science and Mathematics in the Lab., that the Head Master then taught English, History and Geography in 'B Room', that Miss Burrell in 'D Room' was responsible for French and Latin, and that every Friday Mr. E. J. Head took Art in the other upstairs classroom. The ages of the pupils and the diversity of their previous schooling, together with the scarcity of equipment unthinkable in a modern secondary school, must have presented a serious challenge to the staff. Yet the Inspector reported: 'The Staff is adequate. The School premises are suitable and provide sufficient accommodation. The School is provided with the necessary furniture and appliances.'

At this stage the pupils were not yet prepared for the Junior and Senior Certificates of the Central Welsh Board but some of them took the examinations of the College of Preceptors and the Science and Art Department. Nevertheless sixty-four pupils were examined in July 1897 and in the Inspector's Report there appeared detailed comments on the work in English Grammar, Composition, English Literature, History, Geography, Scripture, Arithmetic, Algebra, Euclid, Trigonometry, Latin, French, Theoretical Physics, and Domestic Economy. Mr. Owen Owen, Chief Inspector, concluded: 'The School appears to be conducted in accordance with the Scheme under which it was established except that Drill, or other physical exercises—an obligatory subject—does not appear on the Time Table.' However, note had been taken that there were separate playgrounds for boys and girls, that there were swings on the trees in the girls' section of the grounds, and that there was a field for cricket and football. Football was first played on the Maudlins where the Serpentine Building Estate now stands.

Most of the boys and girls recorded in the earliest years of the first Admission Register have been called to mind by some surviving contemporaries and by other old Tenby residents; many were followed in the school by their own families and they, in turn by their offspring; some were later married to fellow pupils; of several it would be possible to build up detailed biographies. The majority of the first generation are identifiable on the earliest photograph of the whole school, taken in front of the doorway of the Head Master's residence in the summer of 1897. A few who were then Juniors are also recognisable on a second group photographed in the grounds in 1903.

A comparison of the two pictures is interesting, with regard to numbers, costume and personnel. On the 1897 photograph there were thirty-six boys (all being present) and thirty-one girls (four were absent). All but four boys were wearing the regulation mortar-boards with red and black tassels. ('To be seen without a mortar-board on a Sunday was to incur the certain displeasure of J.W.B.A. ! '). All the boys wore boots as was then the fashion; the Juniors with one exception, were clad in jackets, waistcoats, knee breeches, stockings and Eton Collars; the Seniors had jackets, waistcoats, turn-over low hard linen collars with either ties or bow-ties, and long trousers. A few wore watches and chains. While some of the girls were wearing skirts and blouses, the rest of them appeared in a variety of woollen or cotton frocks of below-calf length, several having the fashionable 'leg of mutton sleeves' and a number ornamented by an assortment of late Victorian lace collars. In the centre and dominating the scene was the Head Master, J. W. B. Adams, wearing his Oxford hood. To his left sat the small prim-looking Miss Alice Burrell wearing a high-necked blouse and pince-nez with cord attached; to his right was the first Science Master, Mr. Kirkman, and beyond him the Junior Master, Mr. Robert Phillips. In the foreground reclined Mrs. Adams' dog, Nebuchadnezzar.

The 1903 group has a background of trees. There were thirty-four boys (1 being absent) and twenty-three girls (1 being absent—a drop in numbers). Some changes in clothing should be noticed. The mortar-boards had given place to dark blue school caps with badges adapted from the Tenby Borough Seal. Most Junior Boys were wearing Eton Collars, but one had a woollen jersey and another a striped 'sailor blouse'. The senior boys had high-button jackets with short lapels; one of them sported a double-breasted waistcoat and a 'button hole'; several wore the new style starched double tall collar, which contrasted with the single 'drain pipe' collars of the Head Master, of Mr. Spencer (Science Master in place of Mr. Kirkman), of the Junior Master Mr. Roberts and Art Master E. J. Head.

96

A number of the girls dressed in round-necked blouses and skirts; some had a high-necked blouse as did Miss Camilla Thomas (successor to Miss Burrell); some wore frocks varying in style but no longer with voluminous sleeves, while the lace collars had disappeared from the scene. Two of the girls were adorned with their lockets and chains and one had a watch suspended over her blouse, a fashionable practice on into the years before the First World War.

A brief mention will be made of a cross-section of town and country pupils who were enrolled during the earliest period, from 1896 to 1904, embracing the years of the above photographs. More detail will be provided of a few sample careers. It should be pointed out that the entries in the first Admission Register were inconsistent and, on occasion, erratic. During the first Session were entered the pupils' names and addresses, the names of their parents or guardians, the pupils' dates of birth (the month and day not always noted) and the previous school attended. However, this Register was overlapped by a new one, beginning in the Spring Term 1903. From then onwards the basic information about each pupil, from entry to leaving, was recorded on a separate page in accordance with official requirements.

The very first name in the first Admission Register was that of Bertie Morley, born in 1883, son of Mr. H. T. Morley, the Borough Surveyor who resigned along with the Town Clerk, C. W. R. Stokes, following upon the bitterly fought elections to the Borough Council in 1895. Bertie left school in 1899 to take up office work. Later he followed in his father's footsteps and became Borough Surveyor. His sister Connie entered the school in 1900 and his son was a senior pupil at Greenhill in 1928. The son of another local government official, Mr. T. Aneuryn Rees, Stokes' successor as Town Clerk, was William Aneuryn Rees, who left the County School in 1899 to continue his education at Llandovery College.

The names of children of local business and trades people are to be seen among the early admissions:—

Charles and Winifred Jeffreys, son and daughter of Mr. C. Jeffreys, taxidermist in the premises now occupied by the Tenby Jewellers in the High Street.

Arthur William, Edwin and Harold Parrott, sons of T. Parrott, baker, Tudor Square, the first of whom trained as a dentist, while the other two carried on the family's flourishing confectionery business in a shop later acquired by the Midland Bank.

Trevor Thomas Tucker, Ruby and Charles, part of the family of five sons and two daughters of Tom Tucker, tobacconist and hairdresser next to Barclay's Bank, and one time bathing machine and chair operator on Tenby's beaches.

Reginald Farley and his sister Dorothy, children of Charles Farley, local councillor, bookseller and for many years supplier to the school in a shop subsequently occupied by Melias the grocers, and now absorbed by the 'Bib and Tucker' café. Reginald became a dentist with a surgery in Tudor Square and he contributed reminiscences to the 1946 Jubilee issue of *The Greenhillian*.

Then there were the Truscotts, Harold, Beatrice and Mildred—to be followed later by Dolly and Douglas in turn—the family of James Truscott, Jeweller of 13 High Street at the junction with St. Nicholas Lane, forty years a Churchwarden at St. Mary's. Beatrice married Percy Yeomans, dentist above the Jeweller's shop, then at 'the Priory' where St. Theresa's Convent now is, and finally at 'Tenby House', Pembroke. Mildred married Charles Victor Solomon, who took on her father's business from 1916 until his death in 1937; she died at Newton Abbot in 1974; her daughter, a Greenhillian, now lives with her husband, John Evans, in the Old Coastguard House on Castle Hill.

There were several Davieses. Kate Mildred was the youngest daughter of the original Stephen Davies, outfitter in the High Street and was to be the aunt of Kit Hearn and Eve Fletcher-Evans, both of whom attended the County School during and after the First World War. Also registered were Alice and Muriel Davies, the daughters of William Davies who built Minwear House at the corner of Deer Park and Warren Street; their brother was Walter Davies, the baker, in Frog Street, and their nephew and niece were Wallace and Isabel. Alice Davies married a Greenhillian, Bob Thomas; Muriel pursued a musical career, Walter was for some years organist at the Tenby Congregational Church and Isobel passed the L.R.A.M. examination as a pianist.

Charles Henry and Eva Brookman were the offspring of Mr. A. H. Brookman, Manager of the Tenby Gasworks, of which Charles later became Manager. He married a former fellow pupil Gwen Evans, one of the daughters of John Evans, the saddler in Tudor Square, and sister of Nellie Powys Evans, musician, artist and photographer, who at a later period had her studio at St. Julian House.

From St. George's Street came Gilbert Gwyther, whose father had a millinery and drapery business at Manchester House, and his neighbour Florrie Georgina Rees, a grocer's daughter. Emily Winifred Bassadona was the niece of another grocer in the same street, Mr. Henry Williams, whose business at the junction with Upper Frog Street passed to the Sandercocks; they eventually sold out to Rapaccioli, who altered the premises and installed a clock at the corner.

Alfred Grieve lived at the bottom corner of Tudor Square, where the 'Pam Pam' restaurant now is. His father kept a bazaar and ran a system of payment by instalments at the rate of one shilling per week.

There was the first of the line of Lillycrops in the School, namely Robert, son of T. H. Lillycrop, fishmonger in Lower Frog Street, while the latest, also a Robert, was a pupil at the new County Secondary School in the nineteen-sixties.

Also registered was the first of the Mabes, namely James, brother of J. E. L. Mabe, butcher at Cobra House, Upper Frog Street. James, whose report for the Easter Term 1899 still survives, left to go to the Dockyard at Pembroke Dock. In due course all J. E. L. Mabe's family attended the school—Marjorie, Wynford, Iris, Kenneth, Dilys and John in the twenties and thirties. Wynford married another Greenhillian, Winnie Diment, and the career of their son Keith spanned the move into the new premises in Heywood Lane, where there followed Michael and Heather, son and daughter of Dilys.

Others of this early vintage were associated with the west end of the High Street:— George and Margaret Grabbam, son and daughter of Edward Grabbam, ironmonger (afterwards Griffiths Bros. and now Squibbs Outfitters); Archie and Claire Palmer of Palmer's Stores next to the Market; Dorothy Lord, eldest of the family of three daughters and a son of George Lord, draper, between Palmer's Stores and the Cobourg Hotel (Palmer's and Lord's premises were eventually bought by T. P. Hughes and Son Ltd.); the three Hoffmanns Willie (1899), Carl (1901) and Gilbert Boodie (1903), sons of C. J. Hoffmann, jeweller of Goldsmith's Hall, opposite to George Lord's, and whose family name was changed to 'Stone', the maiden name of Mrs. Hoff-

99

mann, on account of anti-German feeling during World War I. From the North side of the High Street, opposite St. Mary's Church came Boysey Allen, son of Mortimer Allen, a notable local photographer; Boysey's sister, Frances Nesta joined the school in 1908 but left the following year to take up a stage career—the first Greenhillian who is known to have done this.

The early admissions include children of Ministers of Religion:— Leonard J. W. Babb and his sister Mildred, son and daughter of the Rev. H. Babb, Wesleyan Minister and for a while a Governor of the School; Keyworth and Trevor Lloyd Williams, sons of the Rev. John Lloyd Williams, Congregational Minister, a founder Governor of the County School and later author of the Greenhill School Song— the elder boy had a distinguished career in the Congregational Ministry and the younger Trevor, who was admitted to the School in 1901 at the age of 10 (by special concession in respect of the Regulations), took his Senior Certificate in 1907, his London Matriculation in 1909, his Central Welsh Board Higher Certificate in 1910, an Honours Degree in History at the University College of Wales, Aberystwyth, in 1913 and who eventually joined the staff of *The Times* and became the Editor of its Trade Supplement; Beatrice Bancroft, daughter of another School Governor, the Rev. George Bancroft of Bethesda Presbyterian Chapel, became a dressmaker on leaving School.

The following are representative of other walks of life in the town:— Violet, William and Ruth Norman, part of the family of a Master Rigger of 5 Clareston Road; John Rees Jones, son of the gardener to Edward Laws of 'Brython', Narberth Road, (author of *Little England beyond Wales*); John Devereux Mack, a brilliant pupil admitted under ten years old in September 1897, who gained the C.W.B. Senior Certificate (with five Distinctions) in 1902 and the Honours Certificate in 1904 (the only one in Pembrokeshire that year), who was placed 35th out of 1,600 candidates in the Civil Service Examination (Second Division), was awarded a County Exhibition and a King's Scholarship, went to University College, Cardiff, won a scholarship to Jesus College, Oxford, but on his guardian's insistence he began work at the National Health Insurance Office in Cardiff. Subsequently he had a distinguished career in Inland Revenue, terminating in Whitehall. He was refused release for military service in World War I ; Ida Jones, then living at 7 Harding Street was to become an able water-colourist, working mainly in the Tenby area but who also painted her impressions of Canadian scenery during an extended visit to British Columbia; Jessie and Lily Kirkman, daughters of science master J. C. Kirkman; George Bolt of Scarborough House, whose mother was Head Mistress of the Girls' section of the National Parochial School, who in his turn entered the profession and married Claire Palmer (mentioned above); Charles Reginald Hughes, son of James Hughes of Picton Road (Clerk to C. W. R. Stokes and first Clerk to the County School Governors), who went to work on Wyman's Bookstall on the Great Western Railway Station and later had his own bookshop at Westgate House opposite the South Gate—his son, Owen, went to Greenhill and after the Second World War took over his father's business; Arthur Rees, whose father had carriages and horses stabled in Cresswell Street, was small of stature with the appearance of a jockey, who subsequently ran his own riding school with his horse 'Lancer' and his ponies 'Fox Trot', 'Tango' and 'Two Step'—favourites with some of the young Greenhillians—and who contributed his First World War recollections to the 1938 issue of the school magazine, then in its second year as a printed publication; George Sinnett of Worcester House, Esplanade, and his sister Elizabeth were the offspring of George Sinnett, who had a blacksmith's shop in St. Florence Parade (on a site now covered by Jeremy's Petrol Station), where George (Junior) learned his trade and shoed horses after his father's day.

Among the 1896 admissions was Robert ('Bob') Thomas of 3 Langdon Villas, Warren Street. His father worked in H. M. Dockyard at Pembroke Dock. Bob became an employee in Ace's motor business, then in its infancy, but later he did some free-lance car maintenance and taught a number of Tenbyites to drive. During World War II he was a familiar figure about the town in the uniform of War Reserve Constable. He married Alice Davies of Minwear House (see above) and they made their home at 'Windermere', St. Julian Street. Bob's sister, Jane Elizabeth, also entered the County School in 1896. Some time after leaving she was married to Willie Morris, an employee at Ace's. Subsequently she had a grocery and confectionery business at the junction of Clareston Road and Warren Street, her shop being well-known for many years as an unofficial 'tuck shop' for the school pupils.

101

One family specially linked with the school from the very beginning down to the 1970s was that of William Husband, Master Plumber, who served as 'architect' to the Local Governing Body after the Greenhill property was first acquired and who was involved with sundry alterations and extensions to the premises during the first decade of the present century. William Husband's eldest daughter, Eleanor Elizabeth, was the first girl to be entered on the Admission Register on 24 September 1896. There followed at intervals down to 1920 her brothers John, Thomas and Alec and her sisters Marjorie and Dora. Records made available by Eleanor's daughter, Helen Bleines, contain details of the education of members of the family. It so happens that from these data, Eleanor's career can be followed, beginning at the Elementary School, continuing through the County Intermediate School and onwards, through training and entry into the teaching profession, so illustrating the various stages and requirements for the attainment of that goal.

Eleanor Husband was born on 1 August 1883. She became a pupil at the Tenby Wesleyan School in Warren Street. Her Attendance Card for the year 1888 survives, the inside being divided into squares for the marking of attendances, morning and afternoon for each day the school was in session. The pupil's name was written on the front and, on the back, the parents were notified in print: 'Parents are requested to examine this card every evening.' 'The School Clock is regulated by railway time. School opens at 9 a.m. and 1.30 p.m. A star indicates an early attendance—a circle a late attendance.' Eleanor's card was star-spangled. She reached Standard 7, sat the examination for a County Scholarship on 16 September 1896 and was one of the nine successful candidates who entered the new Tenby County School to pursue the course of study provided under the terms of the Welsh Intermediate Education Act. No doubt she appreciated the closing event of her first term, which was reported in the local press as 'a very interesting and enjoyable entertainment given by the members of the Staff and School.' The programme and the report are indicative of contemporary taste:—

Vocal Duet: 'I have wandered in dreams'
    Miss M. Davies and Miss W. Bassadona
Violin Solo: 'Life let us cherish'
    Miss Gwen Evans

Flute Solo: (a) 'Rose of Allandale' (b) 'The old folks at home' (with chorus)

Master B. Morley

Recitation: 'A New Year's Dialogue'

Miss W. Jeffreys and Master P. Jones

Song (with chorus): 'The Torpedo and the Whale'

Mr. Kirkman

Piano Duet: 'Selections from the Gondoliers'

Miss M. Davies and Miss W. Bassadona

Then came a performance of 'A Proverb in One Act' in which the parts were taken by Mr. Kirkman and Masters Willie Baker and John W. John, Trevor Tucker, Claude Jeffreys and Leoard Babb. There followed a surprise item:—

One of the scholars, dressed as a postman, entered and, from his well-filled post bag drew envelopes addressed to each of the scholars. These envelopes were found to contain Christmas Greetings and New Year's Wishes from the Principal and Staff. After a hearty cheer had been given for the senders the whole party adjourned to the Girls' Classroom for tea. One could not fail to be impressed with the fact that there exists between the Principal and the Staff on the one hand and the Scholars on the other those feelings of esteem and confidence, which with a very clearly manifested enthusiasm for the work of the School, are so highly calculated to make it a success. . . . Judging by the marks given for home lessons and the examination, there is every reason to congratulate the Principal and Staff on the amount and quality of the work done during the term.

When the first School Prize Day was held on 3 December 1897, Eleanor Husband was one of the eight recipients of books at the hands of Mrs. Clement Williams, wife of the Chairman of the Governors, they having allotted a sum of £2. 10s. 0d. for purchases. In 1899 she and Leonard Babb were the first two Tenby pupils to gain the Senior Certificate of the Central Welsh Board. At Christmas that year she was awarded another prize, a leather-bound copy of Macaulay's *Essays and Lays*, with the cover bearing a gilt impression of the Borough Seal (the Castle) with the words 'Tenby County School' and, inside, a decorative Book Plate inscribed with her name. Two years later she received a similarly embellished copy of *Concise Latin Dictionary* by John T. White (1037 pages).

In 1900 Eleanor was awarded the Matriculation of the University of Wales on the strength of her Senior Certificate, taken the second time, having satisfied the Examiners in English Composition, English Language (with Distinction), English Literature, History (with Distinction), Latin (with Distinction), French (with Distinction), Elementary Mathematics (with Distinction) and Elementary Science. Already she had gained Certificates of the Department of Science and Art, South Kensington, including a Pass in Theoretical Mechanics. In December 1900 she sat what was then called the Queen's Scholarship for Admission to Training Colleges and for the Office of Assistant Teacher. Candidates had to be over 18 years of age on 1 September in the year of the Examination and had to produce a medical certificate in a form approved by the Board of Education. The Examination was held at the Wesleyan Sunday School Room, Haverfordwest, an approved local centre, on four days in December, her subjects being Domestic Economy, Elementary Science, Geography, Latin, French, Needlework, Theory of Teaching, History, English Composition, English Language and Literature. She was successful. In June 1901 she qualified for the Matriculation of the University of London. The following September she took up residence at Aberdare Hall as a Normal Student attending the University College, Cardiff, where she pursued part of the B.A. Degree Course alongside her training for her chosen profession. However, after her recognition as a Certificated Teacher in August 1903, she accepted a post at Cwmclydach Girls' School in the Rhondda Valley, where she remained until 1912, the year of her marriage to William Morgan John, a colliery official at New Tredegar. Eleanor and her husband lived at Phillipstown, New Tredegar until his declining health led to their retirement to Tenby in 1934. Their family of five had the remarkable distinction of all becoming university graduates. The two youngest became pupils at Greenhill, Catherine Helen (1935-1941) and William David (1937-1943). The latter was awarded his Degree at Jesus College, Oxford where he became a student after serving as a 'Bevin Boy' during World War II. Helen graduated at the University College of Wales, Aberystwyth, qualified as a teacher and for one period came to teach in her old school. She married Norman Bleines, of the same profession,

THE AUTHOR
WILFRED HARRISON, M.B.E., M.A.
photo: Douglas Hardy

W. H. Richards, J.P., C.C.
d. 1895

C. J. Williams, J.P.
d.1912

C. W. R. Stokes, C.C.
d. 1933

C. F. Egerton Allen, C.C.
d.1928

FOUR 'FOUNDER FATHERS'
Drawn by Terence Johns, from photographs

J. W. B. Adams, B.A. (Lond.), M.A. (Oxon)
1896-1910

J. T. Griffith, J.P., B.Sc., (Lond.), F.C.S.
1911-1942

G. C. Gibson, J.P., M.Sc., (Wales), F.C.S.
1942-1963

L. G. Hill, B.Sc., (Lond.),M.Ed. (Nottingham)
1964-1977

FOUR HEAD MASTERS

SCHOOL PHOTOGRAPH 1897

with Staff, left to right: Messrs. R. Phillips, J. C. Kirkman, J. W. B. Adams (H.M.) and Miss Alice Burrell

photo: H. Mortimer Allen

SCHOOL PHOTOGRAPH 1903

with Staff, left to right: Mr. E. J. Head, Miss C. M. Thomas, Messrs. J. W. B. Adams (H.M.), C. H. Spencer and J. R. Roberts

photo: H. Mortimer Allen

SENIOR PUPILS c. 1897
with Head Master, Miss Alice Burrell and Mr. J. C. Kirkman
photo: H. Mortimer Allen

STAFF c. 1910
back row, left to right: Mr. J. R. Roberts, Mrs. J. W. B. Adams, Messrs. J. T. Griffith and
E. J. Head, in front: Miss Gaynor R. Jones, Mr. J. W. B. Adams, Miss Gore Lindsay
photo: H. Mortimer Allen

COOKERY CLASS c. 1906-07
with Miss Margaret E. Thomas, first Cookery Mistress
photo: H. Mortimer Allen loaned by Miss M. Beynon

CAST OF 'RUMPELTSTILTZKIN' AT THE ROYAL GATEHOUSE ASSEMBLY
ROOMS, 1908
with Mrs J. W. B. Adams, centre back
photo: H. Mortimer Allen, loaned by Miss M. Thomson

and their three children, David (after one year at Greenhill), Eleanor and Katheryn all attended the County Secondary School in Heywood Lane. Katheryn, the youngest and the last link in the family connection dating back to William Husband in 1896, left in 1973.

A similar dossier of certificates and academic successes could be quoted in respect of William Husband's two older sons, John and Thomas, did space permit. One of the early members of the family left behind an undated list of books together with new and second-hand prices. The list is interesting, not only from the point of view of costs but as a sample of textbooks in use at the time:—

	£	s.	d.
Latin			
2 *Forum Latinum* at 1/4 for 1/-		2	0
1 *Roman History* at 3/6		2	8
1 *Jerrams' Anglice Reddenda* at 2/6		1	11
1 Cicero *Pro Roscio Amerina* at 2/6		1	11
1 Perthas' *Atlas Antiquus* at 3/-		2	6
English			
1 Coleridge at 2/-		1	6
1 Wordsworth at 2/6 nett		2	6
2 Keats at 1/- and at 4d		1	1
1 Carlyle at 1/-			9
1 Lamb's *Essays of Elia* at 7/6		1	6
1 *Student's Manual of English Literature* at 7/6		5	8
1 Sweet's *Anglo-Saxon* at 2/6		1	11
Logic			
1 Jevons' *Elementary Logic* at 3/6		2	8
Mathematics			
1 *Higher Algebra* at 7/6		1	11
3 Exercise Books at 10d		2	6
6 ,, ,, 4½d		2	3
3 ,, ,, 2d			5

These prices were very similar to those being paid for books during and after the First World War.

Attention should now be directed to the country pupils. There were, of course, a few boarders, the boys usually six in number, being accommodated in the Head Master's house and the girls in approved lodgings. On 1 February 1897 the Governors agreed that Mrs. W. H. Saies of Ripley House, Tenby, should take not more than six boarders at not less than £8 and not more than £10 per term, Mr. Husband having inspected the house and having found the sanitary arrangements satisfactory. On 23 February, Miss Broadstreet of Warren Street was licensed to receive not more than four girls at £8 each per term. Although the names of some of the girls who boarded in the town are known, there survives no official record of how many availed themselves of the approved facilities. As for the rest of the pupils who lived in the country, they made their way to school either by train, many of them having to walk some distance to the nearest railway station, or by horse drawn trap, on bicycles as these came into vogue, or on foot over distances ranging from one to seven miles. It should be remembered that there were no smooth roads such as have been constructed to serve modern motor vehicles. The surfaces even of main roads were rough and specially suited for the convenience of horses drawing carriages or carts and were liable to be dusty in the summer and muddy in the winter, while many of the side roads and lanes were never given more than an occasional scattering of chippings to be run in by the iron rims of passing cartwheels. The boys and girls who traversed these routes had no waterproof coats, though they were advised to bring with them a change of clothing. In February 1897 the Principal reported that he had placed two rooms in his residence at the disposal of pupils for drying and the Governors then made an allowance of £2 for coal for the necessary fires.

As will be seen from the following sample of country pupils, most of them were the children of farmers in the catchment area:—

Thomas Charles Murray and his brother John Claude came from Griffithston Farm, Saundersfoot. On leaving School Charles made farming his career. In 1931 he moved to Buckspool Farm, Bosherston, where he was a pioneer of early potato growing in Pembrokeshire. John went to a Training College, became a teacher, served as an officer in the Welsh Guards during the First World War and was killed in France in 1917. Hugh Williams of Ralph Dairy was the son of John Williams and father of Jean, another Greenhillian, who is now one of the staff of Mathias Thomas and Lewis, Solicitors. From Beaconing Farm, Begelly, came David Watts Williams and his sister Alice, both of whom entered the teaching profession—Alice recalled that they walked all the way to the County School, a distance of six miles.

Others from local farms were George Williams of Wedlock, Eva Protheroe of Skrinkle, James Protheroe of Bubbleton followed later by his brother Albert, a succession of Beynons of Holloway—Ethel, Evelyn, Florence, May and Harold, William Smith of Trevayne, Phoebe Thomas of Ivy Tower, and Aiden Lewis of Carn Rock, St. Florence. Also within this period, coming to school by pony and trap and giving lifts to fellow pupils when possible were the brothers Thomas, George, Hugh and David John of Elm Grove, St. Florence. So far as is known the majority of the above returned to work on their family farms.

Among the Saundersfoot pupils at this early stage were Charles Ormond of the Cambrian Hotel, Arnold Bennett of Bay View and Reginald Read of Saundersfoot Post Office, whose sons Leslie and Harold eventually came to Greenhill and were well-known for their prowess as soccer players.

Fortunately, there are reminiscences supplied by Old Greenhillians who were boarders during this early period, Sir Frederick Tymms and the Rev. Oswald Calvin Thomas.

Frederick Tymms' father, William Henry Tymms, Headmaster of Jeffreston National Parochial School at Cresselly from 1888 to 1923, had come there from Durham, and his mother, née Jones was the daughter of a farmer at Martletwy. Frederick was born at the School House on 4 August 1889. He was admitted to the Tenby County School in September 1902 and remained until July 1904. He was a boarder during the week, being one of the five or six boarders taken in by Mr. and Mrs. Adams:

> Exceptionally I was allowed to go home at week-ends. I sup-
> pose my father insisted and I don't suppose it was a popular
> arrangement with the Head Master. I was allowed to leave
> promptly on Saturday to catch the one o'clock train to Saunders-
> foot, from where I walked to Cresselly. On Monday morning
> there was no train. I started about seven o'clock and walked to
> Tenby (7 miles). The train saved me a couple of miles walking
> on Saturday.

The Boarders lived in the Head Master's house, which although only part of the original building (the west end), was fairly commodious. Nevertheless, I have often wondered how two sensitive adults could have put up with the invasion of their privacy by half a dozen somewhat obnoxious stranger boys, who, although to some extent segregated, even used their bathroom. We had access to the house, either down the area steps through the basement kitchen, or more usually by the back stairs which connected the house with the School, at a lower level. The front door was forbidden. We had lunch, and were on our best behaviour, at the Head Master's table, but other meals were judiciously timed so that we were kept out of sight. As to that bathroom—the régime prescribed for us was a cold bath every morning and it was difficult to evade, since the bathroom adjoined the Head Master's bedroom. On very cold mornings there was enough blowing and stamping to simulate a dozen cold baths. Make believe quickly became reality if either the Head or Mrs. Adams came to the door. I don't suppose anyone was deceived.

Sir Frederick recollects that his fellow boarders were Charles Collard (Carmarthen), Leo Pellowe (Pembroke Dock), William Smith (Amroth), Cecil Thomas (St. Clears) and later, his elder brother. Mr. Roberts, the Mathematics Master (Junior?), also lived in the House and Mr. Spencer, Science Master, came to lunch. Roberts kept a disciplinary eye on the boarders, supervised Prep. in the evening and, in the summer, conducted the early morning bathing parade to the beach.

We boarders must have appeared to be a united lot, always together and segregated, out of school hours, from the day-boys and the girls. There were not, so far as I knew, any specific rules; nor did it result, so far as I remember, from any conscious attitude on the part of the boarders. (It may well have been the other way round). One factor was that the boarders had a specific prep. hour to keep in the School; another was that the Town was out of bounds—that is to say, the principal streets were. We had to use the more obscure streets, or the shortest cut across the more frequented, to reach our permitted wandering places— including the North Sands, the South Sands, the Burrows and Giltar. We also had a well-marked trail to the bottom end of

108

Tudor Square to St. Julian Street, where Rabiotti dispensed ice-cream and fried potatoes, but pocket money only allowed this about once a week. Incidentally, they were consumed on the premises, never on the street or the sands. Another reason for this apparent segregation was that, while we were not excused football practice when that was the order of the day, the boarders were permitted to play hockey with the girls. I don't think any boarder ever got into the school football team. The football and hockey ground was where, I believe, the School now stands.

He notes that, apart from the Head 'a very austere figure' the Masters were: Mr. Spencer, the Science Master 'an easy going and humorous man, in spite of his approaching blindness', Roberts already mentioned, 'young, sinewy and athletic and consequently much admired by the small boys'. Miss Thomas, English Literature and French, was 'young, attractive, well-loved in spite of her attempts to appear a stern disciplinarian. She was held in particularly high esteem by the boarders because of her annual invitation to tea in her rooms in Warren Street—a feast they could only match in their dreams!' Mr. Head, the artist, came only at particular times to give drawing lessons. The boarders thought his more interesting occupation was to paint portraits of the prettier girls in the school, including Maggie Grabbam and Mildred Truscott. It was recalled that Mr. Spencer was succeeded by Mr. J. T. Griffith(s), who was then young 'full of knowledge and ability to teach, but clearly also, then, a new broom, which did not make for his immediate popularity'.

When Tymms was a pupil in the Fourth there were seniors in the Fifth Form, one or two of them carrying on for another year in a sort of super Fifth (there being no Sixth) under the care of the Head Master. Among them was the top Scholar, John Devereux Mack, who passed into the Second Division of the Civil Service, (as already noted). Tymms used to see him later when they walked from Battersea to their respective offices in Whitehall. Another senior, looked up to as a footballer, was George Bolt:

As to football, the greatest was, in fact, an Old Boy—'Teddy' Parrott. (His brother 'Harry' was a contemporary of mine.) To us, standing on the sidelines at an inter-school match, the sight of 'Bobs' (i.e. Roberts), perhaps George Bolt, as they came tearing down the field displaying what seemed their magnificent physique, turned them at least for the afternoon into demi-gods.

Other contemporaries were Charlie Tucker, William Norman (who became a Naval Artificer), Archie Palmer, William Murphey (afterwards a Post Office Sorter), Bevan Thomas (who joined the Merchant Navy) and Maurice Whitten, one of the best scholars, whom Tymms met later during the Second World War in Delhi when Whitten was Correspondent for *The Times,* covering the Eastern Front.

There were among these respected elder pupils two young ladies—I cannot refer to them otherwise—Enid Saies and Tina Simlett. Both were scholars and both commanded our respect and even awe. (Both became teachers. W.H.) A few years later, Enid, who was living with her mother in a house in Torrington Square collected a small group of the Tenby boys for tea. My abiding impression was of the nicety, in manners and tastes, of their way of life, compared with ours in 'digs' in the outer parts of London.

After Frederick Tymms left school he was coached by his father for the Boy Clerks Examination for the lowest rank in the Civil Service and he passed in 1905. 'A "Boy Clerk" (for many years now an extinct animal!) was in fact an office boy, though before long I had to train myself to become a passable shorthand typist serving an irascible senior architect in the Office of Works, who, when I answered the bell, started dictating at high speed before I could close the door.' At the earliest possible age he passed into the Second Division (38th out of 1700 competitors). Then, after temporary postings to various departments, he was by chance the first and only junior member of the staff of a new department created to run the Labour Exchange and Unemployment Insurance Schemes, just launched by Mr. Winston Churchill, then President of the Board of Trade.

Here I found myself looking after the needs of two joint Managers, who had just moved into new offices in Caxton House—Mr. W. H. Beveridge (later Lord Beveridge) fresh from Toynbee Hall and Mr. C. F. Rey (later Sir Charles, a business administrator). One evening Charles Rey was called over to see the President in Whitehall Gardens and ended by inviting the President to come and inspect the new offices. 'What's the use?', growled Winston, ' There'll be nobody there; it's seven o'clock.' ' Oh yes there will!' The bet was sealed. They came. That is the one and only occasion I have ever stood face to face with the great man. And it cost him ten bob! (I wonder why Winston did not get away with it on the grounds that I was, almost literally, 'nobody'. Moreover, Rey knew my habits and did not reveal that he had asked me to stay).

In due course came promotion to the post of Assistant Accountant to a provincial division, Lancashire, where Tymms became familiar with the employment problems of Lancashire mill-hands and Liverpool dockers.

At the outbreak of war in 1914 civil servants were not immediately allowed to join the forces. Already having five years service in the Territorial Army, he accepted a Commission in the Local Territorial Battalion of the South Lancashire Regiment, joined up in 1915, went overseas to the 1st/4th Battalion in 1916, served for two spells in the Battle of the Somme and then in the Ypres Salient.

One day, a flight of F.E.2D (two seater fighter) aeroplanes flew low over us in the trenches. It happened that another Subaltern and I had the habit of doing things together (a phase that passed). He said: 'That's the way to fight this war! Let's go and join the R.F.C.' I said 'O.K.' or words to that effect.

They applied for a transfer and got it. 'So does a wayward wind shape our course.' There followed training at Brooklands and service with No. 5 Squadron mostly in partnership with Captain J. C. Slessor as pilot (later Marshal of the Royal Air Force), on the Arras Vimy Ridge Sector.

After demobilisation in 1919 he secured a transfer to the newly created Department of Civil Aviation in the Air Ministry. The rest of his career was concerned with the organisation and administration of civil aviation. His distinguished record is outlined in *Who's Who 1974*:

Commanded the Air Section of the Oxford University Arctic Expedition to Spitzbergen 1924; Air Ministry Supt. of the Egypt-India Air route 1927; seconded to the governments of the Sudan, Kenya, Uganda and Tanganyika 1928; Chief Technical Assistant to the Director of Civil Aviation Air Ministry 1928-31; Air Ministry Representative on the Commission to Africa to organise the Cape to Cairo air route 1929-30; Director of Civil Aviation

111

in India 1931-42 and 1943-45; Director General of Civil Aviation in India Sept. 1945-March 1947; U.K. Representative of the Council of the International Civil Aviation Organisation, Montreal 1947-54; Government of India Delegate to the International Civil Aviation Conference, Chicago 1944; Leader of the U.K. Civil Aviation Mission to New Zealand 1948.

Frederick Tymms retired in 1955 and settled at Farnham, Surrey. As might be expected, he is a Fellow of the Royal Aeronautical Society. His war service was recognised with the award of the Military Cross and with his being appointed Chevalier de l'Ordre de la Couronne, receiving the accompanying Croix de Guerre, Belgium. For his services to Civil Aviation the following Honours were bestowed upon him: Commander of the Order of the Indian Empire 1935, Knighthood 1941, Knight Companion of the Order of the Indian Empire 1947. It should be added that he was part author of *Flying for Air Survey Photography* and of *Commercial Air Transport*.

Another family which deserves special mention, if only because it supplied more pupils than any other during the first nine years of the school's existence, was that of the Rev. J. Calvin Thomas, Minister of Frog Street Presbyterian Church and subsequently of Hoylake Presbyterian Church. Seven of his nine children attended the Tenby County School. He had shared a friendship 'based on their mutual liberal nonconformist zeal' with Henry Goward, the former owner and Head of the private school at Greenhill. One of the sons, Oswald, now living in retirement in Tenby, knew much of the County School through his brothers and sisters and from his own personal experience The following information has been supplied by him:—

The eldest son, Thomas Henry, left Mynheer's preparatory school for boys, in Hoylake, to learn farming with his grand-parents at Vatson Farm in the parish of East Williamston. However, the grand-parents insisted that his education should continue alongside his farming training. After attending Pentlepoir elementary school, he was admitted to Greenhill in 1896, after special consideration by the Governors, at nearly 19 years of age. He left in 1898. After Matriculation he took a teacher training course at Borough Road College, London, where J. W. B. Adams had served for a time as resident tutor. He taught in Tottenham until 1916, when he enlisted. After demobilisation in 1919 he was appointed Head Teacher in succession to

112

his younger brother, and there he remained until his retirement. During his Greenhill days he had been universally known to the staff and the boys as 'Captain', a nickname given by the Head, probably on account of his seniority.

The second member of the family to join the school was John Calvin. Following early schooling at a private school in Hoylake, he was at Greenhill from 1897 till 1901, where he gained the Senior Certificate of the Central Welsh Board before going to Birmingham University with a King's Scholarship. He did not graduate but qualified as a teacher, taught at East End School, Pembroke, 1904 to 1911, was thereafter Head of Begelly Council School until 1918, when he joined the auctioneering firm of Mr. George Collins.

The next sons, William Watkin and Joseph Edgar, both of whom had attended the private school in Hoylake entered the Tenby County School in 1898 and 1899 respectively. Both became bankers. The former started as a clerk in the Midland Bank Headquarters in Liverpool and finished his career as manager of the Narberth branch; the latter gained promotion in Lloyd's Bank, becoming in turn manager of the Gorseinon and Wrexham branches.

Two girls of the family followed the pattern of private school education before coming to Tenby. Muriel May, born in 1880, was for a brief spell a Greenhillian from 1897 to 1898. She went to the Counting House of F. W. Cook, draper in Dudley, and thence to the well-known store of Mr. T. P. Hughes, where she was the first accountancy clerk in that business. Afterwards she trained for Christian service at the Clapham Bible College, joined the staff of the District Bank in Wrexham, became a well-known lay preacher in North Wales and later in the South Pembrokeshire Presbytery when the family moved into the area after the death of the Rev. John Calvin Thomas. Muriel, widow of J. B. Jones-Bethen, came to live in Saundersfoot, where at the age of 93 she remembered her days at Greenhill with great interest and mentioned that she lived in lodgings along with Mr. Kirkman's two daughters, lodgings where Miss Alice Burrell had the oversight of these young boarders.

The second of the two girls, Hetty, likewise remained at Tenby for one Session, 1905-1906. She won a scholarship to Grove Park Secondary School, Wrexham, from where she gained a scholarship to the Department of Domestic Science at the University College of

Cardiff. After qualifying as a teacher of domestic subjects, she taught in Wrexham, then at Goodwick Council School and then served as a peripatetic teacher in South Pembrokeshire before taking up her last appointment, as Domestic Science Mistress at Tasker's High School, Haverfordwest, where she remained until her retirement to Saundersfoot.

David Oswald, who provided these notes about the family, was born in 1893, started his education at Hoylake, came to Greenhill as a boarder for the Session 1904-1905, then returned to a newly opened Preparatory School, Kingsmead, Hoylake, When his father moved to a pastorate in Wrexham, the family went with him and Oswald attended Grove Park Secondary School before going on to the University College of South Wales & Monmouth, Cardiff, where he graduated with honours in History. As one of twelve conscientious objectors in the University in the First World War he was sent to do farm work until 1919. Then he was accepted as a candidate for the Presbyterian Ministry, proceeded to theological studies at Cheshunt and Fitzwilliam College, Cambridge, graduated in the Theological Tripos in 1922, and thereafter served in successive pastorates in Aberdare 1927-38, Wrexham 1938-53 and Pembroke Dock 1953-63. He became Moderator of the English Branch of the Presbyterian Church in Wales and made a tour of Presbyteries in Queensland, Australia. Now in retirement he has passed the fiftieth anniversary of his ordination.

Oswald's session at the Tenby County School began the term after Frederick Tymms had left, but some of the six other boarders he remembered were contemporaries of Tymms. He writes:

> Most of my recollections of school centre around life in the Head's house rather than in the actual classrooms and lessons in school. J. W. B. A. was a man of considerable stature. He was an Oxford man. I do not know his origins but he certainly regarded himself as 'county' and was so regarded by the Town in general. His associations were with the 'quality'. I remember him as a very well groomed man of polished manners. He had an aristocratic manner and somehow impressed one as a man of character and culture in whose presence anything shabby or mean wilted at once. We all felt his personal standards set a standard for the School. He was highly respected by us all. He was kindly though strict. He maintained discipline without any difficulty.

114

He was highly thought of by us boys, as a good athlete and an excellent cricketer. We maintained that he was a Cricket Blue at Oxford, though I do not know whence our information came or if it was accurate; certainly we all wanted it to be true, such was our admiration of him. I do not remember any nickname being given to him regularly, though he was occasionally called 'the Boss' in some daring moment of lèse-majesté. But generally we spoke of him to each other as 'J.W.B.' He brought his cricket enthusiasm with him to the School. Of an evening he would get some of the elder boys to bowl at him on the School playing field. He would place a threepenny bit on his middle stump as a bait for the bowlers. Normally, this did not cost him much, but one evening great glee was occasioned when the School's very good fast bowler flattened his middle stump with two successive deliveries.

He mentions that the Head included Music among his cultural refinements:

I have a clear recollection of his music lessons. He was a very patriotic man and constantly reproached the times in which we lived for their lack of patriotism. He strove to correct this deficiency by teaching us songs, mostly of a patriotic nature. Prominent among them were the *Songs of the Fatherland*. He feared the then increasing militarism of Germany and had, I think, little but conservative scorn for the liberalism and pacifism—and even republicanism, which at that time had gained impetus as a reaction from the Boer War.

Mrs. Adams, whom we boarders believed to be of Dutch origin, did not share the regard in which J.W.B.A. was held by us. This arose from the fact that her catering for our meals in the School House was, to be frank, extremely economical and inadequate We were perpetually hungry. We believed that the Head was in some degree aware of this, but as time wore on we believed that, owing to his wife's overbearing manner, he feared scenes before the boys. That was the one field in which I ever heard criticism from any of us directed at the Head. Later events seemed to show that here was his Achilles' Heel. Mrs. Adams' manner was always decidedly overbearing to everybody.

As a result of our frugal fare in the House, much of my memory

115

of Greenhill is filled with recollections of fearful and risky enterprises to supplement the gap in our schoolboy hunger. There were surreptitious journeys into town to the South Wales Temperance Hotel, kept by the parents of Maggie Davies (Mrs. Perry), where massive rock buns could be bought at one halfpenny each or five for tuppence. The first chip shop also arrived in Tenby about 1904 and we took it in turns to sneak down to Rabiotti's after lights out in the 'dorm' . . . a perilous adventure especially when arriving back with an armful of chips, generally wrapped in the *South Wales Daily News*. Another means we used was to sneak down to the fish shed in the harbour, when the Brixham trawlers were in, and to buy for a few pence a supply of fish, which our great friend and ally, Annie, the cook would prepare for us. Annie was a godsend. Every evening, as we returned from our evening meal to 'B Room' which served us Boarders as a common room and prep room, we had to pass Annie's kitchen. Mrs. Adams would not allow us to use the front door of the house. Our ingress and exit had to be by the area steps, which meant we had to pass Annie's kitchen. As we passed, Annie stood behind her half-opened door each evening and surreptitiously passed a parcel to us. The parcel contained left-overs which she had kept for us . . . cake or tart or some such 'eats', always seven pieces, one for each of us. Great was the urgency to claim first pick as soon as we were up the area steps. . .I fear I remember much more of our means of assuaging hunger than of 'lessons'. I think the only text book I remember was Chardenal's first *French Grammar*.

As did Sir Frederick Tymms, D. O. Thomas remembered Miss Camilla Thomas as a great favourite: 'She was extremely friendly and charming, especially for an early century "school marm". We all had a soft spot for her; she had a real sense of fun which did not disintegrate even when, on opening her desk one morning, she found a live bat in it. The bat had been collected from some rafters the previous night by some boarders. If my memory is correct she taught English.' He also remembers Mr. Roberts in charge of the boarders and the early morning bathes: 'He always, I think on Mrs. Adams' instructions brought the bull dog (was it a bull terrier? W. H.) with us. We detested the creature as being better fed than we were. We tried to

116

duck the dog and would have willingly seen him drown, but his fat overfed body was unsinkable. Mr. Roberts was inoffensive and friendly but we had a disturbing intuition that he allowed himself to be something of a lap dog for Mrs. Adams. However, he must have turned a blind eye to many of our forbidden escapades and generally we accepted him as an ally rather than a foe in the School House set up.'

Mr. Head, the Art Teacher, was recalled as having 'a rather artistic, even Bohemian approach to the use of the aspirate, in consequence of which we knew him as Mr. 'Ead the Hartist". (Another old pupil remembers his saying 'I want you to draw a hegg in a heggcup'.). Mr. J. T. Griffith had arrived in the Michaelmas Term 1903. 'He immediately won our esteem by taking the boarders out to tea in the old De Valence Gardens. This he repeated frequently. In consequence, we rated him at once as a "good chap" despite his shocking and cutting sarcasms and his despising of all school boys other than those he made his favourites.'

There were initiation ceremonies:

Playground activities were generally fairly rough and one initiation procedure for new boys was cruel. I experienced in on my second day in school. It was called "fenneling". Fennel weed grew plentifully around the playground. When ripe, the seeds become hard and sharp. The victim whose only crime was newness, was collared in the playground and held, whilst one boy with a handful of the seeding weed would rub his lips and gums until the blood came. It was a brutal practice, much more so than its accompaniment of ducking in the washroom hand-basin but one learned one's place and conceited self-assurance was thoroughly drained. Another strange pursuit arose from the existence of a bank of some size in the corner of the playground overlooking the station. A score of activities would be afoot until an older boy, generally Arrol Davies, would yell 'Rush the bank'. He and one or two others would race on to the bank and hold it against all others. Attack and defence were quite violent, but few breaks passed without this steam-letting battle. (There was still a grassy bank in the south west corner in 1928, when the bole of a nearby tree was used as a wicket during the summer.—W.H.)

117

The older boys, the 'great men' of the School, kept themselves remote from the hoi polloi. They were a rather intellectual breed and particularly politically minded, Keyworth Lloyd Williams ('Kiki'), Jack Husband, Johnny Jones, Wesley Howells; they would sit in corners during break busily discussing questions of religion and politics.

D. O. Thomas adds that his stay in school was not long and had little influence upon him academically:

I came to Greenhill School quite unformed in much of my character. My education had suffered almost beyond repair in the Dame's school which I had attended earlier. I knew nothing when I arrived at the County School, Tenby; academically I had made no progress when I left but in dormitory and playground I had learnt much of human relationships and much of human friendship amidst the juvenile barbarities and general rough house therein. One thing I am glad to record in favour of the School House in its boarding school atmosphere. It was free from the perversions which are recorded as obtaining in many of the great Public Schools of the time . . . .

He remembered nothing of any religious influence in such activities as Assembly prayers. This may have been due to the fact that he spent his holidays at Vatson Farm and experienced the then quickening influence of the Welsh Revival in the chapel that he attended. 'The intensity of that experience overshadowed every other religious impression of my Tenby schooldays.' However, looking back over seventy years, he stated: 'My recollections are almost entirely enjoyable and I am grateful,' and, 'to me one of the most inexplicable facts is the way in which John Calvin Thomas managed to provide the type of schooling which we all enjoyed, considering the meagreness of his salary as a Minister of the Gospel.'

It will have been gathered from the comments of the former pupils that the Head Master, Mr. J. W. B. Adams, was generally liked and respected. By the end of the Michaelmas Term 1896 he had already created such a favourable impression in the town that the author of a 'Local Note' in the *Tenby Observer* of 28 January 1897 was almost 'carried away' in his eulogy:

Under the spirited mastership of Mr. J. W. B. Adams, B.A., the Tenby Intermediate School is making a progress which must be

118

regarded by all concerned as more than satisfactory. The number of pupils has increased since the opening; whilst the course of instruction is of such a character and imparted with the greatest success so that those privileged to attend so excellent an educational institution are bound to leave it carrying with them a knowledge which will stand them in good need throughout life—intellectual, physical and general well-being being all looked after.

Two important events of the year 1897 should be noticed as relevant to the School's story. On 29 June the Governors granted the Head Master leave of absence so that he could go to Oxford to receive the Degree of Master of Arts. Soon afterwards came the news of his wedding On 5 August the *Tenby Observer* reported that on the previous Saturday, St. Saviour's Church, South Hampstead, London, was the scene of an interesting wedding, when Mr. J. W. B. Adams M.A., (Oxon.), Principal of the Tenby Intermediate School and son of Mr. W. B. Adams of Orielton House, Willow Road, Hampstead, was married to Miss Pauline Alberta Frank of Haverstock Hill. The Rev. Gerard Herklots, M.A., the vicar, was the officiating clergyman, whilst the musical arrangements were under the able direction of Dr. Greenish (brother of Mrs. W. G. Parcell of Manorbier, a Governor of the School), organist of the church. The bridegroom was attended by Mr. F. Bettany, B.A., of Christchurch College, Oxford, as Best Man. The bride, who wore a soft white silk dress, trimmed with white plumes, and carried a bouquet of white flowers, the gift of the bridegroom, was given away by her uncle, Mr. Frank Brown of Red House, Langley, Bucks. After the wedding the happy pair left for Harwich en route for Holland and the Rhine. The report mentions the valuable presents and the names of the distinguished people who gave them including Sir George Keke, K.C.B., Chief Secretary of the Education Department, and General Laurie, Conservative M.P. for the Pembroke and Haverfordwest Boroughs.

When the Governors met on 27 July, they congratulated the Head Master on having proceeded to the Degree of Master of Arts and agreed to express their appreciation of his services by making a presentation to mark the occasion of his wedding. Mr. and Mrs. Adams received from them a handsome grandfather clock. Mrs. Adams was destined to play a prominent part in the life of the school, other than

119

that already mentioned, throughout the whole of her husbands' head-ship which lasted till December 1910.

Over against this euphoria must be set the very serious problems which confronted the Head and the Governors. Speaking at the Luncheon given by Clement Williams on the day of the official open-ing of the school, Adams had been careful to give warning of dis-couragements which would have to be faced. Doubtless he had in mind the many set-backs which had been experienced over the prev-ious six years before the school was launched on its career; he would have been aware that some financial questions were as yet unanswered. Some problems arose from the nature of the 1894 Scheme itself. The difficulties which dogged Mr. Adams and, to some extent, his successor were closely interwoven: staffing, the provision of the cur-riculum required by the authorities, equipment, accommodation and, underlying the rest, the perpetual inadequacy of the maintenance allowance under the Scheme, which came to threaten the very exist-ence of this school and of some others in the county and elsewhere.

Attention must be drawn to some important changes which affected the administration of education during the time Adams was in Tenby.

Administrative Changes

During the period of Adams' headship of Greenhill, two important Acts of Parliament affected the relationship between schools and the central and local authorities.

First there was the Board of Education Act 1899. The Board, consisting of a President and other members designated in the Act, was to supervise matters relating to education in England and Wales. It was to replace the Department of Education, which had been est-ablished in 1856 to bring under one authority the Privy Council Com-mittee (set up in 1839 to supervise grants to the National and British Schools) and the Department of Science and Art in South Kensington (created after the Great Exhibition of 1851).

The Board could inspect any secondary schools, but schools est-ablished under the Welsh Intermediate Education Act were to be inspected by the Central Welsh Board. Regulations were to be framed for a register of teachers and, significantly, it was to be lawful for Her Majesty to transfer to the Board any powers of the Charity Trustees or the Board of Agriculture. So the Board of Education became the channel through which central government grants came to schools in Pembrokeshire, as elsewhere.

Of special importance were the Board's Regulations for 1907, among them the provision that in all schools where fees were payable (except in Public and Private Schools), a proportion of free places, ordinarily 25 per cent of the yearly admissions must be open to scholars of Public Elementary Schools. There were to be approved entrance tests of attainments and proficiency for all applicants for free places. Other provisions were concerned with the curriculum and with the length of the secondary course, four years for pupils of about 12 to 17 years of age, though a three years stay in school with a leaving age of 15 would be an advantage in small towns and rural areas.

Secondly, attention should be drawn to the Education Act 1902, known as the 'Balfour Act'. It provided that the council of every county and every county borough was to be the local education authority. Provision was made for the management of elementary education. The Local Education Authority, in consultation with the Board of Education, was to supply or aid the supply of education other than elementary. For this purpose use was to be made of revenue under Section 1 of the Local Taxation (Customs and Excise) Act 1890, on condition that the amount raised by a County Council in any one year out of the Rates did not exceed the amount raised by a Rate of two-pence in the pound, or such higher Rate as the County Council raised with the approval of the Local Government Board. Regard was to be had to the existing supply of schools or colleges.

The County Council was to set up an Education Committee or Committees under a scheme approved by the Board of Education. The constitution and powers of the Education Committee were defined. All powers under the Act, except the raising of the Rate, were referred to it. The supply of education, other than elementary, included secondary schools, the training of teachers, the provision of vehicles or reasonable travelling expenses for teachers attending school or college, should circumstances make it necessary.

This Act came into force on 24 September 1904 and the first meeting of the Pembrokeshire Education Committee was held on the 30th. Among the members were those two old Tenby antagonists, C. W. R. Stokes and C. F. Egerton Allen. The first Chairman was Mr. S.

B. Sketch. Mr. H. E. James was appointed Director of Education and Clerk to the Committee as from 1 September 1904. Various sub-committees were set up, including the Higher Education Sub-Committee of which Mr. Palmer Morgan became Chairman. The L.E.A. were informed by the Secretary to the Public Works Loan Board that the Board's loans under the Welsh Intermediate Education Act 1889 were to be transferred from the Pembrokeshire County Governing Body, (of which the last meeting was held on 20 September 1904) to the County Council. The administrative work of the Local Governors/Managers of the County Intermediate Schools would only be effective with the support and approval of the Education Committee, the Central Welsh Board and the Board of Education.

One important task of the Education Committee was to agree upon a Scheme for Intermediate and Technical Education in Pembrokeshire to replace the one dating from 30 April 1894. By 24 March 1903 the Board of Education had published a proposed Scheme and by 6 October 1904 appeared an amended version of this 'Finally settled by the Board of Education'. However, this was found to be not in accordance with the wishes of the County Schools and the matter became the subject of protracted negotiations between the L.E.A. and the Board.

The objections of the Tenby Governors were outlined in the draft of a letter written in December 1904. It was stated that the Governors had recently submitted to the County Education Authority suggested amendments of the Scheme:

> That the unit of accommodation be increased from 70 to 80 on the following grounds. During the term now ended, including 17 Pupil Teachers, the actual number in attendance has been 78. As is well known, a School for 50 or 60 pupils requires as large a grant as one for 40 pupils; in fact numbers do not tell until 80 pupils or more attend the School. All schools below 80 require the same treatment, as only those over that number can afford to receive less Capitation Grant. For some years past our school numbers have exceeded Narberth School, yet our unit of accommodation according to the present Scheme is 10 less.

The letter went on to suggest a scale of amendments to the clause fixing the Capitation Grant and then added: 'The Governors also suggest that the area of Tenby School should be increased to include the Parishes of Amroth, Begelly, Jeffreston and the remainder of the Parish of St. Issell's, so re-iterating the views expressed when the earlier 1894 Scheme was being prepared.

Objections received by the Education Committee were produced at their meeting with Mr. J. L. Casson, representing the Board of Education, on 3 February 1905. The following month the Board agreed not to proceed with their Scheme and asked the L.E.A. to submit their own proposals. The L.E.A., in turn, referred the matter to a sub-committee. Negotiations and discussions with those concerned dribbled on over a period of seven years and it was not until 14 May 1912 that the new Scheme received the approval of H. M. George V, two years after Mr. Adams had left Tenby.

It should be pointed out that, while Tenby and other County Intermediate Schools in Pembrokeshire benefitted financially through recognition as Secondary Schools in due course, as provided by the Balfour Act, and while they received Technical Grants as well as allowances for Pupil Teachers introduced during this period, their hopes of additional help under a revised Scheme remained for long unrealised owing to the long drawn-out negotiations. And in the end, Tenby's catchment area, with a population of 8,000, remained the same as under the 1894 Scheme.

The requirements of the curriculum and accommodation were closely associated with official recognition of the Tenby County School as a Secondary School and as an approved centre for the training of Pupil Teachers. For the sake of convenience the last two will be dealt with separately and there will follow an account of improvements of the accommodation including extensions to the premises.

Recognition as a Secondary School

The question of 'recognition' and the possible financial advantages were first mentioned to the Tenby Governors by Mr. Owen Owen, Chief Inspector of the Central Welsh Board, on 6 July 1904. He considered that the minimum income from the Board of Education would be £100 per annum. Application for recognition was made and in consequence Mr. B. B. Skirrow, H.M.I. met the Governors on 14 April 1905. Mr. Skirrow explained the Regulations, stating that the increased grant earned would be about £60 a year and that it would be necessary to provide accommodation for Manual Instruction. This would be waived for the first year but must be provided in the future. The basement could be used for Manual Instruction but only as a temporary measure, it being too low and, obviously, underground. At this stage a separate wood and iron building was suggested. H.M.I. Skirrow expressed his satisfaction with the extensions, which included the science department and the gymnasium, already in progress.

On 19 May 1905 the L.E.A. received from the Board of Education 'Forms of Application for Recognition as Secondary Schools' and a letter inviting the Committee's observations. Mr. C. W. R. Stokes moved and Mr. Daniel Davies seconded this resolution, which was carried: 'That the Board of Education be informed that this Authority have no objection to the recognition of Tenby County School and that they have no desire to make any observation on the application of the Managers.'

On 6 July the Governors were discussing plans for Manual, Cookery and Laundry Instruction and received a copy of a letter of 30 May from the Board of Education to the Central Welsh Board, approving, recognition of the school as a Secondary School, but it was added. Manual Instruction must be provided in 1905-6. On 25 August Mr. Owen Owen forwarded a copy of a further letter from the Board of Education, following a report of its Inspector, concluding: 'Upon H. M. Inspector's recommendation the Board have confirmed the recognition granted provisionally in their letter of 30 May.'

The above recognition was provisional and temporary. There was of course the all-important question of eligibility for receipt of grants. On 22 January 1906 Mr. W. N. Bruce of the Board of Education wrote to the L.E.A., in answer to an enquiry, that the Board were of the opinion 'that the County Council have the power to aid Intermediate Schools in the County out of the rate raised under Section 2(1) of the Education Act 1902 in addition to the sum raised for that purpose under Section 8(2) of the Welsh Intermediate Education Act 1889.' On 10 February the Governors at Tenby were informed by the L.E.A. that the Tenby County School had been recognised as eligible to receive grants under Paragraph 32 of the Regulations for Secondary Schools and that the School Number was 11764. On 2 July the Education Committee received from the Board of Education a request for their observations on this list of Secondary Schools—Fishguard, Milford Haven, Narberth, Pembroke Dock, St. David's and Tenby. The L.E.A. offered no observations. Meanwhile plans for the Manual, Cookery and Laundry buildings at Tenby were being prepared.

The last stage came in 1907. On 18 January the L. E.A. received the report of its Higher Education Sub-Committee in which it was stated that Tenby County School had been recognised as a Secondary School. Finally, on 4 October, Mr. Owen Owen of the Central Welsh Board wrote to T. M. Eastlake, Clerk of the Governors, Tenby County School:

> I am directed to state that the above named School will be placed upon the list of Secondary Schools recognised for Grant during the year beginning on 1st of August, 1907, and Grant will be payable at the rates laid down in Chapter III of the Regulations for Secondary Schools (Wales) provided that the requirements of Chapters I and II of those Regulations have been observed throughout the year. The recognition now given will be continued unless and until it is withdrawn by the Board under Article 14 of the Regulations.

Pupil Teachers, Probationers, Bursars and Student Teachers

In 1846 the Privy Council Committee proposed a new system of training to replace the use of 'monitors', a practice which the Inspectors considered unsatisfactory. The new proposal was to apprentice Pupil Teachers for five years to schools approved by the Inspectorate. Any Pupil Teachers who went on to training colleges were to receive government grants. An important feature of the early history of the County Intermediate Schools was their recognition, temporary at first, by the Board of Education, as Pupil Teacher Centres for their respective catchment areas in Pembrokeshire. Whilst gaining practical experience as assistants to the teaching staffs of the Elementary Schools, the Pupil Teachers continued their own education by attending part time at the Intermediate Schools, so adding to the numbers on the rolls there as well as to the grants available both from the L.E.A. and from the board of Education.

Information about the emergence of Tenby County School as a Pupil Teacher Centre is to be found in the Minutes of the Local

Governors and of the L.E.A., in Central Welsh Board Reports, official circulars, some surviving correspondence and in a few notes made by the Head Master and the Clerk to the Governors.

An early reference to Pupil Teachers, in the Governors' Minutes, was on 24 April 1900, when they received a copy of the County Governing Body's resolution urging Managers of County Schools 'to communicate with Managers of Elementary Schools in their respective Districts and offer facilities for the education of their Pupil Teachers in accordance with the Scheme . . .' . By October 1902 most of the Managers of the schools in the Tenby area had approved of a proposed Centre at the County School. The Central Welsh Board Reports include in the December figures each year the number of Pupil Teachers on the roll: 1902—6 Girls, 1903—6 Girls, 1904—3 Boys and 13 Girls.

Of course the Governors were interested in the prospect of obtaining additional grants and on hearing of a new arrangement made by the Board of Education that the grants to be paid in respect of each Pupil Teacher attending a full course would be £7. 0s. 0d., they applied to the Education Committee requesting that Tenby County School should be an official Centre for the local area. This was in September 1904. On 12 October the L.E.A. resolved 'That Pupil Teachers be trained at County Intermediate Schools and that the County School Managers be paid by the Education Committee the sum of £5 per head for each Pupil Teacher, in addition to Grants earned for 12 months, and that the School Managers be instructed to give facilities to attend the Intermediate Schools in their area.' The Committee also resolved that, subject to the approval of the Board of Education, each County Intermediate School should be recognised as a Pupil Teacher Centre.

There followed temporary and conditional recognition by the Board of Education of a number of Centres, including Tenby, as from 1 August 1904. The conditions were that half-time instruction of Pupil Teachers must be given without interfering with the work of the full-time pupils, that Time Tables, Syllabuses and qualifications of teaching staff were to be submitted and that regulations concerning attendance at the Centre and Public Elementary Schools must be satisfied. When the Tenby Governors were informed of this conditional sanction they asked the Head Master to prepare a recommend-

126

ed report on remuneration for teachers for extra work. As some concern was expressed about the transport of Pupil Teachers from Saundersfoot and schools in that area, the Clerk was instructed to write to the Divisional Superintendent of the G.W.R., asking whether a coach could be attached to the goods train arriving after 8 a.m. so that Pupil Teachers could be picked up at Kilgetty and Saundersfoot. This enquiry was unfruitful, but by December 1904 Mr. Adams had been able to arrange transport with Mr. Ormond of Saundersfoot, for the conveyance of pupils daily at a cost of 25/- per week. By the beginning of 1905 the L.E.A. had agreed to meet this cost.

Proposals concerning the instruction and recruitment of Probationers (boys and girls who wished to become Pupil Teachers) were put before the Education Committee by the Director, Mr. H. E. James, on 6 January 1905. To illustrate the need for the encouragement of more Probationers the Director quoted figures from the latest Blue Book. There were 108 Pupil Teachers employed in the county 'last year' plus 74 'monitors' or candidates. The normal number of Pupil Teachers was about 100, or about a quarter of the teaching staff of the Elementary Schools. More Pupil Teachers must be engaged each year so as to cope with the demand and the situation could be helped by providing more Probationers. The Board of Education were offering a Grant of £4 per annum for each Probationer who made 250 attendances at an approved Centre during the year. The £4 per head to be handed to the Managers would cover the fees in most schools, while the County Council could pay 3/6 per week for lodgings where travel was impossible and train fare where desirable, daily or weekly. Contributions could be made towards the cost of books and stationery. The numbers of Probationers would be based on a 10% ratio of 'present' attendance at the County Schools, with five scholarships attached. This would give Pembroke Dock 17, Milford Haven 5, Narberth 7, St. David's 5, Fishguard 5, Tenby 8, Cardigan 5, Tasker's 7, Haverfordwest Grammar School 6, making a total of 65. Candidates should be 14 years of age before 1 August last. The teachers' recommendation of special aptitude for Probationerships would be needed and a parent would be required to refund the cost of schooling etc. in the case of a child who did not become articled as a Pupil Teacher.

On 20 February the Director of Education reported on the Probationers' Examinations which had been held on 28 January. 85 candidates had sat for 70 Exhibitions and 61 passed. At Tenby 5 were successful, though one of these wished to go to Narberth.

A Board of Education letter of 20 February 1906 informed the Local Education Authority that Tenby County School Pupil Teacher Centre had been placed on the list of those recognised by the Board for the year beginning 1 August 1905 under Article 11 of the Regulations for the Instruction and Training of Pupil Teachers. Attention was drawn to the conditions laid down in the Regulations and it was stated that the duty of inspecting the Centre would be the responsibility of B. B. Skirrow and J. Bancroft. This recognition was renewed for the Session 1906-1907. When the school was given Secondary School Status for grant, as from 1 August 1907, the Governing Body were informed that this status would be continued and that Bursaries would be tenable at the school with the approval of the L.E.A. Meanwhile the Education Committee decided that for the year 1 August 1907 to 31 July 1908 they would pay, in addition to the grants available from central sources, £3 for each Pupil Teacher and £4 for each Probationer.

Overlapping the recognition of the Pupil Teacher Centres came a change of policy, which is summed up in the 1939 *Report of the Consultative Committee on Secondary Education*: 'In 1906-7 the Board of Education began to abandon the pupil teacher system and issued Regulations for an alternative system known as "the Bursary System" whereby the general education of future teachers might be continued uninterrupted in Secondary Schools until the age of 17 or 18. Boys and girls who intended to become Elementary School Teachers and had received their previous education at a Secondary School might receive a special grant from the Board as bursars to continue at that Secondary School for an additional year.' One result of this policy was that a large proportion of pupils who remained in school beyond the age of 16 were intending teachers.

The above change was adopted in Pembrokeshire on 27 September 1907, when the L.E.A. decided to discontinue the appointment of Pupil Teachers as soon as possible and to adopt the Bursar Scheme. The Governors of each County School were to be asked to submit annually a list of eligible pupils who had passed the C.W.B. Examination and wished to become Elementary Teachers Those who had passed the C.W.B. Junior Examination might receive County Scholarships tenable for one year previous to becoming Bursars, the scholarships being worth £5 per annum, including free tuition, books etc. 'All Bursars were to become Student Teachers for the year following their Bursarships in approved schools. The salary of a Student Teacher was to be £26 per annum, and attendance at a County School for one day or two half days weekly would be required. The Governors were to receive not less than 30/- per year in respect of each student.' On 26 June 1908 came a modification of these proposals: "All Bursars may become Student Teachers for one year following their Bursarship, but the L.E.A. may if thought desirable allow Bursars to go to Training College.' The salary of Student Teachers was to be £25 per annum and they were to attend a County School for 2½ days a week.

The Board's Bursar Scheme was recommended for Tenby County School by H. M. Inspector following his visits on 28 September 1906 and 6 June 1907:

In view of the small number of Pupil Teachers attending the School the Authority would do well to consider the practicability of the Bursar Scheme.

A letter from Mr. Owen Owen of the Central Welsh Board stated:

Bursaries will also be tenable in the School upon the recommendation of the Local Education Authority . . . and Bursars following an approved curriculum will be included amongst the Scholars on account of whom Grant will be paid to the School.

It should be emphasised that these Bursaries, which were the subject of Special Grants and were to be available to intending Student Teachers, under the Board of Education's Regulation 1907, should not be confused with the earlier awards payable out of the District Fund by the Governors to enable a small number of pupils to continue their education. These earlier Bursaries had been introduced as a result of a suggestion made by the C.W.B. Inspector in 1897. Thereafter, the Central Welsh Board's returns included year by year a record of these awards:—For Example

1898   5 pupils at the School—4 boys and 1 girl—receive Bursaries of the aggregate value of £11.

1899   4 pupils at the School—3 boys and 1 girl—receive Bursaries of the aggregate value of £9.

1900   3 pupils at the School—2 boys and 1 girl—receive Bursaries of the aggregate value of £6.

129

Although many of the records of the Tenby County School have been either lost or destroyed, there have survived a few papers of the years 1905, '6 and '7, from which three samples will now be taken.

The first is a rough draft of information prepared by Mr. J. W. B. Adams for entry on Board of Education Forms 9P and 23P, relating to claims for grants in respect of Pupil Teachers (not to be confused with Student Teachers) for the period from 1 August 1904 to 31 July 1905, that is for the first year of recognition for this purpose:

During the Session 1904—5 twelve Pupil Teachers for the Board of Education Grants under Art. 24 of P. T. Regulations. Eleven of these attended regularly during the *whole twelve* months of Session 1904-5 as below:—

(a) 1st of 3 yrs. Engagement at £4

Name	No. Attendances	£	s.	d.
B. Moss (Tenby)	166			
M. Bennett (Saundersfoot)	151			
A. James (Penally)	152			
M. Williams (Amroth)	151			
		16	0	0

(b) 1st Year of 2 yrs. Engagement or 2nd of 3 yrs at £7.

Name	No. Attendances	£	s.	d.
S. Evans (Pentlepoir)	152			
R. Allen (Stepaside)	161			
E. Davies (Stepaside)	155			
C. Parry (Stepaside)	154			
J. W. Howells (Tenby)	160			
		35	0	0

(c) 2nd year of 2yrs Engagement or 3rd yr. of 3yrs Engag. at £7.

Name	No. Attendances	£	s.	d.
E. Nicholls	126			
(Illness prev. making 150)				
R. Davies	150	14	0	0
A. Rogers (took K.S. Xmas 1904)		2	6	8
		67	6	8

Five P.T.s after working whole twelve months of Session 1904-5
were then transferred to Narberth.

They were M. Williams   £4   As this sum makes up deficit both
          E. Davies   £7   in money and no. of P.T.s claimed
          R. Allen   £7   on, is it possible that grants were
          C. Parry   £7   alloted to Narberth—where these
          R. Davies   £7   P.T.s are under instruction now?

                      £32

Until the above transfer took place seven out of the twelve P.T.s
were country pupils. Adams' query underlines the controversial
division of the catchment areas as between the Tenby and Narberth
Districts. It is significant that the Pupil Teachers were from Stepaside and Amroth.

The second document is *Circular* 150 of the Pembrokeshire Education Authority, dated 21 February 1907, accompanied by an official
list of Pupil Teachers for whose instruction provision was being made
by the Tenby Governors. In this case the list names the schools to
which the Pupil Teachers were apprenticed.

Name	*School*	*Date of Engagement*			*Years*
Bennett, Muriel	Saundersfoot Cl.	Jan. '03	—Dec.	'06	4
Burrel, Beatrice	Tenby Cl.	Aug '04	—	'07	3
Davies, Mary A.	Pentlepoir Cl.	,, '06	—	'08	2
David, Margaret E.	Saundersfoot Cl.	,, '06	—	'08	2
James, Alice M.	Penally N.P.	,, '04	—	'07	3
Morris, Eleanor	Tenby Cl.	,, '06	—	'08	2
Moss, Eliz.	Tenby P. G.	,, '04	—	'07	3
Norman, Ruth	Tenby P.G.	,, '06	—	'08	2
Protheroe, Eva	Tenby P.G.	,, '05	—	'07	2
Thomas, Arthur E.	Pentlepoir	,, '06	—	'08	2

Except where stated, the period of Grants terminated on 31 July.
(*Note:* Cl.—Council; P.G.—Parochial Girls).

It should be added that a letter from the L.E.A. to the Governors
written on 5 January 1906 made it clear that the Authority would not

131

be paying for books, as in the past, but this would be the responsibility of the local Managers.

The third item is a letter dated 11 August 1907 from the Director of Education notifying the Governors of the results of the Probationers Exhibitions Examination for the Tenby District.

'Out of 11 candidates who sat the Examination on July 6th, five have done sufficiently well to enable me to recommend the Education Committee to make them Probationers . . .'

The Examination Numbers and marks were included:—Alice Maud Davies, George James Weymouth, Angus Thomas and Henrietta L. Yarrow of Tenby County School and Alice M. Withers of Tenby Wesleyan School.

The Director added:

These candidates may be admitted as Provisional Probationers when your school re-opens. I shall endeavour to call at the School to test their Reading early in the term. It should be noted that Henrietta C. Yarrow and Angus Thomas were over 15 years of age on 1 August 1907. They will therefore be Probationers for one year only—they should be able to qualify by passing the Junior Certificate Examination of the Central Welsh Board in 1908.

Section 2: The Extension of Premises and the Struggle for Survival

From the earliest days it was necessary to fulfill the requirements of the curriculum under the Scheme so that the school would be eligible to receive the grants available both before and after the Balfour Act of 1902. These requirements could only be met by the provision of additional accommodation and equipment for the science department, physical education, cookery, laundry and manual teaching. The necessary extensions to the premises were made in two stages and opened in October 1905 and March 1908.

The first mention of the need to bring Cookery into the curriculum was in February 1897, when the Governors considered a letter from Miss Silcox, teacher of Cookery, under the Pembrokeshire Technical Education Committee. However, at the next Governors' meeting, in March, it was decided that no classes were possible that year. On 21 December, following the first Central Welsh Board Inspection the

Head Master was asked to make provision for 'Drill' so as to comply with the Scheme. On 22 February 1898 he reported that 'Drill' had been arranged—'musical' for the girls and 'military' for the boys.

In the C.W.B. Report of the Annual Inspection 1898 it was stated, under the heading 'Apparatus': 'The School is well supplied with the usual furniture. There are good facilities for practical work in Sound, Light and Heat and also in Electricity and Magnetism. There are some appliances for teaching Chemistry. There is, however, no separate Science Lecture Room. There is the beginning of a School Library.' Then, under the heading 'Recreation and Physical Training', the Report continued, 'A field of about five acres is available for School Games. Drill forms part of the School Curriculum. The physical exercises that came under my notice were very efficiently done. It would have been well perhaps to introduce a little more variety into the movements.' In May and June 1898 the Governors had been attempting to comply with the Report of the Inspector of the Science and Art Department with regard to apparatus for the Laboratory. In consequence Mr. Spencer had worked out a requisition amounting to £17. 0s. 0d.

The Central Welsh Board Inspector returned to the question of 'Drill' in 1900: 'Boys and Girls are drilled three days a week when it is fine; there is no place for Drill in wet weather.' Then the following section was significant: 'The development of the School is greatly handicapped through lack of funds. If the District could be thoroughly roused to support the School, the existing debt on the building would soon be cleared off, and the Governors would then be in a position to consider such a scheme of extension as would enable them to place the scientific and technical work of the School on a satisfactory basis.' 'There is a physics laboratory. Any scheme of further extension should include an assembly hall, a chemical laboratory and lecture room, a workshop and a kitchen.'

Matters appear to have drifted until October 1902 when the local Governors were informed that the County Governing Body were insisting that Cookery Classes be held at Tenby. It was resolved to take up the Head Master's offer of the use of his kitchen for this purpose and to leave him to make the necessary arrangements. Fortunately he was able to secure the services of Miss Margaret E. Thomas, an old pupil of Tasker's School, Haverfordwest. She had attended the

South Wales and Monmouth Training School, where she was awarded First Class Certificates and Diplomas in Cookery and Laundry work. She became an employee of the Pembrokeshire County Council and was already teaching the Domestic Arts at Narberth County School before taking up duties in Tenby for two days a week.

1903 brought further discussions and further reports. On 5 February the Governors resolved 'that the Clerk draw particular attention to the need of a Building for use for Physical Exercises, Cookery and other classes and that the County Governing Body be asked to vote funds for the erection of a building . . . which is absolutely essential'. Their case was strengthened by Temporary Inspector for the C.W.B., Mr. Bond, reporting on his visit to the School on 25 May: 'This School is housed in buildings which are quite inadequate for school purposes. A building should be added to contain (a) a hall and gymnasium, (b) a room for cookery, (c) a smaller room where the Head Master may receive parents and (d) a classroom.' 'There is no hall or gymnasium; for physical exercises the pupils must stand on the benches. There is no field for games. The playground is in a rough neglected condition.' (When they read these last remarks in the printed Report the Governors took exception to them and informed the C.W.B. and the C.G.B. that there were in fact two fields in which the pupils had a right to play and that it was an error to say that the school grounds were in a rough and neglected condition). Mr. Bond noted that a dark room had been constructed in the laboratory for instruction in Optics and that a cupboard had been added to contain appliances for Cookery. He concluded: 'If the School is to continue its work it must receive prompt and large assistance in the provision of new buildings, in the extinction of debt and in increase of grant from the County Authority. In his meeting with the Governors after the inspection he had recommended orally, that plans and rough estimates be got out and submitted to the County Governing Body. Accordingly on 29 July the Governors inspected the buildings and the position of the additions required and decided to submit a scheme for a gymnasium and other rooms and for the removal of the boys' latrines, the position of which had been condemned, as the Board of Education would insist on their removal.

By February 1904, William Husband had drawn up a 'General Specification of proposed additions to the County School, Tenby', and tenders for the additional buildings were received on 28 September:

(1) Adams & Parcell £583. 11s. 0d. and (2) W. H. Thomas £659. 17s. 6d. The first tender was accepted but no work was to commence until a loan would be obtained. By the time the Local Governing Body met again on 30 November, a Draft Order of the Board of Education had sanctioned a loan of £865. 14s. 0d. at three and three quarters per cent repayable in 60 half-yearly instalments of £24. 8s. 0d. and Mr. Stokes reported that the County Council had authorised their Seal to be affixed to the Mortgage when ready. Also at this November meeting it was agreed that application should be made to the Technical Education Committee for a grant of £25 for apparatus to fit up one of the basement rooms for Manual Instruction.

On 22 March 1905 the Governors were informed that the loan, amounting to £856. 2s. 6d. had been received. Mr. W. J. Husband's tender of £92. 18s. 0d. for fitting up the new Science Room and the old Laboratory was accepted. The Head Master was asked to prepare specifications for equipment, although it had been estimated already that the following would be required: Desks £18, Lighting £10, Drainage of Cheminal Apparatus £2, Physics Table £40, Chemical Appliances £30, Fume Chamber £8, Apparatus £40, Furnishing the Masters' Room £20, Fitting up the Gymnasium £20.

Soon afterwards, the work of construction was begun and it continued throughout the summer of 1905. The new premises were built to the east and south-east of the old School. The Science Lecture Room, adjacent to the Laboratory and linked to it by a communicating door, was furnished with a demonstration bench and with desks arranged in tiers. A new entrance, at the front of the building, gave access to an entrance hall, the Masters' Room, the Gymnasium and the other ground-floor rooms. The Gymnasium was built parallel with Greenhill Avenue.

The official opening of these extensions and the School Prize Day were fixed for Wednesday, 25 October 1905. A full account of the proceedings was given in the *Tenby Observer* of 26 October:—

The ceremonies took place in the Gymnasium, where a large company was presided over by the Mayor, Clement J. Williams, J.P. (Chairman of the Governors), supported on the platform by Sir Lewis Morris, Mr. Benjamin Harries J.P., Mr. C. W. R. Stokes, C.C., Mr. S. B. Sketch C.C. (Chairman of the Local Education Authority), Mr. Egerton Allen C.C., Mr. Thomas John J.P., C.C., the Rev. Lod-

135

wig Evans and Mr. J. W. B. Adams M.A.   There were present parents
and friends, together with scholars who numbered over 80.   The
Mayor's speech of welcome was followed by the Head Master's Report
of the most satisfactory progress of the school, outstanding distinctions
having been achieved by the scholars John D. Mack and the brothers
Whitten.   Sir Lewis Morris then distributed the prizes and certificates.

After the presentation, Sir Lewis Morris expressed his pleasure in
being there to distribute the prizes.   He recalled that he had been
present at the official opening of the school and he was gratified to
note its success.

While storms and stresses had been features of the history of Primary
and Collegiate Education in Wales, he was pleased to know that no
denominational difficulty had arisen in connection with Intermediate
Education.   Sir Lewis eulogised the Head Master and said how
fortunate the Governors were in having his services.   Mr. Adams had
the virtue of heredity, his late father having been a great schoolmaster
who did good work in London.

Messrs. Stokes, Sketch, Allen, Harries, Hicks, Whitten and the Rev.
Lodwig Evans also spoke and the proceedings, which were of a most
interesting character, terminated with votes of thanks.

A week later on 2 November the *Tenby Observer* carried a special
Editorial almost bursting with compliments:

> With the completion and opening of the additional buildings to
> the Tenby County School a new era of usefulness opens for this
> excellent educational institution . . . which it must not be for-
> gotten, however, has passed through a somewhat protracted period
> of trial and difficulty, the termination of which as regards the
> financial aspect is not yet reached.   Despite administration
> being handicapped by the incubus of debt, it is a gratifying fact
> that, in an educational sense it has made remarkable strides and
> achieved a series of distinctions which may be justly described as
> brilliant.   Many have carried off the highest honours which come
> within its compass . . . its roll of successes is one of which any
> school might pardonably be proud . . . the sum total of the ad-
> mirable results achieved is one upon which Mr. J. W. B. Adams
> M.A., the Principal, can reflect with unpretentious pride.   Under his
> experienced guidance masterly scholarship and highly developed
> organisation the School has won for itself a front rank position

in the County, and with the increased facilities which the new buildings undoubtedly supply, the future should be still more productive of good results. The equipment of this School is admirable in every respect, and this, combined with an excellent Staff singles it out for special commendation . . . The importance to the town of such an institution cannot be overestimated, and we trust that in future the County School will receive more public acknowledgement than has been the case in the past.

The above 'Observer' editorial should be read alongside the more professional views of the Central Welsh Board Inspectorate. In his report to the Local Managers on 25 May 1903 Temporary Inspector Mr. Bond, regretted to say that the school was not up to the average of Welsh schools. However, in the Report of the Triennial Inspection of 25 March 1907, the Governors and teaching staff were complimented, the gymnasium was 'the best they had seen this side of Glamorgan,' and 'The new wing which has been added to the School provides an excellent laboratory, a demonstration room and a large hall and it is in contemplation to build a new Cookery and Laundry room . . . The best work in the School is of high standard, and there is good material to work upon. There seems to be plenty of enthusiasm in the teaching staff, and when the buildings receive the needed additions the School ought to do well.'

To return to the year 1905. The Minutes of the Local Governing Body, dated 8 November include several matters of interest.

There were the arrangements made for instruction in gymnastic exercises; it was resolved that, subject to the approval of the Board of Education Inspector, Mr. Roberts, the Junior Master, be paid 2s. 6d. per hour 'for the present' as Instructor. Mr. Adams explained that a certain amount of grant could be obtained from the Board for this purpose.

At this same meeting there were significant changes affecting the Board of Governors. Mr. T. M. Eastlake was appointed Clerk in succession to Mr. George Hughes, who had indicated his intention to resign on 6 September, the very day on which Mr. C. F. Egerton Allen came back to the Board after an absence of a few years, this time as County Council representative in place of the late Rector, the Rev. George Huntingdon. Before long, Mr. Allen returned to his former roll as constant critic of his fellow Governors, particularly over financial matters, and, of course, the old animosity between himself and Mr. C. W. R. Stokes, (to whom Mr. George Hughes was Clerk) continued. The Governors were concerned with finding suitable furniture for the Head Master's room and partly for the convenience of their own meetings. It was on this occasion that the Chairman made a gift of a roll-top desk, which was destined to occupy a prominent position in the Head's room down to the termination of the school on the Greenhill site in 1961!

Lastly, there were the plans which the architect had prepared for a red brick building, south of the Gymnasium, with accommodation for Cookery and Laundry and Manual Instruction. Approval was given to these proposals. Mr. Stokes observed that, as the premises would be used by the Elementary Schools as well as by Greenhill pupils, four-fifths of the cost would be borne by the Education Authority.

As a first step, the Governors decided to forward the above plans to the Education Committee for their approval, but it transpired that nearly two years were to be occupied with formalities and negotiations before building work could be set in motion. The main stages in the history of the project have been extracted from the Minutes of the local Governors and of the Education Authority;

On 28 February 1906 the Tenby Governors were informed by letter that the L.E.A. had consented to a loan of £700 for the erection of the further new buildings and, subject to the approval of the Director of Education, to provide appliances for Manual Instruction; also it was stated that the plans had been sent to the Board of Education. When the Board enquired how the cost of the extensions were to be met, the Clerk to the Governors wrote to the L.E.A. on 12 May 1906, developing the views previously advanced by Mr. Stokes: ' . . . as you are aware, the Cookery, Laundry and Manual Instruction Rooms are to be erected not only for Pupils of the County School but also for the Pupils of the Elementary Schools and therefore the Governors expect the Education Authority to bear their proportion of the Annual Instalment in respect of the loan for the new Buildings or to be permitted to receive the Grant earned by the children of the Elementary Schools for instruction in Cookery, Laundry and Manual Instruction.' Incidentally, the Head Master had reported on 10 May that part of the appliances for Manual Instruction had arrived and, in consequence, the Governors had agreed to arrange with Mr. Parry of Narberth about fitting up the appliances—presumably in the basement—and that he should act as Instructor 'for the current term at 2/6 per hour and railway fare.' By the end of the Summer Term the Head was able to speak of the keen interest the boys were taking in Woodwork. There were two classes of sixteen pupils, each class receiving two sessions of two hours per week. Moreover, five Probationers had taken the course and had passed the Pupil Teachers' Examination. On 21 November Mr. Stokes told the Governors that the Board of Education had approved of these plans, and in December there were discussions concerning the size of the proposed buildings.

On 18 January 1907 the Education Committee received a letter from the Board of Education agreeing that the period for repayment of loans in respect of Narberth and Tenby County Schools would be extended to 30 years. On 26 February the Governors considered tenders for the construction of the new premises and accepted that of Messrs. Davies and Griffiths for £707 subject to the usual approvals. Arrangements went ahead for the purchase of the necessary furniture and apparatus which would be needed in the Cookery and Laundry Room and in the Manual workshop.

On 20 January 1908 the Governors were notified that Mr. Parry, who looked after the Manual work would be leaving. However, they were able to find a replacement in the person of Mr. Austin Thomas, an Old Boy of Whitland County School, who had passed the City and Guilds Examinations in Woodwork, who had gained the N.U.T. Diploma in the same subject and who attended courses at Barry before and after taking up an appointment to teach this subject at Tenby for four hours a day for one day a week at the rate of 2/6 an hour.

The official opening of the Cookery and Laundry and Manual Instruction Rooms took place on 18 March 1908. As on the occasion of the opening of the previous extension, the ceremony was accompanied by the Distribution of Prizes in the Gymnasium. The *Tenby Observer* reported the proceedings at some length in their issue of 26 March.

Referring to the newly erected cookery, laundry and woodwork rooms, which had been added to the already extensive school buildings the report stated: 'For some time those responsible for the administration of the School have agitated to secure such a building . . . which will be devoted exclusively to all that concerns the technical side of the school's curriculum. The contractors were Messrs. Davies and Griffiths—the building is the best proof that they have done their work creditably. Modernness is the prevailing note throughout.' The writer went on to extol the qualities of Mr. J. W. B. Adams during whose period of office '. . . buildings used for teaching purposes have more than doubled themselves, while the subjects added to the curriculum have marked an advance which is highly commendable to all concerned.' The proceedings were conducted in the gymnasium 'a large and commodious building . . . packed with parents, friends and scholars.' (Actually the internal measurements of this 'large and commodious building' were 34ft × 23ft 6ins. The length, including a small stage, was increased in 1928.) 'A successful effort at decoration had been made. The walls in addition to being hung with flags and evergreens were hung with a number of works of art and water colours executed during the past term by pupils attending an Art Class held in connection with the County School of which Mr. E. J. Head, an artist whose talents are so well known, is the Principal.'

The Chairman (the Rev. Lodwig Evans), paid tribute to Mr. C. W. R. Stokes 'who knew more about the Tenby County School than anybody else', who had declined to take the Chair in the absence, through a bereavement, of Mr. Clement J. Williams, Chairman of the Governors.

Referring to the new premises the Chairman said: 'Here the boys would learn how to make furniture and other things and the girls cooking and the dusting of furniture' and, he continued, they were looking forward to a splendid generation of men and women who would make happy homes as a result of these new facilities in education.

The Head Master delivered his Report on the last year's working of the school. He spoke of the good progress made. . . They had again endeavoured to give the children as much individual attention as possible, especially the backward ones. Besides really trying to instruct children to do and think for themselves, it was something beyond the mere acquisition of knowledge. Education should not only be a means of helping children to help themselves but a little beyond that; and as far as possible they were endeavouring to keep that ideal before them. While underlining the importance of the new facilities for technical instruction, Mr. Adams drew attention to the fact that they were going to form classes in Cookery, open to residents in the town, whether they belonged to the School or not. With regard to the formation of Laundry classes they were not in a position then to give any more information 'as to whose washing they were prepared to take in'. Speaking of the Gymnasium and Physical Education, he asked for the co-operation of parents to make organised games a success, and underlined the disadvantage of having no playing field adjacent to the school. On the whole, scholastic successes were well up to those of the previous year. One boy had passed the London Matriculation Examination, six had passed the Senior and eleven the Junior Examination of the Central Welsh Board, which was of the same standard as the Oxford and Cambridge Locals.

There followed the Distribution of Prizes and Certificates by Mrs. Herbert Lewis, wife of the High Sheriff. In introducing her, the Chairman referred to her connection with the family of Sir William Thomas Lewis, 'a household name throughout Wales, a family which had always taken a deep interest in educational matters'.

At the conclusion of the meeting Mr. C. W. R. Stokes proposed a vote of thanks to the Head Master and staff of the school for their invaluable services. After speaking of the advantages of the new facilities and praising the work of the school, he said that it was the ambition of the Governors to do everything they could to forward education in the town. It was always a pleasure for him to go to Haverfordwest and advocate the claims of the school. He was always pleading something for Tenby County School, which, as far as its finances were concerned, had been shamefully treated in the past. The Director would bear him out in saying that Tenby did not get the maintenance it deserved. Considering the large number of children, they should have had more money over the last twelve years. The consequence was a banker's overdraft, extra interest and a burden on the school. If Tenby had been treated in the same way as Narberth when opened, instead of being in debt they would have had £1,000 on their back.

A Matter of Maintenance—The Fight for Survival

'Tenby did not get the maintenance it deserved.' These words, used by Councillor Stokes at the official opening of the Cookery, Laundry and Manual premises in 1908, echoed what had been said again and again from the inauguration of the County School in 1896 and even before that date. The school at Tenby, along with some others in the county, was placed in a well-nigh impossible position because the Maintenance Grant was only £252 at first, and, of that, one fifth was allocated for scholarships and bursaries. The total income from grant and fees was barely enough to pay the salaries of the Head Master and staff. Extracts from the Accounts will be quoted to illustrate the problem at two different dates under Adams' headship.

Understandably, the Governors had to be cheese-paring in dealing with certain items of expenditure. For example, on 29 March 1898, they approved certain recommendations from their finance committee. Among the items for payment were £1. 1s. 0d. to Mr. James Truscott for winding clocks and £2. 0s. 4d. to Tenby Gas Co. for gas. It was recommended 'that in future the Caretaker wind the clocks'. Also they considered 'the quantity of gas used in the quarter ended 31 December last very large and that care be taken that no more is used in the laboratory than is absolutely necessary'. The sum involved seems trivial when compared with so-called economies at the present time.

On 24 July 1900 the County Governing Body Areas Committee reported 'That the present allocation of the funds does not appear to be fair, having regard to the number of pupils attending each School on the average of the past 5 years. The Committee propose considerable alterations in the boundaries of several School Districts.' This report was adopted and forwarded to the Charity Commissioners, by resolution of the County Governing Body. However, so far as the Tenby District was concerned, the boundaries remained unchanged even under the Revised Scheme which eventually materialised ten years after the Balfour Act of 1902.

On 12 December 1900 the School Governors discussed the audited Accounts, a statement of Capital Expenditure on Buildings, the Laboratory and School Furnishings, outstanding accounts and a letter from the Manager of the National Provincial Bank concerning an overdraft. The Governors decided to appeal to the County Governing Body to help with a grant from the County Funds. There was also the problem of a guarantee being given in respect of the overdraft. The situation is illustrated by 'A Statement of Receipts and Expenditure for the Year ending 25 March 1901.'

EXPENDITURE	£	s.	d.
Salaries of Staff, Clerk etc. including capitation	537	1	6
Cleaning School and Grounds	30	5	0
Coal, Gas etc. etc.	11	3	3
Rates, Taxes, Insurance	32	8	1
Stationery, Books, Printing etc.	17	10	8
Repairs and Maintenance of Buildings	30	13	8
Instalments on Loans	33	3	10
Furniture and Laboratory Plant etc.	23	12	6
Science and Art Department for Examination Papers	5	6	6
Miscellaneous Bills	4	1	9
Carriage of parcels, postages, incidentals	3	19	7
Bank Charges	11	19	6
	741	5	10

RECEIPTS	£	s.	d.
Maintenance Grant	294	0	0
Grant in Aid of Art Classes	20	0	0
Science and Art Grant	84	5	5
School Fees etc.	211	0	0
Rent of Master's Residence	35	0	0
Deficit for year	97	0	5
	741	5	10

The following 17 June a Special Meeting of the School Governors received a Report from Mr. Headlam, the Central Welsh Board Inspector, who noted that the expenditure on the school and working expenses exceeded income by about £80. The Governors saw no prospect of an improvement in the situation and drew the Inspector's attention to the unequal distribution of the Grant.

By 1902 the situation was worse. On 29 November the County Governing Body received the Accounts of the County Schools, audited by Fred J. Warren. In the case of Tenby, the payments for the year amounted to £846. 3s. 6d. while the income reached only £719, leaving a debit balance of £127. 3s. 6d., which with the previous overdraft (the debt on the School at the end of the last financial year) amounted to £368. 9s. 8d. Owing to the lack of funds, no allocation of income to the Repairs Fund had been made. 'Bank Charges in this last Statement amount to £31. 16s. 6d. This is an item which should not appear in the School Accounts.', wrote the Auditor, 'The state of the finances of this School will doubtless have your attention and that of the local Managers.'

By 1903 there had been a further deterioration. On 19 May the County Governing Body were told that the overdraft had increased 'from £388. 9s. 8d. last year to £890. 2s. 7d. on 31 March this year. This growing debt may occasion some difficulty when the new Authority takes over.' Bank Charges for the year were £23. 10s. 6d. and Outstanding Fees amounted to £41. 6s. 8d. The Auditor's Report to the Finance Committee of the County Governing Body on 17 November included the note: 'New books have been adopted and the Accounts are now in order. The Debit Balance is now £390. 9s. 9d.'

The situation at Tenby County School was also a cause for concern to officials of the Central Welsh Board throughout this period. Following an Inspection on 6 July 1904, Mr. Owen Owen, the Chief Inspector referred to the possibility of improved prospects by the recognition of the school, under Schedule B, by the Board of Education, since this could be expected to bring in a minimum income of £100 from the Board. This, along with a grant from the Technical Education Committee would amount to an extra £140. Mr. Owen undertook to pay particular attention to the financial position when making his report. Eventually, the 'recognition' was made retrospective to August 1st 1904. However, despite the additional funds available following the implementation of the Balfour Act, technical grants and grants in respect of Pupil Teachers, financial worries persisted. Further demands upon the resources were necessary to comply with the requirements of the curriculum, the cost of staffing and extensions.

The 'Statement of Accounts for the Year Ending 31st March 1905', audited and found correct by Fred J. Warren, Incorporated Accountant, County Education Authority, sums up the state of affairs at this stage (see Appendix A).

From the time of its first meeting on 30 September 1904, the Pembroke-shire Education Committee absorbed the functions of the County Governing Body and, on 21 July 1905, it was agreed that the balance of £640 standing to the credit of the C.G.B. should be distributed among the County Intermediate Schools. Tenby's allocation was the sum of £100. No doubt this money was welcome but the basic problem remained and on 3 August the Local Governors resolved 'That the County Authority be urged to proceed with the Amendment Scheme as speedily as possible as, in view of the inadequate Grant to Tenby School, it will be impossible to carry on the School with its present income, having in view the additional expenditure the Governors are being put to meet the requirements of the different authorities.'

The fight for survival was not confined to Tenby County School. On 28 March 1906 the Clerk to the Governors of Fishguard County School (Head Master: O. Gledhill, B.Sc., Lond.) wrote:

> At a regularly convened meeting of my Governors held on March 16th inst. it was unanimously resolved, that in consequence of our financial difficulties & that of several of the County Schools a communication be sent to the Governors of the Haverfordwest Grammar School, Tenby & St. David's County Schools, asking them to unite with the Governors of the Fishguard County School in taking joint action, with the object of seeking some means of removing these difficulties & obtaining more equitable treatment. thus enabling the work to be carried on with less worry & consequently more efficiently. My Governors would be glad of a reply as soon as possible with suggestions as to the methods to be employed.

Mr. T. M. Eastlake, Clerk to the Tenby Governors, replied on 12 May, following their meeting the previous day, stating that the Tenby School would be represented at the proposed meeting. The Tenby correspondence and Minutes contain no record as to when the meeting was held. However, the Fishguard letter serves as an illustration of the anxieties which were being shared by School Governors at this period.

The Tenby School's financial position was considered sympathetically by the Central Welsh Board Inspectors at the conclusion of the Triennial Inspection on 25 March 1907. They expressed surprise at the smallness of the Grant paid to the school; this worked out at only £11 per pupil, whereas the school ought to receive at least £15 per pupil;

in their opinion it should be £17. They were not surprised at the deficiency in the Maintenance Account and promised to approach the L.E.A. on the matter. This deficiency was underlined in a letter from Mr. Fred J. Warren, 3 Victoria Place, Haverfordwest, dated 21 May 1907, and addressed to the Tenby School Governors, following the Annual Audit:

> I beg to report that your Clerk attended here on Wednesday when I and an assistant checked the whole of his accounts, including Cash book, Fees book and Pass Book, and saw that all the payments were in order and duly vouched, and I am satisfied that everything is in order. I have therefore certified to the correctness of the financial statement which is submitted herewith and which reveals the serious position of a debit balance of as much as £632. 2s. 7d. on your Maintenance a/c.
>
> There are old outstanding fees amounting to £14. 4s. 2d.
>
> A Stock account should be kept of all loose apparatus and furniture.

This communication was received by the Governors at their meeting the following day and they resolved 'That the serious attention of the L.E.A. through the Higher Grade Committee be drawn to the deficit of £632. 2s. 7d. on the Maintenance Account, as shown in the financial statement and that the Governors consider that this deficit should be paid by the L.E.A., as in the opinion of the Central Welsh Board the funds allocated for the maintenance of the School are totally insufficient, our income only amounting to about £11 per pupil, whereas in their opinion it should be from £15 to £17. The Governors desire to point out that unless additional funds are forthcoming it will be impossible to carry on the Schools.'

At this same meeting there was discussed the necessity of insuring the staff under the Workmen's Compensation Act 1906.

The pleading of the Governors for assistance met with no success during the following two years. On 31 March 1908 the Audited Accounts showed a Debit Balance of £769. 1s. 4d. on the Maintenance Account and that the blance due to the Treasurer at the National Provincial Bank was £578. 12s. 0d.

Matters came to a head in 1910. Following the Central Welsh Board's Inspection there was a Special Meeting of the Governors on 15 March. The financial position was discussed. When Mr. Owen Owen, the Chief Inspector, suggested that the Local Education Committee might make a Grant of a farthing of the Rate to assist in wiping out the deficit, Mr. Stokes observed that this was unlikely, since the County Council's policy was to keep the rates down. At a further Special Meeting on 24 March. Mr. Thomas John C.C., one of the Governors spoke of an interview he had had with Mr. Palmer Morgan, Chairman of the Higher Education Committee; Councillor John had been led to understand that there was a large sum of money in the hands of the L.E.A. The Governors then resolved 'That application be made to the Higher Education Committee for a Grant towards the deficiency of the Tenby County School consequent upon the receipts not being sufficient to meet the expenditure.' The Clerk's letter embodying this application was received by the Higher Education Sub-Committee on 22 April. The letter contained the statement '. . . the Governors felt that the time had arrived for them to consider seriously whether they could continue to carry on the School, as there was an Overdraft at the Bank of £550 and the expenses of the School every year exceeded the income by over £150.' The Higher Education Committee considered this and then recommended 'that a Grant of £200 be made as in the case of Fishguard towards this overdraft and that the question of paying off of the balance of £350 with a loan by the Authority be referred to the Board of Education.' Here was a little help but this was only buying time. In fact the Audited Accounts for the year ended 31 March 1910 had shown a deficit on the Maintenance Account of £627 with a balance of £531 15s. 1d. due to the Treasurer.

On 24 June Members of the L.E.A. had an interview with the Inspectors of the Central Welsh Board, as a follow-up of the recent Triennial Inspection. It was then resolved that the Chairman, Vice-Chairman and Mr. Palmer Morgan, (Chairman of the Higher Education Sub-Committee), should meet the representatives of the Governors at a conference to discuss the adverse conditions of the finances of the school, as suggested by Mr. Hammond Robinson of the C.W.B.

Before the conference was held the *Tenby Observer,* as might be expected, made a meal of this situation in the issue dated 30 June 1910. 'Tatler', commenting upon the *Daily News* report of the L.E.A. June meeting in which it was said by some that unless some action were taken the school might become bankrupt, wrote; 'Surely such a serious statement as this requires prompt explanation from the local Governors of the Tenby County School. Does the evil influence which has been the curse of Tenby these five and twenty years predominate also in the affairs of the School?' Here once more was the old animosity between Mason and Stokes. 'Tatler' went on to point out that the Press had been excluded from Governors' meetings for some years, in contrast to what happened at Narberth, Pembroke Dock, Whitland and other towns.

The Special Meeting of the Local Governing Body, together with the sub-committee of the L.E.A. and Inspectors of the Central Welsh Board was held on 6 July. Those present from the L.E.A. were Mr. Sketch (Chairman), Mr. Whicher (Vice-Chairman), and Mr. Palmer Morgan; the Governors were represented by the Chairman, the Rev. Lodwig Evans, Messrs. Stokes, John, Allen and Parcell; from the Central Welsh Board came Messrs. Owen Owen and Hammond Robinson; also attending were the Director of Education, the Head Master and the Clerk. They gave careful consideration to the financial position of the school over the previous five years and, in the end, urged the Governors to devise some scheme to reduce expenditure.

The 'Observer' returned to the attack on 14 July. With reference to the investigating Committee, it was stated that the Governors had agreed to guarantee a considerable sum owing to the National Provincial Bank. (Egerton Allen had refused to be a party to this.) 'It is further suggested that the bank overdraft is in a sense illegal and beyond the assistance of either the Education Committee of the County Council or the Board of Education; it can only be liquidated by voluntary effort.' The County Council's recent grant of £200 towards reduction of the debt was also challenged. A week later, the same newspaper published a letter from 'A Parent', urging that Mr. Egerton Allen, as a Governor, should make a statement on the financial affairs of the school. The letter mentioned the disquiet felt concerning the management, while commending the success which the school had achieved on the educational side '. . . it would be a thousand pities if for financial reasons its good work should be crippled'. On 28 July came a reply from C. F. Egerton Allen, who was one of the three County Council Representatives of the Local Governing Body. He stated: 'The School Managers are bound to render yearly accounts and to exhibit, for public inspection, copies of such accounts, giving public notice where and when the same may be seen, and are bound at all reasonable times to allow accounts to be inspected and to allow copies or extracts to be made . . .' Mr. Allen pointed out that six weeks previously, advertisements had appeared informing the public that accounts might be inspected at Mr. Eastlake's Office on a given date between 10 a.m. and 4 p.m. He added, characteristically, 'It will surprise me to hear that anyone but myself took the trouble to look at them.'

Meanwhile the Governors were tackling their difficult task. On 20 July they set to work by reducing staff. They resolved that the Science Master, Mr. J. T. Griffith, 'be requested to undertake the duties of Woodwork Instructor at the same salary as he now receives, the Woodwork Master's engagement to terminate at the end of the present term.' (Mr. Griffith's salary was £155 p.a. having been increased by £5 on 6 November 1907.) 'In the event of Mr. Griffith declining he be given one term's notice; also that the Assistant Mistress, Miss Lindsay, be requested to take the Art Class at no increase of salary and that Mr. Head be given one month's notice in any event.' The Governors then appointed a sub-committee comprising Messrs. Clement Williams, Parcell and Stokes to report on the finances.

The sub-committee met on 2 September and reported to a full meeting of the Managers on the 7th, proposing the following economies:

		£	s.	d.
1.	Salary of Head Master	20	0	0
2.	Salary of Woodwork Teacher	25	0	0
3.	Salary of School Cleaner and upkeep of Grounds	10	0	0
4.	Gymnastic Apparatus	5	0	0
5.	Prizes	5	0	0
6.	Estimated saving on Rates	15	0	0
7.	Estimated Interest on Overdraft (i.e. through reduction)	15	0	0
		105	0	0

		£	s.	d.
By the Amended Scheme the Maintenance Grant from the General Fund was expected to be increased by		77	0	0
	Total	182	0	0
Less Stationery for pupils		15	0	0
		167	0	0

Other recommendations were that Mr. Head's evening Art Classes should be discontinued so as to save coal and gas and that the Head Master was to instruct boarders in the evenings in his own home.

The issues of the *Tenby and County News*, dated 2 and 9 November 1910, contain detailed accounts of the heated discussions, concerning the school's finances, which took place in the County Council meeting held on 1 November. Councillor Egerton Allen moved that a payment authorised by the Education Committee on 22 April of £200 to Tenby County School Governors, to be used by them in reduction of a bank overdraft, was irregular and ultra vires, and that the payment be reported to the District Auditor. Mr. Allen maintained that the payment was illegal. He stated that the Tenby Managers had been 'out-running the constable' by illegally contracting an overdraft of £550; he had no part in guaranteeing the overdraft but some of the Governors had and they would have to bear the loss. The L.E.A. had made them a gift of £200 without any authority and had undertaken to borrow £350 for them. He maintained that the 2d Rate never ought to have been levied—they used to do very well with ½d Rate. Now the Committee went about the country paying debts which were illegally contracted. It was the duty of the Council to draw the attention of the Auditor to the matter. Mr. Sketch, Chairman of the Education Committee, stated that the L.E.A. was bound to provide for secondary education. He said that Mr. Allen was on bad terms with his Governors and that it would be better for him to go and take part in their meetings like a man than to come and throw mud at the Education Committee. Mr. W. Palmer Morgan, Chairman of the Higher Education Committee, argued that they were empowered to make a grant, under the Act of 1902. When Allen's resolution was put to the vote and lost, he protested against votes of members of the L.E.A. being counted. 'No man has a right to be judge in his own court', he said.

It transpired that Mr. J. W. B. Adams did not stay to see the results of the economy measures taken by the Governors or of further pruning of expenditure by the County Council. On 30 December 1910, the Local Governing Body received a letter announcing the Head Master's resignation to take up an appointment as Head of a larger Secondary School at Ashford, under the Middlesex Education Authority. His successor at Tenby, along with the Governors, had to continue the struggle for the school's survival.

150

Section 3: Staff, Curricula and Pupils

The Staff Register at Tenby County School was brought into use under 'Rules 42 (Wales) January 1909'. The volume contains directions for filling up Staff Registers for Secondary Schools and Pupil Teacher Centres. For each member of staff entries were to be made under headings requiring the following particulars:—surname, Christian name, date of birth, appointment, definitive appointment, date of leaving, schools and colleges at which educated with dates, names and types of institutions, public and university examinations taken and certificates and degrees with dates, list of teaching posts with dates, external teaching undertaken in addition to duties in school, special subject or subjects, principal duties assigned and subject taken (any changes to be shown in red ink), total emoluments, particulars of retiring allowance if any, post if any taken up after leaving. As the keeping of this Register was not officially required until thirteen years after the school was opened, eleven earlier members of the staff were not included in it. However, the names of these were recorded in the Governors' Minutes and in the Annual Reports of the Central Welsh Board. In the Register there were retrospective entries for the Head Master and those of his staff already appointed and still in service at the time this volume was first introduced.

With the financial resources then available, the provision of enough qualified staff was always difficult. Throughout his headship, J.W.B. Adams received an annual salary of £120 plus £2 capitation fee on each pupil and a residence free of taxes but for which he paid a rent of £35 per annum. In the early years the Science Master received £100 together with half of the Science and Art Grant, a method of payment which was criticised by the C.W.B. Inspector in 1899: 'Attention is also drawn to the undesirable character of the arrangement under which one of the Assistant Masters receives, as part of his salary, a portion of the Grant earned in connexion with the Science and Art Classes; and the arrangement under which he receives partial board requires further explanation.' In spite of this criticism, this practice persisted until 22 March, 1905, when the Governors, faced with insistence from the C.W.B. Inspectorate, resolved to fix the Science Master's salary at £150. The first Mistress on the staff Miss Alice Burrell, was paid at the rate of £100 a year. Her successors, on appointment, were to receive £90 per annum with the prospect of an increase should their services prove satisfactory. At no time during the Adams period did the salary of a Mistress exceed £110 and not until September 1905 was an additional Mistress added to the full-time staff.

The whole issue of professional qualifications and remuneration is well illustrated by the chain of events which followed the decision of the Governors to appoint a Junior Assistant Master. In his Report to the Local Governing Body on 23 February 1897, Mr. Adams stated that 23 subjects were being taught and that, in view of many sub-divisions an assistant was needed to take the Lower Forms so that other members of staff could attend to the Upper ones. As a result a temporary assistant, Mr. Robert Phillips, was engaged at a salary of £30 per annum. Apparently he had had some experience in an elementary school for a number of years. On 21 December the Governors received a letter from the Charity Commissioners stating that the Central Welsh Board had drawn attention to the employment of an unqualified assistant. The Governors agreed that a reply should be sent, pointing out that they could not engage a fully qualified teacher 'on account of funds not permitting'. Following the 1898 Central Welsh Board Inspection on 18 April the Governors were informed: 'The Board find that one of the Assistant Masters has no qualifications and receives a remuneration of £30 per annum together with tuition from other members of the Staff. The Board expect that the Staff will be put on a better footing before the next inspection . . . ' There was more to follow. On 24 May Mr. James Hughes read to his Governors this letter from Percy E. Watkins, Clerk to the C.W.B.:

> Your letter dated the 30th March was laid before the Executive Committee at their last Meeting when I was directed to state that the Committee cannot answer for what the action of the Board may be, if they find a similar state of things existing on receiving the Report of the Chief Inspector on his Inspection for the present year.

In face of this forceful reproof the Governors appear to have 'played it cool'. They resolved 'That the matter in question remain in abeyance until we hear again from the Central Welsh Board', and Mr. Phillips' services were retained until Half Term in the Michaelmas Term 1898, that is six months after the Board's rebuke of the Governors.

There was still further trouble in store. On 24 October the Head

Master was authorised to engage a resident assistant at a salary of £40, half to be payable to the teacher and half to Mr. Adams for Board and Lodging. On these terms Mr. E. H. Southall was appointed and he, in turn, was succeeded by Mr. J. Griffiths in the Easter Term 1901. In 1899 and 1900, apparently with no effect, the Inspectors drew attention to the lowness of the salary being paid. Then, in the Central Welsh Board Report for 1901, came a warning: 'The Board are of the opinion that the arrangements made in the case of one of the Assistant Masters are not satisfactory, and they trust that the arrangements will be brought to a termination as speedily as possible.' By January 1902, Mr. J. R. Roberts had come in place of Mr. Griffiths. The vexed question of the salary payable to the Junior Master was brought to a head by a letter from the Board of Education, signed by W. N. Bruce and dated 14 February 1902. He referred to the report of the examination of the school for the previous year:—

> I am directed to remind you that the attention of the School Managers has already been called more than once by the Central Authority to the irregularities in connection with the teaching Staff of the School, and, that, as a result of the previous report of the C.W.B., the School Managers were warned by this Board of a reduction of the Treasury Grant unless the arrangements as to one of the teaching Staff were modified.

Then came the ultimatum:

> The Report recently under consideration shows that the irregularities complained of still continue and the Board have consequently recommended to H.M. Treasury that a reduction of one tenth shall be made in the amount of the Treasury Grant claimed in aid of the School.

The Governors approved a reply to be written by their Clerk, the Head had an interview with the Chief Inspector of the Central Welsh Board, and on 3 June reported that, to get over the difficulty, a salary of £75 would be paid. After further prodding by the Central Welsh Board, Mr. Roberts' salary as Second Assistant Master was increased to £80 in 1904. In December of that year he was due to be paid £2. 16s. 0d. for fourteen hours instruction of Pupil Teachers at the rate of 4/- an hour. What were his qualifications? According to the

Admission Register, he was born in 1880, educated at William Borlase's School at Marlow and at Cheltenham College. He had taught for one term at a private school before coming to Tenby, where he served at the County School until December 1911, teaching Arithmetic, Gymnastics and Latin. He passed the London University Matriculation Examination in 1904 and the Intermediate Arts Examination as an external candidate in 1908. Mr. Roberts has been identified on the School Photograph of 1903. Impressions of him as a resident Master will have been gathered from the reminiscences of the Rev. Calvin Thomas and Sir Frederick Tymms. Various 'Old Girls' have called him to mind too:— 'He got very angry with us but he was a dear.' 'They all loved him but were very naughty in his classes. I remember throwing his names register across the room.' 'He was resident and evidently part of the Adams set-up.' One recalled that he used to take Mrs. Adams' pet dog on a lead after school hours, and 'Mrs. Adams sometimes brushed the dog in class when she deputised for him to go on some errand.' Yet another remembered, sadly, that 'Captain Roberts' was killed in the First World War.

Three Science Masters served at Greenhill during Adams' tenure of office; each of them also taught Mathematics. First there was Mr. J. C. Kirkman, B.Sc. (Durham), Honours Prizeman in Physics and Medallist of the Science and Art Department, South Kensington. During his stay, 1896-1899, the establishment of the Laboratory was barely begun and the equipping of it was left to his successor, Mr. C. H. Spencer, B.A. (Cantab.) who was at the school five years, September 1898 to July 1903. Spencer is remembered as a very nice man, whose short-sightedness sometimes caused him a little disciplinary trouble: 'We girls sat right at the back of the room. We spent much of the lessons out of our seats picking up mercury between the floorboards. We got it up with steel pen-nibs and put it in our pencil boxes.' The third Science Master appointed was a Welshman from North Pembroke-shire, Mr. John T. Griffith, who dropped the final 's' from his name, as being an undesirable Anglicised form. Apparently circumstances at home prevented him from continuing his academic studies at the University College of Wales, Aberystwyth and the Royal College of Science and it was not until the autumn of 1910 that he took his London Degree as an external candidate. Before coming to Tenby he taught at Henley Castle Grammar School from 1900 to 1903. At

Greenhill he taught Science and Mathematics. One who called to mind his arrival at the school wrote: '. . . he was then young, full of knowledge and ability to teach but clearly also, then, a new broom, which did not make for his immediate popularity.' At this stage in his career he was an outstandingly good player of Association Football notably in the position of 'centre half'. More will be written of the future Head Master in a later part of the story of the school.

During the Adams period eight-full-time Mistresses held appointments at the school. The first of them, Miss Alice Burrell, B.A. (London), who taught Latin and French, stayed the longest—from September 1896 to July 1901. She was followed by Miss Camilla L. Thomas, B.A., (Wales and London), who taught the same subjects from September 1901 to July 1905. Several Old Pupils have remembered her as a very popular member of the staff. After Miss Thomas' departure the Head Master had difficulty in finding a suitably qualified teacher of Languages. However, for the first time, two women were appointed to the staff, namely Miss J. Tait, B.A. (London), who taught History and Literature, and Miss L. Townsend, who took Geography and Nature Study. Both these ladies stayed from 1905 to 1907; Miss Townsend is recorded in the Staff Register as having gone to Bedales School on leaving Tenby. Meanwhile, stop-gap measures were taken to retain Latin and French in the curriculum. Mr. Roberts taught some Latin. Mr. Adams, who included French among his subjects, found it necessary to teach Senior French at this time. Some small efforts were made to relieve the pressure. In February 1906 a Tenby resident, Miss Saies was called in to give lessons in French Conversation and the arrangement was renewed, her fee being four guineas a term. When the Head Master discussed the problems with his Governors at their July meeting, it was stated that they could not afford a specialist on the permanent staff and Mr. Adams was to enquire into the possibility of securing a student teacher from France 'as had happened at Pembroke Dock'. The problem appeared to have been solved with the appointment of Miss J. Salmon B.A. (Wales), French and Latin, in September 1907, but she left after a year, as did her contemporary Miss G. Wrigley, B.Sc. (Wales), Geography. Miss Gladys Wrigley (a native of Aberdare) emigrated to the United States and became assistant editor of the *Geographical Review*, one of the four leading geographical journals in the world when it was under the editorship of the famous Professor Isaiah Bowman. When Bowman left for the Paris Peace Conference in 1919, she became Editor in Chief and remained so in New York until 1947—a major influence on geographical scholarship the world over.

At last came a prospect of stability with the arrival of Miss Gaynor Jones and Miss Marguerite Gore Lindsay, who served from September 1908 to July 1912 and July 1911 respectively. Miss Jones had studied at the University College of North Wales, Bangor, and was awarded the Degree of B.A. (Hons. French) of the University of Wales in 1908. Writing from Bethesda, Bangor, in September 1975, at the age of 89, she describes how she took up her duties in Tenby: 'Mr. Adams handed over the French to me. He himself had taught the subject and I was very grateful for his help in my first year of teaching—a time when advice meant so much. Mr. Adams was an enthusiast and the 5th Form he handed over to me were in such good form that they did very well in the examinations at the end of the School Year.' 'No one was aware of the authority of the Head Master but it was a quiet authority and he allowed his Staff to get on with their work without interference and anyone who has taught knows what a boon that is. Mr. Adams, as a French scholar himself, would have had every excuse for coming in to my lessons to see how things were going on, but I can remember no occasion when he did so, and I assure you I would not have forgotten. Helpful advice he did give me but *not* in Class.' 'We had *no* Staff room in those days, so you understand there was little opportunity for the Staff to meet or exchange ideas. I found the atmosphere of the School a happy one, though there were none of the facilities of today, and even then space was cramped.' Among the members of the Staff Miss Jones called to mind were the Cookery Mistress 'Miss Thomas . . . dark, very nice looking and a fine singer', the Art Teacher Mr. Head '. . . of medium height, slim and grey-haired and a favourite with the pupils'. And she continues 'I should expect a good many of the pupils of those days to have done very well in life.' She remembers in particular the son of The Manse, Mr. Trevor Lloyd Williams, who became Editor of the Trade Supplement of *The Times*. In addition to her main subject Miss Jones taught English and Latin. She moved to Narberth County School in 1912.

Miss Gore Lindsay, two years older than Miss Jones, had attended Knightsville Training College, had matriculated, had passed the First

Arts Examination (R.U.I.) and had taught in London, Coleford and Liverpool. At Tenby her subjects were Geography, Nature Study, Science and Drill. The Nature Study Lessons were recalled by A. R Gunter in the 1946 Jubilee issue of *The Greenhillian*: 'Nature Study was a fresh addition and the younger classes greatly enjoyed the rambles for specimens, visits to Hoyle's Mouth, the Museum or the shores. One amusing pastime was the making of "skeleton leaves".' Miss Jones succeeded Miss Lindsay as Senior Mistress in 1911.

Of the fifteen full-time members of staff who were appointed during Adams' headship, eight were already University Graduates and one graduated as an external candidate seven years after taking up his teaching duties at Tenby. From 1897 to 1905 there were three full-time Assistants, one of them being a Junior Master, and, from 1905 to 1910, four full-time. These teachers, together with the Head Master and the part-time staff, had to try and meet the requirements of a varied and widening curriculum, to reach the standards required by the Central Welsh Board, and to be responsible for the work of an average of 68 pupils during the first fourteen years of the school's existence. (The smallest number was 48 in the session 1899-1900 and the largest 92 in 1908-'9.) At this stage, of course, there was no official salary scale. From time to time the L.E.A. received representations on the subject from teachers' organisations. The first record of anything of the sort in the Minutes of the Tenby Governors was on 2 April 1908, when a circular from the Assistant Masters Association, concerning fixed salaries was placed before the meeting.

Of the part-time staff some have already been mentioned in the story of the extensions to the school premises—Miss Margaret E. Jones (Cookery and Laundry) and Messrs. Parry and Austin Thomas (Woodwork). One who was there from the beginning until 1910 was Edward J. Head, a product of the Scarborough School of Art, who had settled in Tenby and took in private pupils. For his services at the County School he was paid £20 a year, being half the Science and Art Grant, for giving two lessons a week. Although the name of W. Cecil Williams was given as visiting Music Teacher before the official opening of the school, there was no mention of him in the Governors' Minutes after that time. There was an early attempt to begin commercial work when Mr. E. H. Leach, son of John Leach of the *Tenby and County News*, agreed in June 1898, to teach Shorthand for a fee of

157

£2 2s. 0d. per term of which half was to be paid by the Governors and half by the pupils. How many took the subject is not known, but the number examined by the C.W.B. was very small—1 in 1900, 2 in 1901 and 1 in 1904, after which date Shorthand is not mentioned in the Official Reports. From 1901 to 1907 a small nunber of girls took examinations in Needlework. The 1910 Report of the Inspectors strongly urged its re-introduction into the curriculum.

Also there was an interesting but short-lived effort to include Agricultural Education in the Time Table. On 2 April 1909 the Director of Education, discussed with some of the Governors a circular he had previously sent out on this subject. For their part the Governors expressed their willingness to carry out the wishes of the L.E.A. in this matter 'as far as circumstances would permit.' By September, Mr. Reginald Grant had taken up duties as Agricultural Instructor under the Education Authority. On 1 October the Head Master told the Managers that 5 boys had indicated their wish to join a class should one be formed. Ten days later Mr. Grant attended a Special Meeting of the Tenby Governors and stated his requirements. The minimum number for a class would be five. At first no theoretical lessons would be given but, for practical demonstration he would need 3 square yards of ground for each pupil. He suggested that the boys from the Woodwork classes should fence in a plot either by the north or the west wall. The Head Master pointed out that there would be problems, since his Time Table had been submitted to the Board of Education. However, he thought it possible that one hour each Monday could be set apart for the class. On 24 November Mr. Adams reported that there were 6 pupils and 1 outsider in the Agricultural Class. Mr. Grant's Quarterly Report to the L.E.A. on 13 December stated that 7 pupils and 1 outsider had attended 7 classes. Apparently work was resumed at the end of January 1910 and the fee for the outsider was fixed at 5/- per year. Then, following the Triennial Inspection in the same year, a Special Meeting of the Governors agreed to consider whether it was worth while to continue with Agriculture. The printed Report of the Inspectors included this observation: 'Six boys in Form IIIB are following a course in Agriculture, or more strictly speaking, in Horticulture. Very little actual work in the School garden has yet been done, and it is most important that the technical work in Agriculture should be based upon a sound foundation of Chemistry and Botany.'

Mention must be made of two requests concerning the teaching of Welsh. The first was noted in the Governors' Minutes of 1 February 1897, when they had before them a letter, the authorship of which is not clear, suggesting that Welsh be made a compulsory subject in all Intermediate Schools. The second was recorded in the Minutes of the Local Education Authority, dated 16 November 1906, when they received a letter from the Welsh Language Society asking the Committee to pass resolutions, and forward them to the Board of Education, to make Welsh compulsory in all Elementary and Secondary Schools of the Principality. The matter was deferred. Such proposals would have had scant consideration among the 'Little Englanders' in Tenby and other parts of South Pembrokeshire at that time.

The central figure at Greenhill, John William Bateman Adams, has been described as 'tall, slim, clean-shaven, light brown hair—impression—quite definitely elegant—without being obtrusive'. One Old Pupil has remarked that J.W.B. brought a superior quality into the town. Several remembered that he had a maxim: 'There will always be hewers of wood and drawers of water.' This seems to be well suited to one, who, with the 'father founders' looked upon the Intermediate Schools as imitations of the Public Schools. Surely it was Adams who introduced the practice, which was continued under his successor, of the pupils saying 'adsum' when their names were called at registration. By all accounts the discipline under his regime was very good. Words which he used, when rebuking a pupil in class stuck in the mind of an 'Old Girl'. The culprit was never referred to by name but as 'that silly fellow in the corner over there'. He came to the school with a fine athletic record and continued to play cricket along with the boys against local teams. His musical activities ranged from teaching Class Singing with the aid of a tuning fork to supporting Mrs. Adams in the production of school entertainments at the Royal Gatehouse Assembly Rooms. The Head had to be something of a 'general practitioner'. As occasion demanded, he taught Scripture, Music and French, but his main subjects were English and History. One former pupil says that he taught her Scripture and that he was the best teacher she ever had; another, that 'he taught us to love poetry. He was rather romantic and became dreamy.' An official

159

assessment of his teaching qualities is to be seen in the Central Welsh Board's Report following the Triennial Inspection in 1910: 'In the Upper Forms History is taught by the Head Master whose teaching is most scholarly. The methods of instruction are excellent and include constant references to historical and other atlases and the use of original documents; while wall pictures and standard works convert the classroom into a real History room.' Later generations of Greenhillians down to 1924 would remember the presence of these historical pictures as a part of the décor of 'B Room' opposite the Laboratory. For many years there were on the shelves of the School Library reminders of Mr. Adams' scholarship—his editions of Shakespeare's *Henry V* and Scott's *Lay of the Last Minstrel*, his *Heroes of Medieval England* and his *Illustrated Histories* of the Stuart and the Hanoverian Periods.

The Promotion of Culture—The Library, The Magazine, The Stage

The earliest mention of the School Library was on 23 February 1897, when the Principal reported that the Chairman and others had promised gifts of books. A month later on 23 March the Governors were told: 'A library has been started'. The Central Welsh Board Report for 1899 took note that a Library Fee of one penny a week, or three shillings a year, was being charged, but there was no subsequent reference to this practice. From time to time additions were made, notably through gifts from Mr. Clement Williams, and from these small beginnings were eventually accumulated two collections of books, housed in two book-cases, one for the boys in 'B room' and one for the girls at the east end of the upstairs corridor—a far cry from the Library of works of Reference and of Fiction, which was built up by 1961, the last year of the Greenhill Grammar School. The Head's Report for the session 1903-1904 referred to the popularity of the Library and its usefulness in encouraging children to read for themselves, but went on to state that most of the books had been read and re-read. As the School Library was an indispensable accessory to school work, it was hoped that the Governors, as soon as funds permitted, would give a small sum towards additions every year or every term. His Report for the following year contains the note: 'The School Magazine is published as often as practicable, but it is not possible to make it self-supporting at a moderate price in a school of less than 100 pupils.' It is not known how long this venture lasted, or for that matter, what happened to subsequent ephemeral productions which appeared from time to time, but, even after *The Greenhillian* became permanently established from 1938 onwards, the problem of making it self-supporting at a moderate price still remained. The above Report continued: 'The School Library is a great boon and in this connection, as well as the School Magazine, we are much indebted to the kindness of our Chairman.' According to the C.W.B. Inspection Report for 1910, there were by then about 60 works of reference and about 250 works of general literature on the shelves.

During her husband's Headship, Mrs. J. W. B. Adams was responsible for the entertainments given by County School pupils at the Royal Gatehouse Assembly Rooms (now known as the Royal Playhouse), then the local Mecca for vocal and instrumental concerts, Gilbert and Sullivan Operas, Hunt Week Theatricals and performances by visiting celebrities. The school productions might appear unsophisticated or even childish to our present generation, but they called forth fulsome praise from the local press and they are remembered with affection and nostalgia by many old Pupils of the period. The *Tenby Observer* accounts of two of the series will serve as illustrations.

The first, a 'Christmas Entertainment', was given on the afternoon of Wednesday 27 November 1901, under the patronage of the Mayor, (Mr. C. J. Williams, J.P.) and his fellow Governors and in the presence of a large and appreciative audience. The proceeds were in aid of the Tenby Cottage Hospital. The first portion of the Programme was devoted to a 'miscellaneous selection' comprising a Piano Solo by John D. Mack, a Recitation by Arthur Smith and a Song sung by Boysie Allen, followed by the Duologue 'Hearts or Diamonds' between 'the Hon. Augustus Fitz Clarence, fourth son of Stonybroke', played by George Cheveley, and 'Mrs Blobbs (Christina) relict of Ebenezer Blobbs, tallow merchant, City', by Enid Saies.

Part Two of the Programme was given up to the musical extravaganza 'The Tinder Box', adapted from Hans Andersen. 'This was the pièce de rêsistance and from every point of view—musical, artistic and dramatic—it was an unqualified success, various roles being taken with great ability by scholars who had been very carefully trained by Mr. and Mrs. J. W. B. Adams. To Mrs. Adams in particular special praise is due for the great success which attended the efforts of the young people,

161

some of whom exhibited considerable histrionic abilities. Mrs. Adams was also responsible for the costumes which were very pretty and the scenes, whilst Mr. Reginald Truscott produced the limelight effects. The appreciation of the large audience was shown by repeated outbursts of applause and recalls.' The music was described as being 'light and catchy'; Mr. Adams played the accompaniments while Mrs. Adams was responsible for the stage arrangements. The 'Observer's report of a second performance given on Tuesday 11 February 1902 mentions that the 'Copper Castle' scene was designed by E. J. Head. 'The 'List of Characters' was calculated to appeal to the senses of humour of readers of the Programme:—

King of Hanky Panky Land (a dignified but irascible potentate)
.... George Bolt
Queen of Hanky Panky Land (a 'Home Ruler')   Maggie Grabbam
The Soldier, afterwards Valoroco de Swaggeroso (better to be born
    lucky than rich) ....   William Murphy
Princess Dulcibella (marries the soldier and lives 'happily ever after')
.... Mildred Truscott
The Landlord (a 'Liberal Onionist' with an eye to business)....
.... Arnold Bennett
The Landlord's Daughter ....   May Evans
The Witch (as usual mysterious and wicked 'Loses her head on this
    occasion'.) ....   Enid Saies
The Jester (only 'jester' small part) ....   Devereux Green
The Herald ....   George Long
The Pages (who turn over to Queen Dulcibella)....   Boysie Allen
                                              Arthur Smith
The Watchman (a 'rattling good fellow') ....   John Mack
The Dog with the Eyes like Saucers (a bow-wow worth knowing)
....   Carl Hoffmann
The King's Footguards (warranted 'dandly lions')....   Herbert Morris,
    Charles Collard, Frank Whitten, Arthur Scott, William
    Norman, Leopold Pellowe, John Husband, Gilbert Gwyther
Ladies in Waiting (who have little to say but who look very nice)..
    Claire Palmer, Dorothy Farley, Constance Morley, Violet
    Norman
The Scenes were (1) A High Road, (2) & (3) The Hotel Cecil, Hanky
Panky Land.

The February performances included a repeat of 'The Tinder Box' but the first half of the Programme was replaced as follows:—Miss Gertrude Macaulay, contralto, late of the Savoy Theatre, London, 'and now of the Queen's Hall, London', sang 'The Enchantress', 'Angus Macdonald' and 'Songs My Mother Sang'. A duet was sung by Messrs. Richard Williams and Mr. J. W. B. Adams. Mr. Williams also sang the two little Irish songs: 'I remember meeting you' and 'You'd better ask me'. Mr. Zahradka, violin, accompanied by Walter Davies, performed a 'Fantasia of Balfe's Bohemian Girl'.

The *Tenby Observer* of 5 March 1908 reported another successful entertainment, equally well patronised on 3 March, in aid of the Sports and Library Funds of the County School. Seats were priced 2/6 (reservable at Cowtan's Music Warehouse), 1/6, and, at the back 1/-.

The Programme consisted of two parts: 'The Dream Lady' (a romantic fairy play in one act), and 'Rumpeltstiltzkin' (a musical fairy extravaganza). The principal roles were as follows:—

'The Dream Lady'

The King	Devereux Green
The Queen	Lottie Llewellyn
Princess Fiametta (their daughter)	Bessie Bond
Princess Amolette	Thelma Farley
Princess Astore	Violet Craven
Denise and Nanina (Ladies of the Court)	Ivy Ace, Trudy Hancock
The Prince of Goldacres	Archie Yardley
Pages	Arthur Lord, Graham Ace
The Dream Lady	Phoebe Lord

'Rumpelstiltzkin'

The King	Clifford Hicks
The Prime Minister	Madge Thomson
The Minister of War	Devereux Green
The First Lord of the Admiralty	Archie Yardley
The Chief Miller	Norman Thomas
Milanda (his daughter, afterwards the Queen)	Nesta Allen
Lollipop (the Queen's Page)	Graham Brown

163

Jester......................................	Vee Evans
Elves	Graham Ace, Gordon Thomson, Reggie Gunter Arthur Lord.
Cradle Bearers	Baden Powell, Leslie Cooper
Guards	Charlie Thomas, Arthur Williams
Heralds	Gerald Bond, Edgar Vaulk
Ladies in Waiting	Stephanie Wills, Connie Yarrow
Two Baby Coons	Lola Brown, Thelma Farley
Rumpelstiltzkin	Alfred Hicks

In both pieces, the production of which was very ably undertaken by Mrs. J. W. B. Adams, who is to be warmly congratulated upon her success, the acting was maintained at a high standard of excellence, the youthful performers sustaining their respective parts with marked ability. Where all did so well it seems invidious to single out any for special attention but we cannot refrain from referring particularly to the acting of Alfred Hicks in the title role of 'Rumpelstiltzkin' which was brilliantly sustained, of Devereux Green as the King in 'The Dream Lady', Nesta Allen as Milanda, Clifford Hicks as The King and Lola Brown and Thelma Farley as Baby Coons in 'Rumpeltstiltzkin'. The last two convulsed the audience at every appearance and, in spite of their tender years, carried themselves with marked success throughout. The audience were delighted with them as they were indeed with the whole performance. The scenery which was exceptionally effective, was painted by Mr. E. J. Head, Principal of the Tenby Art Class, while limelight effects were kindly undertaken by Mr. R. H. Tuck. The throne and cradle were made by Wilfred Glanville and looked extremely well. During the evening, Dolly Truscott, was enthusiastically received in her dancing interludes.

Thanks to Madge Thomson, who played the part of 'the Prime Minister', a copy of the photograph of one of the scenes in 'Rumpelstiltzkin' has been made available to accompany this text. One of the principals, Nesta Allen, left school at the age of 14 to study for the stage, the first pupil of Greenhill to take up this career.

These detailed press reports are social documents. They record the team work involved in these early and very popular school entertainments and call to mind the names of pupils from well-known families in the town. The accounts of these performances are period pictures in themselves and their subjects a reflection of contemporary tastes.

Entrances and Exits

According to Adams' own entries in the Admission Registers 253 boys and 176 girls, a total of 429, were enrolled from Michaelmas Term 1896 to Michaelmas Term 1910, inclusive. The lowest admission figures were for the years 1897-8 and 1901-02—10 boys and 7 girls in each of these sessions. Statistics given in the Central Welsh Board Reports, year by year include the total number of pupils in attendance. The figures were low in the Sessions 1899-1900 (31 boys and 17 girls) and 1901-'02 (35 boys and 11 girls). This called for comment from the Inspector on 15 May 1899, regretting that there were not more pupils on the roll and remarking upon the small number of girls. The largest number of admissions was 34 in both 1907-'08 and 1908-'9, while the biggest number of pupils on the roll was in the Session 1908-'9, with 44 boys and 48 girls in attendance. This last mentioned Session and the previous one (35 boys and 36 girls) were the only occasions when the girls outnumbered the boys during the Adams period. An interesting social comment is to be seen in the C.W.B. Report for the year 1900, when the Inspector noticed that in the Tenby County School there was at that time a larger proportion of pupils coming in from Private Schools than in other Districts, and gave the comparisons:

Tenby County School		*Average Elsewhere*
from Elementary Schools	69%	92 or 93%
„ Private Schools	31%	7 or 8%

A number of Private Schools, some of them Dame Schools, persisted on into the twentieth century and during the first three decades provided a proportion of the admission to the County School, more girls than boys.

A reflection of the social background of the pupils is to be found in the parentage recorded in the second Admission Register, for the

165

years 1902 (Michaelmas Term) to 1910 (Michaelmas Term) inclusive with a solitary entry for the Easter Term 1901, that of Trevor Lloyd Williams, second son of the Congregational Minister, admitted at the age of 9 years 9 months and who remained in School for 9 years and two terms—a record surely! These statistics reveal that the largest numbers admitted to the school during this period were the offspring of farmers—26 in all. The other numbers were as follows:—

6 Builders/Contractors; 4 Plumbers/Sanitary Engineers, Jewellers, Commercial Travellers, Grocers/Provision Merchants, Independent Means, Police Constables, Bakers, Boot and Shoemakers; 3 Drapers, Coal Merchants, Fishermen, Stone Masons, Veterinary Surgeon; 2 Master Rigger, Gardener, Shipwright, Sports Depot, Doctor, Fishmonger, Roadman, Clerks, Photographer, House Decorators, Wine and Spirit Merchants, Licensed Victualler, Solicitor, Butcher, Post Master, Minister of Religion, Carpenter. 1 *each* Farm Bailiff, Coal trimmer, Steel worker, Carpenter/ Undertaker, Army Pensioner, Naval Pensioner, Sergeant Major R.A., Army Officer, H. M. Coastguard, Cab Proprietor, Bootmaker Journeyman, Plumber's Journeyman, Hotel Keeper, Lodging House Keeper, Motor Engineer, Marine Engineer, Engine Driver, Station Master, Railway Packer, Tailor, Chemist, Music Hall Artist, Auctioneer's Clerk, Solicitor's Accountant, Furniture Remover, Rate Collector, Chiropodist, Stationer, Retired Banker, Organist and Professor of Music.

From the beginning there had been Entrance Scholarships available to children from the local Elementary Schools. In 1896 eight free scholarships to the value of £6 each had been awarded, five for boys and three for girls. These were tenable for one year, but were renewable on the recommendation of the Head Master. Some time later an arrangment was made for the Entrance Scholarship Examinations to be supervised by one of H. M. Inspectors. In addition to scholarships the Governors granted bursaries each year to necessitous pupils. An example of the allocation may be taken from the Minutes of 5 October 1898, when the Governors approved on the basis of the examinations held the previous July and on the Head Master's recommendation, the award of 4 Scholarships to Elementary School pupils, 3 Half Scholarships to the value of £3 each to pupils in school and 3 renewal Scholarships of £2 each to first year pupils. However, on 18 May the Chief Inspector of the Central Welsh Board took exception to this practice and told the Governors that the 'present' system of awarding scholarships was not in accordance with the Scheme and that renewals should be for the full amount and not for half. The total number awarded should not exceed 9 'with the present numbers'. Accordingly, when 6 boys and 4 girls had sat on 27 July that same year, the Governors awarded 4 at £6 and renewed 3 at £6. But in subsequent years the Inspector's recommendation was not always strictly observed. Some time after the setting up of the Pembrokeshire Education Authority in 1904, the Director of Education became responsible for the County Scholarship Examinations in which the subjects included Arithmetic, English, History and Geography. Extracts from the Central Welsh Board Reports for three separate years will serve to illustrate the increase in the number of places occupied by scholarship holders following the issue of the Board of Education Regulations in 1907.

In the Session 1907-'8, when there were 35 boys and 36 girls on the Roll, it was stated:

5 pupils at the School—2 boys and 3 girls—hold Scholarships to the value of £24.

7 pupils at the School—5 boys and 2 girls—receive Bursaries of the aggregate value of £28.

In the Session 1908-'9, when there were 44 boys and 48 girls registered the Report stated:

5 pupils at the School—3 boys and 2 girls hold Scholarships of the aggregate value of £21. Of these 2 boys and 1 girl receive augmentations of the aggregate value of £9.

10 pupils at the School— 4 boys and 6 girls receive Bursaries of the aggregate value of £31.

Free Places

7 pupils— 2 boys and 5 girls—hold Free Places at the School.

In 1909-10, with 45 boys and 37 girls on the roll the situation was:

Scholarships and Bursaries

7 pupils at the School—3 boys and 4 girls—hold Scholarships of the annual value of £33. Of these 2 boys and 1 girl receive augmentations of the aggregate value of £9.

167

8 pupils at the School—5 boys and 3 girls—receive Bursaries of the aggregate value of £30.

From Secondary School Grants

13 pupils at the School—6 boys and 7 girls—hold Scholarships to the aggregate value of £78.

From the County Education Fund

6 pupils at the School—2 boys and 4 girls—hold Scholarships of the annual value of £33.

Thus, leaving aside bursaries, the number of pupils holding scholarships or Free Places had increased from 5 in 1907-8 to 12 in 1908-9 to 26 in 1909-10. These Central Welsh Board Returns do not give the numbers of those who held renewals or internal awards.

The number and quality of Entrance Scholarship candidates was not always satisfactory. In July 1907 the Local Governors found that there were only 3 candidates for 5 Scholarships. The Reports of the Director of Education, which were included in the L.E.A. Minutes, were critical of the state of affairs. He drew attention to the fact that, out of 10 girls and 9 boys who sat the July Examination at Tenby, only 3 qualified. A similar situation prevailed in the Fishguard, St. David's and Milford Haven Districts where the places were barely filled The Director maintained that the minimum of 200 marks was sufficiently low to enable any intelligent child to pass. (The maximum was 600.) Only two candidates had over 400 marks and they were both from Narberth. He urged that more advertisement of the advantages of Secondary Education was needed. In 1909 the Director reported that at Tenby 5 girls and 6 boys had sat in July and that out of 4 County and 5 District Scholarships, only 2 were awarded. The Entrance Scholarship Examinations were the subject of comments from the C.W.B. Inspectors reporting to the Tenby Governors on 5 March 1910. They were of the opinion that the papers were too difficult and Mr. Owen Owen suggested that there should be a conference of the Governors with the Head Teachers of the District.

How long were pupils remaining in school at this stage in its history? This question can be answered through an examination of 151 entries in the second Admission Register, covering the years Michaelmas Term 1902 to Michaelmas Term 1910 inclusive, together with the single entry for the Easter Term 1901. The longest stayer, Trevor

168

Lloyd Williams, was there for 9 years and 2 terms, while at the other end of the scale there were three pupils who were in school for but a single term. It should be borne in mind that at this time the school leaving age was 13 and that for various reasons, (some of them domestic) when a child was needed at home or when a family left the district, the stay in school was necessarily short. The following list gives the number of pupils and the duration of their stay in school, in years:—

One 9+, two 7+, five 7, nine 6, six 5+, fourteen 5, eight 4+ ten 4, six 3+, sixteen 3, sixteen 2+, thirteen 2, seventeen 1+, sixteen 1, nine 2 terms, three 1 term.

Bearing in mind, that according to the Board of Education Regulations 1907, a three-year school life and a leaving age of fifteen might be accepted in rural areas and small towns, figures drawn from the above analysis show that 55 pupils stayed the full four years, which was considered desirable, while another 22 were in school for three or three plus years, making a total of 77 for all who continued their studies for three years and upwards. Of the remainder, 29 were there for two or two plus years, 33 for one plus years and 12 under one year, making in all 74 who did not remain for the course of three years.

Among those who remained in school long enough in the period from 1899 (the first year any sat the examination) to 1910, 71 gained the Junior, 61 the Senior, and 2 the Higher Certificates of the Central Welsh Board. Among them also were pupils who passed the Oxford Local Examinations, those who secured the Matriculation of the University of Wales, and/or of London University, those who passed the Examinations of the Science and Art Department, and those who gained Queen's/King's Scholarships and County Exhibitions.

Using no other source of information than the entries (not always complete) in the second Admission Register down to and including the Michaelmas Term 1910, the occupations of 'Leavers' may be noted:—

University Colleges 4; Teaching (including 5 known to have gone to Training Colleges) 27: to Public Schools 6 (Wellington College 1, Scholarships to Christ's Hospital 2, Scholarships to Christ's College Brecon 2, Cranleigh School 1); to other Secondary Schools 4 (Sutton Coalfield G.S. 1, Pembroke Dock, Fishguard and Cardiff Intermediate Schools 1 each); to Westminster Abbey School 1 (the son of W. Cecil Williams, Organist of St. Mary's Church); Clarke's Secretarial

College (Madge Thomson, who later had Secretarial posts in Trinidad and then with the I.C.I. in London); Clerks (1 GWR, 2 Solicitors, +1 other) 4; Bank Clerks 4 (including 1 in Canada); Drapery Business 2; Commercial Traveller 1; Engineer Apprentice 1; Engineering 3; Motor Engineering 3; Motor Engineering Apprentice 1; Pharmacy/ Chemist's Apprentice 2; Licensed Victualler, home, 1; Wine and Spirits Merchant, home 2; Canada 1; Designer 1; Farming 8 (2 home + 6); Farming 2 (Canada 1, Australia 1); Post Office 5 (4 clerks, 1 messenger); Merchant Service 3; Grocer's Assistant 1; Greengrocer's Assistant 1; Private Soldier R.E. 1; Tailor's Apprentice 2; Milliner's Apprentice 1; Dental Mechanic 1; Apprentice Jockeys 2 (Dick and Bilby Rees, both of whom became winners of the Grand National); Building Trade (home business) 1; Stationery 1; Fishmonger (home) 1; Furniture Removal (home) 1; Home 20; not known 30.

The events of the year 1910, his last as Head of the Tenby County Intermediate School brought to Mr. Adams, on the one hand the satisfaction of the outstanding academic successes of his pupils and, on the other the sheer anxiety and exasperation caused by the precarious plight of the school's finances. Special meetings of the Managers in March and July (with the Inspectorate and representatives of the L.E.A.) resulted in September in the economies, referred to in a previous chapter, which included the dismissal of part-time staff, the cavalier treatment of Science Master J. T. Griffiths and a substantial cut in the Head Master's own salary. In these circumstances the prospects of preferment which came his way at the end of the year must have been a 'godsend' to Mr. Adams. When the time came for his departure he had the knowledge that his work was appreciated in Tenby and that, following the Triennial Inspection on 15 March, the Central Welsh Board Officials thought very highly of his capabilities both as a Head and as a teacher. A fitting conclusion to this account of his period of office will be provided by brief description of his last Prize Day and his last Governors' Meeting, both of which were held in the last months of the year, and of the Presentation for which he returned to Tenby in May 1911.

A report of the Prize Day, held on 16 December 1910, appeared in the *Tenby and County News*. It was stated that despite the tempestuous weather the function was well-attended. The Gymnasium had been tastefully decorated for the occasion. Owing to the adverse weather conditions there were notable absentees, including the Chairman of the Governors (Mr. C. J. Williams J.P.), and Miss E. M. Milward, who was to have presented the Prizes and Certificates. The Chair was taken by Mr. C. W. R. Stokes, C.C., who had the company of two of his fellow Managers, the Rev. R. T. Lodwig Evans and Mr. W. G. Parcell, while Miss Stokes deputised for Miss Milward. Letters of apology were received from Mr. Palmer Morgan (Chairman of the Higher Education Committee), who sent a message of congratulation on the school's excellent report and splendid success during the year from Mr. Whicher of Milford Haven, from Lady St. David's (who had distributed the Prizes the previous year and who now promised a prize for Literature), also from Sir Marchant Williams, Mr. Seymour Allen and Mr. Marley Samson.

The Head Master was pleased to present a statisfactory report for the Session 1909-'10, the results of the public examinations being specially good. He spoke of the high tone of the school and of the discipline 'at once firm and easy', which had favourably impressed the Central Welsh Board Inspectors when three of them, along with two from the Board of Education, in the course of the Triennial visitation had discussed staff, curriculum, organisation and finance. The number of pupils, then 80-90, was the average to be expected for a District of about 8,000 population, said Mr. Adams. As in the past a great deal of hard work was done with the backward pupils, though this did not bring credit in the public examinations. Speaking of the curriculum, he mentioned the introduction of Agriculture into the Time Table, though progress had not been encouraging; the Gymnasium was popular, but Games still suffered on account of the field not being close to the school; the pupils played football and hockey and netball was being introduced 'as not so dangerous as hockey'. Turning to the examination successes, the Head Master said that they were exceptional. On the results of the Central Welsh Board Examinations 'this year' the Local Education Authority awarded 3 County Exhibitions, tenable at any place of higher education, each to the annual value of £20. All three were carried off by pupils of Tenby County School. In addition there were 3 London Matriculations (the examination was becoming harder every year), 4 Welsh Matriculations and 1 Higher School Certificate (which was equivalent of Intermediate

171

B.A.), 11 Senior and 5 Junior Certificates, and 1 Entrance Scholarship to Christ's Hospital.

After the Head Master's speech, the prizes and certificates were distributed by Miss Stokes. On the conclusion of these presentations the Rev. R. T. Lodwig Evans proposed a vote of thanks to the Head Master and staff and, in the course of his remarks, emphasised the fact that the past year had been better than any in the history of the school despite the financial difficulties, adding that the people of Tenby would be prepared to help in the reduction of the debt when the L.E.A. discharged their obligations. There followed brief speeches from Mr. Parcell and Mr. L. Thomas, a parent of two of the pupils, and, when the formalities were over, a gymnastic display was given by the boys and girls and the visitors were entertained to tea by Mrs. Adams.

The last Meeting of the Managers attended by Mr. Adams was held on Friday, 30 December. Part of the Head Master's Report dealt with the successes already referred to on Prize Day. Other items were the gift of a handsome pair of Entrance Gates from the Chairman and the replacement of Saturday morning School by sessions on Wednesday afternoons for the convenience of country pupils and to make possible the introduction of a period of organised Games. Tribute was paid to the work of the Senior Mistress, Miss Lindsay, who, for the past two terms had voluntarily devoted some of her private time to taking the Girls' Gymnastics and Games. The main business was the Head Master's resignation, conveyed to the Governors in a letter dated 22 December 1910. Obviously the offer of a new post at Ashford had arrived since the Prize Day.

> I am placing my resignation in the hands of the County Education Authority on my appointment to a larger Secondary School under the Middlesex Education Authority. I have as you know, been Head Master of this School since its opening in September 1896 and during this long period I have done my utmost to promote the interests of the School in every possible way. I take this opportunity of thanking the Governors (and especially our worthy Chairman) for their kindness and sympathy to me all these years. I need not say how much I regret leaving the School, but, if I am ever to obtain preferment, I must perforce to do so now, as before long my age will begin to tell against me in my application for Higher posts.

On receiving this notification, the Governors expressed their regret at the resignation and testified their warm appreciation of Mr. Adams' work during the past 15 years. A sub-committee was formed to arrange for an appropriate Testimonial and the Governors then turned their attention to a letter from the Director of Education concerning the appointment of a successor and gave consideration to their part in the proposed arrangements.

At the time Adams resigned there were still six of the fourteen Governors who were on the Board when he was appointed in the summer of 1896. By the turn of the century, Subscribers of £5 and over to the original funds had served their full term of office and no further representatives of that category were invited to serve. Thereafter, the number of Managers remained fixed at twelve. There had been changes in personnel, either through deaths or through resignations when members left the District. In 1910, Mr. Clement Williams, J.P., was still in the Chair, though by that time in failing health; Charles William Rees Stokes, C.C., was still there; the Rev. John Lloyd Williams, Congregational Minister, who wrote the words of the School Song, held office throughout this period and saw his two sons distinguish themselves while in School; Mr. Benjamin Harries, J.P., who was Mayor at the time of the Official Opening was still a member and so was Mr. William George Parcell, J.P., of Fernley Lodge, Manorbier, Mrs. W. G. Parcell (née Greenish), one of the original co-opted members had kept up her service, but Mrs. Edel A. Rowe of St. Andrews School, North Cliff, had resigned in April 1899, her place being taken by Miss E. M. Milward of The Paragon, Tenby. Egerton Allen, always a controversial figure was a member from 1895 to 1897, and again from 1905. From 1900 onwards one of the co-opted members was Dr. Beamish Hamilton of Tudor Square. An important addition to the Board was Thomas John Esq., C.C., of Elm Grove, St. Florence, a representative of the Poor Law Guardians since 1899, in place of the Rev. George Bancroft, deceased.

Whilst some of the Governors appear to have taken their duties seriously, there were occasions when the necessary quorum of over two thirds was not available. For example, on 15 May 1899, Mr. Headlam, the C.W.B. Inspector referred to the return of attendances of the Governors and raised the question as to what should happen to those who had not attended for the qualifying period. On 26 March 1900 only four were present, on 2 April only three, when the Chairman and the Rev. J. Lloyd Williams and Mr. W. G. Parcell decided to send out a circular emphasising urgently the necessity of attending. The Chief Inspector's Report of 18 May stated that the Governors' attendances was not high enough and that there should be an occasional notification that non-attendance was a disqualification. In spite of this the poor record for the year continued when only three were present for the Meeting on 24 November. Thereafter, there were isolated occasions when the same thing happened. By the time Mr. Adams left, there had been over 130 meetings of the Board of Governors, apart from the sub-committees.

J. W. B. Adams had been appointed to the Tenby Headship a year before Queen Victoria's Diamond Jubilee in 1897. His resignation came not quite seven months after the death of King Edward VII and the accession of George V in May 1910. Within the fourteen years of Adams' tenure to office there had been important changes in the administration of education through the passage of the Board of Education Act 1899 and the Balfour Act 1902, the establishment of the Welsh Department of the Board of Education in 1907 (with Owen M. Edwards as its distinguished Chief Inspector), and the beginnings of wider opportunities for Secondary Education embodied in the Board's Regulations 1907. His last four years coincided with the Liberal Reforms of the Campbell-Bannerman and Asquith administrations, culminating in the rejection of Lloyd George's Budget of 1909 by the House of Lords and the constitutional clash between the Upper and Lower Houses of Parliament and the two elections of 1910. Abroad there was the confrontation between the Dual and Triple Alliances; there came into being the Anglo-Japanese Alliance of 1902 and the Anglo-French Entente in 1904; there was the armaments race, including the German challenge to British naval supremacy, and there occurred a number of 'international incidents' which might have sparked off a conflict between the great European powers. Moreover, this was a period of a continuation of the late Victorian hey-day of the British Empire, when pupils in their classrooms, which smelt of carbolic, were proudly shown 'red on the map' indicating world wide possessions, the period in which the provinces of Alberta and Saskatchewan were added to the Dominion of Canada and Dominion Status was attained by Australia 1901, New Zealand 1907, the Union of

South Africa 1910, and in which the British Raj remained supreme in India. The proprietors of the local newspapers in Tenby kept their readers informed about many of these events, and awareness of the Empire is well illustrated by two letters, which have survived, (in the context of the School).

These letters were written during the Mayoralty of Charles William Rees Stokes 1906-1907. The first, dated 4 May 1907, was from George Lort Stokes (the Mayor's son), Solicitor and Town Clerk, to Mr. Eastlake, Clerk to the School Managers.

> It has been decided that Friday 24th instant shall be observed in Tenby in connection with 'Empire Day' Movement instituted by the Earl of Neath.
>
> Will you please take the necessary steps to obtain permisssion for the Pupils at the County School to have a half holiday so that they may take part in the proceedings also to obtain permission for the erection of a Flag Staff at the Schools for hoisting the Union Jack on.

The other letter, dated 18 May was from the Mayor to the Chairman of the Governors.

> By Royal desire Friday the 24 instant is to be observed at Tenby as 'Empire Day' and it has been decided to ask all public bodies to take part in the ceremonial.
>
> A procession will be formed in the South Parade, leaving there at 2.30 o'clock in the afternoon, in which I hope you will be able to take part, meeting me in the Town Hall at 2.15 o'clock.

The Governors agreed to take part in the celebrations as requested. Mr. Adams' own patriotic outlook has already been noted, as remembered by former pupils, and he doubtless shared the flag-waving enthusiasm which was common in all parts of the country at this time.

Mr. and Mrs. Adams returned to Tenby for the Presentation which took place in the Royal Gatehouse Assembly Rooms on Monday, 1 May 1911 in the afternoon, in the presence of parents, pupils and friends of the school. After the ceremony, the company were provided with tea in the side-room on the invitation of the Chairman, Mr. C. J. Williams who unfortunately was absent through illness. The following details have been extracted from the *Tenby and County News* of 3 May:

Mr. C. W. R. Stokes, who presided, said that he regarded Mr. Adams as an old friend, with whom he had been associated over the

175

past fifteen years, during which time there had been numerous difficulties, but no trouble had been too great to give support to the Head
Master in carrying on the successful work of the school. Mr. Adams
had worked many hours late at night (when most of them were in their
beds), studying the interests of the children placed in his charge. A
schoolmaster had not only to teach but to inculcate good principles
into the children and that had been one of the aims of Mr. Adams, most
ably supported by his dear wife. He impressed his pupils with a sense
of dignity and that they should not do anything to bring disgrace upon
the school. Not only had Mr. Adams brought a large number of
Honours, Mr. Stokes continued, but he had encouraged cricket, football, hockey and any other games which created manliness. There
was nothing, in the speaker's mind, 'so disgraceful as an effeminate
boy'. They had tried to make Mr. Adams feel that Tenby was his
home, but he was a young man with a future before him. Mrs. Adams
also had taken a deep interest in Tenby and many had enjoyed the
entertainments she had put on, revealing that she had a marvellous
power with children. Mr. Stokes concluded by presenting Mr.
Adams with a cheque for £39 and an 'Address' which had been illuminated by Mr. E. J. Head.

There followed a number of speeches, the first two being from
Governors. The Rev. T. Lodwig Evans echoed the sentiments expressed by Mr. Stokes and went on to talk of the affection felt for Mr.
Adams by pupils past and present, some of them scattered widely
over the world. Mr. Evans produced a letter and a donation received
from a former pupil, Enid Saies, who lived in Sweden and who was
married to a Swedish schoolmaster, the Head of a large public secondary school there. Mr. W. G. Parcell, a Governor for fifteen years,
gave his full support to all that had been said. Then three Old Greenhillians spoke. First, Mr. J. Calvin Thomas, schoolmaster of Begelly,
the second of the seven children who had attended the County School,
said that having become a member of the teaching profession himself
he had a greater understanding of the kindness, tireless energy and
keen interest of his former Head Master. He also had to say a word
for Mrs. Adams, but for whom he would have been in hot water many
times, and he apologised for all the trouble he had given her His own
name was not on the Honours Board but he hoped that the School
would go from strength to strength and be head of the County Schools

in Wales. Mr. Calvin Thomas was followed by Mr. Reggie Farley, who recalled that he was in the school when it first opened, and by Mr. Clifford Hicks, who expressed appreciation of what Mr. Adams had done for school games and of his efforts to secure the provision of the Gymnasium, which was such a great acquisition. Other speakers were the Rev. G. C. Rowe (Proprietor of St. Andrews Preparatory School) eulogising Mr. Adams as a good teacher because he had tried 'to turn out not merely scholars but men', and Mr. T. P. Hughes (draper) who brought in a sartorial note, saying that Mrs. Adams always gave local tradesmen the chance of supplying her with goods before going any further afield!

When Mr. Adams himself rose to speak 'he was heartily received'. He referred to his former pupils, several of whom he saw walking around with their wives and families and said that he had first known the Old Pupil, who had married a Swede, as a small girl in the lowest Form. He spoke of a Greenhillian living out in Alberta and of another in the way of becoming a prosperous solicitor. Mentioning his departure from the town, he said that a captain was always particularly fond of his first ship and he did not think it possible that he would ever feel the same affection for any other school as he did towards Tenby County School. He and his wife intended to spend a great deal of time in Tenby. (It turned out that this idyll did not last, for they later parted company; Mrs. Adams became the wife of George Stokes, Town Clerk, son of C. W. R. Stokes). Mr. Adams concluded by voicing their thanks for the kindness shown to them during fifteen years and for the gifts they had just received. Miss Milward then presented Mrs. Adams with a bouquet and told her and the audience that Mrs. Adams' production of 'The Water Babies' was the most beautiful thing she had ever seen in her life.

The 'Address' given to Mr. Adams was worded as follows:—

To J. W. B. Adams, Esq., M.A. (Oxon), B.A., (London).

We, the Governors of the Tenby County School, have great pleasure in testifying to the marked success, energy and zeal shown by you during the fifteen years you were Head Master of the Tenby County School, as shown by the Honours Board of the School, on which appear 8 County Exhibitions, 25 Matriculations and 1 King's Scholarship besides other Honours.

And we, the parents of the children who have been educated

at the Tenby County School, also beg to thank you for the painstaking manner in which you have educated our children and the
care and attention that you have devoted to their welfare.   And,
we, the undersigned, sincerely regret your leaving Tenby, and
wish Mrs. Adams and yourself every success in the future.

Dated this 1st day of May 1911.

After leaving his Middlesex post Mr. Adams moved to Hampshire
and it is pleasing to recall that in the New Year Honours List for 1933
he was awarded the M.B.E. in recognition of his services as Headmaster
of Christchurch School, Hampshire.   He died on 12 January 1946.

CHAPTER IV

THE MIDDLE PERIOD

Section 1: The Changing Scene—The Background to the Griffith Period

Mr. John Thomas Griffith, B.Sc., (London), F.C.S. was appointed Head Master of the Tenby County Intermediate School on 27 January 1911. The new Head was a Welshman, the son of the Rev. John Griffith(s), Calvinistic Methodist Minister at Cilgerran, close to the North Pembrokeshire banks of the river Teifi. Whereas J. W. B. Adams, the first Head, was of Pembrokeshire stock, he was English through his upbringing and education in London and Oxford and through his early teaching experience in the capital. On the other hand, J. T. Griffith had been a pupil at Pencadair Grammar School and a student at the University College of Wales, Aberystwyth, before proceeding with a scholarship to the Royal College of Science. He pronounced his name 'Griffith' after the Welsh 'Gruffudd' and, when in authority, he made it clear that he objected to the addition of a final 's' as an unfortunate Anglicised form. However, this appears to have made little impression upon the editors of local newspapers— who for the most part used their own spelling either through ignorance or in one case at least through sheer 'cussedness'—or upon those who wrote the Governors' Minutes, or, for that matter upon those responsible for the L.E.A. Minutes, in which he was recorded as 'Griffiths' down to the time of his resignation in 1942. On the other hand, the Central Welsh Board Reports from 1906 onwards, while he was Science Master, dropped the final 's', and the present writer will do the same.

How was this 30 years old Assistant Master, who but recently had been awarded his B.Sc. Degree, appointed Head of the Tenby County School from among the galaxy of graduates who were candidates for the post? The course of events was as follows:

On 30 December 1910 the Tenby County School Governors received a letter from the Director of Education, stating that Mr. Adams' resignation had been received and that, in due course, an appointment

179

would be made in accordance with the Scheme. The Managers were asked to consider 'whether the Capitation Fee of £2, which had been paid to Mr. Adams will, in view of the present state of the finances of the school, be offered to the new Head Master', and to appoint three of their members to serve on the Special Committee of eight, who would report to the Education Committee on the applications received. The Governors' response to these requests was to reduce the Capitation Fee from £2 to £1. 10s. 0d. and to appoint their Chairman (Mr. Clement J. Williams), the Rev. Lodwig Evans and Miss Milward as their representatives on the Special Committee. Also it was decided that the new Head Master was to be let the House and Garden, including the Greenhouse, at a rent of £35 per annum, he to pay all rates and taxes and to be responsible for internal repairs. On 6 January 1911 the Education Committee adopted a resolution of their Higher Education Sub-Committee 'That the resignation of Mr. J. W. B. Adams, Head Master of the Tenby County School be accepted and that the necessary steps be taken to fill the vacancy'. Mr. H. E. James, the Director wrote to the Governors notifying them that the L.E.A.'s representatives on the Special Committee would be C. W. R. Stokes (of Warwick House, Tenby), Thomas John (of Elm Grove, St. Florence,) Alderman W. Lawrence (of Pentlepoir), Dr. G. Griffiths (of Bunker's Hill, Milford Haven) and Mr. W. Robinson (of 19 Church Street, Pembroke Dock). It should be noted that the first three of these were also Governors at Greenhill.

The post was duly advertised at a salary of £120 per annum plus a capitation allowance of £1. 10s. 0d. Candidates were required to send 10 copies of their applications to the Director by 19 January. There were over 50 applicants in all, among them graduates with two and even three degrees, scattered over the whole of Britain. From these the special committee was to draw up a short list and the local Education Committee to appoint. The appointment went to Mr. J. T. Griffith and was well received by the local press.

J. T. Griffith's period of service at Greenhill lasted 39 years, 8 as an Assistant and 31 as Head Master. He had joined the staff in 1903, the year of the then almost unnoticed first aeroplane flight by the brothers Orville and Wilbur Wright, over in the U.S.A., the year following the conclusion of the Second Boer War, and his resignation in July 1942 came a year after Sir Frank Whittle's first jet-propelled aircraft had made its début foreshadowing a revolution in air transport, and when the Second World War had already lasted almost three years. 1911, the year of Mr. Griffith's appointment to the Headship, was an eventful one, which he and, to some extent his pupils would remember, partly through personal interest and involvement and partly through coverage given in the local press to happenings at both local and national level, at a time when news was not squeezed into corners by a proliferation of advertisements. Statutes of that year deprived the House of Lords of the power to reject Money Bills, limited the life of the House of Commons to five years before the holding of a General Election and inaugurated salaries for Members of Parliament at the rate of £400 per annum; Lloyd George's National Insurance Act paved the way for the Welfare State. The Irish Home Rule Bill was given three Readings in the Commons and so was a Bill to Disestablish the Anglican Church in Wales; the latter provoked a great protest rally of Welsh churchmen at Shrewsbury on 2 August.

On 14 June the *Tenby and County News* reported that His Majesty the King was graciously pleased to accept a copy of *Memories of the Crimean War* by Dr. Douglas Reid of Tenby, published that day. On 28 June the same newspaper reported the local celebrations on Coronation Day, Thursday 22 June—the decoration of the town, the procession, the church service, the Mayor's dinner for 300 guests in the Market Hall, the children's entertainment, the Coronation Mugs, a carnival, the splendid bonfire on the hill west of Waterwynch Lane, to wit a hexagon 16 feet at the base and shaped like a sugar loaf 30 feet high; the Mayor, Captain D. Hughes Morgan, and the local dignitaries were photographed on the lawn of the De Valence Gardens and the Mayor, in his speech, laid great stress on the importance of the British Empire. Likewise, His Worship marked the occasion of the Investiture of the Prince of Wales at Caernarfon by entertaining the school children and arranging for sports to be held on a field in Heywood Lane. Two days later, on Saturday 15 July King George V and Queen Mary were at Aberystwyth to lay the Foundation Stone of the National Library of Wales.

On 4 August, the Mayor who was also prospective Unionist candidate for the Pembroke Boroughs, was present at the Royal Gatehouse Assembly Rooms when Mrs. Emmeline Pankhurst, accompanied on a return visit to Tenby by Miss Rachel Barret, (Organiser of the Suffragettes in Wales), gave an adress on 'Women's Suffrage'.   The same month pleasure was given to the members of the Tenby Golf Club by the presence of the crack golfers, Braid and Vardon, at the Summer Meeting.   The same month, Tenby was badly hit by the railway strike, which lasted three days, while George Ace, pioneer cyclist (whose Penny Farthing still hangs in Ace's showroom), was advertising a garage for 100 cars in the old skating rink premises in South Cliff Street.   On 6 September appeared an advertisement in respect of a double-decker bus, rejoicing in the name of 'Dreadnought' leaving any day, by arrangement, for St. David's Cathedral, return fate 6/-.   Tenby Post Office announced 3 deliveries on week-days: London and General 7.30 a.m., North and Pembrokeshire 12.00 noon, and London and General 7 p.m.   Press reports recall the short-lived attempt which was being made to capture ocean going traffic for the Great Western's port at Fishguard.   On 2 January the Cunard liner 'Lusitania' had been unable to land passengers and mail there from New York, on account of the severe north wind.   A further 'County News' report on 4 October underlined the difficulties encountered at Fishguard and noted that the Cunarder 'Caronia' had failed to call the previous Saturday and that a Blue Funnel Line vessel could not pick up passengers because of the north-east wind.   On 18 October the same newspaper carried a letter from a ratepayer, complaining of the hooliganism of Tenby boys and urging more action by the police: 'Old men and women are molested in the street by day and night; doors are burst open and stones flung at them, and it is well-known that no respectable people will bring their young children and nurses to the town to be criticised and have audible remarks made about them every corner they turn.'   These comments are valuable in reminding us that present day hooliganism is no new phenomenon.   There had been an earlier reference to unseemly behaviour on 16 August when there were complaints that bathers had been guilty of 'indecent exposure' on the North Walk.   However, mention had been made of matters of a more erudite nature.   There was the newly formed West Wales Historical Society, members of which were being enrolled by Mr. Francis Green of St. David's, and during the last week in July there had been meetings of the Royal Archaeological Institute in the town and district.

Readers of the 'County News' of 1 November were informed by Mr. C. F. Egerton Allen that he intended to fight Mr. Stokes in the forthcoming Borough Council election. He stated that he was determined to purge the Council of Mr. Stokes and added that he (Allen) had entered the Council '20 years ago as a blind puppy' but that his eyes had afterwards been opened—'the Council was worked on a conspiracy of silence, it was worked from Bellevue Chambers (Stokes' office) and the Council were not allowed to know their own business.' In the event, Allen was returned to the Council third, with F. B. Mason and Stokes ahead of him in the poll. Unfortunately this antagonism continued with embarassing consequences both in the County School Governing Body and in the Pembrokeshire Education Committee during the early years of J. T. Griffith's Headship. That same issue of the 'County News' announced the death of Mr. Davies George, Deputy Clerk of the Peace, who had acted as Secretary to the Pembrokeshire Joint Education Committee from 1890 and subsequently to the County Governing Body of the Intermediate Schools until its powers were absorbed by the Local Education Committee. Earlier in the year 1911, on 19 April, the Tenby Governors had lost a notable member with the death of Mr Benjamin Harries, J.P., of St. Bride's, Saundersfoot, who was Mayor of Tenby at the time of the official opening of the County School and who had figured prominently in the proceedings.

Within the long span of J. T. Griffith's headship, fundamental changes in outlook towards education in England and Wales were reflected in Official Reports and Regulations, in Acts of Parliament, in the work of Local Education Authorities and in the schools themselves. The task of interpreting and implementing official policy for the Pembrokeshire Education Committee was undertaken by a succession of three Directors of Education: Mr. H. E. James (1904-1919), Captain E. T. Davies (1919-1927) and Mr. D. T. Jones (1927-1957). Also there were two Assistant Directors: Mr. H. J. Lewis until 1920 and then Mr. Tom ('Tim') Davies, who was also appointed Librarian in 1924, when, with the help of a grant from the Carnegie Trust, the Pembrokeshire County Library was inaugurated as a branch of the educational service, a service which over the years, Mr. Davies succeeded in building up for the benefit of the general public and as a valuable aid to teachers and schools at all levels. Within this period there were, of course, serious set-backs following the outbreak of war in 1914, through economy cuts in 1922 and 1931, and through the incidence of war again in 1939. Hardships endured during each of the two World Wars gave a stimulus

183

to the efforts of idealists, who hoped to create a new and better society, of which improved and extended educational facilities would form a prominent part.

This period was one of momentous changes which resulted from outstanding achievements in science and technology, from the speeding up of transport and notable advances in other means of communication. Discoveries ranged from the astronomical to the sub-microscopic, from Albert Einstein's Theory of Relativity and conception of the universe, to nuclear physics, the splitting of the atom and exploration of the living cell. Such discoveries were understood by few beyond the specialists and few, if any, of them could have foreseen the rapidity of further developments leading to the hydrogen bomb and the 'Space Age'. In this period also there were new prospects for the prevention and treatment of disease—slum clearance, improved sanitation, X-rays, the discovery of vitamins, blood transfusion, T. B. injections and the discovery of anti-biotics, notably of penicillin. The work of educational psychologists and the study of child development pointed the path to the introduction of intelligence tests in schools, to reforms in classroom practice, to changes from the rigid disciplines and drab premises of the early part of the century to more pleasant conditions, and to 'child centred' instead of 'curriculum centred' education. Material progress paved the way for vacuum cleaners to replace brooms and brushes, for washing machines in place of copper boilers, for cheap fountain pens instead of steel pens and powdered ink, for the introduction of type-writers into schools. Changes in fashion liberated the female figure from tight corsets and trailing skirts, lounge suits with coft-collared shirts and trilby hats became common wear for men and box-pleated gym tunics for school girls were firmly established until challenged for their inelegance.

Improvements in the internal combustion engine and the mass-production methods of Henry Ford and William Morris led to the popularisation of private motoring and to the use of road transport at the expense of the railways, which reached the peak of performance in steam locomotion in the 1930's. During this golden age of the giant ocean liners arose the challenge of the aeroplanes as a future carrier of passengers and freight, as oceans and continents were traversed first by pioneer long-distance fliers such as Alcock and Brown across the Atlantic in 1919 and Alan Cobham to Australia and back in 1926, and then spanned by the regular air routes of British Imperial Airways, founded in 1924, and which became B.O.A.C. in 1940. Technical processes were developed to ensure safety in flight including the vital invention of 'radar' by R. A. Watson-Watt in 1935. Then in 1941 an aircraft powered by Frank Whittle's jet engine gave birth to the possibility of popular travel under conditions of speed and comfort not realised at the time. On the ground, the motor tractor furthered the mechanisation of farming and in the factories changes in industrial techniques were leading the way to automation. However, between the Wars the greatest impact was made by a revolution in visual and oral communication. While popular newspapers battled for custom, bombarding their readers with banner headlines, dramatic opinions, tabloid news, and pictures, the cinematograph, first the 'silents' and then the 'talkies' lured the devotees into darkened picture palaces where they could sit at the feet of their celluloid idols. Beginning in 1922, the British Broadcasting Corporation transmitted radio programmes which, in due course, were extended and elaborated in coverage and content to bring instant news, entertainment, drama and music into the home. Whereas early listeners marvelled at the intermittent sounds brought to their ears by use of 'cat's whisker' wireless sets, a new generation took for granted the sophisticated radio receivers which formed a part of the household furniture. The experiments of Marconi and Baird prepared the way for the B.B.C.'s first television transmissions in 1936, so opening up new horizons, which would not be further explored until after the Second World War. The educational potential of these oral and visual media was soon recognised, but their introduction into schools was on a limited scale until some time after World War II, when more substantial financial grants led to a widespread use of ciné-projectors, radio receivers and television sets.

The above reference to some of the changes which occurred within the space of thirty years sets the scene for a short account of progress in the provision of education during the period beginning at the time of World War I and concluding with the emergence of proposals which were eventually adopted and implemented during and after World War II. Although the present writer's main concern is with secondary education as illustrated by the history of Greenhill School, Tenby, notice will be taken of changes affecting schools administered under the Elementary Code, since as in the Tenby catchment area, not only

185

did they provide boys and girls for admission but, as reforms eventually materialised, their fortunes became more and more closely linked.

The impact of the Great War (1914-1918) was unprecedented in scale, bringing involvement and anxiety into every home and every school and tragic loss to many. In the course of the struggle some five million men from the United Kingdom were brought into the Armed Forces, at first by voluntary enlistment, and from 1916 onwards by conscription. Of these forces three quarters of a million either were killed or died as a result of active service. (Tenby lost 133 dead— a high proportion for a town of less than 5,000 inhabitants.). In addition the influenza epidemic in 1918-1919 carried off 150,000 of the total population of the country. In the course of the War, as men were called away on active service, women were required to take their places on school staffs, in clerical jobs, in transport undertakings, and to serve in auxiliary services of the Armed Forces as nurses, land girls, or in munitions and engineering works. Hitherto unknown restrictions on civil liberties were imposed by the Defence of the Realm Act (D.O.R.A.) which gave the government power to take control of industry and transport. The familiar gold sovereigns and half-sovereigns were replaced by Treasury Notes (the 'Bradburies'), a 'daylight saving' Bill introduced the public to British Summer Time, the publication of news was censored, air raids led to lighting restrictions, 'U boat' attacks caused some shortages of food and clothing, marginal land was brought under cultivation and eventually rationing was introduced in 1918. Economies held up school building programmes and the supply of equipment, and in some areas school premises were used for billeting or for hospital purposes. School pupils were exhorted to support the war effort by selling flags, by contributing to War Savings, by knitting socks and yards of scarves for soldiers and by working on farms when help was needed.

In the midst of the struggle it was realised that an important aspect of reconstruction after the war should be an overhaul of the educational system. Lloyd George brought in as President of the Board of Education H.A.L. Fisher, a historian from Oxford, perhaps best known to a wide range of students for his *History of Europe*. Assisted by a group of experts, Fisher prepared plans to reorganise educational facilities into a national system and to provide for teachers' pay and pensions on a national basis. His Education Bill of 1917, which incorporated increased powers for the Board of Education, was watered down in face of opposition so that his measure, when it became law on 8 August 1918, contained too little that was obligatory and left too much to the discretion of the Local Education Authorities. However, the 'Fisher Act', with its 52 clauses and 2 schedules, appeared impressive in intention, as stated in the first Clause: 'With a view to the establishment of a national system of public education available for all persons capable of profiting thereby, it shall be the duty of the council of every county and county borough, so far as their powers extend, to contribute thereto by providing for the progressive and comprehensive organisation of education in respect of their area, and with that object any such council from time to time may, and shall when required by the Board of Education submit to the Board Schemes showing the mode in which their duties and powers under the Education Acts are to be performed and excercised, whether separately or in co-operation with other authorities.'

There were important provisions concerning attendance at Elementary Schools, but which also affected pupils in Secondary Schools through the raising of the school leaving age. Attendance was now obligatory between the ages of five and fourteen. Moreover, the Local Education Authorities could make by-laws requiring attendance at school until the age of fifteen and even longer; 'The Board of Education may authorise instruction of children in public elementary schools till the end of the term in which they reach the age of 16.' These last two steps in the raising of the school leaving age, being but permissive, were destined to remain untaken until they became binding under the 'Butler Act' of 1944. Complementary to school attendance were important clauses affecting the employment of children. No child under 12 was to be employed; children of 12 and upwards were not to be employed on any Sunday or for more than two hours on any day, or on any day on which they were required to attend school before the close of school hours or on any day before 6 o'clock in the morning. No child under 12 was to be employed for the purpose of singing, playing or performing or being exhibited in public or offering anything for sale. Also there were prohibitions against the employment of children in occupations, which, in the opinion of the schools Medical Officers, were prejudicial to health. It was the duty of Local Education Authorities to provide, at appropriate stages in public elementary schools, practical instruction 'suitable to the ages and abilities and requirements of the children' and courses there for older or more intelligent children, including those staying beyond the age of 14. The Authorities, either separately or in conjunction with other L.E.A.s, had the duty to establish and maintain continuation schools, 'in which suitable courses of study, instruction and physical training are provided, without payment of fees'; attendance for 320 hours per year was to be compulsory. The intention was for young people to spend part time in industry and part in school, but it transpired that there were problems of staffing and of finding co-operative employers.

Special concern was shown for physical and mental well-being. Local Education Authorities were empowered to supply for elementary school children and for persons over 18 in educational institutions, especially those in continuation schools, holiday and school camps, centres and equipment for physical training, playing fields, swimming baths and other facilities for social and physical training in the daytime or in the evening. Medical inspection and treatment, already introduced into the elementary schools under Acts of 1907 and 1909, were now to be compulsory in the secondary schools. Recognition of the pioneer work of Froebel and Maria Montessori, and of Rachel and Margaret McMillan in Britain in respect of young children, is reflected in the Fisher Act whereby Authorities could supply nursery schools for children over two and under five years of age 'whose attendance is desirable for their healthy physical and mental development.' There were also provisions concerning physically defective and epileptic children and for the education of children in 'exceptional circumstances'

Lastly, it should be noted that the Act included important financial provisions. State grants paid to a Local Education Authority were to be not less than half the net expenditure of such an authority recognised by the Board of Education. These grants came to be known as 'Deficiency Grants.' Education Committees were enabled to pay maintenance grants to holders of scholarships at secondary schools and fees in elementary schools were to be abolished. The Board of Education was to pay yearly to the Managers of non-provided schools the average yearly sum paid to such Managers under the Education Act of 1902. Apart from these financial clauses and the compulsory legislation for school attendance and limits on the employment of children, much of the 'Fisher Act' remained a plan on paper, albeit a plan containing indicators for further reforms. That some of the clauses remained inoperative has been variously attributed to reluctance on the part of Local Education Authorities to operate schemes as laid dow in the Act, to public indifference following upon a temporary stimulation of interest in educational reform, but largely because of financial stringency. After a short-lived post-war boom there came a slump, strikes, widespread unemployment, the problem of 'reparations' and a National Debt amounting to some £7,000 million. In 1921 the Committee of National Expenditure, under the chairmanship of Sir Eric Geddes, imposed drastic economies. Geddes' notorious 'axe' slashed grants to Education by one third, so causing a halt to L.E.A. building programmes strangling the scheme for continuation schools and reducing staff salaries by five per cent.

Ironically the cut in salaries was made in the very year that the scales arranged by Lord Burnham's Committee, through their negotiations with education authorities and teachers' organisations, were due to come into operation. The Burnham Committee had been instituted in 1919 through Fisher's recognition of the importance of attracting suitable candidates to the teaching profession by paying higher salaries and standardising scales throughout the country. Before 1821 Loc al Education Committees were arranging their own salary scales, with the result that the wealthier Authorities were able to make more attractive pay offers than was possible in other areas. In these circumstances salaries for graduate assistants in secondary schools ranged from about £120 to £200 per annum. The situation in the Intermediate Schools may be illustrated from what happened in Pembrokeshire. In Tenby County School, in the Session 1917-1918 for example, the maximum being paid to a graduate on the staff was £130, while the Head Master received a fixed salary of £120 per annum plus a capitation allowance of £2. 0s. 0d. On 25 January 1918, the Pembrokeshire Education Committee received a reminder from the Board of Education of the minimum salary payments which were a condition of the Fisher Grant. During a period of three years there were intermittent negotiations between the L.E.A. and representatives of the Intermediate Schools. The views of the Governors, Heads and Staffs of eight Pembrokeshire County Schools (together with Cardigan) were stated at a joint meeting with representatives of the Authority on 28 February 1919. There was stressed the urgent need to form a

189

scale of salaries and to increase salaries, though the Governing Bodies could do nothing about the matter without additional financial aid. It was pointed out that 'it was exceedingly difficult to keep teachers on staffs or to secure more experienced teachers, as higher salaries were being offered by English and Welsh authorities'. By July the Higher Education Sub-Committee recommended a salary scale, which was amended and then approved by the full committee. By May 1920 further amendments were being pressed by the secondary school assistants and Head Masters. Over the Burnham proposals the L.E.A. played for time. On 26 November 1920 their Higher Education Sub-Committee recommended 'that consideration of the Burnham Report on a Scale of Salaries be postponed for the present' and it was agreed that representatives should be sent to a conference of Rural Education Authorities to consider the Burnham Report.

On 1 April the Director of Education submitted a report on this conference and the Sub-Committee now proposed that the maximum for all assistants should be increased by £50 in two instalments. However, the struggle was not over. On 2 May a Deputation from the County's Secondary School Teachers came and pressed the case for the adoption of the Burnham Scale. The Education Committee then confirmed an amended version of the Secondary Scales, which were adopted as hereunder:

(1) *Salaries of Head Masters*—based on the average attendance of pupils.

		Min.	Max.
(a)	*Grade I* under 200	£550	£600
(b)	*Grade II* 200 and over	£600	£650

(excluding children on whose behalf the Secondary Grant is not received.).

All were to proceed to maxima by annual increments of £25. The minimum for women to be the same as for men. The maximum for women to be £20 below that of men.

(2)   *Assistants with University Degree or equivalent*

	Min.	Max.	Annual Increments
Men	£220	£450	£15 to £210
Women	£220	£400	£20 to the Maximum

No University Degree or equivalent

	Min.	Max.	
Men	£170	£350	£15 to the maximum
Women	£170	£300	

(3)   *Additional* £20 for 1st Class Honours Degree
        £10 for 2nd Class Honours Degree
                          For Heads and Assistants

(4)   Arrangements were made for transition to the new Scale.

(5)   *Domestic Science Teachers* were to be on the non-Graduate Scale.

(6)   *Scale to come into operation* on 1 April 1921.

It should be added that on 25 April 1922 the Committee received Board of Education Circular 1253 stating that additional payments for 2nd Class Honours must be made in strict accordance with the principles laid down by the Burnham Committee. A '2a' or 'Upper Second' was to be classed as a 'good Honours Degree'. Later in the 'twenties' the Pembrokeshire Authority agreed to pay an additional £15 per annum to any holder of a University Diploma in Education in their service.

Alongside the establishment of salary scales Fisher was concerned with teachers' pensions. His Superannuation Act of 1918 applied to all grant-earning schools and initially was operated on a non-contributory basis. However, from the time of Geddes' economy measures the teachers were compelled to pay 5 per cent of their salaries as a contribution towards their superannuation. There were certain extensions and modifications of the scheme under a further Act of 1925, which applied also to such independent schools as came in voluntarily within some special provisions. The qualification for benefits was 30 years' full-time service, of which 10 must be pensionable. The pension and the lump sum payable on retirement were to be x/80ths and x/30ths respectively of the average annual salary for the last five years of service, x being the years of pensionable service. No further changes were made until 1937.

191

Mention must be made of the facilities which became available in the universities for the professional training of graduates who wished to become teachers. Between 1890 and 1900 training departments had been introduced at a number of universities and university colleges, including Aberystwyth and Cardiff. At the latter some of the earliest pupils at Tenby County School took advantage of the opportunity to pursue Degree courses parallel with their training as prospective elementary school teachers. The University of Wales received its Charter in 1893 and in the first five years of the twentieth century Charters were granted to the 'red brick' universities of Birmingham, Manchester, Liverpool, Leeds and Sheffield. In these and others was instituted a four year course, comprising three years for a Degree and one for a course in Education, including teacher training. The sequel was that in 1926 the Board of Education began the practice of granting its Teaching Certificate to graduates who had taken the University Diploma in Education. This four years scheme, which included free tuition and a modest maintenance allowance of £30 a year, provided a university education for many Intermediate/Secondary School pupils whose financial circumstances would have excluded such a possibility. Also through this course the Intermediate Schools in Wales were to be assured of a supply of graduates, with teaching qualifications, who were to be the backbone of staffs for years to come. The present writer was among the early intake of students, who benefited from this scheme at Sheffield, where in the mid-twenties, in the presence of Vice-Chancellor Sir Henry Hadow, they were required to give a solemn undertaking to enter the teaching profession, regardless of the fact that there was no guarantee that posts would be available. Commenting on the supply of teachers between the years 1921 and 1938, W. Kenneth Richmond, in his *Education in England*, wrote:

> With jobs so insecure and hard to find, the profession seemed more attractive than it had ever been before. Since 1921 seventy-eight Training Colleges and twenty-two Departments of Education attached to the Universities had been turning out teachers at the rate of anything from 7,000 to 8,000 a year. For the first time the market was overstocked. Graduates, unable to secure the posts they had hoped for in Secondary Schools, had to seek less remunerative employment in the elementary service. Many of them found their way into Selective Central Schools, which were springing

up in most areas; others into the common-or-garden all-age schools.

The present author recalls graduates of the 1927 vintage, who felt a loss of face by having to knock at the doors of Education Offices in search of such 'less remunerative employment', and who were somewhat taken aback by what seemed to them a sarcastic and abrasive welcome at the hands of certain education officials. It should be added that a parallel to that first overstocked market came again in the 1970's.

An important event of the First World War period was the standardisation of the School Certificate Examination. The background to this and a comment on its consequences are contained in the 'Spens Report' 1939. At the onset it was pointed out that the Board of Education inspections, from 1902 onwards, tended to show that external examinations were having unfavourable repercussions on the work of many schools, often leading to cramming and over-pressure, besides being an impediment to improvements in method. In 1904 the Board's Regulations for Secondary Schools included a prohibition of entry of pupils under 15 for any external examinations. In 1911 the Consultative Committee of the Board produced a report on examinations in Secondary Schools, condemning as mischievous the presentation of young and immature pupils for external examinations, recommending co-ordination of the various examinations, that each school should be connected with one examination and that the University Examining Bodies should be approached for a solution of the problem. Prolonged discussions during the first three years of the War led to an agreement by the various examining bodies that they would modify their existing examinations. 'Fourteen examinations were accordingly recast or brought into existence between 1917 and 1919, seven of which, known as the First School (Certificate) Examinations—were for pupils of about 16, and seven—known as the Second School Examinations— for pupils of about 18.' In September 1917, the Board established the Secondary School Examination Council to advise and to co-ordinate these examinations.

The School Certificate Examination, as standardised in 1917, was destined to become a focal point and often a 'bogey' in the Secondary Schools. A panel of investigators set up by the above Council in 1931 stated that 'the primary purpose of the examination was to provide a suitable test of the ordinary work of a Secondary School at the Fifth Form stage, suitable in the sense that whole Forms, and not only picked pupils, would probably be presented for it, with the expectation that a large proportion would pass, and that without special preparation or undue disturbance of the normal work of the Form'. What constituted a 'large proportion' was not defined. Experience showed that in many schools whole Forms would be entered with the prospect of certain failure for a number of the candidates, varying according to the abilities and aptitudes of the Fifth Form pupils from year to year. In many cases the prospect of success was bedevilled by the Group System. A Pass was required in at least five subjects, including one from each of these Groups (1) English Subjects (2) Foreign Languages (3) Science and Mathematics. Other Passes would be acceptable from Group (4) Music, Drawing, Manual Work and Housecraft. Only too often a candidate would gain as many as six Passes and fail the whole examination by missing out one of the first three vital Groups. A Board of Education Circular (1034) issued in March 1918 had stated 'a cardinal principle that this examination should follow the curriculum and not determine it.' In actual practice the reverse was the case. While this examination prevented specialisation by pupils during their school career down to the age of 16, their syllabuses throughout the school were geared to the requirements of the School Certificate. Here was a goal to be reached, a measure of attainment, a certificate on which a number of 'Credits' in the appropiate subjects would provide exemption from Matriculation—and for many employers 'matriculation' became the yardstick by which applicants for posts would be measured. The examination provided an incentive for pupils, among whom the more conscientious suffered from strain and overwork, and for staffs whose professional success was likely to be judged by results, regardless of the capabilities of the human material at their disposal.

A footnote should be added about the fate of the Central Welsh Board's Junior Certificate Examination. Although the Consultative Committee's Report in 1911 had condemned as mischievous the presentation of young and immature pupils for external examinations, there was considerable and prolonged resistance to the proposed abolition of the 'Junior' in Wales, both from staffs of Intermediate Schools and among members of Local Education Authorities. Older members of staffs looked upon the 'Junior' as a stimulus to effort and as a pre-

194

liminary training for the stiffer hurdle of 'the Senior' the following year. However, thay had to bow to the inevitable when the Junior Certificate Examination was set for the last time in 1920. Thereafter the School Certificate became entrenched as the first external examination, taken at the end of a four years course, and following it, after an interval of two years, the Higher Certificate Examination. Such was the pattern until after the Second World War.

A prominent figure in the history of education in the inter-War period was Sir W. H. Hadow, who was Chairman of the Consultative Committee of the Board of Education which produced the three Reports: *The Education of the Adolescent* 1926, *The Primary School* 1931 and *Infant and Nursery Schools* 1933. Critics have maintained that these Reports should have been prepared and published in the reverse order, as the procedure adopted led Education Authorities to give priority to the needs of secondary school pupils at the expense of those of the younger children. However, some attention must be given here to the 'Hadow Report' of 1926 because of its influence upon the development of secondary education and also because of its shortcomings. Investigations by the Consultative Committee began at the time of MacDonald's first Labour Government in 1924. The President of the Board of Education, Sir Charles Trevelyan, who was able to end some of the Geddes economies, wished to examine the possible application of the views expressed by Dr. R. H. Tawney in his *Secondary Education for All*, advocating that 'the only policy which is at once educationally sound and suited to a democratic community is one under which primary and secondary education are organised as two stages in a single continuous process; secondary education being the education of the adolescent and primary education being preparatory thereto.' Significantly, Tawney's dictum was echoed in the recommendations made by the Committee in their Report and in its title *The Education of the Adolescent*. The Report recommended that the education of boys and girls should consist of two stages, primary and secondary, that all pupils should remain in the primary school until they reached the age of 11 and then, at 11 plus, proceed to the secondary stage in either Secondary 'Grammar Schools' following the more academic curriculum laid down in the Board of Education's Regulations for Secondary Schools until the age of 16, or in well-equipped 'Modern Schools' (which term could be taken to embrace 'Senior Schools',

195

Selective Central Schools and Non-selective Central Schools) until the age of 14 or possibly 15. Besides giving a general Education, the 'Modern Schools' were to make special provision for practical work. Post-primary technical and trade schools were recognised but not dealt with in this Report. The method of deciding which kind of post-primary education would be best suited to the abilities and aptitudes of the boys and girls would be an examination comprising written work, an oral test and a psychological test, the last to be used for determining borderline cases.

The translation of theory into practice raised problems. Although the Report insisted on complete equality of status between the different types of secondary school, parents, teachers and young examinees themselves came to look upon success in the examination (later to be known as the 'eleven plus') as an 'Open Sesame' to the Secondary 'Grammar School' while pupils proceeding to the 'Modern Schools' were regarded as being of an inferior category. The break at the age of eleven-plus came under fire from educationists, who called it an administrative convenience designed to make possible a four years course on the assumption that the leaving age would be raised to 15. Also the application of the term 'adolescent' to children of 11 plus was considered arbitrary, and one which did not allow considerable variations in the physical and psychological development of young people. As the leaving age remained at 14 less pupils stayed on to benefit from the courses provided in either the 'Modern' or the 'Grammar' Schools than the authors of the scheme may have hoped. The response of Education Committees to the recommendations of the 'Hadow Report' varied widely. Some enterprising Local Authorities, especially in urban areas, were able to embark upon the task of reorganisation and the building of new secondary schools before being overtaken by a further wave of economy measures in 1931. On the other hand, progress by some of the poorest rural Authorities was almost non-existent; their financial resources were inadequate; they were faced with the problems of decapitating existing elementary schools to provide pupils for the proposed new 'Modern' schools, of locating such schools at centres which would be most convenient for scattered rural communities, of transporting pupils to and from those centres, of the viability of small village schools and their possible closure should they lose their 'tops', and of dealing with strenuous opposition from the

Church Authorities. The Minutes of the Pembrokeshire Education Committee provide evidence of how these problems were being approached in a largely rural county. On 11 May 1926 the L.E.A. received the Report of their Reorganisation Sub-Committee concerning a memorandum called for by the Board of Education. Having in mind the possibility of receiving from the Board a Block Grant for each of the years 1927-1930, the Sub-committee had prepared a statement of the probable costs of providing for the further development of elementary education, including Junior and Senior Schools, of buildings and equipment including a new school for 400 Seniors at Milford Haven (which was opened as Milford Haven Central School in 1931), of the provision of advanced and practical instruction, of the reorganisation of existing schools, including Tenby Council School. However, much of this remained a programme on paper and on 18 March 1930, the Reorganisation Sub-Committee were addressed by the Permanent Secretary of the Welsh Department, Board of Education, Sir Percy Watkins, whose subject was the extension of Secondary School facilities and the provision of suitable courses; he informed his audience that the county schemes were by then out of date. In July, there followed further pressure from the Board of Education in their Circulars 1397 and 1404 and the L.E.A. then agreed to certain proposals of which those affecting the Tenby District—the catchment area of the Tenby County School will serve as an example:

The proposed reorganisation was to involve the decapitation of a number of all-standard schools namely Begelly, Stepaside, Pentlepoir, Amroth, Saundersfoot, Manorbier, Penally, New Hedges, St. Florence, Tenby Council School and Tenby N.P. School. It was recommended that there should be a non-selective Senior School for 360 to 380 pupils at Tenby Council School, independent of or in association with Tenby County School. All Infants and Juniors in Tenby Council School were to be transferred to Tenby Parochial Schools. New Hedges and N.P. Schools were to be closed and their pupils transferred to the Tenby Schools. But needless to say there was strong opposition from the Diocesan Religious Education Committee over the possible fate of their schools. In the case of the Tenby N.P. School the L.E.A. and the Managers reached a modest agreement in 1932 whereby the Boys' and Girls' Departments would be amalgamated to form a Mixed School, accommodation would be rearranged to improve the housing of the Infants and some structural alterations would be made in the old stone building at a cost not exceeding £400.

Meanwhile, the programme of the Pembrokeshire Education Committee, along with those of other Authorities throughout the country, became a casualty of the economic crisis of 1931. Philip Snowden, Chancellor of the Exchequer in the 'National Government' introduced a National Economy Bill in which he sought to meet £70 millions of a deficit of £170 millions by cuts in national expenditure, and as usual, Education was the most convenient victim for the knife. With rare exceptions, no new school buildings could be commenced and projects in the 'pipe line' were to be abandoned; all salaries paid by the State were to be reduced by 10 per cent; hardest hit by the economies were the teachers who suffered a loss of fifteen per cent.

These emergency economies also had repercussions upon the Free Place System. By 1930 the Local Education Authorities had the discretion of increasing the percentage of Free Places in Secondary Schools from 40% to 50%, but under new Regulations in 1933 the Special Place Examination replaced the Free Place Examination for admission to grant aided Secondary Schools. As before, children were selected on the basis of their performance in examination. Only those boys and girls whose parents' income was below a certain amount, taking into account the number of children in a family, could have full remission of Fees. For the rest there was a scale of Fees, fixed in accordance with the income of the parents, the categories requiring either full payment or giving partial remission. The practice in Pembrokeshire may be illustrated from the Report of the Director of Education, Mr. D. T. Jones, on the Examination or Special Places in Secondary Schools 1937:—

Preliminary Examination

All pupils in the Elementary Schools in the County (excluding Pembroke Borough Schools) between the ages of $11\frac{1}{2}$ and $12\frac{1}{2}$ on 1st April 1937 were duly examined by a Preliminary Examination in Language and Arithmetic held in the Elementary Schools under the supervision of Head Teachers on February 19th 1937. Some pupils were exempted on various grounds by the Director of Education. In practice those who had not reached the standard of attainment of the old Standard IV were excluded. The number of children in the age class referred to amounted to 1973, of whom 128 (13%) were exempted ...

The Preliminary Examination ... acts as a preliminary sifting of candidates for the Final Examination, familiarises the children with printed papers and sometimes encourages parents, where good work is done by their children at the preliminary stage, to give consideration to the possibility of sending their children on to the Secondary Schools.

The papers are set by the Director of Education and printed and sent to the various schools in accordance with the numbers required. The Heads of the Schools are instructed to hold the examination on the specified day and within the time stipulated on the printed paper. General instructions for marking are also circulated by the Director of Education. The Head Teachers mark the papers and submit the results. Unless a parent so wishes, no candidate who receives less than 40% of the marks obtainable can proceed to the Final Examination. As the Preliminary Examination is a test of attainment, and the questions set have attainment rather than order of merit in view, no allowance for age is given at this stage.

Copies of the papers set at this stage were included in Mr. Jones' Report. The times allowed were for Arithmetic $1\frac{1}{2}$ hours and for Language (printed in English and Welsh) 60 minutes. Statistics of the number of candidates examined since 1928-9 were set out in a table, from which three sample years are quoted:—

In respect of Age Class $11\frac{1}{2}$-$12\frac{1}{2}$

Date	Total Examined	No. Exempted	Per cent Exempted	Per cent Qualified	Total Age Class
1928-29	823	260	24·0%	46%	1083
1933-34	1102	86	7·2%	52%	1188
1936-37	1221	128	10·5%	57%	1549

The Final Examination

This was held on 24 April 1937, as follows:—

Language (Eng./Welsh) 10 a.m. to 12 noon, *Arithmetic* Speed and Accuracy Test 1.15 to 1.30 p.m.

Arithmetic General Paper 1.30 to 2.45 p.m.

The Director reported that 584 candidates were presented for these Final Examinations but that 478 were actually examined. A Table provided the percentage of candidates who gained 50% of marks or more and were placed in Grade I in the nine Centres concerned in the years 1931—1937. The position at the Tenby Centre and the County Average of percentages are compared as follows:

Area	1931	1932	1933	1934	1935	1936	1937	Average 7 Years
Tenby	53	50	62	53	65·3	74·0	85·1	63·2
County Av.	47	53	70	63	74·7	65·9	78·8	60·7

According to these figures, the standard of attainment in the Tenby District was below the average for the county for the years 1932 to 1935 but shot ahead during the last two years of the period and finished above the average for the whole seven years.

The Director's Report continued with a comment upon the use of 'age marks' to correct the handicap of age in establishing an order of merit, and gave notice of the Authority's intention to enforce the Board of Education's recommendation that no child under 12 in an elementary school should be given any Homework—a term which also included private tuition for a fee. Furthermore the Director suggested a new form for the Examination 'to avoid the entry into our Secondary Schools of pupils who have been intensively prepared'; for this purpose he had in mind the inclusion of a Group Intelligence Test, as a check rather than the main test, and of school progress reports on all subjects.

Attention was again focussed upon the problems of reorganisation, following the passage of the Education Act 1936 and the Physical Training and Recreation Act of 1937. In consequence, Mr. D.T. Jones completed a detailed Memorandum for the Pembrokeshire Reorganisation Sub-Committee by November 1937. He outlined the legislative and administrative developments since the Fisher Act of 1918 and referred to the financial crises and then he added, in characteristic vein, 'gradually, however, the nation has righted itself and the valuable merchandise, which for Educationists seemed lost has been partly re-collected and the voyage resumed under the recent Education

MR. J. T. GRIFFITH (H.M.) WITH GROUP OF PUPILS c.1918
photo: Arthur Squibbs

CAST OF THE OPERETTA 'THE BURGOMASTER'S DAUGHTER' 1918
photo: at west end of School House by Arthur Squibbs

SCHOOL ASSOCIATION FOOTBALL ELEVEN 1919-20

with Mr. J. T. Griffith (H.M.) seated and Messrs. H. J. Williams and 'Eddie' Parry standing, left and right respectively

photo: Arthur Squibbs

SCHOOL CRICKET ELEVEN c. 1920-21
with Mr. J. T. Griffith (H.M.) and Tom Griffiths, Captain
photo: Arthur Squibbs

GIRLS' HOCKEY TEAM c.1920
with Miss 'Frankie' Howells, seated, and Miss Vincent and Miss Edmunds, standing left and
right respectively
photo: Arthur Squibbs

GIRLS' HOCKEY ELEVEN 1926
photo: Arthur Squibbs

SCHOOL PHOTOGRAPH 1928

with Staff, left to right: Messrs. W. Harrison, W. C. Bennett, H. J. Williams (Sen. Master),
J. T. Griffith (H.M.), Misses 'Frankie' Howells (Sen. Mistress), M. G. Bowen, M. Heap,
'Maggie' Williams (Cookery)

photo: Arthur Squibbs

CAST OF 'SHE STOOPS TO CONQUER' (GOLDSMITH) 1932
in School Hall
photo: Arthur Squibbs

PART OF CAST OF 'ST. JOAN' (SHAW) 1934
in School Hall with Olwen Richards in the title role
photo: Arthur Squibbs

PART OF THE CAST OF 'RICHARD OF BORDEAUX' (DAVIOT) 1937
in the Super (later 'Little') Theatre with Kenneth Griffith in the title role
photo: Arthur Squibbs

CAST OF 'THE MERCHANT OF VENICE' (SHAKESPEARE) 1938
in the Super Theatre with William Henwood as Shylock
photo: Arthur Squibbs

Act of 1936.   In this Act lies the possibility of challenging the view that democracy has proved inefficient, and that the only successful form of government which can live in the modern world must be that of the totalitarian state'.   The memorandum continued with a short analysis of the 1936 Act and a detailed discussion of its implications for Pembrokeshire, including a suggested reorganisation, District by District.

Under the provision of the 1936 Act, (a) the school leaving age was to be raised to 15 plus, subject to the alternative of "beneficial employment" from the age of 14; the Local Authority to grant employment certificates under certain conditions which were stipulated, (b) the Local Education Authority was empowered, for the first time, to make grants from 50% to 75% of the cost of premises of non-provided schools, either new buildings for senior pupils or modifications of existing ones, provided such proposals were submitted to the L.E.A. before either 1 April or 1 September 1938.   Also the proposals must be capable of being put into effect before 1 April or 1 September 1939—the Authority to have choice of date, but thereafter no proposals would be entertained, (c) to facilitate reorganisation denominational religious instruction was to be given by 'reserved teachers' in denominational mixed schools but there was also to be provision for non-denominational instruction on an 'agreed syllabus.'   The Director noted that the provision of post-primary education for all Seniors, according to the Act of 1936, should be almost mature by September 1939 and the full effect of raising the leaving age be felt in September 1940.

Mr. D. T. Jones set out in detail arguments in favour of alternative methods of dealing with post-primary education, being particularly concerned as to whether institutions for post-primary education were to be provided in the centres where they already were in the form of secondary schools, or whether the number of centres should be increased.   'Concentration', he stated, 'will mean larger post-primary schools, a more economic application of staffing, equipment and other necessary facilities, and possibly a greater variety in the kind of work that can be planned and achieved, but human luggage is the most difficult kind of luggage to move, and the geographical conditions and public opinion will play their parts.   Nevertheless, the decreasing child population, tending to increase the total number of small schools, with the attendant increase in prime costs, points the way to some concentration.' There were problems of transport to consider: '. . . as long distance travel has its physical disadvantages, seven miles as the crow flies, should normally be the longest distance children should come to attend a post-primary school centre.' He remarked that while the ultimate aim of educational policy implied a leaving age of 16 years and the provision of secondary schools for all children, the conditions did not appear to be ripe for the coming adjustment between the trend of economic progress and the need for a better education for the increased leisure that was to come. But it was necessary to avoid consideration of Senior children only ' . . . children are no more important at 13 than they are, say at 3, 7 and 9 years of age. Infant, Junior and Senior Schools should be equally suitable for the kind of instruction and training given in each of them.' The Director's Report also considered the provision of Nursery Schools, the Bi-lingual problem, the Physical Training Act of 1937 and the need for co-ordination between District and Parish Councils and the Education Authority in the establishment of community services, including child welfare centres within extended school premises.

The Memorandum included proposals for reorganisation, based on the school rolls for the Session 1936-1937. It was suggested that there should be twelve Districts, namely: A. Fishguard and Goodwick, B. Letterston, C. St. David's, D. 'Precelly', E. Maenclochog, F. Narberth, G. Begelly-Kilgetty, H. Tenby, I. Pembroke and Pembroke Dock, J. Milford Haven, K. Neyland, L. Haverfordwest. In each District, the schools to be affected were listed, together with the numbers on the roll and the proposed re-arrangements. Within the scheme, the additional requirements of the community in each area were to be allowed for. Part of District G and the whole of District H, it should be noted, came within the catchment of the Tenby Intermediate School. In the Begelly-Kilgetty Area (G) there were 12 schools with a total strength of 689: Begelly Council 58, Loveston Council 23, Jeffreston N.P. 92, Carew N.P. 47, Rhydberth N.P. 35, New Hedges N.P. 36, Saundersfoot Council 85, Amroth Council 33, Crunwere N.P. 30, Ludchurch Council 32, Lawrenny N.P. 51. (It was suggested that Martletwy 27 might prefer entering this in preference to the Narberth Area.) The above schools had between them 138 Seniors over 12; for them an independent one-stream school could be established at Kilgetty, with a Child Clinic, Full Hall-gymnasium, Evening Activity Room and Library Branch.

In the Tenby Area (H) there were 3 town schools and 3 neighbouring schools with a total strength of 529 pupils: Tenby Council (all Standards) 271 Tenby Parochial (Mixed) 94, Tenby Parochial Infants 46, Penally N.P. 22, St. Florence N.P. 48 and Manorbier N.P. 48.

In the Tenby town schools there were 115 Seniors over 11 and in the rural schools 22 Seniors over 12, making a total of 137 Seniors, which would constitute a one-stream Senior School or Division, with premises containing a Hall-gymnasium, Evening Activity Room and a Child Clinic. There were also 46 Infants in the Parochial Schools and approximately 65 Infants in the Council School (of whom 23 were under 5). These two could be combined to form a single Infant Department of 111 Infants with a Nursery Class of 23. The Tenby Council School had 123 Juniors and the Parochial School 55 Juniors, constituting a total of 178.

The proposal for Tenby was that independent Infant and Senior Departments be placed in the Council School, for the extension of which a site had been purchased and that the Juniors should be placed at the Parochial School. This would leave Penally School with a strength of 22, as practically all the seniors from the village went into Tenby. Manorbier and St. Florence N.P. schools were not included in the Tenby area for this purpose.

Although this scheme of reorganisation was not the one eventually adopted after the Second World War, it provided a basis for discussion and a starting point for the incorporation of new ideas which had been evolved in the meantime.

The Director added an interesting supplement to his Memorandum, containing his opinions about school buildings, opinions which could have been applicable to counties other than his own:—

> Many of the problems which now confront this Authority arise from the substantial character of the out-of-date buildings at present existing. Many of them have been in existence for half a century. Had they been built to give a satisfactory service for from 25-30 years they would have been built at a lesser cost and could have been abandoned without the qualms which come when contemplating the abandonment of sound and substantial structures.

School premises reflect the educational ideas at the time of their erection. The ideas of 50 years ago have been greatly modified. . . The educational wisdom of this present age is, let us hope and believe, not final. To build structures of a considerable permanency assumes that this age has the monopoly of wisdom in educational matters. Our schools, therefore, should be so built as to last for little more than 20 to 25 years, and in such a way as to be easily adaptable to changing regulations and improved educational methods.

These were the views of Mr. D. T. Jones, part poet, part philosopher. He went on to recommend:

not ugly and makeshift premises of the timber type but of semi-permanent and attractive structures, which must be suitable for the purpose for which they are built . . . The real economy, however, lies in the fact that no unnecessary expense need be incurred, and to encumber education with school buildings which overstay their highest usefulness is not economy or good administration.

This Memorandum, drawn up in 1937, is of interest because it reveals the difficulties which confronted the Education Authority of a largely rural area and the outlook and reactions of its Director of Education when faced with official policy concerning the reform of Schools administered under the Board of Education's Elementary Code.

Meanwhile, the Board's Consultative Committee, with Mr. Will Spens, C.B.E. as Chairman, had been compiling its *Report on Secondary Education with Special Reference to Grammar Schools and Technical High Schools,* which was completed by 1938 and published in 1939. The distinguished Committee, originally 22 in number, began its work in 1933 and sat on 74 days between then and September 1938, while sub-committees dealt with various aspects of the Terms of Reference: 'To consider and report upon the organisation and interrelation of schools, other than those administered under the Elementary Code, which provide education beyond the age of 11+, regard being had in particular to the framework and content of the education of pupils who do not remain at school beyond the age of about 16.' The main body of the text, occupying 385 pages, is assembled under the following Chapter headings: Sketch of the Development of the Traditional Curriculum in Secondary Schools of Different Types in England and Wales; The Present Position (i.e. 1937) in Respect of Provision for

Secondary and Junior Education in England and Wales; A Brief Outline of the More Salient Features in the Physical and Mental Development of Children Between the Ages of 11+ and 16+; The Curriculum of the Grammar School; Scripture; Certain Other Subjects in which the Committee had recommended substantial changes, namely: English, Classics, Mathematics, General Science; The School Certificate Examination; Technical High Schools and other Technical Schools; Administration Problems; Welsh Problems; Principal Conclusions, Suggestions and Recommendations.

Brief reference will be made to the most important considerations and principal recommendations which are outlined in the Introduction to the 'Spens Report' followed by a summary of the main features of the Chapter headed 'Welsh Problems'.

In the first place reference was made to the Consultative Committee's previous publication *The Education of the Adolescent* 1926. While the Spens Committee accepted the two stages 'primary' and 'secondary' as successive periods in education with the change from one to the other at the age 11+, and while they adhered to the terms 'Grammar' and 'Modern' Schools as used in the 'Hadow Report', they included in their own final chapter a more satisfactory definition of 'adolescence' than the notion of it which had been too easily taken for granted earlier. So according to the Spens Report 'Adolescence or puberty is now regarded by psychologists not as a sudden interruption overtaking all children at the same age, but rather as the culmination of a slow process of growth which has been proceeding steadily from birth at varying rates in different invididuals'. There were matters which had been left over by the Hadow Committee, for example certain schools of a vocational or quasi-vocational type, problems of curriculum for Grammar School pupils leaving at 16 and the interrelation of schools other than those under the Elementary Code.

The Spens Report contained critical comments on Multilateral Schools, schools which by means of separate streams, would provide for all types of secondary education with the exception of that provided by Junior Technical Schools in so far as these depended upon their association with a Technical College. The characteristics were a good general education from 11+ for 2 or 3 years in a given area, with 4 or 5 streams, so that pupils at the age of 13 or 14 could follow courses best suited to their individual needs and capacity; there was a common core in the course, though it differed in time and emphasis, including, for example, a literary and linguistic course, mathematical and scientific courses and other courses leading on to technological studies, to commercial studies or to practical or artistic pursuits. The policy of substituting such Multilateral Schools for Grammar Schools, for Modern (Senior) Schools and to some extent for Junior Technical Schools had been recently advocated and had received considerable support. One of the attractions was the association of pupils with varied interests and abilities and the possibility of transfer without a change of school. Over against these advantages, the Spens Committee raised the following objections:—

(1) To provide a satisfactory number for each stream in the school its numbers would have to be 800 or more. 'We believe that the majority of pupils gain more from being in smaller schools.'

(2) The traditional part of the Sixth Form in the life of the school would only be possible if it contained a reasonably high proportion of the pupils in the school. This would be unlikely if only half or less were on the Grammar School side. It was generally difficult to secure adequate Sixth Forms in ordinary Grammar Schools on account of the large proportion of pupils leaving school at 16.

(The authors of the Report appear to have not taken into account the possibility that courses other than those of the academic Grammar School kind might attract a new element into the Sixth Form, as in fact happened when Greenhill School, Tenby, was reorganised on 'comprehensive lines' in the nineteen-sixties.)

(3) Where geographical and other conditions would admit of relatively large schools, there was much to be said for their being wholly of the Grammar School type, so making economically possible a considerable variety of Sixth Form Courses.

(4) Equal importance must be attached 'to the steady evolution of the curriculum and methods of teaching in Modern Schools' and 'to carrying further certain reforms in the curriculum of the Grammar Schools with which this Report will be concerned'. There was the risk, moreover, that if a 'Grammar' and 'Modern' curriculum existed in the same

school the former might, as a result of its long established prestige, exert an excessive influence on the latter. Therefore it was, in general, best for Grammar Schools and Modern Schools to exist and develop independently. If both were to be brought within the Multilateral Schools, there would be the additional problem of finding Heads capable of controlling and inspiring both developments.

(5) The special value of Junior Technical Schools depended upon their contact with the staff and the equipment of a Technical College. In consequence special 'courses' in Multilateral Schools would not be a satisfactory substitute for Junior Technical Schools.

The further argument was added that any general policy of establishing multilateral schools would 'now' be very expensive and 'it would be justified, more especially in view of the "Hadow reorganisation", only if it were clear that a substantial advantage would result. For the reasons given above we do not think this would be the case, and we cannot therefore recommend the general creation of multilateral schools, even as the goal of a long range policy.' Fortunately, or perhaps unfortunately, the Spens Committee had no crystal ball to enable them to see into the 'sixties' and 'seventies', when, at considerable cost premises for Comprehensive Schools were being constructed, including Pembrokeshire, when the fate of the Grammar Schools was the subject of hot debate and the future of secondary Education became a political issue, both in Parliament and in the constituencies.

From multilateral schools, the Report went on to discuss the problems of the Grammar School Curriculum. It was pointed out that the existing arrangements did not correspond with the structure of modern society and the economic facts of the situation. The Grammar School curriculum was still largely planned in the interests of pupils wishing to go to the university, despite the fact that 85% did not remain in school after the age of 16. However, it was important that the interests of both the Sixth Form and the 85% must be safeguarded. Pupils leaving school at 16 should have pursued courses complete in themselves. But in the interests of those who wished to continue an academic education at school or elsewhere and ultimately go to the university, it was important, that in the last year or possibly the last two years before the School Certificate Examination would be taken, such pupils should have instruction in the subject or subjects on which they would later specialise, of such a character as to lay the necessary foundations for their Sixth Form work. Part of the Report would be devoted to a detailed discussion of this problem.

It was emphasised that the prime duty of the Secondary School to provide for the needs of children passing through the adolescent stage: '... it is useless if not harmful, to try to inculcate ideas, however valuable they may be at a later stage of growth, which have at the time no bearing on a child's natural activities of mind and body and do nothing to guide his experience.' The traditional grammar school curriculum was 'still coloured by obsolete doctrines of the faculties and formal training.' Time-tables were overcrowded because of the endeavour to teach a wide range of subjects to the same high level. It was essential for this burden to be lightened and, that from the age of 13+ or as soon as special interests or aptitudes became evident, a pupil should concentrate on a smaller range of subjects, so long as these would include English, a language, and Science or Mathematics. To meet the conditions of modern life there should be changes in the emphasis to be laid on particular subjects and in the content of these subjects. Some of the changes recommended are noted briefly here.

First the English subjects: '... a curriculum, even for pupils up to the age of 16, gains greatly from being anchored round some main core or branch of study. This used to be provided by the study of the Classics. We share the opinion that in modern conditions it should be secured in and through what are often described as the English subjects. By these we mean careful training in comprehension of what is read and in the expression of ideas both orally and in writing; History; Geography (which is however, closely related also to the scientific subjects); English Literature and Scripture'. Neither Public Schools nor Grammar Schools had done all that might be done to educate the powers of comprehension and composition. While the importance of the classic periods of British history and ot the histories of Greece and Rome for an understanding of our own institutions and literature was recognised, there should be greater attention paid to the study of recent history by pupils under 16; recent political economic history would afford the best introduction to an interest in politics and should be so taught as to induce a balanced attitude and sound judgement. With regard to English Literature, it was recommended that set books should not be prepared for examinations, as the form of study involved did real harm to the growth of an interest in literature which ought rather to characterise a grammar school education. The important place to be occupied by Scripture in the curriculum would be dealt with in a special chapter as well as in the Report's discussion of 'Welsh Problems'.

Secondly, apart from the English subjects, it was desirable to see the study of at least one foreign language, but it was urged that the efforts of those pupils with relatively little linguistic ability should be concentrated on acquiring a capacity to read rather than to write the language in question.

Thirdly, the sciences: As alternatives to courses in particular sciences there should be courses in General Science, which should aim at relating science to everyday life and explaining its general principles and laws in a more popular manner than was possible in the early stages of a systemic study of any particular science. It was proposed that substantially less time than 'at present' should be given to Mathematics; but it should be taught to all and, so far as possible in such a way as to lead to the recognition that mathematics constituted one of the main achievements of the human mind.

Fourthly, the tendency to give more time and attention to physical education, to the artistic subjects and to handicrafts was considered to be of great importance and should be further developed.

One of the other recommendations of the Spens Committee should be mentioned. They were anxious that in country Grammar Schools a rural background and colour should be given to the teaching especially in General Science. For the most part they had in view not vocational training for agriculture, but rather the restoration of a widespread understanding of the countryside. But they hoped that local authorities would undertake the provision, in a certain number of the Country Grammar Schools, of courses with a definite 'agricultural bias' which would afford from about the age of 15 a preliminary vocational training. This proposal has a special local interest, in that part of the reorganisation programme of the Pembrokeshire Education Committee after the Second World War included the establishment of a Grammar School with agricultural courses on the Bush Estate at Pembroke.

The Committee recognised that their recommendations followed lines along which successful experiments had already been made; but they believed that reforms along the lines indicated should be concerted, general and more radical than hitherto. They had in mind particularly the contrast between courses primarily designed to lay the foundation for further study and those which were suitable when further academic study was in fact improbable, the relief of the curriculum for the individual pupil and the teaching of English composition They recognised also that carrying out these proposals would be impracticable without further and drastic reform of the School Certificate Examination, as indicated in the main body of the Report.

The discussion of the Grammar School curriculum was followed by observations about Vocational Schools, preparing for single definite vocations, and Junior Technical Schools, Junior Commercial Schools and Junior Art Schools each of which prepared for a variety of occupations. It was advocated that Vocational Schools in the narrow sense should not recruit before the age of 13 (14 with the raising of the school leaving age) and that in all the above schools a general education ought to be the primary concern until, at most, two years before the normal age of leaving school. Those Junior Technical Schools, which were based on engineering and the building industry demanded different treatment and it was recommended that they should be converted into Technical High Schools, equal in status to the Grammar Schools, providing a five years course from the age of 11+ with provision for engineering and other subjects in the last three years.

Importance was attached to the interrelation of schools of different types. There should be parity of status among secondary schools and, so that the transfer of pupils at the age of 13+ if found desirable, should be possible, the courses of study between the ages of 11 and 13 should not differ to any marked extent. While the provision of a modern language course might prove to be a problem in a Modern School, there should be some space for this in the curriculum to meet the needs of those who showed academic ability. Family circumstances often determined that pupils were destined to work 'with tongue and pen', even when their aptitudes pointed elsewhere. For pupils who

210

combined intellectual ability with a practical and especially strong mechanical bent the Technical High School would be a better alternative than the Modern School. As parents were still influenced by the prestige of the Grammar Schools, it was vital to establish parity of status and a uniform leaving age for Grammar Schools, Technical High Schools and Modern Schools. It was therefore recommended that three types of school should be conducted under a new Code of Regulations for Secondary Schools, that there should be similar standards for the size of classes and for the planning and assessment of school buildings, save in so far as differences in curriculum justified different requirements. Another measure to secure parity of schools would be a reform of the salary scales so that a teacher's remuneration would no longer depend upon the type of school in which he was serving; posts paid on the higher Secondary Scale should be made available in all schools, though not in the same proportion. Then there was the question of what should be done about fees, which were chargeable in the Grammar Schools but not in the Modern Schools. It was desirable that the Grammar Schools and Technical High Schools should be placed on an equal footing with the Modern Schools through the abolition of fees as soon as the national financial situation would permit; in other words, the Committee were advocating free secondary school education for all. But meanwhile the Special Place System should be overhauled. Where the cost of education in a school was being reduced for all parents by substantial grants from public funds the children whose parents were being thus assisted should be those who would most benefit from the schooling in question. The conclusion was reached that the system known as '100 per cent. Special Places' should be generally adopted in such schools, subject to the reform being undertaken gradually and subject to certain safeguards, including the method of selection and regard for the practice of granting maintenance allowances.

It was appropriate that the Spens Committee devoted a special Chapter to 'Welsh Problems'. The Committee recognised that, in addition to those common with England, Wales had problems of its own. Reference was made to the Welsh Intermediate Education Act 1889 as evidence of the great demand for this type of education, which bridged the gap between the elementary schools and the university colleges, a function which had previously been only partly performed by the few

211

endowed grammar schools. It was observed that when the school leaving age had been raised to 14+, the Intermediate Schools ceased to be 'Intermediate' in their original sense and that they tended to grow at both ends by admitting more pupils at 11 and even 10 and by retaining pupils until 18 or 19. Some county authorities, in framing schemes under the Intermediate Education Act had paid less attention to the 'technical' side of education than the Act appeared to intend. (as defined in Clause 17). In fact, there was a deficiency of Technical Schools of all kinds and there was a great need, especially in rural areas, for schools which would undertake both Intermediate and Technical education: 'Until recently few schools have provided courses "applicable to the purposes of agriculture, industries, trade or commercial life and practice" for pupils who cannot follow, or do not require ordinary courses in literature, science and mathematics'.

One of the obstacles to the provision of alternative 'intermediate' and 'technical' courses had been the small size of many of the schools. A Central Welsh Board investigation in 1916 had revealed that about 25% of the schools had less than 100 pupils and a further 25% between 100 and 125. Limitations of staffing, curricula and general facilities were common to all small County Schools. Numbers on school rolls had been limited to some extent through the handicap of late admission. There had been a marked tendency for boys and girls to enter at the age of 12, or even later, so shortening the course. Parents, teachers, and school managers in rural areas had been inclined to restrain children from entering at an ealier or more appropriate age, a situation to which parents and Governing Bodies should give their close attention. Statistics giving the number of pupils in grant-aided Secondary Schools on 31 March 1937 showed an improvement in the situation since 1916. The figures for Wales (with the number of schools in brackets), were as follows:— Under 100 (3), 100 and under 150 (11), 150 and under 200 (17), 200 and under 250 (18), 250 and under 300 (134), 300 and under 400 (38), 400 and under 500 (30), 500 and under 600 (2), 600 and over (nil). According to these returns, 183 out of a total of 253 of the schools had less than 300 pupils on the books and there were still 14 schools with less than 150. However, the Spens Committee stated: '. . . it may be found that the schools generally are now in a position to carry out more completely the schemes of education which were foreshadowed by the authors of the Welsh Intermediate Education Act'.

Elsewhere in the Report, the Committee had suggested the establishment of small Grammar Schools which could incorporate Modern Schools,and they considered that such a proposal might be found specially applicable to conditions in some Welsh areas. A Departmental Committee's enquiry into secondary education in Wales and Monmouth in the year 1929 had already brought forth the advice, concerning Welsh rural areas, that alternations in the Secondary Schools Regulations should be made to render it permissible to carry in the same building the two types of education (a) that for children up to the age of 16 and over, and (b) that for children up to the age of 15. In the light of this and of various memoranda issued by the Welsh Department (Board of Education) after consultation with a Joint Committee representing the Board of Education, the University of Wales, the local education authorities and the teachers, the Spens Committee recommended 'that the whole question be re-examined, and that the particular solution of the problem contemplated by the Departmental Committee in 1929 be seriously reconsidered in the light of the suggestions we have made for the establishment of "Small Grammar Schools which incorporate Modern (Senior) Schools" '.

The Spens Committee noted that the Welsh language was being given a prominent place in the curriculum by local education authorities and that various methods had been adopted to cope with the problem of bilingualism. (Though many Welshmen would deny that enough prominence was being given to their language in the schools at that time.) It was suggested that the standard in English to be expected of boys and girls in Welsh Grammar Schools need not be lower than in the Grammar Schools of England. In view of the bilingual problem, it was strongly recommended that there should be a more generous provision of books in English and Welsh for class use and for library use in the Welsh schools.

Another feature of Welsh education was that a high proportion of the child population already attended the Intermediate Schools. There were fewer fee-paying pupils in Wales and the 100 per cent special place system had been more extensively adopted there than in England. Witnesses had drawn attention to the insistent demand for free secondary education, which was not surprising in view of the depression in the industrial parts of South Wales. Because of these characteristics the

213

Welsh Intermediate Schools appeared ripe for the form of development which had been outlined in the Report.

Also there were recommendations concerning the curriculum. It was proposed that liberal provisions should be made, as had already been done in some places, for the teaching of Arts and Crafts, Speech Training, Music and Dramatic Art and the History of Wales in connection with Welsh Literature and with physical and economic geography. In particular, it was suggested that the teaching of Art should be given a measure of attention similar to that given to the teaching of languages and science. The Committee commended to the Welsh schools the full use of the methods of religious instruction prescribed in the Report. Witnesses representing the Federation of Welsh Education Authorities insisted that the Welsh Sunday School tradition clearly demanded this: 'There is probably no part of the country where there is so general an agreement in favour of Biblical instruction for the children as in Wales. It is the view of the Federation that Religious Instruction and a knowledge of the Bible should be an integral and active part of the curriculum for Secondary School pupils.'

This Welsh section of the Report closed with a reference to the Central Welsh Board, mentioning its origin and constitution and its close co-operation with the Welsh Department of the Board of Education and with the University of Wales. The authors of the Report did not feel themselves able to offer a definite opinion on a proposal which had been made to convert the Central Welsh Board into a National Council of Education.

The Spens Report looked back to Hadow and pointed the way forward to R. A. Butler's White Paper on *Educational Reconstruction* 1943 and to the Education Act of 1944; but meanwhile came the second World War in September 1939, the muddle of evacuation, the 'black out', National Service, the 'phoney war', Dunkirk, the Battle of Britain the Blitz and an almost unrelieved series of disasters down to 1942.

In July of that year J. T. Griffith retired. Under the provisions of the Education Act of 1936 the school leaving age was to have been raised to 15 on 1 September 1939, but this and other educational reforms had to be shelved, but only temporarily, for the social impact of evacuation, the bombs, the destruction of property and the civilian casualties were accompanied by the resurgence of hope, so that once again, in the midst of war the educationists were at work with their plans for the future. Between the period of the First World War and the Second, thousands of pages and millions of words had been poured out in the form of Reports on Education, Education Acts, Official Regulations, books and theses, examination scripts, Inspectors' Reports, Head Masters' Official Returns and Reports to their Managers, not to mention Minutes of Education Committees and School Governors up and down the country. During all this time, while generations of pupils had come and gone at Tenby County Intermediate School and membership of the staff there had changed again and again. J. T. Griffith had remained in charge, changing yet unchanged during a period of social revolution, epoch-making discoveries, military and political upheavals. It is time to return to the year 1911 so as to trace the development of the school and follow its fortunes during the long period of J.T.'s tenure of office.

Section 2: Greenhill Problems in the Griffith period

The first problem was related to the cleavage between Messrs. Allen and Stokes, key members of the Governing Body of the School. This must have been a considerable embarrassment to Mr. J. T. Griffith for some time after his appointment. For about twelve years the Head faced a succession of difficulties, which made his task a daunting one. From 1911 to 1914 there was a long drawn-out struggle before the School's Maintenance Account could be placed on a satisfactory footing; then came the stresses and strains caused by the Great War, followed by post-war adjustments and economies, and, in 1922 an unfortunate dispute between Mr. Griffith and members of his staff.

The story of how the Managers, the L.E.A. and the Board of Education dealt with the financial situation at Greenhill is illustrative of what happened in some of the other intermediate Schools, although there were variations in local circumstances. An outline of the main events will include a reference to the new Scheme regulating the Pembrokeshire Intermediate and Technical Education Fund, which was brought into operation in 1912. That financial worries were not peculiar to Tenby is revealed in the County Schools Audit Report made to the Higher Education Committee on 28 July 1911; it was stated that there were Debit Balances at Fishguard £479. 6s. 9d., at Pembroke Dock £395. 11s. 9d., Tenby £448. 13s. 6d., and St. David's

£13. 14s. 1d.   In Tenby there were uncertainties over the payment of salaries, the permanent staff was restricted to four in 1911 and reduced to three the following year.   Matters were brought to a head in 1912 by Mr. Egerton Allen, whose letter dated, 23 March and addressed to the Director of Education, was placed before the Education Committee at its April meeting and, in consequence, before the Governors at a Special Meeting on 6 May.   The main points of Mr. Allen's letter were as follows:—

(1)   On 15 February he had written to the Clerk of the Education Committee, finding great fault with the financial administration of the Tenby County School, pointing out an overdraft of £337 at the Bank and urging the L.E.A. to interfere in the financial interests of the School.

(2)   At a meeting of the Governors on 23 March, when there was no quorum, he was informed that the Bank Account was overdrawn £303. Although a number of accounts were on the table, he was refused information on the total amount due.   Among them was the sum of £89. 13s. 8d. for services of a Loan.   Two of the items on the Agenda were the Head Master's Report and the signing of cheques.   As there was no quorum, neither was dealt with.

(3)   The Head Master's Annual Report was presented at a meeting on 13 December 1911, when there was also no quorum.   His (Mr. Allen's) copy of the Report was enclosed; it revealed a sufficiently serious condition of the school, yet no mention of this Report was made at the January Meeting in 1912.   'As you are aware, I have continually protested against the way in which the School is managed and today I am determined that I should not rest until the present system is completely altered by all the Managers taking part in the management and withdrawing from Mr. Stokes the uncontrolled power which he at present exercises.   I allege that the Managers are completely shut out from any knowledge or control of the affairs of the School and every effort I make to obtain knowledge is frustrated by Mr. Stokes.   I will not continue to hold my position as a Representative Manager of the County Council unless I am supported by the Education Committee and I hereby resign my position if the Education Committee decline to interfere.'

(4)   Mr. Allen asked that two steps should be taken:
    (i)   that an enquiry should be held by the Management.
    (ii)   that no money should be paid to the Managers of the School

216

until an enquiry had been held. That all monies due and payable to the School should be held by the Education Committee and all claims and accounts for payment should be sent to the Education Committee and satisfied so far as the Education Committee thought right, out of the monies so withheld.

(5) He was sending a copy of his letter to Mr. Stokes.

In addition to Mr. Allen's letter, there was before the Meeting of the Governors a statement, which had been signed by six of them and addressed to the Director of Education:—

We the undersigned Governors of the Tenby County School protest at the statements contained in Mr. Egerton Allen's letter to you, dated 23rd March last, as Mr. Stokes has never in any way interfered in the management of the School other than with full approval and consent.

Mr. Clement Williams is the Chairman and Mr. Stokes is the Vice-Chairman and both have done their best for the welfare of the School. In fact, if it had not been for the financial assistance that they have given to the maintenance of the School, it would have been impossible to carry it on as long as we have.

Only about 12 months ago an Enquiry was held by your Board when the Governors were recommended to cut down their expenses and in order do do so they reduced the Staff by one Assistant Master and the Manual Instructor, who came one day a week, and the Art Master who came two days a week. Unfortunately the number of pupils attending the School has, during the last year, been between 60 and 70, whereas during the previous year the number was 80 to 90 and consequently the earnings of the School have considerably diminished, the total loss on the year being £133, as compared with the year before, made up as follows:

	£	s.	d.
Loss on Technical Grant	22	7	8
School Fees	63	0	0
Board of Education Grant	46	0	0
S. T. Fees	1	13	4
	133	0	7

From this you will see how impossible it was to keep the Assistant Masters that the Head Master requires.

We should mention that the debit balance due to the Treasurer on 31st March 1911 was £448.13s.6d., on the 31st March 1912 the debit balance was £262, to which should be added about £133 unpaid bills, the principal sum being £89 instalment on loans, which in the ordinary way would have been paid, but, in consequence of Mr. Egerton Allen's opposition, Mr. Williams and Mr. Stokes declined to sign any cheques, either in payment of these accounts or for salaries until the decision of the Education Committee is come to in the matter, which we need not say is most injurious to the School.

Yours faithfully,

W. G. Parcell, May Parcell, E. M. Milward,

N. Chetwode Ram. T. Lodwig, Evans, John Jones.

After the above letter had been read, Mr. Allen said that he had not received a copy. The Governors then resolved that he should be sent one and then turned their attention to the next important business, which was the payment of salaries.

The manoeuvres of the Governors in dealing with the payment of salaries were to have interesting consequences later. Since Mr. C. J. Williams and Mr. C. W. R. Stokes had declined to sign any cheques, and as these had to be signed by the Chairman, Mr. Williams vacated the Chair and Mr. T. John was voted to the Chair 'pro tem'. Mr. Lodwig Evans then proposed and Mr. Allen seconded 'that cheques for salaries be signed'. and they were signed in respect of the Clerk, the Head Master and staff.

On 16 May 1912 at the Head Master's House there was a joint conference of the L.E.A., the Director of Education, and members of the Governing Body. Following a lengthy discussion it was decided to refer the situation at the School to the Board of Education. Matters were now overtaken by events for the Governing Body was reconstituted under a new Scheme which had received the official approval of His Majesty in Council on 14 May 1912. Under this Scheme the Clerks of the County Schools were required to make arrangements for the election of Representative Governors, in the course of July and August. Much of the 1894 Scheme was retained, but there were changes, some of which will be mentioned briefly, while a more detailed account will be given in Appendix C.

The Charity Commission was replaced by the Board of Education, as the channel through which central funds would be made available and as the body to whom the County Council would be responsible for their appropriate use. The County Council was to continue to pay into the General Fund the product of a halfpenny rate, the Exchequer Contribution, the Treasury Grant and certain stated endowments as before. After deductions for the purposes of administration, examination, inspection, scholarships, exhibitions and liabilities in respect of endowments, the County Council were responsible for all disbursements payable out of the General Fund to the Intermediate Schools. As provided by the Balfour Act of 1902, there were powers delegated by the County Council to the Local Education Committee. The School Districts listed in the Second Schedule of the Scheme remained the same as before and so did the arrangements for the administration of District Funds. There were clauses concerning the governing bodies of the Intermediate Schools. The qualifications for membership were defined and so were the Governors' responsibilities, and the rules for the conduct of business and the holding of elections. The composition of the Boards of Governors was set out in the Third Schedule. In the case of Tenby the representation was to be as follows:— County Council 4 (of whom at least one must be a woman); the Town Council, after whom the District was named 2; District Councillors representing the Parishes included in the School District 1; Managers of Public Elementary Schools in the School District 1; Bodies of Managers of Non-provided Schools in the District 1; Co-optative 3 (including at least one woman). The total of 12 members was 2 less than under the 1894 Scheme, which had included subscribers of £5 and over. The County Council now had 4 representatives instead of 3 and the District Councils, which came into being under the Local Government Act of 1894, were represented instead of the Boards of Guardians. Part VI of the Scheme dealt with requirements for the County Schools: buildings, accommodation, facilities, the Head Master and Staff, organisation and curriculum, the conditions concerning the admission of pupils. In Part VII there were certain changes affecting Free Places, Maintenance Allowances and County Exhibitions.

The election of Governors of the County Schools took place in July-

August 1912, and during the rest of the year the newly elected Governors and the Education Authority continued to wrestle with the financial problems, including the refusal of the Governors to accept responsibility for the debts of their predecessors, the payment of salaries and charges of interest on overdrafts.

After much wrangling the full Education Committee agreed that the Technical Grant due to Tenby County School should be paid at once, and the Director informed the Governors that this payment was being made immediately 'in view of the fact that teachers had not been paid for some time.' In consequence, when the Governors met on 13 November, cheques were drawn in favour of the Head Master and staff. Meanwhile in October, the Governors of Fishguard County School had sent a letter to the L.E.A. and copies to all County Schools in Pembrokeshire, calling attention to the serious financial difficulties of some of the schools, challenging the power of the Local Government Board's Auditor to surcharge interest on overdrafts, and proposing a joint meeting of representatives of the Intermediate Schools and the Higher Education Sub-Committee. The meeting was held at the Shire Hall, Haverfordwest on 20 November and was attended by representatives of the Governors of Fishguard, Milford Haven, St. David's, Pembroke Dock, Tasker's and Tenby—but not Narberth. The proceedings of this conference were reported to a full meeting of the L.E.A. on 22 November; and here at last, came a piece of good news for Tenby. The Education Committee had received a telegram from the Board of Education, stating that the Board were of the opinion 'that the proposed grant of £250 to Tenby County School may properly be paid.' Accordingly the Committee agreed that the sum of £250 should be paid and that particulars of overdrafts should be sent to the Board of Education and the Local Government Board with a request for advice as to the best means of relieving the schools which were in debt. By 29 November the Special Grant had been forwarded to the Tenby Governors. It was found that this money together with the Term's Grant under the new Scheme and certain other sums would be enough to settle all liabilities except the overdraft due to the former Treasurer.

A letter from the Director of Education asked for details of the disbursement of the Special Grant and one from the Board of Education made it clear that under Clause 2 of the Scheme of 14 May 1912 the Governors were responsible for the administration of the District Fund and for the liabilities of the previous Managers. It was for the Governors to consider the need for a scheme, as already requested by the L.E.A., to provide for the gradual or immediate removal of the deficit. When a further reminder of this matter arrived in December the Governors instructed their Clerk to reply that they were not in a position to formulate any scheme and that they felt compelled to ask the Authority to place the School on a satisfactory basis. This business dragged on through the year 1913 and on into 1914, with the Governors trying to throw the onus on the the Education Committee, who for their part maintained that the income provided under the new Scheme was enough to carry on the school efficiently and that the Governors should arrange their expenditure accordingly. They resorted among other things to a reduction of Fees with the intention of increasing the number of admissions.

Despite all the difficulties, prospects were brightening. According to the Report of the Chief Inspector of the Central Welsh Board on 6 May 1913, the school could be congratulated upon its improved financial position and there was a need for an increase in staff so as to give some relief to the Head Master. Further good news came in July when the Governors were informed that the Auditors were prepared to remit the surcharges which had been made on overdrafts. On the eve of the Michaelmas Term 1913, Mr. T. John, Chairman of the Governing Body, told his colleagues that there was a sum of £700 in the Estimates to put Tenby and Fishguard on a sound basis. However when the L.E.A.'s Finance Sub-committee, on 16 September, considered a recommendation of the Higher Education Committee that £300 should be paid to Fishguard and £100 to Tenby, they cut these amounts to £200 and £50 respectively. On 4 October a Special Meeting of the Governors received this Grant of £50, which had been sanctioned by the Education Committee on condition it was used to reduce the overdraft of £154. 14s. 6d. due to the old Treasurer. A cheque was drawn accordingly, so leaving £104. 14s. 6d. outstanding. By 31 March 1914 the Governors' Finance Sub-Committee were able to report that they had gone into the Receipts and Expenditure for the coming year and thought it possible that they could have a Credit Balance of about £80 in twelve months' time. With this prospect in mind they recommended that the Head Master's capitation allowance should be increased to 35 shillings. The Governors agreed to this proposal and in addition, resolved that in line with the practice in other schools the Head should be admitted to all their meetings.

At last, on 29 May 1914, the outstanding debt to the former Treasurer was cleared. The Chairman explained to his fellow Governors that the Higher Education Committee had considered the financial position of the school a week previously and had recommended that the sum of £146. 13s. 7d. be granted to the Tenby School to wipe out the debt of the old Managers, only to meet with last ditch resistance from the Finance Committee, who threw out this recommendation four days later. The Chairman went on to say that, at a meeting of the Education Committee that very day (29 May), he had protested against the action of the Finance Committee and that he was glad to inform the Governors that the recommendation had been confirmed and that the grant would be received.

The improvement in the situation is illustrated in Appendix B by accounts for the years ending 31 March 1912, 1915 and 1916—a debit balance in the first and credit balances on the other two. By 31 March 1915 the Governors were able to increase the Head Masters' capitation allowance to £2 per pupil and pay the rates on his house.

So it was that by the beginning of June 1914 the school finances had been placed on a satisfactory footing, but two months later came the outbreak of war, with its new and unforseen anxieties.

Some of the local effects of the Great War (1914-1918) may be gleaned from the Minutes of the Pembrokeshire L.E.A. and of the Tenby County School Governors, from the Head Master's Annual Reports to the Governors and from recollections of Old Greenhillians.

On 17 November 1914 the Higher Education Sub-committee received through the Board of Education, a circular from the War Office asking that teachers under 35 years of age, having experience in Physical Exercises and Drill should be given every facility to enlist in the Army; the matter was referred to the local Governors. At a meeting of the Tenby Governors on 5 March 1915, they heard that one of the staff, Mr. John Peate B.A. (Latin, History, English and Drill) had obtained a Commission in the Army and the Governors expressed their pleasure at the fact that Mr. Peate had decided to serve his country. At this same meeting the Head Master reported that the scholars had sold about £7 worth of flags on behalf of the Welsh Soldiers Fund, on St.

David's Day, and that the school had sent a donation of £5 to the County War Fund. At the end of the month the L.E.A. notified the Governing Bodies of County Schools of certain instructions contained in Board of Education Circular 893, stating that Pembrokeshire was within the area of the Western Command (H.Q. at Chester) and that the Army Council had issued instructions that schools maintained by Local Education Authorities were not to be occupied for billeting troops without the consent of the Authorities concerned. The L.E.A. also gave consideration to Circular 88 (Wales), laying down the terms upon which the Army Council would pay compensation for the military occupation of school buildings. Although Tenby was a garrison town for the duration of the war, the school premises were not asked for. In June and July came further instructions from the Board; Education Authorities were to notify teachers of the terms of holiday employment in munitions, as soon as possible; the importance of economy in food was stressed, Cookery Teachers, were to be asked to give lectures to housewives on this subject, and all teachers were to make pupils aware of the necessity for thrift. The Head Master's Report for the Session September 1914 to July 1915 contains the statement: 'The School has a proud record to show in its response to the country's call in this great crisis. It is a difficult task to make the list complete, but up to the present the roll contains 15 "Old Boys" who hold Commissions in the Army or Navy, and over 60 who are serving as private soldiers. We shall doubtless set up a "roll of honour" of these our "old boys" at an early date.'

In October of the new session the Head stated that the staff by that time consisted of ladies only and that he wished to be relieved of classes in Woodwork so as to attend to the supervision of the school. The Governors agreed to authorise the Head Master to appoint a qualified instructor locally at a salary of not over £20. Inevitably there arose the question of enlistment of Head Masters. On 19 November, 1915, the Chairman informed the Governors that the Head Master had been 'waited upon' by canvassers with a view to his enlistment under the Derby Scheme. In the Chairman's opinion Mr. J. T. Griffith's services were indispensable and he could not be spared. It was resolved that Mr. Griffith be asked to inform the canvassers that the Governors regarded the services of the Head Master as indispensable and that for this reason he was unable to offer himself for Military Service.

In the same month, a similar resolution was passed by the Higher Education Sub-Committee when considering a Board of Education circular concerning the release of Masters in Secondary Schools for military service, 'That the Governors of County Schools be notified that the Committee considers Head Masters to be indispensable to their respective schools and cannot be spared for military service, and that if any are called up in accordance with the new scheme of recruiting, the Committee will submit their objections to the local tribunal.' The first stage of conscription was introduced through the First Military Service Act in January 1916, making service compulsory for unmarried men between 18 and 41. The Act included a promise that none would be called up until the age of $18\frac{1}{2}$ and that none would be sent abroad until 19 years of age—a concession which was withdrawn in 1918. On 19 December, the Chairman reported that the Head Master had been attested under the recruiting scheme and suggested that the Clerk should be instructed to take the necessary steps to secure exemption. The Governors agreed that an appeal on their behalf should be lodged with the Local Tribunal. On 2 February 1916 the Clerk informed the Governors that the Head had been put back to Group 27 under the Scheme and that another application would be needed when the call-up came for this particular Group. At this same meeting, when the Rector, the Rev. B. C. Edwards asked whether a pamphlet, entitled 'Patriotism', which the Board of Education proposed as a subject of instruction, had been received he was told that the L.E.A. would be sending copies to schools. On 2 June a Central Welsh Board circular was received, explaining the need to obtain exemption for students of military age to complete their studies and sit their examinations; it so happened that, at that time, there was no pupil of military age at Greenhill. Another circular from the same source concerned the possibility of utilising the services of masters and boys at harvest time. The Head Master was to draw attention to this and advise any who were interested to register with the Labour Bureau. In his Report for the Session 1915-16, Mr. Griffith referred to the difficulties of running the school under wartime conditions:

'The exceptional circumstances ruling during the session presented new and difficult problems. The school has largely increased in numbers, and our numbers were far in excess of the supposed accommodation of the school. Added to this was the experience—unique for a secondary school—of having the assistant staff composed entirely of mistresses. It is hardly necessary to add that the session has been one of great anxiety, and what the ultimate effect of these conditions will be is difficult to estimate, but every effort was made to render the organisation and instruction effective, with as little disturbance as possible of the normal curriculum of the school.'

He returned to the subject of the service record of the school, again underlining the difficulty of finding out how many of the old scholars were engaged. The question of Mr. J. T. Griffith's own 'call-up' arose again at a Governors' meeting on 20 June 1917; he had received a notice from the Tenby Borough Tribunal, intimating that his exemption from military service was subject to his joining Section B of the Pembrokeshire Volunteer Regiment. When the situation was investigated it transpired that the Head's name was not on the list of those heard by the Tribunal, and that appears to have been the end of the matter. The position of women teachers was given attention in a Board of Education circular, reminding them of the national importance of their work and asking them not to move out of the profession. In case of difficulty they could make use of the Professional Register at the Central Office of Employment, Queen Anne's Chambers, Westminster.

During the remainder of the war, the Head Master's Reports mention the anxieties experienced, notably the difficulties of running a dual school and fulfilling the requirements of the curriculum without any assistant masters on the staff. Prominence was given to the 'service record' of past pupils. By July 1918 the list of those who had served in His Majesty's Forces in one capacity or another contained over 150 names. According to the Headmaster's records, the supreme sacrifice had been made by former members of staff J. R. Roberts and J. Peate and by Old Boys Lloyd Davies, Hugh Slater Glanville, Norman Green, Bertie John, Hugh John, Joseph John, J. Wesley Howells, Arthur Lord, John Murray, Charles Ormond, Teddie Richards and Arthur Smith.

At the end of the Easter term 1918 the scholars produced an opera (The Burgomaster's Daughter) at the Royal Gatehouse Assembly Rooms. The proceeds, nearly £70, were handed over to war organisations in Tenby, thus bringing the total raised by the pupils for such purposes since the beginning of the war to approximately £200. Here it is convenient to notice two communications from the Board of Education, concerning school pupils and the war effort, which were not mentioned by Mr. Griffith in his Reports. The first, received by the Governors on 31 August 1917, drew attention to the importance of collecting and preserving horse chestnuts for use in connection with munitions. The second, which could be regarded as a significant comment upon the man power situation, was a circular placed before the L.E.A. on 22 March 1918, concerning the National Registration Amendment Act, calling upon boys of 15 and upwards to register themselves.

In addition to matters associated with the war, the Head Master's Annual Reports provide a cross section of the work of the school in the face of exceptional conditions. The Reports range from admissions and numbers on the roll to examination successes, from staffing problems and inspections to Old Pupils' successes, from Prize Days to recreative interests, from awareness of educational developments to the philosophising and moralising of which J.T. was so fond. For example, in reviewing the work of the school for the Session 1916-17, he wrote ' . . . one cannot but refer to the educational reconstruction which is now in progress, and the part our schools have to play in it. "Our Secondary Schools," declared Dr. Fisher, the President of the Board of Education, (see Chap. IV. Sec. 1) "are the key of the situation. Our Elementary teachers must be trained in the secondary school; our professional men, our University students, and our leaders in industry and commerce should have a full secondary school education." . . . The war, amongst other things, has taught us not least that "the day is with them that know;" that the untrained man or woman relying on accidents of birth or character runs an unequal race against those whose native gifts have been intensified by training at the hands of experts. Our present system of education, with all its merits and faults is, and our improved system will be, the measure of our success in learning this. To our unfaith in education we owe the fact that so many of our people enter upon life's work all too ill-equipped to play their part; and to this also we must attribute many of our social evils, against which we struggle in vain.' Mr. Griffith returned to a similar theme in his Report for 1917-18: 'This school will be called upon in the very immediate future to play its part in the development of our education system and life . . . Up to the present the close limitation of expenditure in all branches of educational organisations has resulted, with the best will in the world on the part of teachers, parents and governing bodies, in the fact that only a small percentage (less than 10 per cent) of the scholars pass to a place of higher education. With this standard the ninety per cent complete their early education without that sound general knowledge, that power to think freely and truly, without that equipment for life, in body, mind and spirit which is essential to a progressive nation. The much increased support from the Treasury which will be forthcoming should provide for the extension of our premises, already taxed to the utmost, and enable us to provide further education of a really productive type for this great number, and assist in the widening of the high road to the University for those who deserve to go there'.

This same report revealed the good progress which the school was making, despite many trying circumstances. The total number of scholarships and free places awarded was 22; these, together with 21 others admitted during the school year made a total of 43 new scholars for the session. The number on the roll had continued to increase, the figure for the three terms being 127, 126 and 123. In recent years there had been improved results in the Central Welsh Board Examinations. In the year 1916-17, 26 candidates had sat and all were successful; in the year under review, 36 had sat and 35 were successful: one at the Higher Certificate stage, 14 at the Senior Certificate level (four of whom obtained the Matriculation equivalent of the University of Wales), and 20 at the Junior stage, with a total of 27 distinctions—10 in the Senior and 17 in the Junior Examinations. On 7 and 8 March there had been a full inspection by three of the staff of the Central Welsh Board and as a result the Inspectorate had warmly congratulated the Governors upon the highly efficient state of the school. As in previous years, the Head made reference to additions which had been made to the library (then housed in two glass cupboards, one upstairs for the girls and one downstairs for the boys), which was much used and greatly appreciated. Every year since his appointment to the Headship Mr. Griffith had lamented the fact that the pupils did not have the regular use of a playing field and he returned to the same theme in the 1916-17 Report. As the playing of cricket was out of the question,

227

efforts had been directed to the success of the swimming club under the supervision of Mr. Dickinson, a local enthusiast who for many years devoted his spare time to teaching local children to swim in the sea.

Within three weeks of the Armistice in November 1918, the Local Education Authority resolved to support a resolution urging the release of teachers as soon as possible. When some staff vacancies were being filled at the beginning of the session in September 1918, one of those appointed was Miss M. F. Howells, B.A.; and then at the commencement of the Easter Term 1919 the Head Master was fortunate in securing the services as Science Master of Mr. H. J. Williams, B.Sc., newly released from a wartime appointment as works chemist in H.M. Factory at Pembrey, and the first assistant master on the Tenby Staff since 1915. Both Miss Howells and Mr. Williams were destined to stay long enough to exert through their own particular qualities an important influence on the life of the school. In the year 1919 it was decided that the practice of having School Boarders would be discontinued and that the Head would be vacating the School House, which would be altered with the object of providing 'more accommodation and better facilities for the working of the school'. The Head, in his Report for the year 1918-19, observed: 'The expanding force of the life of the school has demanded these alterations— even with the larger premises we may be sure that still further extensions will be necessary if the school is to be identified with the bold educational reforms of the recent Education Act.' Of course, Mr. J. T. Griffith did not then realise how limited the 'bold educational reforms' of the Fisher Act were to be in practice; neither could he foresee that during the remainder of his long period in office the only further extensions to the premises would be an insignificant addition to the gymnasium and one hut in the playground. However, the outlook of the 1918-19 Report is forward-looking and hopeful. 'The demands', wrote Mr. Griffith, 'on the staff are ever increasing, and the first essential to a more complete and effective organising of the school, with a view of realising our aims and ambitions, is the provision of a larger teaching staff. This would enable us to develop more fully the varying talents, aptitudes and abilities of the pupils, to exert a wider and a deeper influence, and to secure a larger measure of usefulness. I am anxious that the life of the school shall be a process of discovery, not oppressed by our past achievements, but stimulated by them, conscious of the possibilities before us, believing that our fullest and best is yet to be'.

Among the many reminiscences of this period are those of Doris Davies (née Kingdom) daughter of Harbourmaster Kingdom and younger sister of Mrs. Alfred Hullah (née Grace Kingdom) who was at Greenhill during the last five years of Adams' Headship, and who became an uncertified teacher until her marriage. Her children Denis, Donald, David, Esmé and June attended the school in turn. Doris recalls on tape how '1914 brought war, and to those of us who lived through it, the whole world changed but our Head Master remained. Mr. Peate joined the army and Mr. Hughes went into munitions. In their places we were supplied with three new mistresses. An increase in numbers warranted an extra mistress. Miss Jones' teaching in Chemistry was very good and it obtained excellent results. Miss Olsson, a Swedish lady, tried with a grim determination to squeeze the best out of each one of us and, the classes being small, this was possible then. I remember that a somewhat lazy boy, whom she knew, to be intelligent, was one of her targets and I have a vivid memory of her saying to him: "I'll get you through the (C.W.B.) Exam. if I have to carry you on my back". She did so too—but by sheer personality—not on her back! The third new mistress, Miss Keeting, took History. She was a very hard worker and a real friend of mine, but she had not the same capacity of getting her subject over as the other mistresses (including the French Mistress, Miss Stephens, who had been there since before the war). She was too gentle but we all respected her and gave no trouble . . .

'One incident remains in my mind. We arrived at school one morning in time to see the Head Master rushing off on the back of a motor bike to Carmarthen hoping to be in time to prevent one of his older boarders, a boy named Prydderch, from joining the army. He was about $16\frac{1}{2}$ I suppose but a big fellow—and youths at that time rushed to join by putting their age on. The Head Master was too late. Prydderch had "taken the 1/-" and was in. . . . I would like to think that he survived, for these lads were very brave. Unfortunately they had no idea what war really meant—especially in the 1914-18 Soldiers' War— with the horrors of trench warfare.'

The Head's anxiety can be understood. William Thomas Prydderch, son of a Minister of the Gospel of Nant-y-Moel, Glamorgan, was a new-comer, having been in Form V not quite two terms. According to an entry in the Admission Register, he left on 16 March 1915, and a note in the leaving column reads 'Joined the Army'.

The same old student whose reminiscences have just been quoted had interesting experiences in wartime—many of which illuminate the social life of the time. She sat her Junior Certificate Examination in 1915, the Senior in 1916 and the Senior a second time in 1917, so securing her Matriculation. However, she could not afford to go to the University and decided to do war work, much to the annoyance of the Head Master, who, she recalls, gave her a 'dressing down' in the street, in the rain. On the strength of her Senior Certificate she was accepted for service in a Recruiting Office in Cardiff, where 200 women were employed. The men in the Office in Bute Town were war wounded, the head himself having suffered from shell-shock. There were no typewriters and clerical work was done by hand. She remembers that, at the time colliers were being called up, she read a letter from a collier's wife who begged: 'Please call my husband up; he's nasty to me and he hits me.' She recollects her commuting to Penarth, the troop trains bringing in the wounded—their condition in mud, grime and blood leaving a lasting impression—the landing of the Yanks in buoyant mood singing 'Over there, over there' with no idea of what they were coming to; also remembered were the poor food, the meat rationing, her eating rice, bread and maize cutlets, and her own serious illness during the 'flu' epidemic in July 1918. By this time she was Deputy Supervisor with the prospect of a job in the Cardiff City Hall at the end of hostilities, but she decided to return home after an absence of fifteen months. She was accepted as a Student Teacher by the Pembrokeshire Education Authority—there was a shortage of teachers at the time—and attended at Greenhill part-time while spending her student year at the Tenby Council School. Thereafter she served in Penally N.P. School before going on to Tenby N.P. as an uncertificated assistant.

Another old student, Dr. Tom Griffiths of Saundersfoot, has given me a vivid account of his experiences as a country pupil at Tenby County School from 1915 to 1921. The son of a chemist, he attended Saundersfoot Council School before winning a scholarship to Greenhill. He remarks that in the years leading up to the Great War of 1914-18 there seemed to be a steadily increasing interest in education and that more and more parents were prepared to make the sacrifices necessary to enable their children to attend the local Intermediate or Secondary School.

'In those days families were larger and wages were very low. There were few scholarships and grants and, in many cases, fees had to be paid. In addition, parents had to meet the cost of books and instruments and to face the cost of maintaining their children at school for several extra years. When the decision had been taken, there were further problems to be solved. From the child's point of view there was the anxiety of the Entrance Exam, the terrors of which were in no way lessened by the gruesome accounts of its difficulties given by our predecessors. There were no school uniforms, but the jerseys and trousers of the Primary School were not considered suitable and a suit with collar and tie was almost compulsory. A school cap was absolutely compulsory and no other head gear was allowed.

'For country children there was the additional problem of getting to school. There were no buses and hardly any motor cars. Railway stations were far from the villages and train times did not fit in with school hours. In practice, children often had to walk two to four miles, and this had to be done in all seasons and in all weathers. A good mackintosh and waterproof leggings were essential. In spite of these protections, for a large part of the winter, one arrived in school in a very wet condition. Sometimes, as the result of a bad soaking, we were allowed to dry in front of a large fire in the Laboratory, with the additional compensation of missing the first lesson. Most of the country boys cycled to school, some on new models and some on very old crocks. After a few months, boys being what they were, there was very little difference in the appearance of the machines, and the polished bike with all its machinery intact was regarded as the sign of an inexperienced new boy. When the pleasure of its first possession had worn off, his bicycle became a mixed blessing to the schoolboy of those days. The district is hilly and the roads were bad. Punctures were frequent and often one had to rush through one's homework to repair a puncture before bedtime. In winter it was often past lighting-up time before we arrived home and we only had the choice of an acetylene lamp which tended to burn in all the wrong places or an oil lamp that gave a very poor light and that blew out in the wind. Every effort had to be made to avoid being kept in and this must have helped discipline. Fortunately there was no "Highway Code" then and very little fast traffic, which was just as well, as our brakes were never well-maintained. We rode four or five abreast and at a reckless speed, and it was evident that we were not popular with other road users.

'On the first day of term, we set out with our satchels and water-proofs strapped to the carriers of our bicycles and with some trepidation we entered into a new life. When we arrived, we were a bit overawed by the size and complexity of the building and we were impressed by the fact that the School was on two floors. Coming from small village schools, we were struck by the number and size of the separate classrooms and by the Gymnasium, the Science Laboratory, the Science Lecture Room and the Workshop, all of which were new to us. To new pupils, perhaps, the most awe-inspiring experience was the morning assembly of the whole school at the function known as "Prayers". This was held in the Gym. and the whole school marched in class by class, and lined up with the Juniors in front and the Seniors at the back, with the girls on one side and the boys on the other. The Staff, all ladies because of the War, walked in next, to their seats at the front of the Assembly. They wore gowns and, as most of us had never seen academic dress before, we were suitably impressed. When all were assembled, the Head Master walked in; and even at our tender ages, we were aware that we were meeting a powerful personality. An instinct of self-preservation told us that it would be dangerous to get on the wrong side of such a mighty Authority. After prayers, the School dismissed to the various classrooms.

'In those days the new pupils of 12 started in Form 2A, but there were two more junior Forms composed of younger fee-paying children. This section of the School corresponded in a way to a kind of Prep School and they were designated Forms 1 and 2B. When the previous year's juniors joined the newcomers in 2A, we had the advantage of a nucleus of old hands who knew the ropes and who could instruct us in the arts of keeping out of trouble. Most of the first day was given to the explanation of Time Tables and to providing us with the list of books we had to purchase. These were bought at Mr. Farley's in the High Street and, as most of us had never been in a bookshop before, we were interested to see the pile of text books and such new toys as geometry boxes and pencil cases. There was little chance of a wrong purchase because Mr. Farley had been in this kind of business for so long that he knew the books that were right and proper for each child's age and station. Lunch time posed extra problems for country children. There were no organised school meals and every parent had to provide a packed lunch which was eaten in one of the classrooms. In their early days most children had a thermos flask, but these injury-prone articles had a short life, and often the drinking-water tap was the only means of getting fluids.'

The same past student considers that the wartime staff, entirely female, was of very high quality; it said much for them that, in those very difficult years, they obtained one hundred per cent passes in the Central Welsh Board Examinations on one occasion. Nevertheless, he reserves his greatest praise for the Head Master:

'While the ladies in their different ways were good disciplinarians, they had the massive support of the Head Master . . . Mr. J. T. Griffiths, who at that time was at the height of his powers. He was a man of commanding presence with a strong face and a fine head. He was always well dressed in clothes of perfect fit and fine quality. He always wore a white shirt and a hard collar with a tie of good quality, and his shoes of good leather were always brilliantly polished. Schoolboys have never been interested in dress and there must have been times when the sight of us was very painful to him. He was a rigid disciplinarian, largely by the force of his personality. He had a cane in reserve but he rarely used it, but when he did, the recipient had no wish for a repetition. He never seemed to lose his temper, but when he was displeased he could address the whole school in a manner that made us very thoughtful for the rest of the day. Owing to the shortage of man-power he had to do a good deal of class-teaching, for which he had an exceptional gift. He took Mathematics, mostly in the Upper Forms and at times of staff difficulty he showed his versatility in other subjects. At his best, he could make any subject interesting and it was not entirely due to the fear of discipline that we gave him very close attention. He was greatly concerned with improving what he called the tone of the school and insisted that such clothes as we had were worn tidily, that our hands and faces were clean and our hair decently combed. Possibly because there were a few boarders who lived with him in the Head Master's House, he appeared to adopt some of the features of Public Schools. He appointed a few prefects, whose powers were limited, but to such authority as they had he gave complete support. Later on he started a House system and, by doing so, encouraged competition and gave the younger Forms a chance to get into the affairs of the School. With all his sternness he was always ready to show and express appreciation of anything that the school had done well, and success in examinations and sporting affairs gave him great pleasure.

'With the end of the war . . . we had our first experience of a male member of the Staff in the person of Mr. H. J. Williams, who had charge of the Science Department. He was the right person for the transition and he very quickly established good relations with the boys. He took over the building up of organised sport, which had depended on the prefects and had been very limited in scope. On Wednesday afternoons school ended half an hour earlier, but apart from that, all school matches were played on Saturdays or after school hours. The field then used in Heywood Lane is now built over. There was no groundsman and the pitch had no preparation beyond that carried out by the senior boys under the supervision of Mr. Williams. He organised the buying of equipment, acted as coach and referee and accompanied the team on away matches with neighbouring schools. There were no buses then and the team had to travel by train. As train services were scanty for a few years after the war, these expeditions could occupy the whole of Saturday; so Mr. Williams had to work very long unsociable hours. He was soon joined by Mr. Eddy Parry, who very cheerfully helped him in all extra school activities and readily gave his services to the musical activities of the School. Sport was confined to hockey for the girls and "soccer" for the boys. There were no grants for sport and every child had to pay sixpence a season to meet the cost of equipment, and players had to pay their own travelling expenses. There were no showers and there was very little hot water; we had to content ourselves with a very sketchy wash, with the hope of a bath when we got home. Later, cricket was played on a field off the Marsh Road, and there we had to mow and roll the pitch under the supervision of Mr. Williams. Injuries seemed to be infrequent, but when they occurred there was no transport and the injured player had to be carried home or be placed on a bicycle and be towed home. There was no Sports Day, but there was a paper chase once a year.'

234

Tom Griffiths successfully pursued the course of studies which led to his passing the Junior and Senior Certificate Examinations of the C.W.B. Having gained a London Matriculation Certificate in 1921 he went to the University Medical School, Cardiff, and thence to St. Bartholomew's Hospital, London. In due course he returned to Saundersfoot, qualified as Dr. T. R. Griffiths, M.B., B.S., (London), to become a partner of the late Dr. D. H. Pennant.

Another former pupil has contributed some memories of Greenhill during the years immediately following the conclusion of the 1914-18 War:

'One still remembers the nervous agony of sitting what was then called the "Scholarship Exam." in 1919 just before an eleventh birthday, and anxiously awaiting the results. In the following September, having gained a Free Place, we "scholarship kids" still had the worry of entering into a new school life in Form 2A of the Tenby County School, as it was then called. Fears were somewhat alleviated by the prospect of a smart Gym Slip, white blouse and House Tie. The school was very draughty with open-grate coal fires and smoky chimneys, depending on which way the wind blew; so we were allowed to add to our uniforms white woollen jerseys, usually of our own knitting. Black stockings were a "must", even in summer and even in the gymnasium. Gym slips had to be long enough to just clear the floor when we were kneeling and gym shoes had to be black/grey canvas uppers edged with black rubber. All these matters were supervised by the then Senior Mistress, Miss M. F. (Frankie) Howells, who, along with her own subject, English, looked after our "drill", and gymnastics, which consisted of exercises on parallel bars on a stand which was movable. There was also a rope to climb and a strange ladder spanning the room at a wide angle and dangerous to cross, hand over hand, since there was no mattress below. Occasionally such periods were enlivened by sedate and even sometimes energetic dancing depending on the accompanist on the piano. All such activities might now be called "P.E.". Miss Howells, who was small, energetic, with plump legs, dressed in the same way as we were for gym. She also shared our Games, playing herself or umpiring matches at home and away. When not playing ourselves, we always tried to cheer the boys on in their football matches.

'Different ladies and gentlemen came and went during those years

235

following the War, notably Miss Edmonds, to us girls very beautiful and elegantly dressed, teaching French; Miss Vincent, a dear, whose dress was "different", taught Latin and Maths.; then came Misses Daniel, O'Connor and Clarke, but Miss Howells and Miss Maggie Williams (Cookery, Housewifery and Needlework) were still there long after this writer left school. The men on the staff were Mr. H. J. Williams, who remained here all his teaching years, Messrs. Morgan (Latin), Thomas (History) and Parry (Geography and Art); these last three I understand died quite young soon after leaving, possibly owing to after-effects of the War. I remember that Mr. Parry's successor was Mr. Pritchard. We were relieved to find that all these members of the staff were quite kind and considerate, though strict disciplinarians, but naturally we remember best those who stayed.

'Of course, the Head Master was someone apart, most of us having a healthy fear of him, or at any rate of displeasing him. He had his eccentricities, but upon reflection we must surely realise that he was a considerable character, especially after reading of the difficulties he had to overcome. Many old pupils remember to this day, with gratitude the help and encouragement they had from J. T. Griffith, having stayed the course and gone on to greater things. He married a lady who was always very charming and kind.

'However, Miss Howells deserves a special praise because of her popularity, her teaching and her pleasant disposition. She was sometimes referred to as "Howlly"—an unimaginative nickname, as her initials M.F.H. gave little help in the matter and only suggested to us a well-known blood sport. Most of the Staff had nicknames, some of which were stupid. Probably many of us had been brought up to read good books at home and had a fair acquaintance with the Bible, along with some Shakespeare and the Dictionary, there being no diversions such as Radio and "Telly". But, as for the School, Miss Howells will always be remembered for her wide taste in the then available sources of literature and her knowledge, enthusiasm and fresh good-humoured approach to our studies of anything ranging from prose to poetry seemed at that time, to a child's mind unequalled.

'Miss Maggie Williams was very different, a quite passionate Celt with many sides to her nature, but a good teacher of Cookery of a "Waste not want not" nature, your friend if you were never naughty and worked zealously. In fact, the first lesson she gave to new pupils started with a Ruskin quotation to be copied into their notebooks, which went: "Work should be the end and aim of all Education, for it is the source of true felicity through life", etc. It might have seemed silly at the time but oddly enough we have not forgotten it and we have lived to prove it. Miss Maggie Williams had a very forceful personality and strong political views, together with the courage of her convictions. She will be remembered well and with affection by her old pupils and friends who still remain here, for she was also a founder member of the first branch of the Cymrodorion Society formed in Tenby. When the Society held its inaugural meeting in the old school gymnasium, there was a tea, an Entertainment and Welsh music, and some of us dressed in Welsh costume and waited upon the guests.

'At the time of which I write there were interesting plays acted on the premises with sadly inadequate props and I well remember a senior pupil of that period, Kit Hearn, was already a competent producer of sketches. After some years away in England she returned to join the Staff of the new Greenhill County Secondary School in 1961 teaching English and producing plays.

'In 1922 we pupils of the school were well aware of a condition of unease, and it was obvious that hostilities were active between the Head Master and his staff. The real reasons were unknown to us and we could only conjecture, but I cannot seriously say that the situation caused any disruption of the curriculum. Time Table difficulties were usually overcome and "business was as usual".

'The overall memories are of our happy days at Greenhill, of kind teachers, lasting friendships, an educational grounding and guidance which inspired us to continue at leisure in the search for knowledge.'

These selected reminiscences have been quoted at length because they describe so well some of the basic features of school life which survived, with a little modification, during the whole period of J.T.'s tenure of office. The anxieties engendered by the Scholarship Examination and the experiences of newcomers were shared by successive generations of pupils. The organisation remained that of a Dual School in which classes were mixed but in which the sexes were segregated, the boys on the ground floor and the girls on the first floor for Registration and desk accommodation, while the procedure for Morning Assembly continued unaltered. The curriculum was substantially what it had been in Adams' day, though there were

237

attempts to provide commercial work in the Middle School. Chemistry was the only Science taught until General Science was introduced in the mid-thirties and the appointment of a teacher of Biology brought this subject into the Time Table. The provision for Games in the Time Table continued to be a single period for the whole school on Wednesday afternoons. From 1922 onwards the field on the Heywood Lane side of the present school was loaned by Mr. David Harrison, the Tenby racehorse owner, so bringing to an end the hitherto unsatisfactory situation in which there had been no ground regularly available for organised games. The House system for Games and for Eisteddfod, along with dramatics and other cultural pursuits, continued intermittently until placed on a more permanent footing in the 1930s. For country pupils transportation remained difficult, even after the introduction of bus services on the Saundersfoot and Manorbier routes in the 'twenties' and of more limited services, begun later, en route for Amroth and Pembroke Dock respectively. These conditions involved a sacrifice of time and effort on the part of those boys and girls living in the rural areas and wishing to join in out-of-school activities.

During the first ten years of J. T. Griffith's Headship, the school had survived despite the precarious financial situation down to 1915, the challenge of wartime difficulties had been met, and some outstanding academic successes had been achieved. Prospects were brighter in the post-war period. Board of Education Grants were more generous; an increase in the number of pupils brought a corresponding increase in Capitation Allowances, more income from fees and the need for an addition to the staff, the male side being strengthened as men were released from war service. The introduction of Teachers' Superannuation and of the Burnham Scale offered security and conditions of pay comparable with those in many other parts of the country, so encouraging a more stable situation staffwise. Just when the future began to look rosier, salaries were pruned by the 'Geddes Axe' and the reputation of the Tenby Intermediate school was again put to the test through a serious internal dispute between Mr. Griffith and his staff in 1922. No purpose will be served by dwelling on this matter. As might be expected, official references to the event in the Governors' Minutes reveal their full support for the Head, while in the columns of the *Tenby Observer* he was fiercely attacked as a despot. Over the

238

years, the many references made to this unfortunate affair indicate that, in fairness, blame and lack of understanding must be definitely attached to both sides in the quarrel. Subsequently, when comparative peace and harmony returned, only those who chose to do so remembered the 'skeleton in the cupboard' and dropped occasional dark hints as to its presence.

The graph which appears at the end of the volume is intended to be largely self-explanatory. Certain national and local events are incorporated along with session statistics extracted from the annual Reports of the Central Welsh Board. The relationship between the number of pupils on the roll and the number of assistant staff is shown clearly, and so is the effect of two wars upon the balance of men and women teachers at the school. In each of the sessions from 1911 to 1913 there were only three full-time staff plus the Head and the part-time Domestic Science Mistress. In the years following, it was possible to employ more Assistants until the total of seven was reached after the number of boys and girls in attendance totalled 164. For ten years, from 1925 to 1935, the staff consisted of three men and three women until the growing number of pupils made an addition essential. J.T. went on to finish his career with an assistant staff of nine, and under his successor, G. C. Gibson, further appointments were found to be necessary. It has been remarked already that a more stable situation developed after pay and pensions were placed on a statutory basis. Previously, from 1911 to 1919 inclusive, out of 21 Assistants, 11 (over half) stayed for one year or less and, of those, four stayed for one term only. Of the nine 'long stayers' listed on the chart, six remained in service at the school after J. T. Griffith's retirement and one returned after serving in H.M. Forces during the Second World War, so providing a valuable nucleus of experience, while some others who joined the staff, some of them careerists went on elsewhere after shorter periods at Greenhill.

The statistics provided in the graph should be examined alongside the table of population figures taken from the census returns for the urban areas and the parishes within the County School District. Between 1911 and 1921 there was a striking increase of population in all parts of the catchment area except St. Florence. In Tenby itself the increase amounted to almost 31 per cent, in the St. Mary Out-Liberty to almost 30 per cent, while there were also appreciable

239

increases in Manorbier, Penally and St. Issells (but only the southern part of this parish was in the Tenby District). The net gain for the whole area was 1,485. It is significant that, in the session following the 1921 census, the number of pupils at Greenhill was 164, the most since the school was founded. The process was reversed between 1921 and 1931 when there was a considerable decrease, though the numbers involved were not so large. The biggest losses were 724 from Tenby (about 15 per cent) and from Manorbier 101 (15 per cent), while the net loss for the whole area was 836. Correspondingly, the number on the School Roll had fallen back to 104 in the Session 1929-30. The Head Master's concern about the drop in numbers was stated in his Report for the year 1927-28:

'The number of pupils who left during the year was 31, 13 girls and 19 boys. During each of the past three years the number of pupils leaving has been in excess of the number of new pupils, so that the number on the School Roll is now materially lower than that of the years previous. Also we have suffered rather more than usual through pupils having left the town. The indication at the moment appears to favour a steadying of this efflux and to be towards an increase in the next years.'

The causes of the decrease of population in the area during the 'twenties' await investigation. Account should be taken of the exodus of a number of people, as suggested by Mr. Griffith, and of the vital statistics for the period during and after the Great War. Furthermore, an enquiry should not leave out of the reckoning some speculation as to the adverse affects upon the birth rate of the number of men from the area killed in action—there were 133 from Tenby alone—and, in consequence, upon the number of eleven to twelve year olds available to seek entry to the County School in the years 1925 to 1929.

When the Head's expectation of an increase in numbers materialised in the course of the 1930s he repeatedly drew attention to the inadequacy of the school premises and in his Report for 1936-37 he complained of frustrated hopes and emphasised the need for persistent effort to improve the situation:

'In my last report, I expressed satisfaction that our hopes were being raised by signs of a move towards providing the school with more adequate accommodation and modern equipment—a long overdue reformation. To my great disappointment no tangible advance or

240

progress has been made in this direction during the past year. It is difficult to understand this suspended action. The organisation of the school in all its phases and many-sided activities for the development of a free, expanding invigorating and inspiring life within it, is sadly hindered through the lack of reasonable aids and facilities, which combine to produce in the mind a feeling of inescapable cramp and of oppressive restriction and confinement. I can only hope that efforts, pressing and persistent will be made in the right quarters so that we we may share in some of the privileges enjoyed by schools in other parts of the country.'

At last, on the instructions of the Education Committee, Mr. T. Owain Thomas, County Architect, examined the premises, prepared a report, dated 11 February 1939, and placed it before the full meeting on 17 March. Mr. Thomas stated that, while the fabric of the various buildings was generally sound, there were details of slating, leadwork and dormers of the old house portion which needed attention. He noted that the original building on the site was the Head Master's house, to which had been added certain rooms to form the nucleus of the school and that to these further additions and alterations had been made, with little or no regard for future requirements. The house was ultimately added to the school accommodation and the combined result was a collection of rooms at various floor levels and connected by corridors and staircases of inadequate width, with dangerous points of congestion and without the possibility of proper supervision.

As these old buildings were destined to provide the bulk of the accommodation for the next 22 years, the Architect's description of them is worthy of note:

'(1) *Accommodation for pupils.* The number of pupils on the books is 183 and, calculated on floor space in classrooms and allowing the usual proportion for special subjects, the premises would appear to provide accommodation for that number. There are four classrooms of good dimensions and with good or fair lighting providing a total of 115 places. Two rooms in the house provide temporary classrooms of 16 and 20 places, but the height of these rooms is only 8 ft. 8 ins., and in the larger room a class of 23 is now taken. Neither of these rooms is adequately lighted. The total number of places provided in classrooms may be taken as 143, and with the proportions allowed for

241

Gymnasium (15), Lab. (12), Cookery (12) and Woodwork (12) the total accommodation is estimated at 194 places.

(2) *Assembly Hall—Gymnasium* (23 ft. 6 ins. x 46 ft.) There is no storeroom for chairs and gymnastic apparatus. Therefore furniture/apparatus, according to the use of the room, has to be stored in the main entrance corridor; the corridor is very limited in area without the further restriction of say nearly 200 chairs. There are no changing rooms or shower baths; the boys have to change in their classroom, but the girls have somewhat better facilities in their basement cloakroom.

(3) *Laboratory.* The only laboratory is provided for Chemistry. The room is inadequate in size for a full class and has no preparation room or store attached and no accommodation for advanced students.

(4) *Cookery.* This room and the woodwork room are contained in a detached building; built about 30 years ago, it fulfilled the requirements of those days, but based on present day regulations it is too small. This room is also used as a Dining Hall by 36 pupils and, as there is no service kitchen. Mid-day meals have to be prepared in this room while Cookery classes are in session.

(5) *Woodwork Room.* This is also considered below the present day requirements for a full class. As it adjoins the Cookery Room, it was at one time thought that it could be converted to a lunch room; but its size would be inadequate if the whole of the 88 rural pupils attending were to be accommodated.

(6) *Cloakrooms.* The girls may be said to have reasonable cloakroom accommodation so far as area is concerned, but situated in the basement of the house and approached by a narrow staircase it can hardly be considered satisfactory. A range of six lavatory basins are provided in the Cloakroom.

The boys' cloakroom is dark, badly ventilated and quite inadequate in size; and with its one narrow doorway it must be a source of dangerous congestion. The available wall space for cloaks is only 23 feet for 90 pupils—about a quarter of the requirement. The cloakroom is fitted with six lavatory basins.

(7) *Staff Rooms.* A small room near the main entrance doorway serves as the Assistant Masters' room; it is badly lighted and does not provide reasonable accommodation for the five members of the male Staff.

242

There is no lavatory for Masters. The Mistresses have a room in the House portion, with a lavatory adjoining.

(8) *Sanitary Offices.* A range of four closets (of a type not nowadays installed) is provided for the boys and a quite inadequate urinal space. For the girls three W.C.s are located in a room on the landing of one of the staircases. The number is unsufficient and the position offers little privacy.

(9) *Generally.* The lay-out of the School is such that any attempt to remodel it to fulfill present day requirements would leave so little of the early buildings that, in my opinion, it would be better to (a) erect such new buildings as are required on other portions of the present site and ultimately demolish the existing buildings, with perhaps the exception of the Cookery and Woodwork Block, or (b) to erect new buildings on another site.

The greatest danger to the School buildings is that of fire apart from the fact that all floors are boarded on wood joists, the partitions are mostly wood, and the School is heated throughout by coal fires; to the pupils and Staff by reason of the awkward entrances and exits of the premises, the narrowness and indirectness of the corridors, the number of steps and staircases insufficiently lighted in certain parts and the possibility of the space near the main entrance being encumbered with furniture etc. removed from the Hall.'

When the Education Committee had received Mr. Owain Thomas' Report, they resolved that a new temporary cloakroom for the boys should be built at a cost of £20 and that, to relieve congestion, a wall at the top of the stairs should be taken away. Unhappily, within six months, Britain was at war with Germany and the architect's proposals for new buildings remained unconsidered for years to come. Even the project of a temporary cloakroom was abandoned, while but little satisfaction could be derived when the wall was removed at the top of the stairs. The use of incendiary bombs by German raiders over the neighbourhood underlined the vulnerability of the Greenhill premises in the event of fire, a danger which the architect had emphasised in his Report. Furthermore, the problems of accommodation and the risks from congestion were augmented when the school population was further increased by the arrival of a number of evacuees,

21 in 1939, 14 in 1940, 21 in 1941 and two in 1942 up to July; but it should be added that some of these returned to their homes after spending less than a year in Tenby. By 1941 the pressure on classroom space led the L.E.A. to consider negotiations for the use of the Tenby Congregational Church Schoolroom. However, it was decided to bring up a Maycrete Hut from Pembroke Dock and erect it at the lower end of the boys' playground. Apart from air-raid shelters which were belatedly installed in the two playgrounds, this unpretentious hut with its fancy name was the only addition outside the older premises which Mr. J. T. Griffith was to see, and this was brought into use only some three months before his retirement.

Past pupils and members of the staff would recognise that the County Architect, possibly with some prompting from the Head, had produced a very good description of the school premises. The present writer, and others who worked there, were only too familiar with the difficulties. As the number on the roll increased the two classrooms in the house, one adjacent to and one over the Head Master's room became more and more crowded and uncomfortable. Sixth Formers on the Arts side were housed in the Library, a converted bedroom overlooking Greenhill Road. On occasion, through the pressure upon staff time they had to study on their own while the teacher concerned was in charge of another class.

For much of the year the surroundings were pleasant enough, but from time to time there were spells of inclement weather when gales and rain assailed the inadequately screened back doors, which gave access to the two playgrounds, when the wind blew piles of leaves into the corridor, when doors banged, when a journey to the outside toilets, to the workshop, to the Domestic Science or to the hut was a personal challenge and a menace to clothing and exercise books alike. There were other challenges too for the more exhuberant and venturesome among the pupils; the short flight of wooden stairs between the Laboratory and Classroom B provided an invitation to the energetic, when not under supervision, to make the descent in one flying leap, to the discomfort of any of their fellows who happened to be in their path. The question of warming the building with open coal fires was a special task. In the winter the Caretaker had the unpleasant task of clearing a dozen coal-fire grates, of carrying coal in heavy buckets from the basement through an outside entrance and of lighting fires in time for

244

morning school. There were menaces in the men's staffroom next to the Gymnasium, notably when the wind was in the East and it appeared that less smoke ascended the chimney than blew back into the room. Masters on their way to lessons emerged from a cloud of smoke, feeling thoroughly kippered, having rescued their books and apparatus from a coating of smuts. In the same room the low gas-bracket was a special problem for the tallest, who periodically bumped his head and brought down the incandescent mantles. In fact the frequency of this accident caused J.T., always a little suspicious, to hint that this was being done on purpose. The low position of the gas fittings in the Science Lecture Room was the cause of similar misadventures even for those of less stature.

Such and much else were the physical conditions under which the school functioned. A detailed description of some of the difficulties involved would throw into relief the surprising fact the the discipline and tone of the school were so good and received the most favourable comment following a Full Inspection in 1931 and after further inspections down to the Second World War. Examination results were variable, depending upon the quality of the entrants from year to year. Academic successes will be dealt with in a separate chapter and so will the expansion of cultural and out-of-doors activities, especially from 1930 onwards. Meanwhile, with regard to the premises, J.T.'s vision, often repeated in his speeches and reports, of a new school with all amenities and even a chapel for Morning Assembly, remained but a dream during his lifetime, and the new County Secondary School, when it at last came into being in 1961, was not at all what he had envisaged.

Section 3: The Griffith Period— Personal Reminiscences

'Chance is a single hair on the head' (J. T. G.)

As the writer of this history I have now reached the stage where my own involvement necessitates the use of the first person. In the Michaelmas Term 1927, Mr. Alwyn Thomas resigned from the staff of Greenhill School to join his brother in running a Private School in Swansea. The post of History Master was advertised and I was one of the applicants. Born and bred in Chesterfield, my acquaintance with Wales was confined to two fleeting visits, one to the north coast resorts and the other to the valley of the Ebbw in Monmouthshire. At that time Tenby had attracted but little attention north of the Trent. For ten years I had been a commuter by rail, for six of them six miles northwards to Henry Fanshawe's Grammar School at Dronfield, and for another four, twelve miles to Sheffield as a student at the University, passing daily within view of Tapton House, former residence of George Stephenson at Chesterfield. My father, grandfather, three uncles and an older cousin served on the old Midland Railway in one capacity or another. Railways were 'in the blood' and, at one time in my youth, a journey to London by way of the L.M.S.R. and the splendid span of St. Pancras Station roof appeared to offer prospects of excitement, new hopes and adventures. One day, during the Christmas vacation 1927-28, I made this journey, having been 'short-listed' for the History post at Tenby and having received an invitation to meet Mr. J. T. Griffith in a tailor's shop in Oxford Street. I learned later that Mr. Griffith and his wife Ceinwen, daughter of Sir William Price, frequently stayed at her parents' home in Hendon Avenue, Finchley. The interview took place in a first floor room behind a quantity of rolls of high-class suiting materials. J.T., then 46 years of age, had lost his earlier slim look. He stood, holding a copy of my application in his hand; he was genial in conversation, easy to talk to and ready to listen to my own expression of my aspirations. Here was a mature, shrewd Welshman talking with a forthright young north-countryman, whose knowledge of Welsh History was limited to the Edwardian Conquest and a smattering about the hardships of the South Wales miners. However, the upshot was that early in January 1928 I was offered and accepted the post. This event was to have a profound effect not only on my professional career but upon my social life and, in due course, upon my personal life. I often wondered what caused J.T. to choose me in preference to other applicants, for times were hard for graduates and I heard later that there were about 150 candidates. The Head's keen interest in Music, my own training and a strong recommendation from Dr. J. Frederick Staton, well-known throughout Britain as an adjudicator, a popular figure at the Welsh National Eisteddfod and one of the Bardic Circle, may have tipped the scales in my favour.

On 16 January I travelled to Tenby, reaching Swansea with two and a half hours left and wondering where this time would be spent, considering how the distance appeared on the map. Darkness fell as we skirted the northern shores of Carmarthen Bay. At long last I heard called the names 'Templeton', 'Kilgetty' and 'Saundersfoot', stations all dimly lit by oil lamps, before arriving in Tenby about 6-30 p.m. The Head Master met me at the station and drove me to the Peerless Hotel which had been established by Mrs. Peerless, one of the school Governors. Before retiring for the night, I explored the gas-lighted streets, the stillness and darkness completely blanketing the presence of the sea. When I awoke the following morning and looked out from the window of my second-floor bedroom, I was astonished at the beauty of the scene before me—the winter sunshine, the sea, the old stone pier, the sand-coloured buildings surrounding the harbour and the Castle Hill itself. The first Greenhillian I met was the proprietor's son, Wallace Sweet, wearing the maroon and silver uniform blazer and tie, then in his second year at the school, later to become a well-known architect in South Wales and one of the firm of Sir Percy Thomas and Sons in Cardiff. He conducted me to the school, of which the buildings, the entrance gate, the carriage drive and the surrounding trees gave me the impression of an overgrown private house rather than an academic institution. On arrival, I was welcomed by a fair-haired, fresh complexioned man, wearing pinc-nez, which were then fashionable. He introduced himself as 'Williams, Senior Master and Chemistry Master', and his colleague W. C. Bennett. The latter was tall, large of frame, with a slight stoop, with a twinkle in the eye when amused, and inclined to grey prematurely at the temples; he was in charge of Geography and Woodwork and took some Junior and Middle School Maths. and Scripture at various times. Later on that first day Bennett took me over to 'Longford', Church Park, where Mr. and Mrs. Parcell received me kindly and agreed to provide me with lodgings. Mr. Williams and Mr. Bennett were my mentors, acquainting me with certain aspects of school routine, pointing out pitfalls to be avoided and in due course helping me to know the town and the neighbourhood. The three of us inhabited that small room just inside the main entrance. There we moved, dodging the table, the bookcase, the single armchair and the gas pendant, worked and breathed when the smoky chimney permitted. In an upstairs room were three mistresses: Miss 'Frankie'

247

Howells (Senior Mistress in charge of English and Girls' P.E.), whose parents, Dr. and Mrs. Howells of Rock Terrace, St. Julian Street, kept open house for members of staff on Saturday evenings; Miss Mary Heap (Latin and Art); Miss M. G. Bowen (French and Needlework), a valued colleague who eventually became Senior Mistress and rendered most notable service to the school down to 1963. Across the Boys' Playground in the Domestic Science Centre was Miss Maggie Williams, who had been appointed back in 1917 by the L.E.A. and whose services were shared with the Council School on the other side of Greenhill Road. In addition to her normal duties, Miss Williams had the unenviable task of seeing to the provision of school lunches at a cost of fourpence per head. These meals were eaten by pupils seated on high benches at scrubbed deal-topped tables and my own memory of them is an absence of salt and the frequency of lentil soup and 'spotted dick' pudding.

The Head Master's Room was at the north western end of the old house. When at work he invariably sat behind a large square table, of which all except a working area was covered with books and papers, with his back to the gas fire, facing the full length bay window, with a view of tall trees and a small circular wooden summer house in that portion of the girls playground. To his right, occupying the full length of the wall was a monumental glass book case. Immediately to his left was a roll-top desk, beyond which a window looked on to the grass tennis court, and beyond the window a book press and further shelving—though I recall that part of that area was for some time occupied by an excellent Bechstein upright piano, the property of J.T.'s friend Richard Williams. The piano is mentioned in an inventory made for insurance purposes in 1933 and valued at £50. In the wall next to the fireplace a communicating door was kept locked and through it could be heard sounds from the adjacent classroom, usually occupied by Form 5B. Over the years, J.T., seated in his room, became a familiar figure to members of Staff and pupils alike, whether for consultation, advice or reprimand. He was an inveterate cigarette smoker and often smoked while typing, periodically blowing the ash off the cigarettes to save the inconvenience of any interruption through extracting the weed from his mouth.

At Greenhill, as in other schools, the specialist teacher was also expected to be something of a 'general practitioner'. In 1928 there was no Form 1. The four years course commenced in Form 2, a single form entry until the late 'thirties'. I was allocated two periods a week for History, with sometimes one extra in Form 5. The very few pupils in Form 6 had to make do with whatever periods could be spared after all other needs had been met. Over the years and according to Time Table requirements, I taught English, Mathematics, Scripture and Latin in the Middle School and Civics and Music to Junior Forms for one or two periods of the thirty-five period week. One day Mr. Griffith called me in and said: 'I want you to take a little Book Keeping with Form 3B.' 'But I know nothing about Book Keeping' I replied. 'That presents no difficulty,' said J.T., 'Here is a small book providing you with an elementary course,' and he went on to unfold in simple terms the mysteries of the Balance Sheet, the meaning of Assets and Liabilities, the use of the words 'Creditor' and 'Debtor' and other peculiarities of the system. With considerable patience, my colleagues Williams and Bennett, who at times taught Maths. in the Lower and Middle School, introduced me to Pendlebury's and Robinson's 'Arithmetic', with its 'Bills' based on pre-1914 prices, its ponderous examples of reduction of pounds, shillings and pence to farthings and the conversion of farthings into pounds, shillings and pence—though the small coin had long since passed out of use—with similar exercises in respect of weights and measures. Along with this 'Arithmetic' we used Blackie's *Elementary Algebra* and for some years a 'Geometry' by Godfrey and Siddons. My undergraduate Latin had to be adapted to the use of Macmillan's Latin primer and the tantalising task of teaching declensions and conjugations, translation and construction to the members of a B Form. I welcomed the opportunity of teaching English Language and Literature, the latter from selected prose and verse, including *Modern Poetry* (edited by Sir Arthur Quiller-Couch) and school texts of *The Merchant of Venice* and other Shakespearean plays. The correction of grammatical and spelling errors was everybody's business. Members of the staff were required to see that pupils wrote their corrections, not only in their exercise books but also on their internal examination scripts.

There were problems to be faced in my own Department, not the least of them being the phasing out of old-fashioned text-books. Such an operation was by no means easy. The practice was for Scholarship Pupils to be supplied either from existing stock, or, only where

249

absolutely necessary, by replacements of worn-out copies; fee-payers could either buy new books on order or acquire second-hand ones from their predecessors, Form by Form. To oust a Fifth Form *Matriculation History* whose stolid contents were matched by the forbidding dull green of the cover required time and patience, and there was the inconvenience of introducing a new text, half a set at a time over a period of two years. The dislodgement of books in use in the Middle School, a British History by Morris, Parts 1 and 2, took much longer, while Synge's somewhat romantic *On the Shores of the Great Sea* survived throughout the thirties. As a newcomer, I had the impression that the Head was parsimonious in the matter of supplies, without realising that there had been serious financial difficulties in the past and that expenditure still had to be carefully scrutinised. However, it should be mentioned here that after the inauguration of the South-West Wales Branch of the Historical Association by its founder President, Mr. T. W. Phillips, former Divisional Inspector of Secondary Schools at the Board of Education, J. T. Griffith, who was a bibliophile with a knowledge of Welsh literature and history, became a member of the Committee, gave his support to my work as Organising Secretary from 1934 onwards and sympathetic encouragement to the needs of my subject in school. When funds made purchases possible, wall maps were acquired, historical atlases were introduced throughout the school, and by 1942 the History Reference Library had expanded from a shelf and a half of books to the whole side of a room in the north west corner of the premises. Another problem during my first years was how to acquire a knowledge of Welsh History when the only texts available were Owen M. Edwards' '*Wales*' and H. T. Evans' *History of England and Wales*, when the only substantial work in English was Sir John Lloyd's medieval work, which stopped short at the Edwardian Conquest; in fact, many years were to elapse before the text books of Idris Jones, David Williams and later E. G. Bowen provided much needed assistance to teachers of modern Welsh history. Getting acquainted with local history was a gradual process, but my interest was given great stimulus when Mr. Arthur L. Leach came to Tenby after the outbreak of the Second World War and took on the Hon. Curatorship of the Tenby Museum.

For a few years after my arrival, the procedure for handing out text-books at the beginning of a School Session was remarkable, to say the least. The Head's room was used as a kind of depot for his purpose. A considerable area of the floor was literally paved with books—books returned, second-hand books purchased in London, along with new texts and with the prospect of new orders to come in. As soon as promotions were settled pupils came either during morning break or at the end of afternoon school, queued in the corridor, entered when called and were handed their books, all if they were very lucky, or probably only part with instructions to return the following day. A decision to 'close the shop' for the day would be accompanied by the order 'Come back tomorrow'. According to circumstances, this operation could be spread over many days. How records were kept at this stage I cannot remember, but I do recall one or two members of staff, who were asked to assist, picking their way delicately between piles of books to see to the requirements of boys and girls awaiting their turn for attention. Eventually the Head was persuaded to allow subject teachers to be responsible for giving out texts for the classes they taught and for keeping a systematic record in special books. Not long after I joined the staff, Farleys concluded their stationery business in the High Street and C. R. Hughes of Westgate House, became the official supplier to the school. Regularly at lunch time J.T. walked or drove over to Hughes' shop and regularly could be seen standing in there, perusing the pages of the *Financial Times*—though I never discovered whether he actually purchased a copy.

The first lesson I taught at Greenhill was to Form 3B in Classroom C upstairs. Close to the door was a piano. In 1928 it was played daily by Eileen Thomas (who became Mrs. Cole, organist of Tenby Methodist Church), for the Girls' Morning Service which was held in that room pending the completion of the extension to the gymnasium. During that same period the boys met for Prayers in the classrooms downstairs. There were 108 pupils on the Roll. A list of their surnames shows the preponderance of Thomases, with the names 'Davies', 'Evans', 'Griffiths' and 'John' trailing behind. This was to be a recurrent feature in the Admission Register, though the proportions varied from year to year, with the names 'Phillips', 'Rees' and 'Morris', and a crop of 'Coles' from the country figuring prominently from time to time. In due course I came to know that many of the Tenby Thomases were related to one another and were linked by marriage with various other families in the town. What surprised me, coming from England, was the paucity of Joneses. The complete list was as follows:

Allen	1	Gibby	1	Ormond	1
Badham	1	Glisson	1	Page	2
Bamkin	1	Goodridge	1	Parcell	1
Bennett	1	Griffiths	4	Phelps	1
Brace	1	Hare	1	Phillips	3
Brazier	1	Hodges	2	Read	1
Brown	1	Howells	1	Rees	2
Carr	1	James	1	Richards	1
Clark	2	Jenkins	2	Rowe	1
Cole	1	John	4	Samuel	1
Cooke	1	Jones	1	Sharland	3
Collins	1	Kelly	1	Skone	1
Craig	1	Lawrence	1	Sweet	1
Davies	8	Lea	1	Sweetman	1
Diamond	1	Leach	1	Thomas	15
Diment	2	Luly	1	Thrupp	1
Duffy	1	Mabe	2	Waldron	1
Evans	6	Maroney	1	Walker	1
Garland	1	Morgan	2	Waymouth	1
Gay	1	Morley	1	Webb	1
Garratt	2	Morris	2	Williams	3

In earlier chapters examples have been given of families which had a long association with the school, for example 'Husband', 'Mabe', 'Kingdom' and 'Hullah'. Unfortunately, requirements of space preclude a detailed note of other 'successions' of children, but should one be prepared it would be bound to include a veritable 'dynasty' of Diments.

To the best of my recollection, certain surnames on the above list were never repeated during the whole subsequent history of the school: Bamkin, Glisson, Garratt, Gay, Kelly, Leach, Sharland, Waldron, Sweetman and Thrupp. Certainly I find it easier to visualise the first 108 pupils than some of the later vintage.

The Head Master was a complex personality and was the subject of much criticism. Feelings about him in the town and in the school ranged from down-right hatred to respect, admiration, astonishment and, in some cases, affection. At times it appeared that he was a law unto himself, whether dealing with the Governors, the L.E.A. or the Inspectorate. His Official Returns were often delayed. He was frequently absent on account of various outside commitments—for some years he was Moderator of the South Pembrokeshire Presbytery of the Presbyterian Church in Wales, an active member of the House Committee at the Tenby Cottage Hospital, a member of the Tenby Museum Committee, Treasurer of the County Liberal Association and a County Justice of the Peace, serving on the Bench at Saundersfoot—no wonder there were days when he was seen leaving the premises 'hat and gloves'. He was often unpunctual, whether driving down in his car or coming on foot from his home at Bryn-y-Mor, carrying a stout walking stick, while the school was kept waiting for Morning Assembly; in fact, on one occasion, two Inspectors attending Prayers during the Full Inspection of 1931 awaited his arrival. The Head Master's Report to the Governors for that Session 1930-31 contains the following paragraph:

'During the year we had a very exhausting inspection, lasting more than three days, by the Inspectorates of the Central Welsh Board and the Board of Education. The report of this visit—a lengthy document and as exhaustive as the Inspection itself—has been before you, and I am sure that you have felt a sense of warm satisfaction with the encouraging character of the report, which afforded a striking testimony not only to the work done in the class-room, but to the tone and character of the institution which you have so gladly served and governed. The sympathetic understanding of the members of the Inspectorate of all the difficulties of a School, and the friendly attitude of their counsel and helpful criticism meant much joy to all who bear the responsibilities of the School's government.'

The question has often been asked: 'How did J.T. get away with it?' One can only say that his very presence seemed to carry him through. That 'presence' could be felt in the school or in any organisation to which he belonged, whether people liked him or not.

What of J.T. as a teacher? When he first arrived at the County School it was noted that he was 'young, full of knowledge and ability to teach.' Along with this capability has been remembered his 'shocking

253

and cutting sarcasm'. Several Old Pupils consider that he had no use for mediocrities, and a few, that he despised all others than those he made his favourites. And then another who knew him well said: 'He had an exceptional gift—at his best he could make any subject interesting and it was not entirely due to the fear of discipline that we gave him very close attention'. It should be remembered that during the period of the First World War he had to spend much of his time teaching, and that he and his staff produced some striking examination successes, albeit from a good vintage of pupils. However, another Old Pupil has written of him in the 'thirties : 'Whatever he may have been in his day, he was surely something of a teaching disaster—to us he was responsible for a subject he failed to teach. A lesson too often consisted of a five minutes appearance and a blackboard demonstration of some algebraic diversion before he disappeared to answer the telephone or to go to some appointment.' Be that as it may, he had a gift of clear exposition when he minded to give an explanation of the topic under discussion. This was always recognised by Senior Master Mr. H. J. Williams. Mr. Griffith was a believer in 'chalk and talk' teaching, known to some as 'the funnel method', and set great store by oral questioning. In his view, a member of staff was not teaching unless standing in front of a class and engaged in one of the above activities, whatever the subject or lesson. One favourite routine was to require a boy or girl to work at the blackboard under his direction.

Having been brought up differently, I always used a good portion of any lesson for pupils to do written work, whether English exercises, mathematical examples, or historical diagrams, maps and notes under my guidance and supervision. In would walk Mr. J. T. Griffith, looking down his nose and glaring: 'What are they doing, Mr. Harrison?' 'They are doing work under my direction' was the reply. 'You should be teaching them,' said he, stalking out of the room. From time to time I took up the challenge and visited him in his study to explain what I was about, but without appearing to make much impression. However, my own persistence and probably the observations of the Inspectors seemed to have worn down his opposition to my methods and eventually he ceased to comment, though I was never sure of his reconciliation to my departure from what he considered to be desirable practice. For many years he was responsible for the

Mathematics and Scripture of the Senior Forms, which sat the Central Welsh Board Examinations in these subjects. When the School Certificate Examinations, then held in July, were in the offing—when a Summer Term really was a full Summer Term—the Head would use a substantial amount of time in Morning Assembly to deal with portions of the Scripture Syllabus currently prescribed in the Schedule, obviously for the edification of his own pupils, and on the assumption that all would benefit from the instruction, and regardless of the fact that other morning lessons were being delayed. It should be emphasised that Mr. Griffith regarded the morning service, with the singing of hymns, scripture readings and prayers, as especially important. The hymn book in use was the 'words' edition of *A New School Hymnal*. The Head's enthusiasm led him to purchase the music editions of the hymnals of every denomination and after some years he entrusted me with the delicate task of mapping out the programme of hymns together with appropriate tunes for a whole term. In fact, Music was to some extent the servant of the morning service; otherwise it was a cinderella subject catered for only in the Junior Forms. This and the training of the School Choir 'out of hours' were my own responsibility. The importance of religious instruction was frequently emphasised by Mr. Griffith and he returned to this theme at his last Prize Day in the School Hall on 9 April 1942. In school, for physical training they had a 'Gym', for science a 'Lab', for games a field, for Art an art room, equipment for needlework and other things, for woodwork and metalwork workshops; and yet for religious work they had nothing at all. He would like to see a chapel in every school or a room set apart expressly for that purpose. 'Wales in the past owed much to the religion of the hearth,' he said, 'Were the schools going to save Wales in the future without the provision of religious training?' He would not see a school chapel but it would be a grand thing if they had one in a new building in the future, occupying a central place, to show that this kind of education was the centre and foundation of Education, whatever form it might take. This might be a dream, but dreams sometimes came true. (At least he had the satisfaction of witnessing after his retirement the inclusion of compulsory religious instruction in schools under the provisions of the 1944 Education Act.)

There is no doubt that Mr. J. T. Griffith was a man of considerable potential; in fact a considerable figure, a strong personality, a man

255

whose declared intentions carried conviction, though some of them remained unfulfilled. Periodically he would address the school or talk to the staff with such earnestness on matters of work and discipline that they really believed that he meant business. For the most part he regarded class discipline as the responsibility of the individual teacher. A similar situation obtained in respect of supervision duties on the premises during mid-morning break, the lunch hour and other occasions outside the Form Room. Year by year the Head had the full co-operation of the masters and mistresses in carrying on the work of the School; and it must be stated that he never failed to acknowledge, with great appreciation, the services of his colleagues, whether in public or when reporting to his Governors. During the last dozen years of his Headship the school routine followed much the same pattern. The Session began in mid-September and ended in the last week of July, with vacation periods from just before Christmas until mid-January, and for Easter, according to the date of this move-able Feast. Half-term breaks never exceeded two days and established fixtures were the School Play in December, the Eisteddfod on 1 March and the Annual Sports towards the end of July. Twice a year there were collections for charities, one for the Tenby Cottage Hospital and the other for the British and Foreign Bible Society, the latter being the occasion for a visit from Miss Grant, the local secretary, who was accompanied for many years by 'Crwys', the Archdruid of Wales, as guest speaker. Periodically there were concerts given by the Dorian Trio, whose efforts were appreciated by some, but welcomed by the unmusical as providing a convenient respite from ordinary lessons. On the academic side the pattern was usually the same—the time table of lessons and a monthly check on progress through a system of Mark Sheets compiled by the Form Teachers, who had the task of drawing the attention of their pupils to any short-comings. Boys and girls who were taught by the Head were somewhat mystified by the marks he had given them on the lists and stated that they never received any for their written work. Apparently he had his own method of assessment! There were Terminal Examinations at Christmas and Easter and Summer Sessionals for those who were not sitting the public exami-nations. These internal tests were held as late as possible each term so that teaching could continue as long as possible. During my first three or four years at Green Hill, question papers had to be reproduced on an exasperating and archaic piece of apparatus nicknamed 'the clay'. The procedure was to write out questions in a special violet ink on a sheet of paper, which was then turned over and pressed on to the flat surface of the clay which was contained in an oblong tray. The original paper was removed leaving an impression of the information which was afterwards transferred on to other pieces of paper by pressure with a pad supplied for the purpose. Even with a new clay the result became fainter and fainter after the first 25 copies had been made, and the more the clay was used the more obstinate it became in yielding any results at all. Fortunately, we soon acquired a hand-operated duplicator, a forerunner of the more sophisticated electrically driven machine which was purchased some years later. The marking of scripts was done out-of-hours and the writing of School Reports involved some late nights within about three days from the end of term. It was a ritual for Cecil Bennett to arrive with coffee and sandwiches about 8-00 p.m. and work through until the small hours so as to complete the task in one sitting. The last Assembly of the term closed with the hymn: 'Lord dismiss us with thy blessing' and the girls and boys returned to the hall in the evening for what was known as the 'End of Term Social'. Apparently they were content to play such exciting games as 'Spinning the trencher', 'Stations', 'Charades', 'Clumps' and 'The Noble Duke of York' and to dance 'Sir Roger de Coverley'. During the course of this function the Head would be completing his Reports, recruiting some assistance to address the envelopes, so that as many as possible could be distributed before the party dispersed. The whole affair was very conventional, but no doubt many a lasting friendship derived from the jollifications which followed.

Half-way through the year it was the established practice to enter pupils for the various stages of the Royal Drawing Society Examinations, the end product being an impressive number of certificates. But of course the main event was the Central Welsh Board's School Certificate Examination which was held in the hall and invigilated by certain members of the Governing Body, working on a rota. Most of Form 5B were entered, even when prospects were uncertain, while Form 5A consisted of second timers, who wished to improve upon their previous certificates. An increase in the number of candidates corresponded with an increase in the school's population down to 1942.

257

The vintage varied from year to year and often there were good candidates who met with failure on account of the Group System which then obtained. The smallest number who sat the examination during the period after I joined the staff was in 1931, when 13 sat and 11 were successful. The largest number of candidates before Griffith retired was 38 in 1942, and of these, 29 gained Certificates. The best proportion of Passes was in 1937, 22 out of the 24 who sat, and in that year no fifth former was withheld from entry for the examination. Candidates for the Higher Certificate were few in number, and when there were any, their instruction had to be undertaken in the four periods or less per week which could be spared for each subject, the variation depending upon other pressures upon the Time Table from Session to Session. On more than one occasion I had the experience of having to make do with one period a week and of taking a Sixth Form pupil in with other classes and giving additional guidance to his studies after school. Often First and Second Year Sixth pupils were taught together and this provided a stimulus for the former, but on the whole there was little or no competition and success depended upon the capabilities and ambitions of the boys ar girls concerned, together with their response to the instruction given. As the number of pupils on the Roll increased, so did the number on the Sixth Form Register but even so the total of nine in 1942 provided the school with a very small top.

During his last twelve years in office J. T. Griffith, with the co-operation of his staff, either initiated or revived many features of school life, which became firmly established and could be further developed and extended by the next Head Master. These features were the House System, the School Magazine, the Annual Sports, the St. David's Day Eisteddfod, the Literary and Debating Society, the Dramatic Society and the School Library. After being dropped for a number of years, the Prize Day was resurrected on a modest scale towards the end of the 'thirties'.

From 1929 onwards the School was divided into three Houses which were named 'Glyndwr', 'St. David's' and 'Tudor', and were given their respective colours yellow, blue and green. A handsome shield to be presented annually to the House which gained the most points in, inter-House games, was the gift of the Viscountess St. David's, one of the Governors. Although House Masters and Mistresses were expected to inculcate a sense of loyalty and mutual responsibility through periodic meetings with their members, the main use of the system was in connection with competition in the School Sports, Field Games and the Eisteddfod. When the initial allocation of pupils was made in 1929-30 there were only 15 boys and 20 girls for each House, ranging from the second to the Fifth Form, an unsatisfactory situation which made the selection of teams difficult and often reduced a football match to a contest between a few of the biggest boys. In 1935-36 there were 26 boys nd 26 girls in each House, and in 1941-42, when the number on the Roll had greatly increased, there were 37 boys and 45 girls for each. Each September the apportionment of new-comers depended upon the number of leavites there had been from each House at the end of the previous year; and while the distribution was always carefully studied there was always a risk of unbalance in talent, whether physical or academic.

The School Magazine

The first successful attempt to establish a school magazine began in 1937. There had been two previous ephemeral productions. J.T. himself recalled one of them: 'The first School Magazine appeared in 1903 but was discontinued after three or four issues as it was considered inadequate, and a more ambitious one could not be afforded at the time. Its form was very much like many Church Magazines of those days, an inset of some stories which interested very few; with four pages devoted to School activities.' The other is mentioned in a reminiscence by Dr. Wilfred Hugh who stated that it was produced in manuscript by a number of seniors about 1920, the Editor being Ronald Davies. 'As the Magazine was quite an unofficial production, and was not sponsored by the teaching staff, its contents were free from censorship. In consequence, it contained comments and opinions which I am afraid might not be regarded as suitable for inclusion in the more orthodox magazine for which I am writing now.' (Jubilee Issue 1946). The laborious business of writing out copies and the departure of the editor brought an end to this undertaking.

The first number of the new magazine appeared in July 1937. It owed its origin to the initiative of Miss Evelyn Ward, the English Mistress, and was printed and produced by pupils, the laborious process of cutting stencils and duplicating copies being undertaken by those who were doing commercial subjects. The following term the Head announced to the Governors that he had made 'special and favourable arrangements' with E. H. Leach, proprietor of the *Tenby and County News*, who printed *Green Hill School Magazine*, Vol. II, No. 1, dated December 1937. It was bound in a maroon cover, matching the covers of the school exercise books, with an impression of the Tenby Borough Seal on the front. The production had been entrusted to an Editorial Board comprising two staff—Miss D. E. Ward and Mr. W. Harrison—and two Sixth Form pupils—Margaret Berry and Nicholas Neale.

The magazine became an increasingly important addition to the records, often providing information not available from any other source. Moreover it is almost the only medium through which access can be had to the original work of past pupils. There were two issues in each of the Sessions 1937-38, 1938-39, 1939-40, 1940-41 and, because of wartime economies, one per session thereafter. The first printed copies cost about £6 to £7 to produce and sold at one shilling each. In fact the magazine was run 'on a shoe-string'. The maroon cover and the original title were retained until December 1942, when a grey cover was substituted and the title 'Greenhillian' introduced by Mr. G. C. Gibson, J. T. Griffith's successor. Subsequently, there were minor modifications until 1950, when a green cover with a design by R. A. Dickerson was adopted. From time to time came further changes giving scope for pupils in the Art Department, later in charge of Mr. T. O. Thomas, to make use of their talents. In addition to the publication of news of the school and of Old Pupils, the magazine has always provided the opportunity for girls and boys in all Forms to submit their original contributions whether in verse or in prose, imaginative or factual, serious or humorous, relating to school life or to local or national events, artistic or scientific, sensitive to the sea-shore or to the countryside. It is important that some material from the early issues should be quoted, as apart from a few reminiscences, this is the only way in which a sample of the work of former Greenhillians can be included in this story of their school.

Over the years, in fact down to the present day, there have been contributors expressing their anxiety about the contemporary state of the world. In that first issue of December 1937, a Sixth Former with the initials 'C.A.J.' attempted an analysis of the international situation in a survey entitled *Europe To-day*, beginning with the paragraph:

'I think it is important that now and again we should review the internal affairs of each country and the policy of each government, in Europe especially. From these observations a definite view can be obtained of the international situation. It can be easily seen that today, each country, big or small, is influenced by either Fascism or Communism or both. Thus if a European war should break out, we know roughly on which side the nations would arrange themselves, for in the next war it will undoubtedly be a struggle between Fascism and Communism.'

In September 1938 appeared an article by the same author, headed *Clouds over Europe*, actually written before the Czech crisis and 'Munich', and commencing:

'Everywhere we hear people saying that Europe today is in a more precarious position than ever it was since the war. We ordinary individuals do not know, for only our Statesmen who control the reins can contradict this statement, But the fact remains that the development of a series of dangerous incidents and aggressions since the war is placing Europe and the world in a position comparable to that of 1914.'

'This condition of affairs is due to many things—increasing population, new inventions, lack of trade, but primarily to three—the rise of the dictatorships since the war, the failure of the League of Nations to ensure permanent peace, and individual internal disorders.'

C.A.J. developed his subject by outlining the rise to power of Lenin, Stalin, Mussolini and Hitler and other dictators, their initiative, ruthlessness, fanatical ambition and patriotism, their use of the secret police—the Ogpu, the Ovra and the Gestapo, and their threat to democracy in Europe. He then referred to the weaknesses of certain governments, notably in France, and to the Spanish Civil War, and made a summary of the failures of the League of Nations in the Far East, Abyssinia, the Rhineland and Austria. These were the factors which had hindered the furtherance of peace in Europe.

It is not surprising to find the sea as a recurrent theme among pupils who live not far from the sea shore. Here is an example in prose.

261

Seascape
by E. A. (IIIA) (Spring 1940)

The day was calm and still, and over the sea a haze hung heavy, mantling any sign of life. The sea itself was blue where it met the horizon—blue that could not be distinguished from the sky—and green at the point where the foam-crested waves broke on the silent beach.

The silence was broken only by the gulls, and by waves foaming over rocks, and emptying and filling anew the rock-pools, and slipping back into the sea, as one higher pool overflowed into a lower crevice of sea-weed and anemones, so forming a miniature waterfall and then trickling down to the sea, amid a cascade of bubbles.

Towards the horizon, waves could be seen, foaming and dispersing back into a calm unruffled sheet of blue ocean, which, except for the crested waves near the beach, was as a tranquil lake.

:: :: ::

A strong sea breeze was blowing, and the sky was dark with angry clouds. The sea was reflecting this on its grey, stormy surface. Far out at sea, the waves were rolling, and not for long did the gulls stay at sea; they settled on a rock screeching the while.

On the shore, the waves rose, higher and yet higher, and pounded foam-flecked on to the cliffs, and splashed up in thick, damp spray over the crest of the rocks, until yet another huge breaker surged over the top, carrying foam inland to the shore, where they again pounced on to the beach, throwing up dense spray. Foam was carried swiftly up the beach.

It was as if some undercurrent were dragging the tide inwards, ever inwards, until the wind changed and the moody sea left off its mad rush and once more became peaceful.

Throughout its existence the magazine has contained poetry, ranging from the work of Brian Price and his contemporaries in the late thirties and early forties to that of Tony Curtis, (who is now on the Panel of the Arts Council) in the sixties. The editors have always given encouragement to the inclusion of verse from members of all Forms in the School. Unfortunately only two of the earliest contributors can be quoted here, one from each 'end' of the school.

262

Moonrise
by M.R. (2A) (September 1938)
Shadows are falling and daylight is past,
Beautiful evening is with us at last.
All the wide landscape with silver is dressed,
Cool winds are kissing the flowers to rest.

Forest leaves rustle in quivering light,
All the young birds are now taking their flight,
Over the city and over the hill,
Pale yellow moonlight is hovering still.

Heroes
(Chair Poem, Eisteddfod, 1938) D.G. (5B) (April 1938)
Heroes! The present age surpasses far
All previous eras that the world has known
Since time began. Those seeds of daring, sown
On land, on sea, in air—these heralds are
To deeds of brav'ry, that by force or might,
Make certain nations free—others betray;
Attainments, which by fanciful display
Dupe even conscience to consider right;
Apart, above, beyond this earthly strife
Abides that Supreme Power, looking on.
The common man pursues his simple life,
Doing what good he can, and harming none;
And who shall say, but that, when time is rife,
He yet may qualify for God's "Well done!"

The Editors always welcomed news of Old Pupils and periodically received articles from subscribers to the magazine, among them Arthur Rees, who wrote vivid accounts of his experiences during the First World War in a series 'Away in the Western Desert', or 'With Allenby in Palestine' and 'Aboard a Torpedoed Transport'. Likewise, the vivid description of an entirely different scene appeared in the Autumn 1940 issue from another former Greenhillian. This was Kenneth Griffiths describing a Royal Matinee in which he took part at the Piccadilly Theatre, London.

263

The Annual Sports and School Games

The Annual Sports were held near the end of the Summer Term in July, a homely family affair, well-attended by parents, friends and the Governors, who acted as Judges, and one of them, usually the Chairman, presented the trophies in the early evening at the conclusion of a somewhat lengthy programme. Of course, there was no groundsman and the cutting of the grass and preparation of the tracks and jumping pit was undertaken by W. C. Bennett and a team of boys on the eve of the Sports Day. While the athletic events were contested with keen rivalry between the Houses, there were no 'standards' and no split-second timing. This was a purely domestic function and not influenced by what was happening at the County Level as at present, when even the date of the Sports has to be fixed in May and geared to what is happening outside. Points were awarded and the Captains of the winning House received the J. T. Griffith Cup, which was presented at the same time as the Viscountess St. David's Shield for Games. Most often during this period St. David's won both Cup and Shield. In due course the number of trophies increased, through the generosity of Old Pupils, the staff and friends of the school.

From the earliest days of the County School there had been difficulties and uncertainties about securing the regular and long-term use of a playing field. The problem persisted into the Headship of J. T. Griffith. In fact for his first few years no field could be had. About 1922 Mr. David Harrison, the Tenby racehorse owner of Heywood Grove, came to the rescue with the loan of the ground above the present County Secondary School. Then, in his Report for 1927-28, the Head informed the Governors: ' . . . . we have lost the free use of the Sports Field we have enjoyed for many years due to the kindness of Mr. David Harrison, but satisfactory arrangements have been made for renting the ground.' It transpired that the owner, Mr. J. E. L. Mabe, after a few years found it necessary to introduce certain limitations on account of his own use of the field, and on 17 December 1937 Mr. D. T. Jones, the Director of Education, reported to the L.E.A.: 'The playing field is rented annually and is constantly used by cattle and sheep. The use of it is restricted and it can only be had on two evenings a week and for Saturday matches. The field cannot be mown except for the purpose of preparing a confined cricket pitch. No nets can be put up owing to the animals. Building is encroaching upon the field. The final difficulty is that the Head knows of no other suitable field.' (Those of us who had the task of supervising games under these conditions would have added the effect of long grass upon the style of cricket and upon the scoring rate, not to mention the frequent hazards of cow pads to footwear and newly washed flannels.) The upshot was that the County Council decided to purchase the field and there followed a period of protracted negotiation. In May 1938 Messrs. Mathias Thomas, Solicitors, on behalf of Mr. Mabe, refused to accept the District Valuer's valuation as adequate and the L.E.A. resolved 'That the Board of Education be asked to approve of the site and that the field be bought by compulsory powers.' In July of that year the L.E.A. recommended 'That the whole field belonging to Mr. Mabe except the portion already built on be acquired by compulsory purchase.' On 7 March 1939 it was resolved 'That the completion of the matter be now proceeded with due regard to the valuation of the District Valuer.' At last, on 19 July 1940 the Clerk of the County Council reported that this matter had been completed and that the land was now the property of the Committee as from 19 May. This transaction was important, not only in the acquisition of the playing field but also because eventually it was to provide a base from which the County Council could expand into neighbouring fields to the south and east, when further purchases were necessary for the building of the new County Secondary School in the late fifties.

Until 1941, when the L.E.A. appointed Miss Kathleen Cook, fresh from Nonington P.T. College, to take charge of the girls' physical education, along with Music, there was no Mistress of the staff with specialist qualifications for this work. Previously, the supervision of games and the umpiring of matches, home and away, had been shared by the Mistresses, while one of them took charge of P.T. Ever since 1919 the boys' P.T. and games were the responsibility of Mr. H. J. Williams, who was eventually relieved of the gymnastics when Mr. W. H. Edwards B.Sc., joined the staff and took charge of this work in addition to Biology and General Science. Year in, year out, the Masters along with senior boys followed the same routine—putting up the 'soccer' posts and taking them down in due course, cutting the grass, marking the cricket pitch, sharing the refereeing, travelling by train for matches with neighbouring schools. In his article 'Fifty years of Sport' (Greenhillian 1946), Mr. Williams referred to matches with

Whitland, Narberth, Pembroke Dock and less frequently with St. David's, Fishguard and Milford Haven County Schools of which his records showed a fair proportion of success against the first two. He remarked that the cricket record was rather dismal. We had held our own against Whitland, with only very occasional victories against Narberth, Pembroke Dock and Milford. Other schools had their fields adjacent to the premises and practice was possible at lunch times and most nights, whereas the Tenby field was almost half a mile from the school. 'Harry' Williams, himself a good hockey player, used to assist with the umpiring of the girls' matches: he wrote: 'The Hockey record is very much like the Soccer record. There was a very good team from 1920 to 1925, and they won more matches than they lost. I have no written records—I think the best team ever was the 1934-35 one captained by Ethel Rowe. Beatie Grant was an exceptionally fine centre forward and scored well over fifty goals and I think the team was unbeaten. The most outstanding player I should say was the late Margery Mabe. Whilst at school, she played in the Women's International Trials, playing in goal for the South v North. She played a very fine game, and but for her youth would have probably been chosen. Unfortunately, shortly afterwards, she met with an accident which eventually proved fatal.' During the summer months the girls played tennis on the court behind the school and rounders on the school field.

The School Eisteddfod

The School Eisteddfod, held on 1 March (St. David's Day), became an annual fixture from the early thirties onwards. Pupils, staff, former Greenhillians, Governors and parents assembled in the School Hall for the occasion. With the increase in numbers on the roll and as the event gained in popularity, so the limited accommodation became full to overflowing. Competitions in Music, Literature, Recitations, History, Geography, Art, Crafts and Hobbies were adjudicated by a number of ladies and gentlemen who were well qualified in these particular fields of interest. Every year flower-arrangers saw to the display of daffodils on the platform table and in other parts of the room. The daffodil was the emblem worn by most girls and boys, but there was always an enthusiastic minority who preferred the leek, and always one or two boys had a prescription for growing giants of the species over the winter. Nearly always the sun shone, giving a sense of well-being to the assembled company at the start of the day. For the first of this series of eisteddfodau J. T. Griffith himself was the Conductor and managed to convey the 'Welshness' of the event to the largely English speaking company. The Bard was chaired with traditional ceremony, seated beneath a sword presented by Mr. Meyrick Price, the Town Clerk of Tenby, and in reply to the usual questions whether there was peace came the enthusiastic shout 'Heddwch!' In subsequent years the role of Conductor was undertaken in turn by members of the staff, after suitable coaching, and then by friends from the town, notably the Rev. J. Perry Oliver and the Rev. J. Lumley Williams. During the day House points were chalked up in the appropriate colours on a blackboard by three energetic scorers, who sprang to their task as the winners were announced by the judges. Out of the nine eisteddfodau beld hefore Mr. Griffith's retirement, St. David's House was the winner in four, Tudor in three and Glyndwr in two. In three successive years, the Chair Poem was won by Dennis Griffiths, whose poem 'Heroes' has already been quoted from the Magazine of 1938. St. David's Day brought to fruition some weeks of preparation and chivvying of their respective competitors by House Mistresses and Masters. It was usually my lot to assist with the rehearsals of the rival choirs and to check the standards of the musical performers.

The Literary, Debating and Dramatic Society

Literary and Debating meetings were held once or twice a term down to the outbreak of war in 1939, the number being restricted through the engagement of personnel in other activities such as the School Play in the Michaelmas Term and the Eisteddfod in the Easter Term. There were debates on familiar subjects such as blood sports and capital punishment and on the future of Tenby; there was a Mock Parliament and there were lectures on 'Stamp Collecting', 'Lifesaving' and 'Pacifism'; the School Choir provided a programme of Shakespearean songs from *As you like it*, *The Tempest* and *Two Gentlemen of Verona*; following a current American craze there was a 'Spelling Bee' and a 'General Knowledge Bee'. These and others were reported in the school magazine.

A short history of school stage performances in the Griffith period was given by the 'Old Stagers', under the title 'From Classroom to Playhouse' in the Jubilee Number of the Magazine July 1946. Herein this stated that the regular practice of staging a performance at the end of the Christmas Term dated from 1930. Before that time there had been productions at intervals. In 1918 and 1920 two operattas were staged in the town, *The Burgomaster's Daughter* and *Pocahontas*.

'In 1928 Miss M. F. Howells, then English Mistress, decided, in the face of considerable odds, to put on a performance of "The Rivals". Here Mr. Bennett and Mr. Harrison served their apprenticeships in the presentation of school plays. The town and country parents who attended on consecutive nights must have been as amazed as we were at our own ingenuity: the stage—two (or was it three?) trestle table tops resting on the ever-handy Encyclopaedia Britannica, the curtains complete with runners, and the costumes, including ladies' three-quarter length coats worn inside out by the male characters'.

In 1930 came the first of a succession of productions in the Gym. Miss R. Robinson decided to present *Everyman*, with mediaeval carols to follow. The play was followed by the entry of singers in mediaeval costume carrying the boar's head, after the custom of Queen's College, Oxford. In 1931, Miss Reed had come to take the place of Miss Robinson as English Mistress. Her first play was *Antigone* in which the chorus parts were sung to Mendelssohn's setting. There was an outstanding performance by Patricia Glisson; and Ernest Brown learned and played a long and exacting part at a few days' notice. In 1932 came *She Stoops to Conquer*. By this time there was a number of seasoned players, notably A. H. J. Thomas, who played four outstanding parts in successive years, his last being a dryly exact portrayal of Malvolio in Miss Ward's first production of *Twelfth Night* in 1933.

In subsequent years and with improved stage facilities *St. Joan*, *The Rivals* and *Arms and the Man* were performed. Then in 1937 a great decision was taken—to move back again into the 'real' theatre. 'Half regretting the informality of our improvised stage, we presented "Richard of Bordeaux" at the Super Theatre. Never were there more intensive preparations. On Saturday morning Miss Ellis could be found supervising the making and painting of dozens of shields (what heraldic research that entailed!), Miss Bowen organising the making of clothes, Mr. Chalkley fashioning the pinkest of almond trees, Mr. Bennett constructing what we have always called the "Units", Miss Williams in the kitchen coping with those sixteen feet curtains.

And how justified was all that enthusiastic work when it was realised that we had launched a real actor in Kenneth Griffith(s), whose intense playing of Richard is unforgettable.

'There followed the next year "The Merchant of Venice", with a good Shylock in William Henwood, and an attractive Portia in Joan Ebsworth. Then came the war and for a time blackout and its attendant evils suggested the inadvisability of rehearsals after school'.

The School Prize Day

From 1913 to 1921 it was the practice to hold a Prize Day every two years. On the first two occasions the guest speakers were Sir Edward Anwyl of the University College of Wales, Aberystwyth and Mr. (later Sir) Henry Stuart-Jones of Saundersfoot, respectively. In 1917 the function was merged with the final assembly in July when the speakers were the Chairman of the Governors (Mr. T. John), the Rector (the Rev. B. C. Edwards) and the Rev. J. Lloyd Williams (Senior Governor). The 24 July 1919 was a special occasion, the first Prize Day after the war, and the Head Master requested an extra week's holiday in line with what was happening throughout the country because of the commencement of peace. Staff and pupils had been busy decorating the gymnasium, where Mrs. T. John distributed the prizes for the past two Sessions and an address was given by the Rev. A. W. Parry M.A., D.Sc., Principal of Trinity College, Carmarthen. Prize Day 1921 was held on 21 October, a colourful event for which academic robes were worn in a procession of pupils, staff, the Head Master, and the Governors headed by the new Chairman Alderman Lawrence, the Director of Education (Captain E. T. Davies) and Mrs. Davies, Alderman D. H. Williams (Chairman of the Central Welsh Board) and the Mayor (William Davies C.C., Vice-Chairman of the Governors). In the course of his remarks the Chairman referred to the death of his predecessor in office who had given invaluable service to the school during his tenure of the Chairmanship from 1912 to 1921. After the Head Master had given details of successes in the past two years, prizes were distributed by the Mayoress (Mrs. William Davies), and the guest speaker, Alderman D. H. Williams, congratulated all concerned on the efficiency of the school. As on previous occasions, tea was served for pupils, parents and friends.

269

There followed a long interval. It would appear that the Prize Day was abandoned after the internal dispute of 1922 and that no attempt was made to revive the function until April 1939, when the speaker was Mr. D. T. Jones, M.A., LL.B. Similar domestic Prize-givings were held in the three years following, the last of them being on Thursday 2 April 1942, when J. T. Griffith's decision to retire had been announced. This was the last Prize Day for over twenty years.

The School Library

A library had been started by the first Head Master. It began its existence with two bookcases, one upstairs for the girls and the other down in B Room for the boys. The Central Welsh Board Report for 1911-12 (J. T. Griffith's first session in office), contains a note that there were 65 Reference Books and 260 of General Literature in the Library. The Head Master's Reports for the following three years refer to the lack of funds, and the small additions which could be made, but by the end of 1918 the Library was being steadily added to. About 600 volumes were borrowed in the Session 1916-17. By 1927-28 there were 175 Reference Books and 420 of General Literature. J. T. was a bibliophile, a browser in second-hand book shops in London where he purchased additions to his own library at Bryn-y-Môr and, as much as funds would permit, for the school. An upstairs room in the north-west corner of the premises was set aside for the purpose of housing the Library, which was placed in charge of Miss Evelyn Ward. Generous donations by Mr. T. W. Phillips, H.M.I., and others helped to augment the supply of books for which additional shelving was acquired so enabling all the wall space, from floor to ceiling, to be used. The C.W.B. Report for the Session 1941-42 noted that there were 550 Reference Books and 1,300 of General Literature. So was provided a good foundation on which the new Head could build when more generous supplies of money became available.

The School Staff during the Headship of Mr. J. T. Griffith

In many ways, the Senior Master, Mr. H. J. Williams exemplifies that very fine vintage of Schoolmasters and Mistresses who absorbed and passed on the academic traditions of the Old County Intermediate Schools. He had been educated at Bridgend County School (1903-08) and at the University College, Cardiff (1909-13) where he graduated with Honours in Geology, gained the Teaching Certificate of the Board of Education and some experience in two schools down to 1915. During the rest of the 1914-18 War he served as a chemist in H.M. Factory at Pembrey. He started duties at Greenhill on 10 February 1919 and served there until 10 April 1957. His main work was the teaching of Chemistry and he became responsible for many years for the physical education of the boys. Mr. Williams was dedicated to the task of preparing his pupils, step by step through the school to face their examinations at the end of their fourth session. Year by year he scrutinised the results, and as time went by, he culti- vated a habit of calling on me on the morning the Pass Lists appeared so as to mull over the situation in general and our own subjects in particular. I venture to say that his record of results in School Certifi- cate and the later Ordinary Level Chemistry were second to none in Wales. He was dedicated in another way. The school and its well- being were uppermost in his mind. There was no function without his presence and without his finding a way to be of some service. Always he set a high standard of conduct. Pupils were aware of his meticulous regard for their behaviour in school and of his ever watchful eye outside the walls. As a Housemaster, he was fanatically devoted to St. David's and nurtured the competitive spirit which served them so well in the Eisteddfod, the Annual Sports and on the games field. He was a good cricketer and sound hockey player. Conscientious to a marked degree, he could become tense when tenacious in standing for what he believed to be right. On occasion he could be obstinate or even unbending in argument. Sometimes sarcastic, he was generally genial and had his own peculiar brand of humour.

My other colleague of long standing in the men's Staff Room was Mr. W. C. Bennett, who was a graduate of Birmingham University, having been previously educated at King Edward VI Grammar School, Stourbridge. His main subject was Geography, of which he proved himself a sound teacher within the limits of the practical resources then available. The valuable services of the Woodwork classes under his direction were greatly appreciated. He was well-loved and respected by the pupils and from the start of my own career in the school he proved to be a good friend and companion, both in and out of school. He was a lay-reader and Sunday School teacher and a member of the Tenby Museum Committee. In March 1932 he was married at

Gumfreston Church to Miss May Jenkins, one of the daughters of Mrs. Margaret Jenkins, the first woman Mayor of Tenby (1927-28).

It was also my privilege and happy experience to be working alongside three women of fine character and individuality, dedicated not only to the efficient teaching of their subjects but also to the welfare of their pupils. First there was Miss M. G. Bowen B.A. (Wales) Hons. French, Dip. Ed., who was already on the staff when I arrived in Tenby. Then, in 1931, came Miss E. Ellis B.A. (Wales) Hons. Latin, who taught Art in addition to her special subject. These two Mistresses spent the whole of their long teaching careers in the service of Greenhill impressing those with whom they came into contact with their own personal qualities and passing on the benefit of their experience to new arrivals on the staff and to successive generations of boys and girls. The third was Miss D. E. Ward (London) Hons. English, Dip. Ed. who was appointed in succession to Miss Reed in 1933. Her teaching and influence extended beyond the classroom and was especially felt in improving the quality of production and the standard of performance in school dramatics; her services in the School Library and her initiative and encouragement to the literary efforts of contributors to the school magazine have already been mentioned. Miss Ward remained in the school till 1946, and after a move to Pinner, she was eventually appointed Head Mistress of Cathays High School for Girls, Cardiff.

There were other staff appointments of shorter duration: an addition to the staff Mr. W. H. Edwards, B.Sc. (Wales) Hons. Zoology of U.C.W., Bangor, the first Welsh speaking Welshman in the school for a number of years. The common language brought him into close association with Miss Maggie Williams, who retired from her Domestic Science post in 1939, to be succeeded by Miss Doreen Davies who departed after a year and was followed by Miss Catherine O. Thomas, a Cardiganshire girl who used to sing penillion.

Bill Edwards took up a post in Beaumaris Grammar School in 1937 and his position as teacher of Biology, General Science and P.E. was was filled in turn by Messers. Edgar Chalkley, Donald F. Booth and Leslie Jenkins, the last of whom let to take up National Service in 1940, with the expectation of returing after the war. An important appointment in the history of the school was that of Mr. William John Davies, a former pupil of the Queen Elizabeth Grammar School, Carmarthen, B.Sc., (Wales) Hons. Maths. Dip. Ed. of U.C.W., Cardiff. This was an addition to the staff warranted by the increase in the number of the pupils on the Roll. Mr. Davies left to take up Military Service on 14 February 1940 and he was destined to return after the war. The place of Mr. Davies was taken by Miss Doris Gregory and that of Mr. Jenkins by Miss M. V. Sutherland. One other appointment should be mentioned, that of Miss D. M. Worthington, B.A. (Wales) Hons. English, Dip. Ed. of U.C.W., Aberystwyth, who came to assist in the English Department but who taught General Form subjects and assisted with the Music of the School during the many years of her stay.

The Second World War 1939-1945

For the second time during his Headship, J. T. Griffith was in charge of the school during a period of war. The impending struggle with Hitler was often a topic of conversation in school. Civil defence was organised in the County and a practical reminder that the worst might be expected was the instruction to the Governors that gas masks were to be kept and fitted in pupils' homes. When war was declared on 3 September 1939 the holiday season concluded abruptly with an exodus of visitors, the beaches were left bare and remained so until occupied by families of military personnel and impaled with iron posts as obtacles to the possible arrival of enemy aircraft, premises were blacked out, street lights were doused, hotels and boarding houses were commandeered and Tenby once more became a garrison town. First came infantry units, Herefords, Monmouths, K.S.L.I., with detachments of R.A.M.C. and R.A.S.C., and Sunday mornings were enlivened by regimental bands, heading parades which converged on St. Mary's Church from various parts of the town, among them the Shropshires coming up Cresswell Street at a cracking pace. Soon the bands were heard no more when the Royal Marines, the Buffs and others in turn replaced the original occupants of the requisitioned premises. From time to time the school gymnasium and nearby classrooms were used for evening classes for the troops and inevitably the staff were affected by the call-up which in turn put more work on the women teachers and the Head Master. Mr. W. J. Davies, the young Mathematics assistant had to go first, leaving on 14 February 1940 to join the Royal Engineers, with whom he eventually served in Burma, attaining the rank of Major. On 5 October the call came to Biology Master, Mr. S. L. Jenkins and there were 60 applicants for his post, most of them women. It proved more difficult to keep the Maths. post filled and the Head himself had to take up teaching in more Forms. Other men over the age of 35 were in the category of a Reserved Occupation, but under a new schedule Bennett and I were liable to be called. In fact I was informed that I would be dereserved as from 1 January 1942. On 17 December 1941 the Governors resolved to send to the Board of Education a request for our deferment; as a result we remained in school through-out othe war. Maybe in my own case my service as a Special Constable influenced the decision. Meanwhile, Mr. J. T. Griffith had been appointed Gas Detection Officer, H. J. Williams took up rota duties at the A.R.P. Report Post at Woodlands (in the event of emergency the Head's room was to be used for this purpose). W. C. Bennet and Miss M. G. Bowen had enrolled as Air Raid Wardens.

By 1940, twenty-two schools had been evacuated into Pembrokeshire. On 13 October 1939 Mr. Griffith informed his Governors that there were twenty-three evacuees distributed throughout the school without any inconvenience. Some of these stayed for only a short time, but others came during the following years. The numbers, entered in the Admission Register from various parts of the country before J.T.'s retirement, are as follows, most of them evacuees and a few of them the children of soldiers:

1939
Bletchley 1, Croydon 3, Ealing 1, Edinburgh 1, Greenwich 1, Gillingham 1, Hampstead 2, Kensington 1, Lambeth 1, Portsmouth 1, Runcorn 1, Southgate 1, Sutton Coldfield 1, Swansea 2, Warwick 1, Wembley 2.

1940
Birkenhead 1, Cardiff 2, Devonport 1, Greenwich 1, Liverpool 1, Purley 1, Richmond 1, Rickmansworth 1, Southsea 1, Sutton Coldfield 1, Wandsworth 3, Welling (Kent) 1.

1941
Antwerp 1, Belgian Army 1, Brussels 2, Canterbury 1, Coventry 1, Ealing 1, Hove 1, Hounslow 1, Kingston 1, Lewisham 1, Liège 2, London 1, Leigh-on-Sea 1, Manchester 1, Swansea 1, Wakefield 1, Wallasey 1.

1942
Peterborough 1, Portsmouth 1, Wimbledon 1.

The inclusion of Antwerp, Belgian Army, Brussels and Liège in the list is a reminder that for some time following the summer of 1940 Tenby was the headquarters of the Belgian Army in Britain. Claire Truffaut from Liège, the daughter of a Belgian captain, who was also a Member of Parliament, wrote for the School Magazine of Summer 1941 her impressions of the School under the heading 'As others see us'.

'I have been in Belgian schools and in French schools. I have known big ones and small ones, sunny ones and dark ones. I have liked some of them, but there are some that I have hated. For instance, I keep the worst memory of the last school I was at, in Toulouse. I had not a moment free to play or rest. I got up at half-past six and when school was finished, I had to work enough still to be up at midnight or more. I don't think that was a good way of teaching. I know that I hated going to school after that.

'Some people say that it is because I am in England that I find everything nice about her, but I have good reasons to prefer English schools to any others. It is not only the gay atmosphere I love, but also the way of teaching. I can remember a good deal of what I learnt the last time I was in England, but hardly anything of the Belgian teaching. I think that it is marvellous that for a child; school should not be the dark side of life as I have often considered it. You would never meet, in Belgian or France, with a school with games like rounders or hockey, and yet I believe that the body should be developed as well as the mind.

'But there is something that I find wonderful in the British people. That is the way they receive strangers. Although I don't think I am shy, I always felt bewildered when I first entered a school. But it didn't happen this time. And when Daddy asked me if I wanted to go back to school in Belgium or to finish my study here, I said "Here".'

Meanwhile there had been stern reminders of the horrors of war— the tale of disasters in the summer of 1940, the arrival of evacuated Belgians, followed by bedraggled and exhausted mixed units of the B.E.F. after Dunkirk. Incendiary bombs were dropped in St. Issell's parish, a high explosive bomb was unloaded at Carswell three miles from Tenby, oil-tanks were set alight at Pembroke Dock, and then in

February 1941 that town experienced an exceptionally heavy raid. At 3 a.m. on 12 October 1941 a stick of four bombs was dropped on Tenby, doing extensive damage.

Almost two years was to elapse before "fire watching" arrangements were established on school premises and Air Raid Shelters erected in the school grounds.

One part of the war effort was the 'Dig for Victory' campaign. The plan was to increase the cultivation of allotments. This was discussed by the L.E.A. in January 1941, when it was stated that the Authority would assist with the cost of tools, seeds, plants, fencing, manure and ploughing. On 19 March the Tenby Governors agreed to accept the Town Council's offer of a plot on the north side of Heywood Lane and the Head Master undertook to purchase tools. This long narrow strip of ground was ploughed and the masters had the duty of persuading pupils to stay behind after school and assist with the planting and other necessary chores. This virgin plot turned out to be intractable and at no time was the yield proportionate to the time and effort expended on its cultivation. It should be added that the L.E.A. began its development of the school meals service alongside efforts to increase production in the county. Two School Meals Organisers were appointed on a temporary basis on 20 January 1942.

The involvement of youth, including school pupils, in voluntary service assumed greater importance from 1941 onwards. At this stage it was not possible to establish a unit of the Air Training Corps in school but one was set up in the town. When the question of a proposed Army Cadet Force was raised in a Governors' meeting on 25 March 1942, it was pointed out that the A.T.C. already covered the 15 to 18 group, leaving only the 14 years olds for the A.C.F. The L.E.A. Minutes of 15 May 1942 shed some light on the situation. The War Office was to be asked by the Education Committee not to merge boys of 16—18 in the Home Guard but to organise them in separate cadet units, on the grounds that it was educationally and socially wrong to train boys of 16 to 18 with adults up to the age of 50. It was urged that youths under 18 should not be allowed to join the Home Guard.

In those same Minutes it was recorded that under Board of Education Circular 1577, boys of 17—18 were registered in January 1942 and those of 16—17 in February. Local Committees were set up to interview boys in these age groups who were not connected with any voluntary youth organisations. 624 of them were invited to attend the Tenby Centre and were apprised of the various organisations which they might join. Under Board of Education Circular 1585, girls also were required to register—17 to 18 year olds in March and 16 to 17 year olds in April. There was no parallel with the A.T.C. and the Cadets for the girls, but they were advised of opportunities in Youth Centres and of proposals for special training for the women's services in H.M. Forces. There were possibilities open in Young Farmers' Clubs, the W.V.S. and the W.I., in pre-nursing training for those aged $15\frac{1}{2}$ to $17\frac{1}{2}$; also girls of 16 could join a local detachment of the British Red Cross Society. In fact a most efficient unit of the last of these was formed by Miss Marjorie Knowling in Tenby and many Greenhill girls were indebted to her for the thoroughness of her work on their behalf.

As he approached his retirement (and afterwards from his home, Bryn-y-Môr), J. T. Griffith could look back with satisfaction on the careers of many Old Greenhillians who had attended the school during his headship. Yet there had been times when he had complained to his Governors that there were pupils who did not stay for the full four years' course and that some were leaving as soon as they attained the statutory age of 14. Unfortunately, entries in the careers column of the Admission Registers were not always made. Neither did the Head, in his Reports, consistently note the destinations of leavers, although of course these were not always known. However, the following compilation from the available information bears witness to his complaints. The figures take into account the intended occupations of girls and boys who entered and left school between 1 January 1911 and 31 July 1942, but not any changes from the original intentions: Universities 26; Student Teaching and Training Colleges 50; Commercial Colleges/Schools 6; Technical Colleges 3; Colleges of Pharmacy 3; Domestic Science Colleges 2; Radio College 1; Apprenticeships—local trades 127; Clerks (including Post Offices 22, Railway 15, Banks 13, Solicitors' 9) 110; Home (mostly girls) 141; Home Business 17; Sundry businesses 77; Shop Assistants 37; Farming 50; Australia 2; Canada 2; Engineering and Manufacturing Industries 7; Cashiers 4; Wireless Telegraphy 4; Gardening/Horticulture 3; Domestic Service (including 1 valet) 7; Theatre 1, Journalism 1; Army 5; Royal Navy (including one naval school) 3; Training Ship 'Conway' 1; Merchant Navy 6; Royal Air Force (9 artificers, 6 clerks) 15; Fleet Air Arm 2; Police 3; Nursing 13; Masseuse 1; Golf Professional Training 1; 'National Work' (wartime) 6.

Many of these old pupils either settled in or returned to various businesses and trades in the town or in the neighbouring parishes, serving the community and the needs of holiday-makers; many returned to their own farms in the area; while others became distinguished in a variety of walks of life in a national and even a global setting. Among the last may be mentioned Wilfred E. Hugh, a pupil from 1916 to 1922, who won a County Exhibiton and an Open King George V Science Scholarship tenable at University College, Swansea, graduated with First Class Honours in Chemistry and took the further Degree of M.Sc. With an Industrial Research Fellowship he proceeded to the Imperial College of Science and on the strength of his work was awarded the Degree of Ph.D (London). Some time later he entered the service of Lever Bros. and eventually became Technical Director of the Unilever Chemical Works at Bromborough Pool. He married a Greenhillian, Marjorie Husband, who was gifted with the finest singing voice of any discovered in the County School and who was a dedicated elementary school teacher.

On the Arts side there was A. H. J. Thomas, who was on the Roll from 1926 to 1934. He won a County Exhibition and had the distinction of being the first pupil to go from the School direct to Oxford by winning an Open History Scholarship at Jesus College. As a candidate for the Stanhope History Prize he received an 'honourable mention' and subsequently graduated with Honours and took up successive history teaching posts before becoming Senior History Master and then Senior Assistant Master at the Queen Elizabeth Grammar School, Carmarthen. Other notable performances were those of Enid M. Thomas (1929-36) who graduated in Oxford and obtained a post in the Foreign Office, Nicholas Neale who won a King's Scholarship for King's College, London, and Brian Price who was awarded an Exhibition at Emmanuel College, Cambridge, just before J. T. Griffith's retirement. The last two graduated in English and Mathematics respectively. Ronald F. Walker won a State Scholarship in 1942, completed his Degree Course after serving in the R.A.F., being awarded a First Class Honours in History at University College, Aberystwyth, undertook research at Jesus College, Oxford where he gained the Degree D.Phil., and returned to Aberystwyth, where he is now a Senior Lecturer in the History Department.

A career of special interest was that of Leslie R. Badham (the son of the Head Master of Manorbier V.C. School), who was at Greenhill from 1921-1927. With a Welsh Church Exhibition he went to St. David's College, Lampeter, graduated, continued his studies at Jesus College, Oxford, where he gained a further degree. He became a curate at Pembroke Dock in 1933 and Senior Curate at St. Mary's, Tenby in 1937. For six years he served with the Royal Air Force Volunteer Reserve as a chaplain. He was with Fighter Command during the Battle of Britain and subsequently with Bomber Command, and he was mentioned in dispatches for his conspicuous service as Chaplain to the British Forces in Iceland. During this war period he served as Chaplains' Representative on the Advisory Board of the B.B.C. and published *These Greatest Things*, a collection of addresses dedicated to the Battle of Britain Pilots, of which the royalties went to the R.A.F. Benevolent Fund. He also published *Verdict on Jesus* and *Love Speaks from the Cross*. The Rev. Stanley Newsom was so impressed with *Verdict on Jesus* that he bequeathed a fund for a reprint of the book which appeared in 1972 and of which a copy was to be sent to each new man ordained into the Church of England. After the war, Leslie Badham obtained the Living of Rotherfield Peppard and then in 1958 he was inducted as Vicar of Windsor, where he was Chaplain to the Mayor and Corporation of the Royal Borough. There followed his appointment as a Chaplain to the Queen. He retired in 1963 to Highcliffe-on-Sea. His wife, Effie Garratt, was a former Tenby County School Girl and a London Graduate in Economics. He died early in 1976.

Also outstanding was Kenneth Arthur Graham. He left school in 1916 to be apprenticed as a marine engineer in Glasgow. He emigrated to Australia in 1927, joined the Commonwealth Navigation and Lighthouse service and afterwards joined Qantas Airways as a Senior Navigation Engineer. He then became Inspecting Officer with the Royal Australian Airforce and finally he served with the Royal Australian Navy for about 18 years, was in action against the Japanese and was promoted to the rank of Lieut. Commander.

Lionel Luly, in school from 1916 to 1919, started his career as a

279

dockyard apprentice, entered the University College, Swansea, where he graduated in Engineering, he joined the firm of Babcock and Wilcox, with whom he became a well-known expert on boilers, both at home and abroad. His contemporary, Albert Howells, left school in 1919 to enter the Mercantile Marine, but went on to study at the London College of Pharmacy. He became a well-known figure both in Britain and overseas—Chairman of the National Pharmaceutical Union, President of the Pharmaceutical Society of Great Britain, and Founder President of the Commonwealth Pharmaceutical Association, an office he held for six years. He was awarded the O.B.E. for services to Pharmacy, alongside other honours bestowed upon him—Fellow of the Pharmaceutical Society of Great Britain, Hon. Fellow of the Pharmaceutical Society of Victoria (Australia) and Fellow of the Pharmaceutical Society of Nigeria. While Albert Howells has performed services to pharmacy on an international scale, Enid Chilton (neé Francis, another contemporary in school) has spent most of her life in her chemist's shop, Medical Hall, Tenby, where she has been of service, not only to the local community but to thousands of visitors, including many from overseas.

Over the years, a number of Greenhill girls became nurses. Among them were two sisters, Joan and Violet Parcell. Joan left school in 1929, underwent training at the Prince of Wales General Hospital, Tottenham (1930-34), became Staff Nurse there for two years, did training in midwifery in Edinburgh at the Royal Maternity and Simpson's Memorial Hospitals for one year before serving as Night Sister at the War Memorial Hospital, Andover, until 1938. From 1939 to 1943 she was Ward Sister at the Prince of Wales Hospital, working on general wards and in the Male Air Raid Casualty Ward. After three years involvement with administrative work she became Assistant Matron at the King George V Hospital, Floriana, Malta, where she had the privilege of being presented to the Princess Elizabeth. She returned to England and took up an appointment as Matron of Sevenoaks Hospital in Kent, where she was in charge from 1952 to 1964, when she went back to Malta as Matron of the King George V Hospital and remained there until 1967. She was in Malta for the Independence Celebrations, when the Duke of Edinburgh was present for various functions she attended. She was also there at the time of the 400th anniversary of the Knights of Malta. Appropriately she concluded her career at the Tenby Cottage Hospital, from which she retired in 1972, after 41 years of devoted service in the nursing profession. Commencing in 1934, Violet followed the same course of training as her sister, but thereafter her career followed a different pattern as she decided to devote her life to children's nursing. She did Paediatric training at the Hospital for Sick Children, Great Ormond Street, London, and remained there, holding various posts until here retirement in 1973. She had the pleasure of being presented to H.M. the Queen on the occasion of the Hospital's centenary celebrations in 1952. She attended an International Congress of Nurses in Rome in 1964 and another in Montreal in 1968. She returned home to Tenby after 39 years in the service. She and her sister have a fine record, totalling 81 years between them.

Even the stage was not neglected. The Head had seen the debut of Kenneth Griffith in the school production of 'Richard of Bordeaux' in 1937 and Kenneth recalls that when he announced his intention to enter the theatrical profession the only advice Mr. Griffith could give him was to drop the final 's' from his name and this he did! His subsequent career on stage and screen was known to J.T. but did not live long enough to see his former pupil gain an international reputation, not only for his acting but for his decomentary films on Napoleon, St. Helena, Edmund Keen and the American War of Independence controversial and always stimulating in character. As a bibliophile, Mr. Griffith would certainly have been interested to hear of Kenneth's extensive collection of books and other material relating to the South African War, to read his book *Thank God We Kept the Flag Flying* and to see his film about Tenby, entitled 'Birthplace'.

It seems appropriate to conclude this selection of Old Pupils by referring to the distinguished career of James ('Jim') Cole, a native of this seaside town, who recalls that he entered the school in 1926 and, after acquiring a basic education there, left as soon as possible to become a cadet in the Merchant Navy. In due course he passed a series of qualifying examinations, the last of which enabled him 'to command the largest ship afloat on foreign voyages' or, as the Americans say "any ship any ocean". In 1938 he was commissioned in the Royal Navy. On the outbreak of war in 1939 he was sent to H.M.S. 'Nile', a shore base in Alexandria, Egypt, but soon returned to the U.K. via the Cape running the gauntlet of German bombers in the North Atlantic, two of the ships being badly damaged.   After various courses terminating in a spell at the Royal Naval Barracks, Chatham, he served on H.M.S. 'Aurora', a light cruiser, aboard which he was involved in intensive action in the Mediterranean and elsewhere until mid-1944.   His next appointment was as second in command of H.M.S. 'Eastway', a long range Assault Ship with a crew of nearly 400 Officers and Ratings. This ship took part in the Normandy and Southern France landings and then went out to the Far East until 1947, when Jim Cole left her on her return home.   Thereafter he was appointed to the Marine Service in the Anglo-Egyptian Sudan—the Condominium.   When Sudan became independent in 1955, at the request of the new government, he stayed to take command of the Marine Service, administer the Port of Sudan and train Sudanese Officers to take over senior posts.   By the time he left in 1971, he was the only Britisher in the organisation.   Subsequently he became Superintendent of a shipping company and took up residence in the south of England.   He attained the rank of Commander.   Meanwhile his services received richly deserved recognition:— 1944 the Distinguished Service Cross; 1954 elected to the Honourable Company of Master Mariners (one of the Livery Companies of the City of London); 1960 elected a Livery-man of the Honourable Company; 1961 was made a Freeman of the City of London; 1964 awarded the Reserve Decoration; 1965 was elected a Life Member of the Guild of Freemen of the City of London.

The Retirement of Mr. J. T. Griffith

On 25 March 1942 the Governors received a copy of a letter which Mr. J. T. Griffith had written to the L.E.A., announcing his retirement as from the end of the Summer Term 1942, on the grounds of ill-health.   Previously he had been absent for short spells through indisposition, and in the Easter Term 1938 he had been granted leave for three months because of illness, during which period Mr. H. J. Williams was in charge of the school and a temporary assistant was appointed.   On hearing of the Head's decision the Chairman of the Governors, Alderman H. F. Berry expressed his regrets and his appreciation of the sterling qualities of Mr. Griffith and of the progress of the school under his direction.

On 15 May the L.E.A. appointed Mr. G. C. Gibson, M.Sc., A.I.C., Senior Science Master, Maesteg Secondary School as Head Master as from the beginning of the Michaelmas Term 1942. The Governors resolved to send a letter of congratulation to the new Head Master. The Governors met again on 20 July, when Mr. Gibson was introduced by Mr. Griffith and welcomed by those present. This was J. T. Griffith's last appearance at a meeting of the local governing body. He had seen many changes in its personnel and had served alongside several Chairmen.

A presentation to Mr. Griffith was made on the last afternoon of Term, Friday, 24 July 1942. The current issue of the *Tenby and County News* carried three columns on this event, ander the heading 'Green Hill School closes a proud chapter'. There were present in the Hall pupils, members of the staff and Governors of whom the Chairman, Alderman H. F. Berry presided. The Chairman opened the proceedings with his own tribute to the retiring Head Master. Messrs. W. C. Bennett and W. Harrison, speaking on behalf of the pupils and staff, referred to the considerable developments which had taken place in the life of the school during the time they had been associated with Mr. Griffith and they wished him and Mrs. Griffith many years of health and happiness. The Senior Governor, the Rev. Canon Bickerton C. Edwards, said that behind the presentation there was much gratitude and admiration for conscientious work throughout the years. He had been a governor almost as long as Mr. Griffith had been Head Master and he had the opportunity of watching the school under his very able guidance, in face of very great difficulties from time to time. The Canon then went on to name some of the outstanding pupils produced by the school during the time Mr. Griffith had been there. He wished Mr. Griffith well in his retirement and called upon the Senior Boy and Senior Girl to unveil the presentation. Ronald Walker and Helen John came forward and removed a cloth cover from an elegant Queen Anne Bureau, which Canon Edwards then formally handed over to Mr. Griffith as a gift from the pupils, staff and governors.

In the course of his farewell speech, Mr. Griffith referred to the strength and encouragement he had derived from the presence of Canon Edwards on the Governing Body consistently for so many years and he said: 'I am reminded of a quotation at this time. It is "I'll hear thee and wait until thine accusers come." His accusers never came, but my accusers are here this afternoon in force. You can accuse me of a great deal and my heart will grow guilty to many charges. The minutes of this ordeal seem like hours to me, yet the years, as I look back upon them seem like days. I well remember the first day I came to Tenby. It's quite a long span, but at this moment it stretches before me just like a huge vivid panorama, as you have seen pictures on the screen, changing in character, sometimes a grey sky over them, sometimes with summer, sometimes with winter. . . . one is not likely to forget the impressions that were made on one's mind and on one's heart. For the past six months everything I do seems to call out "This is the last time you are going to do it." I experienced it at the last eisteddfod, at the C.W.B. examinations, yesterday at the sports and just now, when we had our end-of-term gathering. It has been very trying.' He then reminded his listeners of the changes that had taken place—the extensions to the original premises, the growth in numbers from 70 to 250 on the Roll, and of the importance of preserving a sane balance in outlook towards examinations and of helping pupils to sit another examination—the Examination of Life— helping pupils to face life with a little courage, to make up their minds to do a little good, to find a better code of honour, to discriminate between good and bad. He hoped the school had played its part in this grand and noble work. Mr. Griffith went on to pay tribute to his staff, to thank the governors for their co-operation and to express the hope that when the time came to move the school 'from the city to the suburbs' the name Greenhill would cling to it. He expressed his deep appreciation of the beautiful gift he had received: 'I shall make good use of it, but whatever I put in it, it will always be most valuable when it is empty, because it will contain thoughts which are kind from the Governors, pupils, old pupils, colleagues and others amongst whom I have spent some time. I shall always treasure this token of your kind feelings.' He concluded with these simple but nevertheless sincere remarks: 'Thank you very much and may the school flourish and prosper and be rich and worthy of its associations.'

The function closed with the singing of the School Song and with cheers for the Head Master. So far as I know, he never entered the premises again after his successor took over, though he was induced to write for the 1946 Jubilee Issue of the Magazine. Unlike Mrs. J. W. B. Adams, who figured prominently in the life of the school, Mrs. J. T. Griffith, quiet and gentle, remained in the background, appearing very

284

occasionally for school functions. Most of their retirement was spent at Bryn-y-Môr on the Narberth Road. An evening visit would usually find them in the library on the first floor at the back of the house, while the rest of the lofty rooms appeared to remain unused. His retirement came before there was any sign of the war reaching a successful end. J. T. Griffith was a Welsh Nonconformist Victorian at heart; he would have been out of place in the post-war world. Outwardly, at least, he maintained the sobriety of his Age, especially in matters of alcholic beverages. For a member of staff to enter a public house in the town in those days was unthinkable and for the Head Master to do so would have been considered as setting a very bad example to the pupils and to the school alike. Yet whether Mr. Griffith was too broad-minded a man to adopt a conventional nonconformist attitude to the matter in private we do not know. In this book, however, our concern is for the example he set to the school, both staff and pupils, and not with his private convictions if they were, indeed, in any way at variance with the image based on the sterling qualities he displayed in public. He did not withdraw from the social life of the community on his retirement but continued to attend meetings of the West Wales Hospital Management Committee, the Museum Committee and the Historical Association Branch Committee, so long as his health permitted. He died at Bryn-y-Mor on 14 March 1955 and after a funeral service in the Tenby Presbyterian Church, attended by Mr. G. C. Gibson and Mr. W. Harrison representing Tenby Grammar School—and by Mr. H. J. Williams, his former Deputy, he was laid to rest most appropriately at Cilgerran where his roots lay deepest.

CHAPTER V

THE GIBSON PERIOD

Section 1: The Background to the Gibson Period, 1942–1963

Graham Charles Gibson was a Llanelli man. Born there in 1903, he was educated at the local Grammar School and, after graduating at the University College of South Wales, Cardiff, he returned to take up his first teaching post at Stebonheath School, Llanelli. His heart was in Llanelli; his relatives were there; his wife belonged to Llanelli and, had not fate intervened, he would have retired there after occupying the Greenhill headship for almost 21 years. At Cardiff he took a Degree with Honours in Chemistry and for subsequent research in physical chemistry he was awarded the M.Sc. Degree of the University of Wales. Also he gained a Diploma in Education. After three years in his first appointment he became Senior Science Master at Maesteg Secondary School, where he was also principal teacher of Art. His interest in Art had led him to attend the Llanelli School of Art, his special study being etching. As a keen photographer he entered and won a number of open competitions. A keen cricketer, he had been playing Secretary of his University College First Eleven for two years. Twenty years service with the Boy Scout Movement culminated in his being made Assistant Commissioner for Maesteg and District. After the outbreak of war in 1939 he became Commanding Officer of the Maesteg Squadron of the A.T.C., with the rank of Flight Lieutenant, and after coming to Tenby he became attached to the Tenby Flight.

The stringent conditions which prevailed subsequent to his appointment as Head Master of the Tenby County School should be noticed. He took over his new duties in the depths of the black-out and the shortages of the Second World War. He witnessed the comings and goings of various military units, including the American 28th Infantry Division, to some of whom part of the school premises were let for instruction classes and for boxing. Along with the rest of us he saw the Tenby harbour completely cleared of local vessels on the eve of the invasion exercise 'Jantzen', to make way for thousands of troops to pass through there for embarkation prior to landing on neighbouring shores. There came the news of 'D Day' on 6 June 1944 and at last the announcement of 'Victory in Europe', with a declaration from Winston Churchill on 8 May 1945 and a broadcast by H.M. King George VI the same evening. As in the rest of the country, there were celebrations in Tenby and in the neighbouring parishes. *The Tenby Observer* reported 'Flags and banners appeared on every house and shop. The Union Jack of course predominated, but the National Flag was supported by flags of all the allied nations. There were new flags and veteran flags.' In the bright sunshine the Army Cadet Drum and Fife Band paraded the town, the Mayor and Mayoress (Lt.-Col. and Mrs. P. R. Howells) toured the streets and street and district parties were held. On the morning of Sunday, 13 May, a Civic Service of Thanksgiving in Tudor Square was attended by members of the fighting services, the Home Guard, Civil Defence, the Police, the V.A.D., Youth Organisations and hundreds of civilians. On the 24th the Mayor and Mayoress gave teas for young and old in the De Valence Pavilion.

The victory over Japan, officially declared on 2 September 1945, was dramatic, but this time the local celebration seemed to be something of an anti-climax. The atomic bombs dropped on Hiroshima and Nagasaki on 6 and 9 August respectively had brought unconditional surrender in the Far East—but, as A. J. P. Taylor remarked, 'Though they ended the war against Japan, they also foreshadowed the coming of Doomsday'. This marked the ending of the war and the beginning of Britain's post-war troubles. On 14 August the optimistic plans of the Labour Government (in office from 26 July) were interrupted by a warning from the Treasury that the country faced a "financial Dunkirk"; without substantial American aid, it would be virtually "bankrupt and the economic basis for the hopes of the public non-existent". Three days later, on 17 August, American aid was cut off. President Truman directed that lease-lend should end on VJ-Day.' By this time the National Debt had grown to some £24,000 million. The war had brought tight controls of men and materials, controls which could only be relaxed gradually over a number of years. The last vestiges of rationing were not removed until 1954. Alongside the Labour Government's programme of nationalisation of the Bank of

287

England, coal, iron and steel, transport, electricity and gas, the National Insurance Act and the introduction of the National Health Service, had come a dollar shortage, a fuel crisis in 1947 and the devaluation of sterling in 1949. The Marshall Plan for economic aid in 1947, the Festival of Britain in 1951 and the Coronation of Queen Elizabeth II in 1953 provided temporary rays of light amid the gloom of austerity imposed by government measures. The pressure of demand for building materials and manpower to make good war-damage to household and other premises built up a back-log of hindrances to school building programmes which was felt for 15 years and more after the war.

During the 21 years Gibson served as Head Master at Tenby, educational progress was affected by a series of official reports, delarations of policy, Acts of Parliament, regulations and circulars of various kinds, comprising a vast quantity of words which perhaps only a small minority of those engaged in the actual work of teaching had any time to read. We can look first of all at some of the decisions taken at national level since these governed the policy of the Pembrokeshire Education Committee with regard to re-organisation and, in turn, influenced the fortunes of the Tenby County School within this period.

In the midst of war, partly through necessity and partly through a wave of idealism, there was planning for the future. To be taken into account were the postponed raising of the school leaving age to 15 under the provisions of the 1936 Education Act and the recommendations of the Hadow and Spens Reports. A sequel to the Spens Report was that of the Norwood Committee 1943 concerning changes in the Secondary Schools' curriculum and examinations. The Committee advocated parity of amenities and conditions for three rough groupings of children—'the academic' in Secondary Grammar Schools, the 'mechanically minded' in Secondary Technical Schools and the 'essentially practical' in Secondary Modern Schools. It was emphasised that the judgement of the Primary School Teachers should provide the basis upon which the selection of children for the appropriate secondary schools should be made. Consideration should also be given to the results of intelligence and other tests and to the views of parents and pupils.

So far as possible there should be a common curriculum for pupils aged 11 to 13 in these three types of school, with arrangements for transfer where found advisable. After giving an outline of the history of the examination system the Norwood Committee recommended that 'in the interest of the individual child and of the increased freedom and responsibility of the teaching profession, changes in the School Certificate Examination should be in the direction of making the examination entirely internal, that is to say, conducted by the teachers at the school on syllabuses framed by themselves'. ' . . . . pupils would be encouraged to sit those subjects which they wished to take.' It was proposed that the existing Higher School Certificate should be abolished and that the university examining bodies should hold an examination every March. The results and the school records of candidates would provide the criteria upon which 'the State' could award scholarships, including the payment of university fees, and the cost of living, subject to the proof of need. In addition the State would be responsible for half the cost of additional scholarships awarded by local education authorities. Recommendations for both kinds of award should be made by special Boards representing the universities, the L.E.A.'s and the teachers. Some aspects of the Norwood Report were to be reflected in subsequent legislation.

In 1941 the Board of Education issued a confidential document known as the 'Green Book'. Its purpose was to sound the opinions of local education authorities, teachers and other interested parties on such current issues as the raising of the school leaving age, free secondary education and the training and supply of teachers. This supposed confidential publication in fact became widely known and the subject of much discussion, so helping to accumulate information for the Board of Education, of which the new President, Mr. R. A. Butler issued in July 1943 a White Paper entitled 'Educational Reconstruction', which foreshadowed the contents of his Education Bill. The Bill received the Royal Assent on 3 August 1944, three months before the significant Town and Country Planning Act, 'An Act to make provision for the acquisition and development of land for planning purposes, for amending the law relating to town and country planning; for assessing by reference to 1939 prices compensation payable in connection with the acquisition of land for public purposes . . . ', an Act of considerable importance for those concerned with the purchase of land for school buildings.

Because of its far-reaching effects, the principal features of the Butler Education Act 1944 should be noticed. It consists of five parts and contains 122 Sections, together with nine Schedules. An introductory note in Chitty's *Annual Statutes* states: 'Most of the previous Education Acts are repealed, but this is not a consolidating enactment and reproduces only a portion of the substance of the legislation which it repeals. Much of what was contained in the former enactments will be the subject of orders and regulations. It does not apply to Scotland or Northern Ireland. It makes provision for the first time in Part III for the registration and inspection of schools outside the statutory system of education'.

Part I was concerned with the reform of central administration. The Board of Education was replaced by a Ministry of Education. It was to be the duty of the Minister 'to promote the education of the people of England and Wales and the progressive development of institutions devoted to that purpose, and to secure the effective execution by Local authorities, under his control and direction, of the national policy for providing a varied and comprehensive educational service in every area'. With the consent of the Treasury, the Minister could appoint a Parliamentary Secretary and other such secretaries, officers and servants as he deemed necessary. There were to be two Central Advisory Councils, one for England and one for Wales and Monmouthshire. They were to include persons with experience of the statutory system of education and others who had similar experience and were to replace the Consultative Committee of the Board of Education. The function of these Councils was to advise the Minister on matters connected with educational theory and practice and upon any questions referred to them by him. It was obligatory for the Minister to report annually to Parliament upon the powers and duties entrusted to him.

Part II, entitled 'The Statutory System of Education' deals with local administration. ' . . . Subject to the provisions of Part I of the First Schedule to this Act, the local education authority for each county shall be the council of the county and the local education authority for each county borough shall be the council of that borough'. 'Part III Authorities' were to be abolished. Thus the 315 Education Authorities as constituted in 1902 were reduced to 146. In accordance with the recommendations of the Hadow and Spens Reports it was enacted that 'the statutory system of public education should be organised in three progressive stages to be known as primary education, secondary education and further education, and it shall be the duty of of the local education authority for every area, so far as their powers extend, to contribute towards the spiritual, moral, mental and physical development of the community by securing that efficient education throughout those stages shall be available to meet the needs of the population of their area.' ' . . . and the schools available for an area shall not be deemed sufficient unless they are sufficient in number, character, and equipment to afford for all pupils opportunities for education offering such a variety of instruction and training as may be desirable in view of their different ages, abilities and aptitudes . . . ' Accordingly, the Local Authority must have regard (a) for the provision of primary and secondary education in separate schools, (b) for the provision of nursery schools for pupils who have not attained the age of five years—or, where considered expedient, nursery classes in other schools, (c) for the provision of special schools for pupils suffering from any disability of mind or body (d) to the expediency of providing boarding accommodation, either in boarding schools or otherwise, for pupils for whom education as boarders is considered desirable by their parents and the authority. Requirements were laid down as to the standards of building suited to the various types of school.

Within a year of the passage of the Act every local authority was to estimate the immediate and prospective needs of their area, having regard to the provisions of the Act and any regulations made thereunder and then submit to the Minister a 'Development Plan' showing what action the Authority propose to take for securing that there should be sufficient primary and secondary schools available for their area. Furthermore, they were to indicate the successive measures by which they proposed to accomplish their purpose. Proposals could include the establishment of new county schools. All primary and secondary schools maintained by the Authority were to be termed 'county schools'. The separation into stages had certain consequences for the 'Dual Control' system which was modified by agreement. Voluntary Schools were to be of three categories:

(a) Controlled schools, where the Managers or Governors were not responsible for any of the expenses of the school, where secular instruction was in the control of the L.E.A., as was the appointment and dismissal of teachers. In such schools one third of the Governors were to be 'Foundation Governors' and two thirds were to be appointed by the Authority.

(b) Aided Schools, where the L.E.A. provided 50 per cent of the cost of repairs and alterations to the premises, where two-thirds of the Governors were to be 'Foundation Governors' and one third to be appointed by the Authority. In primary schools of this category secular instruction is under the control of the L.E.A., while in aided secondary schools it was to be under the control of the Governors.

(c) Special Agreement Schools, where under the provisions of the 1936 Education Act, reorganisation was being carried out under the Hadow Scheme and in which the L.E.A.'s had agreed with the Managers to make grants from 50 to 75 per cent towards the cost of extending non-provided schools or building new ones for senior pupils. The composition of the Managers was to be the same as in the Aided Schools.

For the first time, religious instruction and daily prayers were made obligatory by Act of Parliament. This was largely the result of pressures from religious leaders during the war. The school day in every county school and in every voluntary school was to begin with collective worship on the part of all pupils in attendance, except where the premises made this impracticable. Such worship was not to be that of any particular denomination. Religious instruction was to be given in every county school and every voluntary school, though there was provision for the withdrawal of a pupil at the request of a parent. In a controlled school religious instruction was to be given in accordance with an agreed syllabus for not more than two periods a week, while in an 'aided' or 'special agreement' school such instruction was to be under the control of the Managers.

The Butler Act contained a provision for the 'compulsory school age', ' . . . a person shall be deemed to be of compulsory school age if he has attained the age of five years and has not attained the age of fifteen years and a person shall be deemed to be over compulsory school age as soon as he has attained the age of fifteen years'.

'As soon as the Minister is satisfied that it has become practicable to raise to sixteen the upper limit of the compulsory school age he shall lay before Parliament a draft of an Order in Council . . . . .'

However, it was also provided that the Minister could, if there was any shortage of staff or accommodation, by Order, keep the leaving age to 14 until 1 April 1947. In fact, a Postponement Order to that effect was made through necessity. S. J. Curtis, in his *History of Education,* noted that 391,000 extra places would be needed with the raising of the age to 15, and a further 406,000 more with the raising to 16. Also enemy action had caused a loss of 150,000 places.

There were also clauses concerning further education and the provision of County Colleges, medical inspection and the treatment of pupils, the provision of milk and meals, board and lodging, clothing, facilities for recreation and social and physical training, transport of pupils, and the powers of the Local Education Authorities to prohibit and restrict the employment of children. There was the important prohibition of fees in respect of any school or county college maintained by an Education Committee, though fees were retained in Direct Grant Schools. The Minister and the L.E.A.'s also had certain duties in the arrangement of facilities for the training of teachers. There were to be special exemptions of buildings approved by the Minister from bye-laws and of voluntary schools from the payment of rates.

Part III of the Act was concerned with Independent Schools, their registration and inspection, the determination of complaints and the procedure for dealing with them.

Part IV contained miscellaneous and administrative provisions, including those affecting the appointment of Chief Education Officers, the remuneration of teachers, the compulsory purchase of land and the audit of accounts. Financial clauses authorised the Minister to pay annual grants to local authorities in the exericse of their functions relating to Education, other than their functions relating to the medical inspection and treatment of pupils, these last being the responsibility of the Ministry of Health. There were certain special financial arrangements relating to Wales and Monmouthshire. Subject to some provisions concerning standards of efficiency: 'The Minister shall pay to the Local Education Authority for every area in Wales and Monmouthshire a special annual grant in respect of any school which is maintained or assisted by the Authority, being a school in which grants were payable immediately before the date of the commencement of Part II of this Act under Section nine of the Welsh Intermediate Education Act 1889.' These grants, which were important for every County School in Wales, were to be of such amounts as would be determined by the Minister's Regulations from time to time and the

293

total sum was not to exceed the amounts payable in respect of such schools for the year ending 31 March 1929.

Part V was supplemental to the rest and contained schedules which elaborated on certain sections of the Act.

The 'Forty-four Education Act' was followed by a number of Statutory Regulations, Amending Acts and further Acts.

During the year 1945-46 there were financial regulations concerning grants for medical inspection and treatment of pupils, the supply of milk and meals, training college grants, the emergency training of teachers and the removal of Air-raid Shelters. There were additional grants for poorer Local Education Authorities comprising a main grant equal to 60 per cent of recognisable expenditure plus a capitation grant of £6 for each unit of attendance, less the product of a 2/6 rate. The purpose was to equalise the burden on the poorer areas.

The definitions of the personnel of primary and secondary schools were amended by the 1948 (Miscellaneous Provisions) Act. Primary school pupils were now defined as those juniors who have not attained the age of $10\frac{1}{2}$ or of those over $10\frac{1}{2}$ whom it is expedient to educate in primary schools, and secondary school pupils as those who have reached the age of ten years six months whom it is deemed expedient to educate with older children, the last being a concession to those teachers who favoured the promotion of the more able.

The provision of satisfactory school buildings was a constant cause for concern. In 1945 were issued regulations and circulars prescribing standards for building whether for extensions or for new primary or secondary schools based on an anticipated leaving age of 16. The best of intentions were subject to set-backs. First, in 1950, these regulations were modified on the grounds of economy, and then in 1952 it was necessary to revise the building programme on account of an acute shortage of materials. Further economies resulted in a reduction of grants for adult education in 1953, but this decision was afterwards reversed on account of the opposition it aroused.

Not only buildings were in short supply, but also teachers. This need was recognised in 1943 when the Emergency Training Scheme was launched, with a view to filling the gap by establishing a one year's intensive course. In 1944 the McNair Committee reported on the training and recruitment of teachers. Among the results was the

294

inauguration of Institutes of Education, each of which was an Area Training Organisation with the task of co-ordinating the training of teachers at colleges within a given university area and of awarding certificates in education to successful candidates who could be recommended to the Minister for recognition as qualified teachers. The Institutes could also provide facilities for advanced studies in the field of education. Recruitment to the teaching profession was to be encouraged by the offer of improved financial prospects. A new Burnham Scale was introduced from 1 April 1945. There was a basic scale of salaries for teachers, irrespective of the type of school in which they were employed and additional increments for special qualifications and experience were to be added at both the minimum and maximum of the scale. Posts of special responsibility were to carry extra allowances. Subsequently the salary scales were adjusted from time to time because of the increased cost of living. In 1956 the unsatisfactory condition of the superannuation fund led to an increase of the teachers' contributions from five to six per cent.

In 1947 there was published a report of the Secondary Schools Examinations Council. This was influenced to some extent by the earlier Norwood Report. One of the features was the proposal to introduce a General Certificate of Education on which would be recorded the Ordinary and Advanced Level results of successful candidates. A five years general course, suited to the ages, abilities and aptitudes of the pupils would lead to the Ordinary Level Examination which they could sit at the age of 16. There was to be no group system and passes in individual subjects would be entered on the Certificates. The Advanced Level Examination could be taken after a further two years course of specialised studies and Scholarship papers would be set for sixth formers with special talents. It was proposed that the examinations should be held sufficiently early for the results to reach the Ministry by 1 August. The Minister approved of the Council's proposals. The School Certificate and the Higher Certificate Examinations passed out of use and the first G.C.E. examinations were held in 1951. Because of objections on the grounds that gifted pupils would be held back on account of the minimum age of entry the regulations were modified in 1952 so that heads of schools would have the discretion of entering promising candidates who were younger than the age limit. At the same time Distinctions were reintroduced at the Advanced Level. The decision to hold the examinations early in the summer had the unfortunate effect of shortening the working part of the term and encouraging a waste of time once the tests were over.

A stock-taking of progress since the 1944 Education Act, along with plans for the future, was contained in a White Paper published in 1958 and entitled *Secondary Education for All : A New Drive*. Hard on the heels of the White Paper came the report of the Central Advisory Council for Education (England) under the Chairmanship of Sir Geoffrey Crowther. This lengthy Report, entitled *15 to 18* was published in two volumes in 1959 and 1960 respectively. The first contains the main report and the second the surveys on which the Advisory Council's recommendations were based. As the title indicates, the concern was with the problem of the older adolescent, within which age group there were some 2,318,00 boys and girls in 1959, with an expectation of a further 700,000 by 1965, when the 'bulge' in the birth rate would have been reached, with the prospect of a further bulge in the mid-seventies. (This further bulge along with the raising of the leaving age to 16 in 1971 created serious problems of accommodation in secondary schools in the mid-seventies.) The main report is divided into seven sections: Education in a Changing World (including a historical survey), Secondary Education for All, The Way to County Colleges, The Sixth Form, Technical Challenge and Educational Response, and Institutes and Teachers.

Among the reforms advocated were the introduction of an examination of lower standard than the G.C.E., suited to about one third of the pupils of modern schools; the raising of the school leaving age to 16 as soon as possible, preferably between 1965 and 1969 (between the 'bulges') and prior to the opening of County Colleges; the reform of the Middle School curriculum to prevent too early specialisation; the easing of congestion in the Fifth Form time-table; measures to attract highly qualified graduates for teaching in the Sixth Form; a better use of minority time of sixth formers so that attention could be given to 'the literacy' of science specialists and 'the numeracy' of arts specialists, while keeping in mind religious and moral education, art, music and physical education. The Report did not favour the segregation of the growing number of sixth formers who were not intending to pursue university careers. It was noted that about a

G. C. GIBSON AND STAFF 1947

standing, left to right: Mr. W. H. Morris, Mrs. Jones, Mr. W. Harrison, Miss B. Toye, Messrs. W. J. Davies, A. S. Richards, Miss R. Merriman (Secretary), Mr. G. R. Samuel, Miss D. Worthington
seated, left to right: Mr. W. C. Bennett, Miss M. G. Bowen (Sen. Mistress), Mr. G. C. Gibson (H.M.), Mr. H. J. Williams (Sen. Master), Miss E. Ellis
photo: Arthur Squibbs

G. C. GIBSON AND STAFF 1950

standing, left to right: Messrs. Forest Jones, H. T. Roberts, S. W. H. Court, Miss R. Burgess (Secretary), Misses G. Morris, B. Jenkins, Messrs. W. J. Davies, J. L. Williams
seated, left to right: Mr G. R. Samuel, Misses E. Ellis and M. G. Bowen (Sen. Mistress), Mr. G. C. Gibson (H.M.), Mr. H. J. Williams (Sen. Master), Messrs. W. Harrison and A. S. Richards
photo: F. A. Rose

PART OF THE CAST OF 'LADY PRECIOUS STREAM' (H. I. HSIUNG) 1943
at the De Valence Pavilion, with Denise Ormond in the title role
photo: *Arthur Squibbs*

CAST OF 'TOAD OF TOAD HALL' (FRASER-SIMSON/A. A. MILNE) 1949
at the Little Theatre, with Lumley Hughes in the title role

photo: F. A. Rose

LAST SCHOOL 'SOCCER' ELEVEN 1948-49
photo: Arthur Squibbs

FIRST SCHOOL RUGBY FIFTEEN 1949-50
photo: F. A. Rose

SCHOOL HOCKEY ELEVEN 1944-45
with Miss Beryl Toye (P.E. Mistress)
photo: Arthur Squibbs

GIRLS' ATHLETICS LONG JUMP c. 1950
photo: P. M. Davies

BOYS' ATHLETICS — TRACK EVENT c. 1950
Photo: P. M. Davies

BOYS' GYMNASTICS c.1950
with Mr. L. Forest Jones (P.E. Master)
photo: F. A. Rose

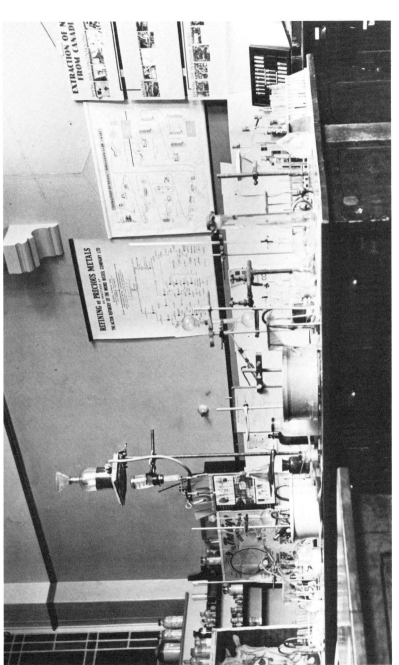

PART OF THE OLD LABORATORY c. 1948-49
used for Chemistry, Biology and Physics
photo: F. A. Rose

FOUNDATIONS OF A BUILDING OF THE ROMANO-BRITISH PERIOD
uncovered at Trelissey near Amroth 1950-51
photo: F. A. Rose

PUPILS AT WORK ON THE SITE
1950-51
photo: F. A. Rose

ARCHAEOLOGICAL ACTIVITIES
by pupils, past pupils and Staff in collaboration with Tenby Museum

quarter of the 15—18 group leaving school at fifteen continued in some kind of further education, and a summary of the institutions providing the facilities included Evening Institutes and 'Sandwich Courses' in Technical Colleges. Following the Report, and with a view to establishing a more stable fourth year in secondary schools, an Act passed in 1962 fixed two leaving dates, namely at the ends of the Easter and Summer Terms.

Parallel with the appearance of the Crowther Report was a special enquiry by a committee appointed by the Secondary Schools Examinations Council. The Beloe Report, named after the Chairman of the Committee, was published in 1960 under the title *Secondary Examinations other than the G.C.E.* It was observed that after the school leaving age was raised to 15 many children in non-selective secondary schools remained longer than they were legally required to do. Some of these pupils, a limited number, were entered as candidates for G.C.E. Examinations, while others who were less able sat the examinations of a variety of bodies, some of them London based. The Certificates generally had a 'local currency' and they were gained by pupils aged 15. As some boys and girls were staying on in school after that age it was necessary to devise an examination for those who had completed a five year course and could be classified in ability range lower than required for the General Certificate of Education. It was also recognised that in the non selective secondary schools there were many pupils whose capabilities made them unfitted for any kind of external examination. It was proposed that a new examination, also a subject examination but not a watered-down version of the G.C.E., should be taken at the end of the fifth year and be geared to the needs and interest of the boys and girls concerned. Some 20 Regional Examining Bodies should have overall responsibility, but the form and content would be devised by the teachers themselves. The Minister of Education should recognise the examination for the Certificate of Secondary Education (the C.S.E.) and the local authorities should pay the fees of the candidates.

After consideration of the Beloe Report, Sir David Eccles, Minister of Education, decided to ask for a further investigation of the problems involved. The Council, together with representatives of Technical Colleges and persons with experience of non-selective secondary schools, under the Chairmanship of Sir John Lockwood, produced a new report in 1962 with the title *Examinations in Secondary Schools—*

The Certificate of Secondary Education. The Beloe recommendations were accepted and as a result the new Minister for Education, Sir Edward Boyle, gave his approval for the new examination to come into operation in 1965.

During the last years of G. C. Gibson's headship at Tenby he witnessed many advances in Higher Education. More opportunities and wider scope were offered with the establishment of Colleges of Technology and the foundation of the new universities of Keele, Sussex, York, East Anglia, Carlisle and Canterbury. Meanwhile, following the Report of the Anderson Committee, which had been looking into the question of university and government grants, the Minister accepted a modification of the "means test" which increased the number of students receiving the full grant. The new rates were to come into operation in 1961. Also State Scholarships were to be abolished after 1962 in favour of open entrance scholarships to universities; the holder of an open scholarship would be allowed to retain up to £100 of its value without any deduction from the government grant. This event led to changes in the G.C.E. Examinations; the Scholarship Level was brought to an end and the Advanced Level candidates had their results in individual subjects graded A, B, C, D, or E, but 'O' if only Ordinary Level standard was attained. These new arrangements were first operated in summer 1963. The year 1963 saw the publication of the Robbins Report proposing an expansion of Higher Education at a cost of £1,420 million, and of the Newsom Report entitled *Half our Future*, dealing with the age group 13 to 16 who were mainly pupils in Modern and Comprehensive Schools. In the same year a Committee, chaired by Lady Plowden commenced its consideration of Primary Education involving the youngest age group in the system of education, but, as in the case of the Hadow series of Reports, it was the last to receive full attention.

That same year G. C. Gibson died in April. During the time he had spent as Head Master at Greenhill successive governments had carried out sweeping changes in Education affecting all stages from the Nursery School to Further Education and the University, with more to follow. We can now turn from the national to the local level during the same period.

Legislation, official regulations, reports and circulars relating to education exerted an important influence upon the work of the

298

Pembrokeshire L.E.A. and its officials. The task of the Director of Education was to inform and advise the Authority on a multitude of matters arising from the decisions of the central government. The key post of Director was held by Mr. D. T. Jones, M.A., LL.B., until his work was cut short by his untimely death in February 1957. His successor was Mr. Wynford Davies, M.A., who had served as Assistant Director since April 1951, and who was promoted in May 1957. The bound volumes of the Minutes of the Education Committee which doubled in thickness after the mid-forties, bear witness to the growing bulk of business which had to be dealt with. The original sub-committees were retained, some of them with additional functions, and others were added so the list included Finance and General Purposes, Staffing, Secondary and Further Education, Buildings, Furnishing, Development—plan, Sites, Medical Services and Meals, Attendance, Library, Youth, Music, and ad hoc advisory committees on such matters as religious education, road safety, and agriculture in secondary schools. Additional responsibilities involved the appointment of additional organisers, advisers and instructors for Meals, Physical Education, Further Education, Needlework, Youth, Music and Horticulture.

The Authority's concern with youth and the activities of its Youth Sub-Committee expanded from an immediate involvement with the registration of boys and girls in January and March 1942 and the problem of pre-service training to a far reaching effort to provide local facilities, activities and premises throughout the County, during and after the war. While the main task of the Education Committee was to carry out the reorganisation required by the central government, from time to time they passed resolutions on certain current questions when they arose, as the following sample from the war period will illustrate. On 20 November 1942 they voted in favour of the need for an efficient system of religious education after the war and for the abolition of the Dual System; on 15 January 1943 they made recommendations for the educational uses of the Welsh Church Fund (under the Welsh Church Acts Scheme); 18 January 1944 they approved the report of their sub-committee which had been considering Board of Education Circular 182 (Wales) concerning the teaching of Welsh. Governing Bodies and Heads of Schools in the South of the county (predominently English) 'should be urged to reconsider the place of foreign languages in the curriculum with due regard to the advantages of selecting Welsh as a suitable foreign language. The sub-committee wishes to draw the attention of the Governors to the following statement in the Norwood Report . . . "Even for those who have learnt no Welsh hitherto it becomes a question whether their first foreign language (in Wales) should not be Welsh—the language of their own country and the language spoken by thousands of their fellow pupils in other parts of Wales. Whatever linguistic discipline is undergone in learning a foreign language will be undergone in learning Welsh equally with other foreign languages." . . . '; on 16 May 1944 there was a discussion about the McNair Report on the supply of teachers and the L.E.A. considered means of avoiding a loss of recruits and of encouraging suitable recruits from the elementary schools; on 15 May 1945 the agenda included Board of Education (Education Pamphlet 119) *Sex Education in Schools and Youth Organisations* and it was agreed that instruction in Sex Hygiene required (a) biological training, (b) a healthy attitude to reproduction and sex, (c) a married teacher with at least a three months course in sex training in schools. This was one of the signposts to the future and the greater freedom of discussion of such matters, whereas in the past the word 'sex' scarcely ever crossed the lips of those who taught in the pre-1945 Intermediate Schools.

The implementation of the provisions of the 1944 Education Act and the evolution of the Authority's scheme of reorganisation occupies much space in the Minute Books, in particular the Minutes of the Development, Sites, and Buildings Sub-Committees. On 30 November 1943 a Special Meeting of the Education Committee had discussed the Director's summary of the Government's White Paper *Educational Reconstruction* and reached the following decisions, which reveal the Committee's attitude and give some indication of the local problems:

They were glad to note the proposed raising of the school leaving age to 15 as soon as possible after the war and that secondary education would be free, and that three types were to be made available.

They noted the government's intention to make the provision of nursery schools a duty of the L.E.A., but concluded that, unless the Board envisaged quite small nursery schools, in one or two districts nursery schools attached to infant schools would meet the situation so far as Pembrokeshire was concerned in smaller towns. But they were unable to make suggestions for sparsely populated areas.

The Authority feared the perpetuation of the Dual System and concern was expressed over the possibility of the retention of 'Single School' areas because there were 41 of them in the county which were denominational. The Committee were of the opinion that the Agreed Syllabus would meet the needs of all children. The decapitation of 'the present' all standard schools would create difficulties through the duplication of small junior and infant schools in small towns.

They appreciated the need for a change in the assessment of pupils entering the secondary schools. A welcome was given to the new status for Technical Secondary Schools. It was anticipated that adjustments would be needed in schemes governing Intermediate Schools and that of the existing ones would become multilateral and some lateral. They agreed with the proposal for continued part-time education up to 18 and envisaged Young People's Colleges being housed in premises for Technical Secondary Education.

They were fully in accord with most of the proposals and felt that the government should by financial assistance make them possible within the territory of every L.E.A. in the land. The heavy recurring cost of transport was one of the strong obstacles to re-organisation in rural areas and special provisions would be needed. The Authority was concerned with the problem of premises—they realised that there would be an allocation of priorities for building materials, if this had not already been done. The L.E.A. had a high degree of priority for the use of public buildings 'at present in the hands of government departments'. These should not be handed over for private use before knowing whether they would be required for educational purposes.

Copies of the Committee's resolutions were to be forwarded to the President of the Board of Education, the Chairman of the Welsh Parliamentary Party, the M.P.s for Pembrokeshire, Carmarthenshire and Cardiganshire and the Permanent Secretary of the Welsh Department of the Board of Education.

The Education Act 1944 had important consequences for the constitution and responsibilities of the Local Education Authority. On 28 September 1945 it was recommended that, under the provisions of the Act, the Education Committee should consist of 35 members when complete, of these; 30 were to be appointed by the County Council including 20 of its own members. The 30 were to co-opt five persons experienced in education and of these, not less than two were to be women. The Committee was to exercise the County

Council's function with regard to Education, determining general policy and having authority to approve of capital expenditure over £500. The term of office would be normally three years, but the term for the first members would end on the day following the termination of their membership of the Council.

The status of the County Intermediate Schools and their Governing Bodies was also affected by the Act. In January 1945 the Higher Education Sub-Committee reminded them that, with the abolition of the payment of fees, the County Schools would become dependent on the L.E.A. and would be classed as Voluntary schools. The position was finalised on 27 September 1946 when the Authority approved of the Director's summary of the Instrument and Articles of Government of the Voluntary Secondary Schools', as defined in Circular 89 Welsh Department, Ministry of Education and other circulars and administrative memoranda: 'With one exception the existing secondary schools in the county will become Controlled Voluntary Schools. The existing schemes are to be revised by the Minister.' It was necessary to have an Instrument of Government and Articles defining the functions of the Local Government, the Body of Governors and the Head Teachers respectively: ' . . . the Instrument of Government for every Voluntary (Controlled) Secondary School shall provide that one third of the Governors shall be Foundation Governors and two thirds shall be appointed by the L.E.A.' This meant that the total number on each Body must be a multiple of three. The co-opted members were to include at least two women in Mixed and Girls' schools. Of course, the Education Authority now exercised a controlling influence in the Board of Governors. The relationship between the Governing Body, the Head and the Chief Education Officer were defined in a Ministry of Education circular in 1944, *The Principles of Government Maintained Secondary Schools* as follows:

(1) There should be free consultation at all times with the Chairman of the Governors.
(2) All proposals affecting the Governors' sphere of responsibility should be submitted formally to the Governing Body.
(3) The decisions of the Chairman should be on matters of policy only and such directions should be reported without delay to the Governors.

(4) The Head is entitled to attend meetings of the Governing Body, except when the Governors decide otherwise 'for good cause'.

(5) Free consultation and co-operation should exist between the Head and the Chief Education Officer 'on matters affecting the welfare of the school'.

(6) The teaching staff should be entitled to submit their views and proposals to the Governors through the Head.

It was stipulated in the Butler Act that the Education Authorities were to provide secondary education for all children of the appropriate age and that as from 1 April 1945 no tuition fees would be chargeable, thus eliminating a separate fee-payers' examination. In March 1945 the Heads of Intermediate Schools and representatives of the elementary schools decided that the examination for admission would be held in May that year. However, in 1946 the Secondary Schools Admission Examination was fixed for Friday 29 March so that staffs of secondary schools could be available for invigilation. There were two groups to be examined at the usual centres with the same papers set for both:

Examination I for pupils not less than ten on 1 August 1946 and not over 12 on 1 April 1946.

Examination II for pupils not less than 12 and not more than 13 years of age on 1 April 1946.

The subjects were to be:

(1) Arithmetic (Mental and Mechanical) 30 minutes;

(2) Arithmetic (Problem Paper) 45 minutes;

(3) Group Intelligence Test, 45 minutes;

(4) Language, 75 minutes.

Provision was made for questions to be answered in Welsh. The syllabuses and allocation of marks were recorded in the Minutes. For success a candidate would need 40 per cent total in Examination I and 50 per cent in Examination II. No age marks were to be allowed. The Heads of Secondary Schools were to be responsible for the first marking, allocating one examiner per subject. The setting of the papers and the final award would be the responsibility of the Director of Education.

The Pembrokeshire Authority's Development Plan was prepared by a sub-committee, accepted by the Education Committee on 18 March 1947 and then forwarded to the Ministry for observations.

303

In the course of his introduction to the plan the Director stated that certain matters remained to be discussed in detail, including the frontiers with neighbouring shires.

'This plan is a long range plan and the Authority is not committed to it down to the last detail, not even when it is finally approved and not even after that . . . . It is also officially declared by the Ministry that the Education Authority itself is free to modify the general features of the plan from time to time as events dictate and high policy commends. The period during which this plan is to develop extends over the next 15 years. What we shall see and know during that period no one knows.

'The estimated gross cost of bringing existing schools into accord with the Ministry's Building Regulations and of providing new schools is, in round figures 2½ million pounds.

'The plan involves (a) the discontinuance of 52 Primary Schools and of nine Secondary Schools; (b) the building of eleven Nursery Schools, eight Infant Schools, eight Junior Schools, eight all-standard schools up to 11 + and eight Secondary Schools, a total of 43 schools. Many schools will be altered and extended to more than double the accommodation . . .

'If priority is given to the provision of secondary education it is because secondary education was never before free and universal, and because the improvements of the present all-standard schools are bound to be of a temporary nature until the senior pupils have been taken out of them. The extension of the leaving age to 15 + also makes it imperative that the education provided for senior pupils should substantially meet their needs.'

An analysis of the distribution of population was given on the basis of the 1931 census and attention was drawn to the language problem due to the predominantly Welsh north of the county and the English south The total number of pupils on the registers in January 1947 was 12,289. The proposals for secondary school re-organisation were based on existing School Districts 'except that the Preseli District will in future be a self-contained district, with a secondary school within the borders of the county'.

The following programme, with a number of modifications, was eventually carried through:

District		Proposed Kind		Sex & Ages	Size
I	Fishguard and Goodwick	Grammar-Modern	M	11—18+	600
II	Haverfordwest	Grammar	B	11—18+	300
		Grammar	G	11—18+	240
		Modern	M	11—15+	700
III	Milford Haven	Grammar-Technical	M	11—18+	400
		Modern	M	11—15+	600
		Neyland Modern	M	11—15+	180
IV	Narberth	Modern	M	11—15+	200
V	Pembroke and Pembroke Dock	Grammar-Technical	M	11—18+	300
		Modern	M	11—15+	600
VI	St. David's	Grammar-Modern	M	11—18+	200
VII	Tenby	Grammar-Modern	M	11—18+	580
VIII	Preseli	Multilateral	M	11—18+	340

(B=Boys; G=Girls; M=Mixed)

It was proposed to provide facilities for training and instruction in Agricultural Science at Preseli (Distr. VIII—based at Crymmych) and at the new Grammar School at Pembroke; Engineering at Milford Haven; Navigation at Milford Haven and Fishguard; Pre-Nursing at Pembroke Dock and Tasker's, Haverfordwest; Commercial Education at Fishguard, Tenby and either Haverfordwest Grammar School for Boys or Taskers for Girls. There were also proposals for Hostels in Haverfordwest, Milford Haven, Preseli and Pembroke Dock. Free transport would be provided in accordance with the distances laid down in Section 39 of the 1944 Act. Public bus services would have to be supplemented by special buses at an estimated cost of £20,000 to £25,000 annually.

Also envisaged were centres for the handicapped and centres where halls could be built with provision for (a) Public and School Health Service, (b) Library Service with Reading Room, (c) Drama and Music, (d) Light Refreshments.

The Plan contained a detailed examination of the eight Districts which would be the catchment areas for the new secondary schools—their extent, economic development, schools and school population, schools to be closed and schools to be provided.

District VII (Tenby) included the following parishes or areas: Tenby (urban), St. Mary Out-Liberty, Caldey, Gumfreston, Penally, St. Florence, Manorbier, East Williamston, St. Issell's, Redberth (Rhydberth), Amroth, Loveston, Ludchurch, Jeffreston. Within these were eight Council Schools and eight Non-provided Schools with a total of 1,206 pupils. The Tenby Intermediate School had 265 on the Roll. The closures and proposals for new schools were not entirely carried out as intended at this stage. Eventually the re-organisation led to the closing of Begelly, New Hedges, Rhydberth and of the Tenby Parochial Schools, while the rest were destined to be the contributory schools for the new County Secondary School at Tenby: County Primaries at Amroth, Sageston (new with Community Hall), Loveston, Pentlepoir (new), Saundersfoot (new recently), Stepaside, and Tenby (new Junior School opened 1977); other County Primaries being Voluntary Controlled schools at Jeffreston, Manorbier (remodelled), Penally (huts added), St. Florence (new). Following the phasing out of the Tenby Parochial Schools a new V.C. Infants and Nursery School was built in Heywood Lane.

The Development Plan suffered periodic set-backs and the fulfilment of all the projects within the 15 years estimated by Mr. D. T. Jones was not possible. On 18 July 1947, four months after the Plan was unfolded, the Education Committee received the Ministry's Circular 143 (Educational Building Programme for 1947-48) emphasising (a) the shortage of labour and (b) the shortage of materials and the 'drastic curtailment of new works programmes generally' but bearing in mind the permanent new accommodation required by September 1947 for the raising of the school leaving age.

Meanwhile, the Development Plan Sub-Committee continued its work and its proposals in respect of secondary schools was approved by the L.E.A. on 19 March 1948:

District No. 1. Fishguard and Goodwick. Consultation at the Ministry in London resulted in the suggestion that the new school be organised as a bilateral school, or if necessary be divisible into two separate schools. This proposal was approved and the County Architect gave 1 January 1949 as the starting date.

District No. 2. Haverfordwest. The proposals here were for two single sex Grammar Schools on adjoining sites and a five to six form entry Modern School at Prendergast. The starting dates were to be Haverfordwest Modern 1948, Boys Grammar 1952 and Girls Grammar (Tasker's) 1950. The tender of Gibson and King Ltd., £221,000 for the construction of the Modern School was accepted on 7 December 1948 and the Foundation Stone was laid on 25 March 1949. Thus was launched the first major building project. The dates in respect of the other two schools were proved to be wildly inaccurate.

District No. 3. Milford Haven.

(a) a bi-lateral four-form entry Grammar-Technical School.

(b) a five-form entry Modern School.

(c) a one-form entry Modern School at Neyland.

District No. 4. Narberth. The proposal was to convert Narberth Intermediate School into a Modern Secondary School (one to two form entry) and to send pupils of the 'Grammar' type to the proposed multilateral school in the Crymych area, to Whitland and to the proposed bi-lateral Grammar-Modern School at Tenby; where appropriate they could go to the two schools in Haverfordwest. The Minister noted that the number of Grammar School pupils would not be large and estimated 25 to 30 in this age group. (This loss of Grammar School status met with vigorous and prolonged resistance from the Narberth Governors and townsfolk, who were proud of the academic record of their school. In the end the catchment area, which had favoured Narberth in the 1894 and 1912 Schemes, was rearranged to the advantage of Tenby.)

District No. 5. Pembroke and Pembroke Dock. The Minister agreed with the proposals to provide a two form entry Grammar-Technical (Agricultural) School and a five-form entry Modern Secondary School. Ministerial approval was given for the purchase of Bush House and 109 acres of land at Pembroke. The property was expected to be in the County Council's hands by March 1949.

District No. 6. St. David's. It was recommended that there should be a bi-lateral Grammar-Modern School and that in order to make this possible the Committee should agree that there should be streams of 20—this in view of the fine record of this small County School.

District No. 7. Tenby. The Minister was of the opinion that the total provision required would be for a five-form (plus) entry and suggested the separation into two, i.e. a two-form entry Grammar and a four-form entry Modern School. Otherwise there should be a solution similar to that at Fishguard. Accordingly the Committee recommended that the school should be planned so that it could be either bi-lateral (Grammar-Modern), or if necessary two separate schools.

District No. 8. Preseli. The Minister appeared to favour a Modern Secondary School only in this District, but he would approve of a multilateral school if the Authority would agree to streams of 20. The Authority accepted this condition and agreed to set up a two to three-form entry multilateral school as planned. Part of their plan was to establish a course for agricultural study and practice. In 1954 the scheme was revised in favour of a three-form Grammar-Modern School.

These were the broad outlines. Many modifications would be necessary in order to convert planning into practice. There were sites to be acquired, 77 of them in all, according to Walter Barrett, the County Architect. The District Valuer's services would be required, and then there were legal formalities and consultations with the County Planning Department, the County Surveyor and others who would be involved. Plans and the acceptance of tenders would be subject to the Minister's approval. There were unforeseen delays caused by government economies in 1952, 1953 and 1956.

In the Pembrokeshire Education Authority's scheme of re-organisation the new bi-lateral school at Tenby did not have top priority. In fact, it was far back in the queue. Prendergast Secondary Modern School was opened in 1952. By the mid-fifties Bush Grammar-Technical and Fishguard Grammar-Modern Schools were completed. Major projects for 1955-56 were Preseli Bi-lateral and the St. David's extensions for bi-lateral, with Tenby bi-lateral and Pembroke Dock Secondary Modern extension to come within the next five years. The new school premises for Tasker's and Haverfordwest Grammar School were even later in the line. Meanwhile the L.E.A. had decided in March 1951 to establish a County Technical College at Neyland and the Minister allocated £55,000 for the purpose of establishing a workshop block there in the year 1951-52, a site of 10 to 12 acres being needed for the purpose. In commenting upon this project the Director of Education analysed in detail the purpose of providing (a) full time and part time education for persons over compulsory school age, (b) leisure time occupations for any over school age who were able and willing to profit, so catering for a social need and the desire for knowledge. In this connection he referred to the work of the Evening Institutes which had been set up in Fishguard, Narberth, Haverfordwest, Pembroke Dock and Tenby (where G. C. Gibson was in charge). At the other end of the scale and on a site to the west of the Tenby Grammar School playing field the new Tenby Infants School had been completed by 1953.

Consideration of sites for the new Secondary School at Tenby appears at intervals in the Education Committee's Minute Books from 30 September 1949 onwards. The decision that the school should be sited in Heywood Lane was made on 24 November 1950, and after discussion as to the amount of land required, the Minister's consent was sought for the preparation of the first plans and for the purchase of the fields required. In July 1953 it was reported that part of the site for the new premises had been approved by the Planning Committee and in November 1954 the Buildings Sub-Committee received a progress report on negotiations with the owners of the land who were considering the prices proposed by the District Valuer. A year later the Ministry of Education had approved the establishment of a new County Secondary School for 500 to 600 children. On 24 May 1957 the County Architect submitted a schedule of areas to be acquired together with the District Valuer's recommended prices. The School Field, Ordnance Survey No. 205, 4·991 acres, was bounded by Heywood Lane on its northern side. The new Infants School had been built on a narrow field O.S. 204 to the east. The fields required for the bi-lateral school lay to the south, south-east and south-west, while further land for an addition to the games field was on the north side of Heywood Lane.

Mr. V. S. Hodges and Mrs. W. Chadwick agreed to sell a small enclosure for £5. 0s. 0d. The figures listed by the Architect do not include Surveyor's and Legal Fees. In due course all the necessary purchases were made and in November 1958 the Clerk to the County Council was able to report that the Tenby Borough Council and the National Parks Committee had approved of the proposed development

O.S. No.		Area in Acres	Owner	Price Agreed
Pt. 200 &	(S.)	6·44	Tenby Borough Council	£1724 5s. 10d.
Pt. 165	(N.)			
Pt. 165 &	(N.)	·33	Mrs. M. Evans	£515 8s. 7d.
Pt. 164	(N.)	·29	Mrs. H. A. L. Adams	£350 0s. 0d.
Pt. 216 &	(S.E.)	3·13	Mrs. V. S. Hodges	£470 0s. 0d.
Pt. 211	(S.)			
Pt. 209 &	(S.)	1·25	Mr. J. E. L. Mabe	£300 0s. 0d.
Pt. 200				
Pt. 208	(S.)	·50	Col. H. Allen	Not yet agreed.
Pt. 199	(S.W.)	1·28	Commander Locke	Agreed to sell at District Valuer's price subject to a way-leave.

in accordance with the plans submitted by the County Architect. It was noted that bus bays would be needed for 'contract buses'.

On 10 April 1959 a Special Meeting of the Education Committee was informed that the Parliamentary Secretary to the Ministry of Education (Sir Edward Boyle) would be in West Wales the following month, that arrangements were being made for him to perform the Foundation Stone Ceremony on 22 May and that he would be invited to a special lunch as a part of the programme. The Development Committee had received from the Ministry a letter dated 13 May 1959 approving under Section 13(6) of the Education Act 1944 the plans for the proposed Tenby County School at a cost of £296,220 and that would start immediately. The plan provided for a six-form entry Grammar-Bilateral School. The Architect stated that work on the school would start officially on 3 June 1959. There was correspondence between the Governors and the County Authority over the title of the new school. The Governors' request that it should be named Tenby Grammar High School brought forth a recommendation from the L.E.A. 'That the Governors be informed that, in common with other similar schools, the new school will be a County Secondary School and that its official title till be "Tenby County Secondary School".' After further discussion it was conceded that the word 'Greenhill' should be retained in the title. The Governors asked for the retention of this name on the new site on account of its associations in the minds of Tenby people with the traditions of the old school and not with bricks and mortar. The school was ready for occupation by 5 September 1961, the beginning of the new Session, but the 'Official Opening' by Mr. Desmond Donnelly, M.P. did not take place until Friday 17 November. Further reference to this event and to the Foundation Stone Ceremony will be made in the following chapter.

By the time G. C. Gibson moved into the new premises he had served 19 years in the old Greenhill School, constantly looking forward to this change of environment.

Section 2: Greenhill with Gibson

'Keep Trust'

(School Motto introduced by G.C.G.)

Along with the Senior Master, Mr. H. J. Williams, I first met the new Head Master at the school prior to the Session beginning in September 1942. Mr. G. C. Gibson was short of stature, stout of figure, well-dressed, with a good head of hair, neatly trimmed, and parted on the left. He wore horn-rimmed spectacles. We were always to find him thus—immaculately clothed and with an interest in the appearance of others besides himself. He had a welcoming and winning smile, a twinkle in the eye suggesting a sense of humour, and a slightly projecting lower jaw with a strong chin which bespoke determination and gave a hint of obstinacy. Fortunately, Mr. Williams took an immediate liking to him, a fact which augured well for their mutual relationship and for the future of the School. At first Mr. and Mrs. Gibson took up residence in Broadwell Hayes before moving to a flat next to the Cawdor Hotel on the Esplanade and eventually to 'Cliff Side' in Sutton Street.

In the initial stages of the new Session G. C. Gibson seemed anxious to establish an easy-going relationship with the older members of the staff, but before long he made it clear that he was just as concerned about his authority as his predecessor had been. An 'enter without knocking' attitude changed to one of 'knock and wait for an answer' on the occasion of a visit to the Head Master's Room. The new broom

311

was soon in evidence in that room, where no books and papers were allowed to lie around. The square table at which the Head sat, where J.T. had sat before, was now covered with a green baize cloth. The contents of the roll-top desk and the large book-case were reorganised and as soon as funds permitted, a metal filing cabinet and other storage cupboards were installed. When the day's work finished, may be one neat pile of papers remained. A long table also covered with green baize was placed near the bay window. This could be used for special purposes.

Changes in the running of the school were inevitable, many of them overdue. There were minor adjustments in the Morning Assembly. Since the early thirties the staff had sat at the back of the Hall, leaving the Head in solitary state on the dais. G. C. Gibson asked his staff to join him on the platform, the men on his left facing the boys and the women on his right facing the girls. Pupil participation was encouraged by arranging a rota of Prefects to read the daily portion of scripture. Mr. Gibson's encouragement was not confined to the School Service. Originally a Baptist, he had been confirmed as member of the Church in Wales and he made it his business to find out all school pupils who were confirmees in St. Mary's Church and invite them to join him and his wife for a monthly corporate Communion there. The arrangements for the beginning of morning and afternoon school were altered. The relics of the so-called 'Dual School', with the segregation of girls upstairs and the boys downstairs for registration were discontinued in favour of the Form Room system, with members of the staff allocated registers according to seniority in ascending order through the school. Weekly totals and terminal additions were to be systematically and neatly entered. An untidy register could result in an angry rebuke. He was always clear and incisive in his instructions whether given verbally or in writing. Supervision duties before School, at Break and Lunch time, and after school were defined along with points of congestion to be watched when pupils were on the move in the noisy corridors of the old building. Whereas Mr. J. T. Griffith had appeared to be neglectful of his own personal punctuality, the new Head was always in his room a quarter of an hour before morning school and almost as prompt in the afternoons. He was equally punctual in his departure for lunch and at the end of the day. Unless it was necessary for him to attend a Governors' Meeting, a Staff Meeting or some

312

special function, he was ready, hat and coat on, as soon as the old hand-bell was sounded to mark the close of a morning or afternoon session. A concession to comfort, unthinkable in the old days, was that shortly after taking up duties he arranged for mid-morning tea to be brought over from the Domestic Science Centre for himself and his colleagues. In the midst of his insistence upon the routine he devised we were appreciative of his tremendous sense of humour and his enjoyment of a good story.

Mr. Gibson was of course entering the school in the middle of the Second World War and its shadow of necessity hung over everything. Indeed, re-reading *The Greenhillian* for the year 1943 just after Mr. Gibson's arrival gives one the impression that the entire life of the school was geared to the War effort. We are told by a sixth form contributor that Greenhill is 'in the front line with those who are doing their bit. The whole aspect of the school has changed. It is now full of varied school uniforms some of which I am sure one never expected to see at Greenhill. The women members of staff display Civil Defence badges and may disappear at any moment to join the ATS or the WRNS. Many of the boys belong to the A.T.C. or the Army Cadet Corps and feel so important as they don their uniforms and go on parade. The girls too play their part. They all belong to some movement or other. The boys rarely fall down during "break" now as they know they will have too many girls willing to render what they call "First Aid". Many of the senior boys leave the school and come back looking "men of the world" in their uniforms with a stripe or two or even "wings" and tell their thrilling experiences of life in wartime beyond the walls of Greenhill. The school puts its back into saving and the slogan "lend to defend the right to be free" meets the eye everywhere. Pupils come on Monday morning with all they can spare to put something into National Savings while in the background Greenhill's team of gardeners helps to swell the nation's food supplies. Some of them indeed, are keen enough to help the neighbouring farmers. Many of the Sixth forms boys spend their lunch hour discussing the war every day and particularly how they think the various campaigns should be run. They plan the world of the future and the Sixth form girls put forward their ideas for the complete freedom of women after the War. Some of the "airminded" boys

313

spend hours learning foreign languages which they say will prove useful if ever they make a forced landing on foreign soil!'

In the later war years it was clear that the status and constitution of the school would be altered as a result of the 1944 Education Act. The Governors were kept informed of impending developments. At a Special Meeting on 10 April 1946 the Head Master outlined the L.E.A.'s scheme of reorganisation under which Grammar-Modern Secondary Education would be catered for in Tenby, though at this stage the Governors were desirous that Technical Education should be provided as well. Three months later the Director of Education explained the main provisions of the Butler Act and the Governors' option to apply for Greenhill to become a Voluntary Controlled School, with two-thirds of the management nominated by the L.E.A. and with one third Foundation members, the actual number awaiting a decision from the Ministry. On 31 October a letter from the Ministry of Education pointed out that there were no Foundation Governors in the Tenby County School and that at least four would be needed to see that the interests of the school were maintained; under the new Act the Ministry could transfer the legal estate, i.e. the buildings and grounds from the Official Trustee of the Charity Funds to the Local Education Authority. At a Special Meeting of the Governing Body on 30 October 1947 five Foundation Governors were duly elected.

The constitutional position was defined in the Education Committee's Circular dated 22 April 1948. In accordance with the requirements of the Education Act 1944, the procedure laid down for the status of the school was now complete and the Instrument and Articles of Government was sealed on 12 December 1947. The School was now a Voluntary Controlled Grammar School maintained by the Pembrokeshire Authority. The following comprised the new body of Governors:

(1) *Representative Governors*, i.e. eight representing the Education Committee of the Authority and two being nominated by the Tenby Borough Council and appointed by the Education Committee.

(2) *Foundation Governors*. These were the five elected by the Board of Governors on 30 October 1947.

The Foundation Governors were to serve for the period allotted to them and Representative Governors were to serve until 31 March 1949. Casual vacancies were to be filled according to the remainder of the

314

terms of office of the Governor responsible for the vacancy. After 31 March 1950 the appointment of Governors for a full term of five years would commence.

The powers, duties and responsibilities of the Governing Body were stated: the submitting of annual estimates at the usual time; the general oversight of the premises, subject to special responsibilities entrusted to the Foundation Managers; responsibility for the general conduct of the School, reporting any defects in the premises or any staffing needs; sharing with the Authority the appointment of the Head Master. All members of the staff to become servants of the Authority, who were also to have direct control over school meals. The finances of the school were to be conducted by the County Accountant. The Governors did not have to provide any monies. The Authority's Organisers of Meals, P.E., Music and Needlework were to report on the situation at the school and to advise, within their spheres of interest. Henceforward, the Chief Education Officer would serve as Clerk to the Governors.

Mr. M. B. Eastlake resigned from this office in May 1947, when a presentation was made by the School.

The first meeting of the Governors of the Tenby Grammar School, newly constituted under the Instrument of Government, was held on Wednesday 12 May 1948. On 17 July the new governing body resolved to approve the idea of a Grammar-Modern School for Tenby—the bi-lateral project already recognised by the Ministry. For eleven years after this the Governors were destined to follow a trail of nego-tiations and delays before the County Architect showed them the detailed plan of a building with accommodation for 810 pupils.

In an appreciation of G. C. Gibson written for *The Greenhillian* in 1963, Mr. H. J. Williams remarked: 'Before his appointment we were wont to regard Greenhill as the Cinderella amongst other Pem-brokeshire Grammar Schools as far as accommodation, teaching equipment, stationery and scientific apparatus were concerned. In a relatively short time by sheer persistence he altered this and we were as well equipped as any.' This persistence was apparent in his inten-tions and efforts during the period of wartime and post-war austerity to expand the curriculum and acquire the staff for the purpose, to refurnish where necessary and introduce new equipment, to increase, and as far as possible extend the existing accommodation to provide

315

for the increasing school population, while all the time, along with his Governors, engaged in a perennial struggle to assert the claims of Tenby for a new school.

On 28 September 1942, at his first meeting with the Governing Body after taking up his new duties, he advocated the introduction of Physics into the curriculum and the addition of a member of the staff qualified to teach the subject. In consequence the Education Committee approved a grant of £150 to be spread over a period of three years for the purchase of apparatus and in February 1943 the Governors agreed to the appointment of Mr. A. S. Richards B.Sc. (Wales), Hons. Physics, a long stayer, fine teacher and a man of culture. There were time-table problems, since Physics had to be taken in the one laboratory, which was already being shared by Chemistry and Biology. This addition to the Science Department necessitated the employment of the first Laboratory assistant at 12/6 a week. In October 1943, commercial subjects, which had been taught when and where possible in the past, now received serious attention for the first time with the L.E.A.'s appointment of Mr. J. L. Williams, B.A. (Wales) to divide his time for this work, one half of the week in Pembroke Dock and the other half in Tenby. Later he became a full-time dedicated member of the Tenby staff. In that same year the L.E.A. appointed the first full-time P.E. Mistress. On the other hand we lost a subject when Woodwork had to be dropped from the Time Table in September 1945 and the workshop was converted into a Classtoom In the Lent Term 1946 we were pleased to welcome back Mr. W. J. Davies, who had served with the Royal Engineers in Burma, attaining the rank of Major, and who was destined to revolutionise the teaching of Mathematics in the School. In the Michaelmas Term 1948 came the first of a series of specialist teachers of Religious Knowledge and Welsh, and the L.E.A. appointed a teacher of Art to be shared by Narberth and Tenby. It was not possible to take on a full-time P. E. Master for the boys until after the Authority had given approval in July 1956. At an early stage Mr. Gibson reorganised the Time Table so as to include double periods of Field Games to be taken together by two or more Forms at a time, depending upon numbers. The old provision of the last part of Wednesday afternoons for the whole school had long ceased to be adequate.

There was much to be done in the way of refurnishing the classrooms and providing the additional desk accommodation needed for the growing number of pupils. Although J. T. Griffith had purchased some new desks he had not been using his full allowance—so Gibson said—thus leaving a quantity of badly worn and incised desks to be replaced. In 1943 expenditure ranged from 'blacking out' several classrooms to obtaining Dutch bulbs for the grounds, to reproductions of pictures by well-known artists to be hung in appropriate places in the school building. Year by year books were added to the Library and members of the staff were invited to submit requisitions for their respective departments, storage cupboards and additional teachers' desks were acquired, the *National Geographical Magazine* was regularly purchased and the School became an Institutional Member of the South West Wales Branch of the Historical Association. Over the years money was spent on equipment for general use—a school radio set in the Head's Room with extension speakers in three of the classrooms, a sound film projector, an 'inter-com' system which enabled the Head Master to speak to the whole school, an epidiascope in B Room, a filmstrip projector, violin stands and orchestral instruments and a new Bluthner overstrung piano in the Hall. When Mr. Gibson arrived on the scene the school premises were badly lit by gas, for which the fittings appeared to be as old as the school itself. The Head eliminated gas by a gradual introduction of electricity. Meanwhile there were coal fires in every classroom until the Michaelmas Term 1955 at the end of which Mr. Gibson was able to report the introduction of electrical heating. Alongside all this he was mindful of the comfort of his staff. The Mistresses were moved across the upper corridor to the south side of the building and their room was refurnished; the Masters were brought out from their former smoky quarters next to the gymnasium into a room on the north side of the ground floor corridor of the house.

G. C. Gibson at his best had the attributes of a good business man. Some considered him to be too 'money minded'. Every school function where appropriate, must pay for itself and if possible bring in a profit, whether it be the School Play, the Eisteddfod or the Annual Sports at which there was an admission charge of sixpence and light refreshments were on sale. Advertisemnts were introduced into the school magazine to help defray the cost of production and the proceeds of letting the School Hall were hoarded for special purposes. All profits

317

when accumulated were earmarked for projects for which the L.E.A. could make only part or no provisions—for example the Jubilee Prize Fund and the School War Memorial. Audited Accounts of all voluntary out-of-school functions were submitted regularly to the Governors. In January 1959 came a new venture. A Tuck Shop was established in the old Masters' Room, where biscuits and sweets were on sale to those pupils remaining on the premises from 9 o'clock until 4. This was a great boon in a school with so many long distance day pupils. The success of this enterprise is illustrated by the net profit of £141 18s. 0d. shown in a statement of account for a year ending on 30 June 1960. Mr. Gibson constantly encouraged thrift among his pupils. In various savings campaigns the school raised considerable sums— 'Wings for Victory' £4,000, 'Silver Lining Week' £1,717, and the Head's enthusiastic membership of the local National Savings Committee led him to make a drive for every boy and girl in the school to become a saver by depositing as little as a penny in a savings account. On 29 May 1952 he proudly informed the Governors that Greenhill was the only school in Wales with a 100 per cent membership of a National Savings Group. The practice of supporting local and national charities, begun by Mr. J. T. Griffith, was continued—such causes as the Tenby Cottage Hospital, Hungarian Relief in 1959, and Guide Dogs for the Blind were among those assisted by school collections.

Pressure upon accommodation accompanied the upward trend of the number of girls and boys on the roll. This process had begun during the last ten years of Mr. Griffith's Headship and reflected an increase in the population of the catchment area from 8,306 in 1931 to 8,909 in 1941 (a gain of 603). Census returns reveal further increases in population from the estimated 8,909 in 1941 to 9,492 in 1951 and to 10,087 in 1961, a gain of 1,178 in the course of two decades. At the time of Mr. Gibson's appointment there were 234 pupils on the registers; by 1945 there were 278 and then, after some fluctuation including a drop to 245 in the Session 1950-51, the number grew to 360 in 1957-58 and remained steady until 1961 at the end of the last year in the old school. From the mid-fifties the effect of the 'bulge' in the birthrate was being felt alongside the full impact of the raising of the school leaving age to 15. The quest for internal improvements and additional accommodation was backed by the Inspectorate after a Full Inspection terminating on 22 May 1947. Among the recommendations were the tarmacing of both playgrounds, shower-baths for the girls and the boys, the reflooring of the gymnasium for reasons of safety, a new dining hall and a classroom in the boys' playground. With the exception of the new dining hall these proposals were eventually implemented.

The first extension to the premises arose from the L.E.A.'s decision, on 20 October 1942 to introduce a School Meals Service by building a Kitchen Centre on the Greenhill Avenue side of the gymnasium at a cost of £700. Here were prepared school dinners at sixpence per head but free in special circumstances, for approximately 300 pupils.

Meals for the Tenby Council and Parochial Schools were sent out in containers, while Greenhill pupils dined in relays in the gymnasium, an unwelcomed complication necessitating the removal of furniture and inconvenience to other users of the Hall, whether for P. E., Music or other subjects. As numbers grew so did the congestion in this general purpose room.

Accommodation problems affected the Fifth Form in particular as they increased in size and had to be moved into the large C and D Rooms upstairs, while smaller Forms of younger pupils were installed in the former house. Every available space was used. A room opposite the Head's room was made into a Secretary's office. A commercial class, temporarily housed in the girls' basement, had to make way for the provision of showers, and was given the old Masters' Room with new heating facilities. In May 1945 the Air Raid Shelters were converted into bicycle sheds. The offer of the R.A.F. Training Branch to establish a School Squadron of the Air Training Corps was accepted on 9 March 1950. The R.A.F. Branch undertook to erect a wooden hut, 80 feet by 20 feet, to install electric light, heat, furniture and equipment and to grant the school free use of these premises during the day time. A site at the bottom end of the boys' playground was approved and leased at a nominal rent. A modest measure to find further teaching space was the division of the old two classroom hut into three by the insertion of a middle room, on the instructions of the L.E.A. in May 1952 at a cost of £210. 10s. 0d. The intention was to provide for upwards of 20 pupils.

The very serious problems in the laboratory were underlined by the Head in his report to the Governors on 20 September 1954. Despite the Head Master's urgent appeal conditions made it necessary for the L.E.A. to delay the project, as was reported in June 1955. Meanwhile, the Manual had been used as a classroom. Mr. W. C. Bennett who taught the subject as an extra had been appointed Head of a Church School in Weymouth. By a mutual arrangement with Mr. S. W. H. Court, Head Master of the Tenby County Primary School, it was made possible for first year Greenhillians to take Woodwork in a workshop which had been erected there. At last, on 23 March 1956 the Authority's Building Sub-Committee's recommendation for the expenditure of £2,015. 10s. 2.d on the conversion of the old woodwork shop into a science laboratory for Physics and Biology was approved and the situation was eventually relieved. Further relief resulted from the erection of a new classroom in the boys' playground. This was brought into use on 6 November 1956 for the accommodation of Form 3A. Mr. Gibson reverted several times to the acute problem of accommodation. In 1957 he made a plea for temporary accommodation in a chapel schoolroom and for an additional member of staff. The 'present' staff ratio with 17.8 teachers, including the Head Master, was 20.2 which was in excess of the needs of a school of that size. Also there was heavy pressure on the three science teachers. The extension of facilities for Physics, Chemistry, Biology, Botany, Zooology and General Science was out of the question on the existing site. The Appointment of an extra science teacher would make the ratio 1.19. After hearing the Head Master's statement, the Governors agreed to press the L.E.A. on the school's problems, but they met with no success. The Head returned to the same theme in January 1958, pointing out that the School could continue, but that after the following September's intake the Congregational Schoolroom and an extra teacher would be needed.

One of G. C. Gibson's outstanding qualities was his single-mindedness. When dealing with matters of administration he would close his doors to all-comers and deal with one task at a time. Having conceived a project he had the determination and drive to carry it through. These gifts are well illustrated by his organisation of celbrations for the School Jubilee Year, 1946, and by his work for the erection of a school war memorial in 1949. In both cases the raising of funds was an essential ingredient.

Proposals for the School Jubilee were put before the Governing Body on 14 June 1945. The scheme included a service in St. Mary's Church, an Open Day, a special issue of *The Greenhillian* and the setting up of a Jubilee Prize Fund by raising a sum of £500 through subscription, concerts, dances and other events, the interest on the capital sum to be used for the purchase of prizes for pupils entering the universities or other agreed institutions. To further this purpose a committee was formed comprising the Chairman and Vice-Chairman of the Governors, the Head Master, representatives of the staff, Old Pupils and parents, with Mr. W. H. Scourfield, Manager of Barclay's Bank as Treasurer. Accordingly various functions were arranged and the proceeds of any school play, Annual Sports or other outside event were accumulated, banked and invested. So greatly did old Green-hillians and others, respond that in less than two years time the Fund was closed at £1,000. Thus Mr. Gibson had been able to envisage a practical and long term method of commemoration and see it carried through to a successful conclusion. On 22 July 1946 the celebrations began with the whole school parading to St. Mary's Church for a special service conducted by the Rector, the Ven. Archdeacon Bickerton C. Edwards, himself a Senior Governor of the school. The following day was an Open Day with all aspects of the school curriculum on view, ranging from experiments in the laboratory to departmental displays of apparatus, text books and exercise books; from gymnastic demonstrations in the playground to dramatic present-ations and short musical interludes by the string orchestra then only two years old. On Wednesday 24 July came the Annual Sports, attended by parents and friends, who watched the events which appeared to be contested even more keenly than usual.

The Jubilee Number of the school magazine, issued in July, con-tained, besides the usual features, a retrospective article by Mr. J. T. Griffith, a view of the future by the Head Master and reminiscences by Old Pupils, one for each decade since 1896. This special magazine contained Jubilee Greetings from people in authority: from D. Brynmor Anthony, Chief Inspector of the Central Welsh Board: 'I learn that your school was designed in 1896 to accommodate 90 pupils. Since then your numbers have grown steadily and in this Jubilee Year have reached 275. The Founders of your school can hardly have anticipated such a result to their efforts. Tenby and the neighbourhood have good cause to be grateful to them for their initiative, faith and devotion.' From W. Thomas, His Majesty's Chief Inspector of Schools for Wales: 'Heartiest congratulations on your fiftieth birthday; may your next fifty years be even more successful.' From Mr. D. T. Jones, Director of Education for Pembrokeshire: 'The school is on the threshold of another half century. A new school is promised on a new site. It will be a secondary school free for all. It will be bigger and stronger and it will bring to completion the promise made by some great men of 1889 who said: "We must build secondary schools for the people of Wales." Nevertheless, as long as there are years and schools, the year 1896 and Green Hill will be remembered with appreciation and affection by hundreds of men and women.'

Appropriately, this magazine included a special feature on the services rendered by old Greenhillians in 'The Second World War (1939-45)', and included the School's Roll of Honour. This, indeed, was unfortunately a very long list for a relatively small school in the Second World War, but the sea claimed its toll as well as the land and air activities where Tenby was concerned.

Roll of Honour

F/Sgt. David Robert Booker, R.A.F. Killed on Active Service.
P.O. Geoffrey Bowen, R.A.F. Killed on Active Service.
Air Raid Warden Ivor Brace. Killed in action.
A.B. Seaman Harold Brummell. H.M. Minesweeper. Killed in action.
Steward Lionel Clarke, H.M.S. 'Jervis Bay', Drowned.
F/Sgt. Dewi Davies, missing after operational flight.
Sgt. Kenneth Diment, R.E.M.E. Died from illness contracted in Burma.
F.O. David Evans, R.A.F. Killed on Active Service.
Major Norman Evans, The Welch Regiment. Killed in action.
P.O. Donald Grant, R.A.F. Missing after operational flight.
Sgt. Air Gunner George Griffiths. Missing after operational flight.
Second Officer (Wireless) Richard James. Drowned at sea.
Marine Richard Nicholl, R.M. Lost in H.M.S. 'Glorious'.
Ord. Seaman Colin Rees, R.N. Died on Active Service.
A.C.2 Stewart Richards, R.A.F.
Trooper Archie Thomas, Royal Armoured Corps. Died from grenade explosion.

Decorations

Sqn. Leader Leslie S. R. Badham, R.A.F. Mentioned in Dispatches.
Lieut. Reginald James Cole, R.N.R. D.S.C. (Later Commander).
Electrical Officer E. Davies, R.N. Mentioned in Dispatches.
F.O. W. R. Jones, R.A.F. Mentioned in Dispatches.
P.O. William Maroney, R.A.F. D.F.M.
Corporal N. Neale, R.A.F. Mentioned in Despatches. B.E.M.
Leading Telegraphist John Richards, R.N. Mentioned in Dispatches.
P.O. John Edwin Thomas, R.A.F. D.F.C.
F. Lieut. John Eric Tipton, R.A.F. D.F.C. and Bar (later Wing Commander).
Segt. V. A. Williams, Survey Unit. B.E.M.

As soon as possible after the war the Head Master turned his attention to the provision of a memorial to those Old Pupils whose names appeared on the Roll of Honour. On 2 December 1948, when the matter was discussed by the Governors, he announced that he had already set aside £100 for the purpose and proposed that parents and others should be invited to subscribe with a view to erecting a suitable tablet on the wall in the school hall. This was done and the Memorial, a plaque in polished oak, was unveiled on Sunday, 6 November 1949 by the Chairman of the Governors, Mr. W. J. Beddoe. The service was conducted by the Foundation Governor, Rev. J. Lumley Williams. There were three short but dignified addresses by the Head Master, Dr. D. H. Pennant, D.S.O. and the Director of Education. Then the Head Boy, Howell Daniels, laid a wreath at the foot of the Memorial and the service concluded with the hymn 'For all the Saints' and the National Anthems. Under the carving of the Tenby Borough Seal was the inscription:

1939—1945
In grateful and honoured memory
of the following Old Boys of Greenhill
Grammar School, Tenby, who made the
Supreme Sacrifice during the World War.

There followed the names, as given in the Jubilee Magazine, but without the ranks or decorations, and below the names the inscription: 'They kept their Trust'.

323

The School Magazine

During the Gibson period much was done to nurture and expand existing institutions in the school and to inaugurate new ones. Because of wartime and post-war austerity *The Greenhillian* continued to appear with its drab grey exterior. At Gibson's instigation, the numbers issued from December 1942 onwards included advertisements and he had the names and qualifications of the staff printed at the beginning of the magazine. Owing to economies there was no publication in 1949, but in 1950 came a renewal with several attractive new features. Appropriately, there was a green cover with a design drawn by Art Master Dickerson, depicting several aspects of school life; there were 47 pages—a concession since there would be only one issue per year; an experiment was made of widening the number of editors; and for the first time there were illustrations, photographs of the school teams and cartoons. Successive Heads of the English Department had the responsibility of guiding the preparation of each number of *The Greenhillian*. Successive generations of Sixth Formers, serving as editors, gained in experience by reading, selecting and arranging a great variety of material for the printers. So far as I can remember, only one of these young people took up journalism as a career, namely Pat Coverley who joined the staff of *The Tenby Observer* on leaving school and who is now Assistant Editor to another Greenhillian, Arthur Ormond.

Outdoor Activities

During the first few years of Gibson's Headship the pattern of outdoor activities was unchanged—girls' hockey in the winter and rounders in the summer, with tennis as a domestic pastime on the single grass court behind the school; boys' Association Football in the winter and cricket in the summer; inter-House matches were played according to season. Fixtures with the usual neighbouring schools had been renewed after some restrictions at the beginning of the War, engagements depending upon distance and the convenience of transport, with variable fortunes generally and not much success against the larger schools. Athletics were confined to competition between members of the rival Houses for a growing number of individual trophies and for the J. T. Griffith House Cup on the Annual Sports Day in July. There were changes during the post-war period. The girls were encouraged to play tennis matches, at first by use of hard courts near to the Golf Course and then after 1953 on courts which had been fenced off at the upper end of the school playing field. Reliance on railways for transport gradually gave way to buses or coaches when the increase in school numbers made possible the formation of additional teams and the carrying away of more than one team at a time. However, the most significant development followed upon the Education Committee's appointment of a Physical Education Organiser for the county. This led to the co-ordination of inter-school activities not only in Athletics but in Field Games. In the past the first and only loyalty had been to the school. Now came new loyalties, with the creation of county teams, membership of which might pave the way to the national level. A beginning was made with Athletics, as reported in *The Greenhillian* in July 1947: 'This year the Secondary Schools of Pembrokeshire have formed a Pembrokeshire Secondary Schools Athletics Association, which is affiliated to the Welsh Secondary Schools A.A.A. for Boys. County Championships Sports will be held each year, and from this event competitors will be chosen to represent Pembrokeshire at the Welsh Championship Sports. In this way it is hoped that the Welsh Secondary Schools will become a cradle for future world champions.' So 'standards' were introduced and the standards of performance were raised in local school Sports, which now served as a preliminary to the County Sports held early in the Summer Term, from 1947 onwards, with parallel arrangements introduced for the girls. Schools, where the facilities were available, acted as hosts for the occasion. Greenhill Grammar School enjoyed a fair proportion of success in these events, with a number of competitors reaching the Welsh Championships. The involvement of Senior Boys in the School and County Sports on the eve of the Public Examinations, themselves advanced in the term, tended to push cricket aside, the game being played only in a fragmentary fashion at Greenhill, though many boys enjoyed success with local clubs in the county. However, County Caps for cricket were awarded and likewise for Rugby when the schools moved over to the Union Code. Over the years a number of Greenhill girls gained places in the Pembrokeshire Secondary Schools hockey teams.

Another important event in the history of sport at the school was the change-over from Association Football to Rugby Union Football in the season 1949-50. Rugby was the game played by the long established club, Tenby United, and the town pupils were nurtured on this game in their previous schools. On the other hand the traditional game in the parishes of the catchment area was Association Football. However, the decision was governed partly by the fact that with the growing number of pupils on the Roll the game of Rugby would involve a greater numbers of boys than had been possible previously, and partly by the prospect of outside help. The first move came on 13 January 1949, when the Head Master informed the Governors of the intended transition and that the Welsh Secondary Schools Rugby Union had sent a cheque for £25 to cover the cost of goal posts etc. Needless to say, this move was welcomed by the town club and, when the 1949-50 season started, Tenby United Committee allowed the use of their showers, with water heating and cleaning to be at the expense of the Governors. Moreover there were occasions when United's field could be used for Saturday morning games in case of need. Over four seasons elapsed before the L.E.A. found it possible to install showers in the front basement of the School House. Meanwhile, neighbouring schools gradually transferred to the Rugby code and in due course fixtures ranged further afield from Pembrokeshire into Carmarthenshire. At first the coaches were Messrs. T. K. Edmonds and Alan Nicholas. Then with the appointment of Mr. Norman Cousins to the staff in 1957 the boys at last had the benefit of a full-time P.E. and Games specialist, and in 1959 he was succeeded by Mr. Denzil Thomas, a former Welsh Rugby International whose skill and experience made a further impression on the school's Rugby Football and Athletics. The school was regularly represented in the Pembrokeshire Secondary School teams. In the 1954-55 Gwyn Robins played in the A.T.C. team for Wales and in 1958-59 two Greenhill boys Toni Chiffi and Brian Rees had the distinction of being capped for Wales. Toni and Brian were the first young Internationals to be produced by Tenby Grammar School. Honours were not confined to Rugby Football. Although cricket appeared to become a Cinderella among school games, one boy, David Morris of Carew, became Captain of the Pembrokeshire Secondary Schools Cricket Team in 1954 and was selected to play for Wales against England at Edgbaston, where he scored a half-century undefeated. In the course of this period there was a continuous and ever-growing pressure upon playing space, a pressure which remained unrelieved until more ground became available on the north side of Heywood Lane after the opening of the new school in 1961.

In addition to Tenby United other local organisations became interested in fostering outdoor pursuits for our school pupils. In the summer of 1954, through the co-operation of the Tenby Golf Club, there were inaugurated Golf Foundation Classes, whereby a number of Junior and Senior boys and girls could receive tuition at the hands of the Golf Professional. Then in 1957, through the good offices of the Tenby Sailing Club, a Junior Section was started with Mr. Cousins in charge of a number of enthusiastic would-be young sailors from the school. The enterprise flourished and by the end of 1958 a 'Redwing' was bought for the Juniors.

Literary and Dramatic Society

Indoor pursuits after school hours had to be arranged so as to avoid clashes not only in demands for the use of the gymnasium but of classrooms at the school and of personnel involved in Field Games. Even when the numbers topped 350 the school was still relatively small and certain pupils were being called upon for a cross-section of activities. Meetings of the Literary and Dramatic Society were usually confined to the Lent Term and from 1946 the newly formed Science Society had to be found a place. Instrumental Classes were started in 1944 and grew in number; there followed classes in Speech Training and Speech Therapy, taken by Miss Madge Thompson and classes in Music and Movement in charge of Miss V. Ellis of Pembroke. In the Michaelmas Term until December every year there were the rehersals of the Dramatic Society; from January to 1 March came preparations for St. David's Day until discontinued in favour of Prize Day in 1952. For most of the year the School Choir rehearsed on a Monday and, after small beginnings the School Orchestra became a fixture on Thursdays.

Those who look back on the story of school dramatics do so with nostalgia and recall with pleasure the talented young actors and actresses, who maintained and handed on the high standards which were traditional in the annual productions, often under difficult conditions. Generally speaking period plays were favoured for their substance and for the attraction of costumes, which also gave added con-

327

fidence to the young players. Production was the province of the Head of the English Department who always had the help of a team of staff, boys and girls engaged in making and painting scenery, manufacturing props, supplementing hired costumes, sewing curtains, devising lighting and providing any other accessories needed in the show, ordering tickets and generally taking care of the business side. The work of the Dramatic Society, which had been suspended on the outbreak of war, was resumed, with G. C. Gibson's encouragement, in the Michaelmas Term 1942. For the first time the temporary stage in the school hall was fitted with electric lighting for the performance of a Nativity Play called *The Child in Flanders*. The following year it was decided to venture once more into the town. The old Super Theatre where *The Merchant of Venice* was staged in 1938, had been closed. The old De Valence Pavilion, the scene of many a drama and opera in the past, had been requisitioned by the military authorities. Through arrangement with them it was found possible for the school to have the use of this theatre, though by that time it was in a delapidated condition. Much of the upholstered seating had dissappeared and what remained had to be supplemented by borrowing. The stage, denuded of its flies and other equipment, had no heating and was as cold as a cavern. The dressing rooms, equally cold, were primitive and uninviting. However, the atmosphere of the theatre was there and so was Tom Rogers "The Jazz", a part of the establishment, who assisted with curtain and lights and who roasted chestnuts on a portable stove somewhere off-stage during the intervals. Here, in these conditions, all went surprisingly well for three years. In 1943 Denise Ormond played the title role in *Lady Precious Stream* by S. I. Hsiung, much appreciated by American allies billeted in the town. A year later, in a pleasing presentation of *A Midsummer Night's Dream*, the large cast included Gaynor Williams and Haydn Mason. Last, on the De Valence stage, was Molière's comedy *Le Bourgeois Gentilhomme*, in which the central character, M. Jourdain, was most ably acted by Gwyn Thomas. At the end of the war the De Valence was derequisitioned and was no longer available. Accordingly, resort was had once more to the school hall for *She Stoops to Conquer* in 1946, Miss Evelyn Ward's last production before leaving for Pinner, having set high standard for her successors. Meanwhile the one-time Super Theatre in Warren Street was brought back into use by Mr. Harry Weight, as a private venture, and was renamed 'The Little Theatre'. Whereas back-stage at the De Valence was a veritable void, behind the scenes at the Little Theatre there was scarcely room to move, with the actors picking their way past props to enter right or left at the right time. Those not on stage somehow found space to quaff imaginary Malvoisie while playing 'five stones' or draughts with 'pop bottle' tops. On a 'matchbox' of a stage, Mr. Ray Samuel successfully produced *Quality Street* in 1947, with Audrey Hughes admirably cast as Miss Phoebe, and *Pride and Prejudice* in 1948, with Anita Davies as an equally admirable Lady Catherine. Next came *Toad of Toad Hall*, Milne's adaptation of Kenneth Grahame's story, with music by Fraser-Simson, the school orchestra being augmented for the occasion. Lumley Hughes, who played 'Toad', proved his versatility when appearing as Molière's 'Miser' in Mr. Alan Nicholas' first production in 1950. Mr. Nicholas staged six more plays in the years 1951 to 1955, some of them in double bills: *St. Joan* (a fine portrayal by Pat Coverley), *Rizzio's Boots*, *A Room in the Tower*, *The Women have their way*, *Cranford*, and then Molière again with *The Imaginary Invalid*. In 1952 the present author produced and conducted Armstrongs Gibbs' opera *The Great Bell of Burley*, with a cast and chorus of 50, with the baritone lead sung by Maurice Cole, the accompaniment on two pianos played by Misses Pauline Osborne and Mary Williams, and the scenery built by Mr. Stef Court and his helpers and painted by Mr. T. O. Thomas. Mr. W. J. Davies was the stage manager during this period. In the same theatre, Mr. Nicholas' successor Mr. Ken Jones, put on two plays, *As you like it*, with Marion Elce as Rosalind, and *The Rivals*, in which Diana Davies, playing the principal comedy role, Mrs. Malaprop, was suitably supported by John Griffths as Captain Absolute and Roy Truman as Sir Lucius O'Trigger. Unhappily the Little Theatre was closed shortly afterwards, ultimately to be converted into an Amusement Arcade. With all its inadequacies it had many happy associations both for players and audiences. After an interval it was found possible to stage *A Midsummer Night's Dream* at the Heywood Lane Infant School, with very limited facilities. Then at last in September 1961 came the move into the new school, where the stage had space and all the necessary lighting, sound and other equipment. There Mr. Jones had the assistance of an additional member of Staff with qualifications in Drama and the first production was *The Lark* by Jean Anouilh.

Appropriately a new star was discovered in Clive Merrison, who played the part of the Dauphin, and who was the second boy from Greenhill to become a professional actor and to make a successful career on stage and television. Between 1942 and 1961 many young performers had appeared in public, varying in talent, taking the parts allocated to them, mastering their lines, following their instructions and becoming part of a team. For all these and for all helpers in whatever capacity, the names mentioned above must be taken as representative.

School Music

The music of the school during this period was fostered out-of-hours through the activities of the orchestra and choir, both of which were Mr. Harrison's responsibility, as a hobby, there being no full-time music specialist on the staff until after the move into the new school. Unlike his two predecessors, Mr. G. C. Gibson had no musicianship. He had no sense of pitch yet he enjoyed listening to any music which had taken his fancy and with which he was familiar. It is to the lasting credit of G.C.G. that he was most often prepared to accept advice on musical matters, even if something did not appeal to his personal taste, and that he took the initiative which led to the formation of our school orchestra, so bringing into a reality a known dream of the late J. T. Griffith. Our orchestra started from nothing—literally. There were no instruments, no players and no instructor. During the war there were temporary orchestras set up among military personnel. On the other hand, at Milford Haven there was a schoolmaster, Harold Lewis, a competent pianist and an all-round string player running the Hubberston String Orchestra. Along with others in the county, we owed much to his example and encouragement, and it transpired that when the National Youth Orchestra of Wales was formed through the efforts of Mr. Irwyn Walters, H.M.I., Mr. Lewis provided many well-trained string players, especially of the viola. On the receipt of a request from the Tenby Governors on 15 September 1944, the L.E.A. recommended a grant of half the cost of the purchase of 12 violins, their contribution to be a maximum of £40. This was two years before the appointment of the County Music Organiser. Fortunately, the Director of Education, Mr. D. T. Jones, was personally keen on such projects and our instruments were ordered and arrived in good condition and there was no difficulty in finding recruits for a class, some of them being prepared to buy their own violins. Our plans could have come to grief for want of an instructor. After some persuasion, Miss Blodwen Griffiths reluctantly undertook the task. In July 1945 the Governors approved the purchase of a 'cello, which had come to our notice locally even before there was any prospect of any instruction on the instrument. By September 1945 membership of the violin class had increased to 26. On the Head's insistence they played, rather indifferently possibly, some incidental music for the school play production 'The Would be Nobleman' in December 1945. By this time pupils improved their progress by taking private lessons. In 1946 a concert was given in the Lent Term and four short interludes were played on the Open Day on 23rd July. From this time onwards a concert became an annual event and so did a week-end school arranged at various centres by the County Music Organiser. In 1947 at the time of the full inspection, the Music H.M.I. for Wales first became acquainted with our efforts and thereafter gave us every encouragement on his regular visits. Other instruments were added in due course. The measure of the advance which had been made is revealed in an Editorial Note in the 1950 issue of the Magazine: 'Congratulations to Miranda Harrison who in April was selected for the National Youth Orchestra of Wales under the direction of Clarence Raybould'. This was after an audition by Mr. Irwyn Walters, who also selected Towyn Mason a year later and then, after he had left school for the Castle School of Music in Cardiff, Kenneth Hewlings, who had taken cello lessons in school. Woodwind and brass enthusiasts followed. In 1958 there were 30 members of our orchestra, A photograph of that year shows eleven violins, two violas, four cellos, one bass, three clarinets, two trumpets and one horn. Periodically the fortunes of the Orchestra had fluctuated when experienced players left school, and in those days there were no Primary School violin classes to provide children with a basic trining and a feed for the Grammar School. At various times notable assistance was provided by Messrs. Leonard Pullin, Misses Nora and Kathleen Rees, and Mr. Joffre Swales. Unfortunately there was an efflux of Senior members a year before the move to the new school and a long period elapsed before a good recovery could be made.

Sometime during the Gibson period, rehearsals of the School Choir became firmly established on Monday afternoons after school. So

331

long as there was an eisteddfod the singers were divided into rival House Choirs in the first part of the Lent Term until 1 March. From 1952 onwards they were always involved in the preparation of three groups of music, mostly part songs, to be interspersed between the speeches on Prize Day. Otherwise there were carols in December and an annual concert, the latter being shared with the orchestra, once that attained a satisfactory standard. The policy was to cast as wide a net as possible, bringing in pupils from the whole school in preference to concentrating on a few select readers of music who could be trained to build up a more sophisticated repertoire, though on occasion a smaller group of singers would be chosen to contribute certain items in a programme. Whenever possible, senior boys were brought in along with a few members of staff, either to sing tenor and bass or a third part written for the changing voice. In 1953 the choir took part in the School's Coronation Festival Celebration Concert on 30 September, then singing in four parts. In 1955 there were 57 members. In 1956 the number had fallen to 45 through the loss of senior boys who had left school. In the session 1957-58 the membership was 63, the highest so far, and once more there were senior boys taking part. The choir sang for the assembled company in Heywood Lane Infants School on the occasion of the Foundation Stone Ceremony, a preliminary to the building of the new school, on 22 May 1959. In 1959 there were three other events: Prize Day, a further District Schools Festival and a School Concert. Vocal solos and duets were regular features of the programmes. At no time did we have the resources to attempt a full-scale work.

The School Science Society

The School Science Society was inaugurated by Mr. A. S. Richards in October 1946, with Terence O. Denney as its first Hon. Secretary, and a committee representing both senior and junior pupils. For some years this organisation also embraced the function of a film society. The general practice during the autumn and winter was to hold monthly meetings at which lectures and demonstrations were given and films on scientific topics shown. A report survives of the programme for the year 1957-58 which included an illustrated lecture on 'Magnetic Recording' by Daniel Evans; a film taken and shown by an Electricity Board Official, Mr. J. E. M. Copland, on the electrification of the Welsh village, Ysbyty Ystwyth, an excursion to the Trostre Cold Strip Mill, arranged in co-operation with the Tenby Rotary Club; a talk and demonstration on colour photography; an illustrated lecture on 'Birds and their eggs' by Brian Harris who also placed his collection on view.

The A.T.C. and Duke of Edinburgh Awards

One of our most effective organisations, both practical and social, was No. 2219 Squadron A.T.C. It owed its origin to an initiative taken by the Air Training Branch of the R.A.F.. The Squadron was formed on 1 May 1950 and was operative from the 17th, the day of the first parade. Apart from the obvious advantage to those being called up for National Service, the aims were (1) To provide service training which would prove useful both in the Air Service and in civil life, (2) To foster the spirit of adventure, to promote sports and pastimes in healthy rivalry and to develop qualities of mind and body which go to the making of a leader and a good citizen. The minimum age for enrolment was 14 for probationers. At the other end, personnel changed as trainees left school, some for the R.A.F. some for other destinations Members of the Staff with appropriate experience accepted commissions with F./L. W. J. Davies as Commanding Officer. Changes in the staff brought changes in the command but Mr. W. J. Davies remained a tower of strength throughout, while Mr. S. W. H. Court, who resigned on his appointments as Head of the Tenby County Primary School, agreed to return as a commissioned officer in 1956 and four years' valuable service was given by Mr. T. O. Thomas. Membership ranged between 28 and 40. There were proficiency tests, parades, camps and inspections.

In 1955 F/Sgt. Peter Emery was selected by the H.Q. Home Command as one of the cadets from the United Kingdom to visit Canada for two or three weeks in the summer. That same year Emery left to take up a Cadetship at Henlow and a Flying Scholarship was won by Segt. Derek Williams. Visits to R.A.F. Stations at Pembroke Dock and St. Athan were arranged and cadets were given flights. In 1957 also came an important innovation when the Squadron took up the Duke of Edinburgh's Award Scheme, in which there are three stages— bronze, silver and gold, each with four sections; rescue, public service, physical fitness and hobbies, plus one night under canvas during a 24 hours expedition. In the following years there was much pre-occupation with this scheme. There were 'silver' presentations in 1958; then in 1959, the school magazine included the following report emphasising the importance of the Award Scheme. The scheme 'certainly has brought new life and enthusiasm into the Squadron and our cadets have really excelled themselves in this field. We have, to date, gained 15 bronze badges, seven silver and six gold, with prospects of several more by next autumn. The gold badge winners were presented with their certificates and badges by H.R.H. The Duke of Edinburgh at Buckingham Palace last November and this, preceded by a Civic Reception by His Worship the Mayor of Tenby, has brought the Squadron more publicity than anything else since the Squadron was formed in 1950.

'Much work in connection with the Award goes on quietly throughout the year, such as Pursuits and First Aid in winter with Fitness Tests and Expeditions in summer. Bronze and Silver expeditions will take place in June, probably in the Marros-Pendine-Laugharne area, while it is hoped to arrange the Gold expedition during the first week of the summer holidays in the Brecon Beacons.'

This work was to set the pattern of much that was to follow: On 26 November 1959 the Governors learned that the A.T.C. Squadron would have to be disbanded in May 1960. The value of the pre-service training, with the ending of compulsory National Service, no longer had the same appeal. Mr. W. J. Davies, on medical advice, was not renewing his commission which was due to expire in May 1960. The Governors expressed appreciation of Mr. Davies' services and heard that he was willing to continue to direct the training for the Duke of Edinburgh's Scheme. This Mr. Davies did through a new organisation, which was to be named 'The Greenhillians'. This society continued to prosper. Its work was carried through into the new school, and it had the advantage that a girls' section was also formed under the leadership of Mrs. Phyllis Davies. Both girls and boys have well maintained the splendid record of the A.T.C. in this kind of activity.

As in the past, the annual eisteddfod was held in the school in 1943 and 1944. With increased school numbers there was little accommodation for visitors, and on 6 February 1945 the Head Master had the Governors' approval to hold the forthcoming St. David's Day Eisteddfod in the South Beach Pavilion Cinema. The first and subsequent occasions were strongly supported by parents and friends of the school. For five years the eisteddfod was conducted by the Rev. Crwys Williams ('Crwys'), Archdruid of Wales. In 1950 his place was taken by Miss Gwyneth Evans, M.A., H.M.I., who was resident in our area. A few quotations from *The Greenhillian* will serve to illustrate the proceedings:

'In 1946 for the second year in succession the annual St. David's Day Eisteddfod was held in the South Beach Pavilion, and again we were fortunate in having Crwys to direct the proceedings. Both at the morning and afternoon sessions there was a good attendance. Those present had the additional pleasure of seeing the varied range of exhibits which filled the corridor leading to the entrance. These included biological collections, woodwork and physics models, knitting exhibits and artistic efforts and maps of every kind. The number of telegrams received this year was an all-time record, and there were also a few cables, one coming from as far as Burma. It is obvious that this custom is increasing yearly.'

'As for the actual House positions, once again St. David's succeeded in winning but, although they led throughout the day, Tudor remained dangerous challengers all the time until eventually the whole issue depended upon the choral competition. This Tudor lost, and with it the eisteddfod, much to the disappointment of both Tudor and Glyndwr, the partisans of the latter House having fallen hopelessly behind much earlier in the day, and supporting Tudor against St. David's. However the close contest made every competition all the more interesting and the standard of compettitions was as high as ever. The Chair Poem, for which there were five entrants was adjudicated by, Crwys.'

In 1948 the magazine gave a list of telegrams from old pupils and friends. These are quoted to illustrate the interest shown by past pupils, well-wishers and partisans.

Ernest Long (Aberystwyth), Owen Morse (Tenby), Gordon Crockford (Plymouth), Ruby Merriman (Tenby), David Griffiths (Yatesbury Camp), Denise Ormond (Aberystwyth), Colwyn Williams (B.O.A.R.), Terence Denney (Aberystwyth), Leslie Truman (Swansea), Haydyn Mason (Aberystwyth), Bryan Hart (Tenby), Neville Williams (Aberystwyth), Joan B. Rees (Tenby), Michael Morris (Camborne), Mary Little (Leytonstone), Joan Davies (Kilgetty), Graham Cole (Saundersfoot), Peggy Lewis (Tenby), Ivy and Violet Davies (Tenby),

335

Vi and Eve (Tenby), Cliff and Johnny Lawrence (Saundersfoot), Brenda Evans and Enid Powell (Tenby), An Old Saint (Tenby), 'Porridge' (Cardiff), 'Toot' (Tenby, the Pat Schoolgirls (Essington, i.e. the Royal Victoria Patriotic School pupils who were evacuated here during the war), C. J. Rees (Runcorn), Beryl Evans (Bristol), the Bennetts (Weymouth).

Lastly, from the 1950 issue:

'The Chairing of the Bard, always a highlight of the Eisteddfod, was carried out with the usual ceremony, except for the reading of the Bardic poem, and of the complimentary poems by other competitors. The winner of the Chair this year was Towyn Mason, who thereby earned six points for Glyndwr House.

'The three cups awarded at the Eisteddfod were presented by Mr. Harold Howells. The House Cup donated by Clr. S. H. Hughes was received by Gaynor Williams and Fred Rose, the St. David's House Captains. The other two cups, neither of which had appeared in an eisteddfod before were the "John Pennant" cup for Art, won by Terence Gill and the William Parcell Cup for the violin solo, won by Miranda Harrison.'

On 8 March 1951 Mr. Gibson reported to his Governors that while the Eisteddfod that year had been successful, there was a certain lack of enthusiasm, and suggested resting it for one year in favour of a Prize Day. In fact the Eisteddfod was rested until some time after the school moved into the new school and the Prize Day was held every year until 1976.

The revival of the Prize Day in 1952 after a lapse of some ten years had to be held in a suitable venue in the town so that parents of recipients of certificates and prizes would be able to attend. The offer of the use of the Tenby Baptist Church of which the Rev. J. Lumley Williams, Chairman of the Governors at the time, was pastor, was accepted. The appointed day was Wednesday 27 February. The guest speaker was Sir Frederick Rees and Lady Rees undertook the distribution of prizes. The Programme on this occasion set the pattern which was to be followed for the next 20 years. The certificates and prizes awarded were those gained by pupils during the previous school session. The programme was built up as follows: (1) A Hymn of Thanksgiving or of Praise, (2) Chairman's Address, (3) the School Choir, (4) The Head Master's Report on the School's progress, studies, societies, games and athletics during the previous session, (5) The School Choir, (6) The Guest Speaker's Address, (7) The Choir, (8) The Distribution of Certificates and Prizes, (9) Vote of Thanks to the Principal Guests, (10) The School Song and the National Anthems. The Head insisted that the conduct and appearance of the pupils were to be impeccable. Recipients of certificates were rehearsed and martialled as precisely as if they were attending an investiture at Buckingham Palace, first the girls, who were trained to curtsey and then the boys how to bow, with due allowances for occasional eccentricities in style, on receiving their presentations. After the first experience, the procedure was speeded up but without any loss of dignity. On that first occasion Sir Frederick spoke to the young members of his audience as the 'New Elizabethans' and urged them to emulate the many and varied achievements of the 'Old Elizabethans'. Prizes were handed to the top two pupils in every Form in the School and Special Prizes as follows in 1952: Head Girl—Anne Richards; Head Boy—Robin Davies; School Drama Prize—Pat Coverley; The Rollings Prize for the best all-round boy in the Junior School—Vincent Seabourne; The John Pennant Art Cup—Gillian Venables; The William Parcell Violin Cup—Towyn Mason; The Kenneth Hewlings Pianoforte Cup—Auriol Hurlow.

From 1953 onwards the Prize Day was held in the Tenby Congregational Church. The Guest Speakers, whose wives distributed the prizes, were as follows, each choosing some appropriate subject of current concern: Dr. William Thomas (former Chief Inspector of Schools for Wales), Mr. D. T. Jones (Director of Education for Pembrokeshire), the Rev. Canon T. Halliwell (Principal of Trinity College, Carmarthen), Professor R. F. Treharne (University College of Wales, Aberystwyth), Dr. Idris Jones (Consultant Physician to the United Cardiff Hospitals and to the Welsh Regional Hospital Board), The Right Hon. The Viscount Tenby of Bulford, Wynford Davies, Esq. (Director of Education for Pembrokeshire), J. A. Davies, Esq. (Director of Education for Montgomeryshire), Wynne Ll. Lloyd, Esq. (H.M. Chief Inspector of Schools, Wales). Mr. Lloyd was the last of our guests to speak in the Congregational Church in 1961. At the first Prize Day in the new school our Guests of Honour were Mr. Desmond Donnelly, Member of Parliament for Pembrokeshire, and Mrs. Donnelly. Then in 1963 came the last Prize Day of the Gibson period, when the speaker was Dr. W. E. Hugh and the prizes were distributed by his wife, Mrs. Marjorie Hugh. This was a unique occasion, for both of them were former Greenhillians performing this special function for a new generation in a new school.

With one exception, on these special days when the school was on show to our visitors, all ran smoothly, except in the year 1957 which was marred by the tragic death of the Director of Education (Mr. D. T. Jones) while in the act of addressing the audience.

As the years went by the Programmes had included, where appropriate, the names of winners of State Scholarships and County Awards, together with an increasing number of certificates, both Advanced Level and Ordinary Level. Then there were commercial successes in the Royal Society of Arts and Pitman's examinations, elocution results of the examinations of the London Academy of Dramatic Art and violin successes in the examinations of the Associated Board of the Royal Schools of Music. Jubilee Prizes were awarded to university entrants and others. The number of Form Prizes increased from 32 in 1960-61, the last session in the old school, to 59 in 1963. Meanwhile, thanks to the generosity of Old Pupils, parents and friends the number of Special Prizes had grown from year to year.

For the first eight years Graham Gibson was in office pupils were pursuing the traditional four years course leading to the School Certificate Examination, with a further two years for candidates to sit the Higher Certificate Examination. The General Certificate of Education was introduced in 1951, with a five years course required for the Ordinary Level Examination and a further two for the Advanced Level. As it was now possible to obtain a certificate with only one subject, a comparison of successes of the new and the old is not possible. When Mr. Gibson took up his duties in the session 1942-43 one of his aims was to strengthen the Sixth Form and to encourage more pupils to offer the sciences in the Higher Certificate Examinations. By agreement with Mr. H. J. Williams he took over Form 6 Chemistry, which he taught in the small laboratory in the corridor of the House and equipped it for the purpose. As soon as conditions were favourable, he introduced Physics, Zoology and Botany into the Sixth Form Time Table, even though the main laboratory was overcrowded. Between 1943 and 1950 the number of Higher Certificates gained ranged from four to eight. The proportion of candidates on the

338

science and arts sides fluctuated. For example in 1946 out of eight certificates three were on the science side and in 1950 there were five out of eight. In the long run the Head's efforts bore fruit when more of the leavers took up science courses at the universities. During this period there were 15 Major Awards. A vintage year was 1945, with Muriel Bowen Evans placed second, Neville Williams third, Haydn Mason fifth and Alan Rodway sixth in the county. Mason, being on the young side, stayed a further year and came top in the county, with Gwyn Thomas not far behind in fifth place. An Agricultural Scholarship, tenable at the University College, Aberystwyth, was won by Victor Hughes in 1943 and in 1950 State Scholarships were won by Howell Daniels and Gaynor Williams, both of whom went to Aberystwyth to read English and History respectively.

After the introduction of the General Certificate of Education the number of Advanced Level Certificates did not show any marked increase until 1956, when there were 16. A peak was reached in 1960 with 24, a notable achievement for the last year in the old school. The figure for 1963, after two years in the new premises, was 19. From 1951 to 1961 there were 49 County Awards. State Scholarships were won by Clive Knowles in 1951 (he went to Aberystwyth to read History), John Searle in 1956 (who went to Bristol to take a science course) and Michael Howells 1960 (who entered King's College, Cambridge to take Mathematics). In 1957 Daphne Davies gained a Lewis Pilcher Scholarship, tenable at Bedford College in the University of London.

During Gibson's first eight years the School Certificate successes ranged from 20 to 30 in number. The best performances were 29 out of 34 entered in 1943 and 34 out of 39 candidates in 1949.

The first three years of the Ordinary Level Examination brought no change in the number of certificates gained. In fact the number dipped to 17 in 1951. From 1954 onwards there was an increase with peak years 58 in 1956, 66 in 1959 and 62 out of 68 entries in 1960. The upward trend coincided with the growth of the school population in the mid-fifties. There was a further leap upwards in 1963, with 91 out of 108 candidates gaining certificates. As could be expected, the quality of the certificates varied greatly, with some good pupils able to pass in nine and ten subjects, and others only able to record one or two.

From Foundation Stone to Official Opening

The place of Tenby's new Grammar-Modern School in the L.E.A.'s scheme of re-organisation, our lateness in the queue for buildings and the Authority's purchase of the necessary fields for the site have already been described. For years J. T. Griffith had had a vision of a new school; year by year G. C. Gibson, becoming more and more pressed for accommodation for his pupils, had raised the subject in his Prize Day Reports and pleaded his case with the Inspectorate and the Education Committee. At last came a 'red letter' day, 22 May 1959, when the Foundation Stone of the new building was laid on a spot to the south-west of the games field. There were present members and officials of the Pembrokeshire Authority, the Mayor of Tenby, school governors, the Head Master and staff, and a number of pupils, parents and friends. The proceedings were opened by Alderman T. R. Joseph (Chairman of the Pembrokeshire Education Committee) and the ceremony was performed by Sir Edward Boyle (Parliamentary Secretary to the Ministry of Education), with a silver trowel which was presented to him by the County Architect, Colonel Walter Barrett. After the site had been dedicated by the Rev. J. Lumley Williams (a senior governor), an invited audience, including a cross-section of girls and boys, assembled in the hall of the nearby Heywood Lane Infants School to hear a number of speeches appropriate to the occasion. Sir Edward Boyle, the principal guest, congratulated the Pembrokeshire Authority on their being near to the completion of a re-organisation, which would enable every child in the county to receive a secondary education in accordance with his or her age, ability and aptitude. This was his first visit to the area, he said; he was delighted with the beauty of Tenby and with the site of the new school which would overlook the Golf Course, Carmarthen Bay and Caldey Island. He had been made aware of the difficult conditions under which the pupils and staff had been working in the old premises and he was very impressed with the notable examination successes and with the variety of out-of-school activities, such as those of the School Choir and Orchestra and of the Dramatic Society. Turning from the locality to a wider horizon, he made an urgent plea for greater interest to be taken in the British Commonwealth and expressed the hope that more attention would be paid to the teaching of its geography and history. In the course of the proceedings, the School Choir sang the madrigal 'My bonny lass she smileth' by Morley, and led the singing of the hymn 'Now thank we all our God'. At the close, votes of thanks were proposed by Alderman Mrs. Anne Norman (Chairman of the Governing Body) and Mr. Wynford Davies (Director of Education).

Commenting upon the above event at the June meeting of his Governors, the Head Master said that it was a 'happy and successful function and singularly free from the artificial stiffness which sometimes attends these occasions'. The Director had since written to him, congratulating the School and stating that the Parliamentary Secretary had been most impressed by the singing of the choir and with the general demeanor of the pupils. The Head remarked that work had already started on the site and that big machines were moving mountains of soil. The Foundation Stone has been removed and would be incorporated in a wall of the entrance hall of the new building.

From mountains of soil, drainage and foundations to a structural steel skeleton and thence to a finished building on the sloping site seemed to us an endless process as it continued for over two years. Eventually, through periodic visits we saw emerge the main three storey building, with the appearance of a rectangular box, constructed east to west with three straircase towers at intervals on the north side. The two gymnasia projecting northwards from the east end and the hall and canteen from the west end gave it the shape of a letter E without the middle arm. On 7 March 1961 it was reported that the governors visited the structure and were very impressed by the careful planning of its accommodation. As the end of the summer term approached at Greenhill the staff in the various departments were making preparations for the move, although the contractors seemed to be lingering tantalisingly with more and more finishing touches to add. The Head's and the Deputy Head's Rooms were still in use as an operational centre by the builders, but on 17 July Mr. Gibson insisted on moving in, on taking over his room, on having his new desk and other furniture brought in and polished almost before the dust had settled on the premises. The rest of us followed in the course of the summer vacation. On 4 September, in the Library, the Head Master met his staff, which consisted of a nucleus from the Grammar School, together with new appointments, most of them drawn from neighbouring Senior Centres and primary schools. The discussion included the plans made for the first day.

341

Arrangements were made for the reception of all the over-elevens in the catchment area, the first allocation to Forms being based on the results of the eleven plus examination and reports from the schools. The new session opened on 5 September. As the Head himself reported to the Governors on 12 October 1961, 'Everything was incredibly smooth. Every pupil, old and new, had been told where to go and to whom to report', with a few masters on point duty, nearly 800 girls and boys were absorbed quietly and without a hitch. The Head then added that the actual numbers on the first day, 766, had grown to 770 and that the total the following year would be 800. On the opening day the first Assembly was at 11 a.m. and the first lessons were given in the afternoon. He announced that the old school had raised nearly £1,000 through various functions and so made possible the purchase of an electronic organ for £625 and special Ceremonial Furniture for the stage in the hall.

The Official Opening took place on Friday, 17 November 1961, after the School had been in session for over ten weeks. The proceedings began at the main entrance to the building with an invocation and dedication ceremony conducted by the Rev. H. J. B. Hallam, M.A., Hon. C.F., Rector of Tenby and a governor of the school. A commemorative tree was planted by Mr. Desmond Donnelly, M.P. for Pembrokeshire; he then opened the door with a key presented to him by the County Architect, Colonel Walter Barrett. The official party entered the main hall, where the guests were welcomed by Mr. Evan Anthony, M.B.E., Chairman of the Pembrokeshire Education Committee, who expressed the hope that the new school would be valued by the pupils and be of service to the youth of Tenby for many years to come. The principal item on the programme was a speech from Mr. Donnelly. He spoke of the new school as marking an important milestone in the history of the county and went on to emphasise the importance of education in our society. He declared that in Wales, which had a proud claim of being and education-conscious nation there was not enough sense of urgency excitement and receptiveness for new ideas. Of teachers he said not only must they be provided with the most up-to-date facilities but they should make fuller use of the universities during vacation periods for refresher courses to keep them abreast of the latest development. However, he concluded that the key to success in our educational system was to be found in the attitude of the pupils themselves and he would like to see emblazoned in every classroom in the country four words: 'Work, work and work.'

Interspersed with the speeches were two songs from the School Choir. The function concluded with votes of thanks proposed by Alderman Mrs. Norman and Mr. W. S. John (Chairman of the Governors).

So the old Greenhill was left behind, but as J.T. had wished, the name was carried up the hill with the new school. Yet it was also retained at the old site which the Education Authority called Greenhill House and converted into accommodation for a Branch of the County Library, a Further Education Centre, a Youth Centre and a Remedial Centre.

The organisation of the pupils in the new school for various purposes had been planned in advance. On 11 May 1961 the Head had spoken to the Governors of the need for an additional House, as the existing three would not be enough for the number of pupils. He said: 'I propose to name this House after Robert Recorde, the Tenby Mathematician, who is said to have been the first to have introduced the sign of equality into Mathematics. Those who seek hidden meanings may find it significant to discuss this association between equality and our new comprehensive school which will, we hope, provide equality of opportunity for all its pupils.' This reference to the comprehensive system was an echo of what Dr. William Thomas had told the Governing Body back in July 1959, when he said, during a discussion of the new bi-lateral school, that it would be best to think in terms of a comprehensive school. Yet, the L.E.A. records show that from the start it had been envisaged as a bi-lateral school—a Grammar-Modern. But at one stage, the Governors, apparently wishing to shun the word 'modern' had requested that it should be called a Grammar High School—though it is doubtful whether anyone knew what this really meant. Eventually the L.E.A. agreed to the incorporation of the word 'Greenhill' in the name—'Greenhill County Secondary School' and honour was satisfied.

Although the term 'comprehensive' had been used, G. C. Gibson's organisation was on bi-lateral principles. There was a five-stream entry, with a sixth first year Form for remedial work in charge of Mr. Roy Davies. The A and B streams followed a five years course leading to the Ordinary Level Examinations of the Welsh Joint

343

Education Committee. The A stream carried a heavier load of subjects than the parallel Form in the examination year. The fourth and fifth streams pursued a 'modern' course extending over four years. The C stream was regarded as a kind of bridge across which transfers could be made during the first three years, but this stream continued into Form 5C, from which boys and girls could be entered for some subjects in the Ordinary Level Examinations. Also in the fifth year was a Commercial Form in which pupils were prepared for the examinations of the R.S.A. and the Pitman's Institute. The Sixth Form, as in the old school, was divided into Arts and Science, first and second year. On the whole, the pupils appeared to settle down under these arrangements, and in the course of the first three years some of them crossed over from E stream to the C stream, some, who would not even have found a place under the former selective entry for the Grammar School, were able to sit the Ordinary Level papers, and at least one boy passed through into Form 6 on the Arts side.

An early analysis and costing of the bi-lateral school, drawn up by the County Architect in 1952, is reproduced in the Appendix D. This was modified in due course, but a comparison of the figures with the total final cost of £265,500 illustrates the effect of inflation upon the project, following the delay of seven years before the building could be started. While the new premises offered so many advantages in respect of accommodation and equipment, light, and warmth in the winter through an oil-fired central-heating system, there were certain defects and deficiencies (which were remedied by later extensions, notably in 1973 and 1976)—for example, the siting of a Rural Science Laboratory on the third floor, showers for after field games on the second floor, the separation of the Arts and Craft Rooms at one end of the building from the Woodwork and Metal Workshops at the other, and the absence of a sound-proof Music Room. Then there was the tunnel piercing the ground floor, with a road passing under it, making the crossing hazardous in wet weather for pupils on their way to the Workshops or to Morning Assembly. Being late in the new buildings queue, unlike Prendergast, Fishguard and Pembroke, where the Assembly Halls were self-contained, Tenby was provided with a hall adjoining the dining area and with a movable partition on the balcony to be operated so as to make available a small hall for use as additional dining space. While the hall was given a good appearance and a well-equipped stage, the latter was too low for good viewing by an audience and the acoustics were unsatisfactory.

The expenditure involved in running the new school is illustrated by the Estimates for the year 1963/64, totalling £79,676, a copy of which is included in the Appendix E. For the sake of comparison, the Estimates for the years 1947 to 1950 and 1960/61 are also included. Although any comparison is difficult on account of inflation, these figures should be set alongside those of the J. T. Griffith period at the beginning of the First World War, and again alongside the items of expenditure quoted in the Adams period.

For so many years G. C. Gibson had looked forward to this new school as to a 'promised land'. Unhappily he did not survive even two full years in his new surroundings, where he had everything indicating full efficiency as in his previous room. Over the years he had suffered occasional illnesses and had undergone an operation at the Royal Masonic Hospital, but otherwise he seldom missed school, even when confronted with a succession of bereavements. He suffered a severe double blow in 1955 with the loss of his wife and sister and other bereavements followed, but he was determined to prevent his personal problems interfering with his work in school.

Since H. J. Williams retired in 1957 I had been serving as Deputy Head Master and regularly spent the mid-morning break in G.C.G.'s company. Occasionally he would become expansive, and admitted how he found it difficult to adjust himself to the task of running the school on comprehensive lines, a feeling he had also expressed to one of H.M. Inspectorate. My wife and I last saw Graham Gibson in St. Mary's Church on Good Friday, 12 April, when he greeted us with a cheery smile. On Easter Tuesday evening, 16 April, I received a telephone call from his housekeeper to say that he had been taken to hospital in Haverfordwest having had a heart attack. At nine o'clock that evening I was informed that Mr. Gibson had died in hospital.

A short memorial service conducted by the Rev. Canon H. J. B. Hallam was held in St. Mary's Church on Saturday, 20 April. There was a large congregation including Governors, staff, pupils and friends. At a Special Meeting of the Governors on 2 May, the Chairman Mr. W. H. Scourfield, in his tribute said: 'Today we are certainly the poorer for the passing of one who, over a long period of years, made himself

345

master of his job, and one who used that mastery so effectively, not only for the benefit of the school which was so near to his heart, but also for the benefit of the whole community.' At the request of the Education Authority I had taken over the responsibilities of Acting Head Master, with Mr. W. J. Davies as Acting Deputy Head and when the school reassembled on 23 April, I explained the situation in Morning Assembly and paid a tribute to the late Head Master.

Graham Gibson's Headship had coincided with some of the most sweeping changes in the history of education—the Butler Act raising the school leaving age to 15 and bringing in secondary education for all, along with the abolition of fees; the re-organisation in the county consequent upon the Act; changes in the Burnham Scale; the institution of Posts of special responsibility; the end of the Central Welsh Board and the beginning of the Welsh Joint Education Committee; the introduction of the General Certificate of Education and the projected C.S.E. Examination, though he did not live to see this established; and he had been involved in the transition of the old County Intermediate School into a Grammar School and the absorption of the Grammar School into the Greenhill County Secondary School. Throughout his single minded service and devotion to duty he had worked with Governors ranging from Mrs. Peerless and Archdeacon Bickerton-Edwards to Miss Anne Norman and Canon Hallam, with the Rev. J. Lumley Williams as a Foundatin Governor providing a link between the earlier and the later generations. He had been well served by a succession of Head Girls and Head Boys, Prefects, Games Captains, Head Master's Secretaries (from Elizabeth Robartes to Jocelyn Lewis) and by a competent staff, some of whom stayed for a spell before seeking service elsewhere and others who provided a backbone of continuity of tradition to be carried through into the new school. Those who either provided continuous service or returned from time to time to be of service were as follows: *Mistresses* Miss M. G. Bowen (Senior Mistress), Misses Ella Ellis (Latin), Mary Williams (Domestic Science) and G. C. East (Biology), Mrs. Jean Williams, née Davies (French), Mrs. Pauline Allen (P.E. and Music) and Mrs. E. Court (General Form Subjects); *Masters*: Mr. H. J. Williams (Second Master who retired and received an appropriate presentation in 1957 but who sometimes returned as a relief even in the new school), Mr. W. J. Davies (Mathematics), Mr. A. S. Richards (Physics), Mr. J. L. Williams (Commercial Subjects), Mr. T. O. Thomas

(Art), Mr. K. J. Lee (History), Mr. Ken Jones (English) and Mr. Denzil Thomas (P.E.) and Mr. W. T. Howells (Physics and Mathematics).

Mr. Gibson always followed with keen interest the careers of the old pupils. The destinations of the leavers in some respects the previous pattern in the time of J. T. Griffith—clerical posts in various offices, farming, home businesses, hotels, the Post Office, the South Wales Electricity Board, H.M. Forces, the Merchant Navy, engineering, journalism, the Civil Service, local trades (building, garages, plumbing, etc.), teaching, and what was a cause of satisfaction to the Head, a great increase in the number following science and arts courses in the universities. For example in 1952 there were sixteen in the universities and five in training colleges. Three had gone further afield by winning Rotary Foundation Fellowships for post-graduate studies in the U.S.A.—Dr. Haydn Mason, who is now Professor of French in the Department of European Studies in the University of East Anglia; Dr. Howell Daniels who is Secretary to the Department of U.S A. Studies in University College, London, and Dr. Tim Rickard who holds an appointment in an American university. Three other old pupils of the same vintage as Howell Daniels secured appointments as lecturers on the staff of the University College, Cardiff—Dr. Fred Rose (Bio-Chemistry), Dr. Fred Thomas (Civil and Mechanical Engineering); while Gwyn Thomas, M.A. (Oxon), F.S.A., (a contemporary of Haydn Mason), on the staff of the Royal Commission on Ancient Monuments, Wales, also became editor of *Archaeologia Cambrensis*.

G. C. Gibson's gifts as an organiser have already been described. He was clear-cut and seemingly unhesitating in his decisions, and once a decision had been taken he could be inflexible and difficult, without always having regard to the possible consequences. On occasions, his passion for discipline led to extremes. For example, there was a period when the staff in charge of school lunches in the gymnasium of the old school were expected to insist on total silence among the pupils during the meal—a tall order to say the least of it on what was or should have been a social occasion. At times, especially before a Prize Day, a School Play, or other public occasion, he would become very tense. Moreover, he had an explosive temper, which naturally aroused resentment. When I became Deputy Head after 'Harry

Williams' retirement I was sharing the Staff-room and sometimes had the unpleasant task of communicating unpopular decisions to my colleagues. In the new school the Deputy Head was allocated his own room, while the Senior Master, Mr. W. J. Davies, served as a kind of liaison officer in the men's Staff Room. Sometimes Mr. Gibson would ask for an opinion from me without thinking that any consultation outside his own room was necessary.

It was written of him in an obituary notice by his Deputy (H. J. Williams): 'He disliked slovenliness in all forms whether in written work or in school attire, and he was very insistent that girls should wear berets and boys their caps at School functions. In the classroom or in a corridor he would usually quickly spot a slightly mutilated desk or damaged wall, and woe betide the culprit when discovered.

'He had a very keen sense of humour which made him very popular as a speaker. Whenever he got up to speak on any big occasion we expected him to do well and rarely were we disappointed. I remember very vividly his speeches at Assembly on the mornings following Staff matches. They were usually in humourous vein and his references to members of the staff were witty, apt and very true.

'He was usually a little worried about his Speech Day Reports, with their recital of all the School activities during the School Year. He fully realised that they were, of necessity, somewhat boring, but he considered them essential in order to bring home to the Public and particularly parents that education meant much more than mere preparation for examinations. It also gave him an opportunity to thank publicly those of the Staff who had devoted much of their spare time to the various social activities which should have a special place in school life. He himself was very interested in these activities and tried to make contact with them as often as he could during the year.

'As his Senior Master for fifteen years I naturally got to know him very intimately, and incidentally this period was the happiest of my teaching career. He always had the best interests of the school at heart. He was always ready to encourage and advise any pupil or old pupil who approached him.

'He never hesitated to make decisions, even though he was aware they might be unpopular once he had assured himself they were in the best interests of the School. I cannot recollect him deliberately attempting to court popularity.

'Members of the Staff always received his warmest sympathy in times of bereavement or illness.

'Outside school he was very active. As a Rotarian he worked assiduously in obtaining Rotary Scholarships tenable at an American University for a one year course of study. He was a prominent Freemason and a very loyal member of St. Mary's Church, where he served on various committees. As a Magistrate he served the Tenby Bench loyally and conscientiously for a number of years.

'One can therefore fully appreciate the very grievous loss the school and town have sustained by his untimely death at the comparatively early age of sixty.

'If ever a History of the School is written, the name of Graham Charles Gibson, J.P., M.Sc., A.R.I.C. will loom large in its pages, and will always command honour and respect'.

For two terms I was Acting Head Master and at the end of the Session 1962-63 Miss M. G. Bowen retired after teaching in Greenhill for 36 years and serving as Senior Mistress for 21 years. She had always expected a very high standard of behaviour and turn-out from the girls. Her sincerity, sympathy and sense of vocation were of great benefit to successive generations of pupils. At a special social function on 16 October 1963, happily attended by all who wished to show their appreciation, Miss Bowen was presented with a framed picture by John Armstrong, a gold watch, a tea service and a cheque, and many sincere and complimentary speeches by Governors, colleagues and pupils were made. Miss Bowen was succeeded in Office by Miss Ella Ellis, who needless to say carried on the tradition of service.

The new Head Master, Mr. L. G. Hill, M.Ed., B.Sc., was appointed by the Education Committee on 28 May 1963, but was unable to take up his duties until the beginning of the Lent Term 1964. In one respect he differed from his three predecessors in being the father of five able children, all pursuing academic careers and his wife, Mrs. Anna Hill was capable of relief teaching when necessary. His experience in organising a new school in the 'new town' of Bracknell was to prove invaluable in his new appointment. He had a clear conception of what was required to re-organise Greenhill on comprehensive lines and I had the pleasure of co-operating with him in this task.

In 1969, my oldest colleague, Mr. 'Harry' Williams died, up to the end of his life still keenly interested in the school.

349

CHAPTER VI

EPILOGUE

It is in many ways appropriate that we have to leave the story of Education in South Pembrokeshire and in Greenhill in particular at this point—abruptly as it may seem. It is clear, however, that the Butler Act and all that followed from it, is as much a milestone in Welsh Education as the Welsh Intermdiate Education Act of 1889 that first brought the school into existence. Travellers of old frequently rested on roadside milestones contemplating the journey so far accomplished and that which lay ahead. It is under such conditions that Epilogues are born. As for as Greenhill is concerned it is relevant to this narrative to recall that I recorded my reflections as I sat in the summer of 1969, having just returned on what was clearly a very important milestone in my teaching career. My reflections are recorded in the form of a letter published that summer in *The Greenhillian*.

Dear Greenhillians,

I hang up my gown with thankfulness, regret and expectancy.

I am thankful for the good health I have enjoyed during $41\frac{1}{2}$ years in the School, for the opportunity of meeting successive generations of pupils and many of their families and for the privilege of service under three Headmasters alongside a sequence of Staff. From all I have learned much and I like to feel that I, in my turn, have been able to make some small contribution to the common stock of experience.

It is obvious that being among young people enables one to remain young in spirit, though not necessarily in appearance. My regret is that I have not found it possible to know our boys and girls better. I first knew Greenhill 50,000 lessons ago. The old building was a rabbit warren of corridors and classrooms, with ten coal fires and two gas fires (one very erratic), the walls streaming with condensation and the whole crowned with a clutter of attics haunted by weird fragments of art models and the ghostly pranks of past Greenhillians. There were then 56 girls and 54 boys, who were kept apart by a high wall in the playground and were not even allowed to exchange marbles. I can still recall them; many of them I still meet from time to time, some correspond from all over the world and two are serving on our staff at this moment.

In due course numbers increased, more rooms were brought into use, two bookcases expanded into a library, hutments were erected in the playground, the coal fires grew to 17 until they were replaced by nightstore heaters. There were additions to the Staff, Biology and Physics made their appearance alongside Chemistry in the curriculum. We gained half a Commercial Master and half an Art Master but no Art Room. The small gymnasium was a 'maid of all work'. It housed Morning Assembly, eisteddfodau, concerts and other functions. Choir, orchestra, dramatics and P.E. jostled for a place and preference, and there were extra complications when it was elevated to the dignity of a dining hall. Inspectors came and went, Prize Day followed Prize Day and so did promises and hopes of the new School. The Foundation Stone was laid in 1959, removed and re-laid, though not in the same place, in the premises which were opened, as you know them, in 1961.

Despite hopes for the future, many of us had regrets when the doors of the old establishment closed behind us for the last time. Already it was difficult to recognise individually some 350 pupils; now these were swallowed up in over 750. At present you are 420 girls and 457 boys. You all know me by sight at least. I have spoken to all sometime or other, even if only in groups. My teaching programme has brought me into closer contact with a small proportion of the School. My other work and the very size of the population, have prevented me from knowing you better. However, I hope that you will continue to greet me on the street, make yourselves known to me as you grow up, and let me know if I can be of any help to you.

My expectancy concerns my own future and yours. I expect to find myself occupied with the Museum and other local organisations to which I belong, with History books, music and of course my family. Who knows? We may travel. I shall be an interested spectator and a regular visitor to the School.

We live in a rapidly changing world. I have witnessed the change from horse-drawn cabs to a proliferation of motor cars, from horse-drays to articulated trucks, from primitive cinematograph to cinerama, from 'cat's whisker wireless' to T.V. Scientific progress has become

351

bewildering in the variety and extent of its implications. Man seeks to set foot on the moon before he knows how to walk the earth; he seeks the control of birth, the origin of life, and the extension of it by artificial means. The speed of communictions has made the world seem smaller without shrinking many of its problems. Visual aids on a massive scale enable us to see more of our fellow human beings without teaching us how to live with them.

During my teaching career, I have been part of a school which has changed its character. The present pupils have arrived on the scene, taking for granted much of what many of us thought impossible even twenty years ago. Staff/pupil relationships have altered too; autocracy is seen to be on the wane, topics once taboo are more easily discussed. Further changes, some not yet even envisaged, are likely to come, and girls and boys of this School will grow up in them and of them.

You now spend your days in a structure of steel, cement and glass, with your half-dozen laboratories and all their sophisticated apparatus. You have your art and craft rooms, your workshops, your other specialist rooms, your radio, T.V., films, projectors, tape-recorders, your canteen, your stage with all its appurtenances, your gymnasia, not to mention playing fields with the grass ready cut for you.

More will be added. See that you value all this and make the most of your opportunities. Remember that the old school had a splendid record without all these refinements. My expectation is that you will do even better. Some of you may even reach the moon. I think I can assure you that it won't be all honey.

My wife, herself an Old Greenhillian, joins me in warmest good wishes to the Headmaster, Staff, Pupils, Governors, the L.E.A.— to all involved in the future of the School.

Yours sincerely,

WILFRED HARRISON

SIXTH FORMERS AT WEST ANGLE BAY DURING AN EDUCATIONAL EXCURSION ALONG MILFORD HAVEN, 1950

photo: F. A. Rose

THE SCHOOL SQUADRON OF THE AIR TRAINING CORPS
with Mr. G. C. Gibson (H.M.) and officers, left to right: F.O. T. K. Edmonds, Flight Lt. W. J. Davies and F.O. S. W. H. Court

photo: Squibbs Studios

THE SCHOOL CHOIR 1956
with Mr. G. C. Gibson (H.M.), Mr W. Harrison and Mrs. E. Court
photo: Squibbs Studios

THE SCHOOL ORCHESTRA 1958
with Leader, Howard Allen
photo: Squibbs Studios

THE SCHOOL HALL, GREENHILL COUNTY SECONDARY SCHOOL.
17 November 1961, on the occasion of the Official Opening by Mr. Desmond Donnelly, M.P. for Pembrokeshire
photo: *Squibbs Studios*

SCHOOL CRICKET ELEVEN 1963
with Mr. W. Harrison (Acting Head Master) and Mr. Denzill Thomas (P.E. Master)
photo: Squibbs Studios

A GROUP OF THE GIRLS' SECTION OF 'THE GREENHILLIANS'
outside St. David's Hostel, during a hike in connection with the Duke of Edinburgh's Award for
Girls. All gained the Silver Award before leaving school. Pamela Sutton, seated right, went on to
receive the 'Gold'

CAST OF 'TWELFTH NIGHT' (SHAKESPEARE) 1964
on the new stage at Greenhill C.S.S.
photo: Squibbs Studios

STAFF PHOTOGRAPH 1964

with Mr. L. G. Hill (H.M.) seated centre, Mr. W. Harrison (Deputy H.M.) and Miss E. Ellis (Sen. Mistress)

photo: D. Hardy

INCOME ACCOUNT

		£	s.	d.
To	Scholarship & Bursary a/c. $\frac{1}{5}$ Grant	61	17	4
,,	Instalment on Loan	45	19	6
,,	Balance carried to Maintenance a/c	976	17	4
		1084	14	2

MAINTENANCE

		£	s.	d.
To	Balance due 31st March 1904	369	0	10
,,	Rates, Taxes, &c.	43	16	11
,,	Expenses of Management	42	3	3
,,	Head Master's Salary, Capitation &c.	279	11	8
,,	Other Members of Teaching Staff	406	3	4
,,	Furniture, fittings, apparatus, Books, Stationery &c.	104	2	3
,,	Examination Expenses	3	5	3
,,	Repairs of Premises	19	18	1
,,	Cleaning Schools &c. Coal, Gas &c.	50	2	5
,,	Head Master, use of Kitchen for Cookery Classes	16	5	0
,,	Treasurers Charges	25	4	0
		1359	13	0

YEAR ENDING 31 MARCH 1905

		£	s.	d.
By	Authority Maintenance Grant	309	6	9
„	Pupils' fees including £26 Evening Classes	370	11	9
„	Scholarships & Bursary Fees	61	13	4
„	Science & Art Grant	133	3	0
„	Technical do. including £42. 18s. balance of 1902-3 Grant	154	18	0
„	Rent of Residence	35	0	0
„	Sale of Books, Stationery &c.	20	11	4
		1084	14	2

ACCOUNT

	£	s.	d.
By Transfer from Income Account	976	17	4
„ Balance due to Treasurer 31st March 1905	382	15	8
N.B. School fees owing £39 11 7			
Pupil Teachers' do. £21 13 4			
	1359	13	0

SCHOLARSHIP AND BURSARY

	£	s.	d.
To Scholarships and Bursary Fees	61	3	4
To Balance in hand 31/3/05	5	2	10
	66	6	2

NEW BUILDING

To paid Contractors on account	362	—	—
To Balance in hand	494	2	6
	856	2	6

BALANCE

To Cash at Bank 31st March 1905	116	9	8
To Debit on Maintenance Account	382	15	8
	499	5	4

ACCOUNT Year Ending 31 March 1905

	£	s.	d.
By Balance in hand on last account	4	8	10
By Transfer from Income Account	61	17	4
	66	6	2

ACCOUNT

		£	s.	d.
By Loan from Public Works	—	856	2	6
Loan Commrs. less costs	—			
		856	2	6

ACCOUNT

	£	s.	d.
By Credit on Scholarship Account	5	2	10
do. on Building Account	494	2	6
	499	5	4

Appendix B

1st Ledger pp. 701-2 Summary

	£	s.	d.	£	s.	d.
Balance due to Treasurer 31/3/11 ..				482	3	6
Principal and Interest on Loans ..	90	1	2			
Treasurer Charges	24	4	3			
				114	5	5
Cleaning Schools and Grounds ..	32	17	2			
Repairs and Maintenance	13	10	4			
Cleaning, Lighting and Heating ..	14	10	0			
				60	17	6
Laboratory Apparatus	3	16	11			
Cookery and Laundry Apparatus ..	5	18	4			
Woodwork Apparatus	2	4	7			
Books and Stationery	13	16	7			
Needlework Requisites		18	0			
				26	14	5
Cost of Prizes					15	1
Travelling Expenses of Daisy Morse						
County Scholar as agreed ..	2	4	0			
Bursars' Maintenance Allowance ..	10	0	0			
				12	4	0
Salaries						
Head Master	120	0	0			
do. Capitation Fees	102	10	0			
Assistant Masters and Mistresses..	311	12	1			
				534	2	1
Examination Expenses					7	0
Insurance	3	12	8			
Rates and Rent	20	0	8			
Petty Disbursements	19	2	4			
				42	15	8
Salary Clerk, three-quarters ..				11	5	0
				£1,285	9	8

Year Ending March 1912

	£	s.	d.	£	s.	d.
Received from Local Education Auth-						
ity Half Services of Loan £732 ..	23	17	1			
Cash refunded by Head Master being						
Salary for Month of January 1911,						
the date of his appointment, he						
having been paid subsequently						
Term's Salary	12	18	4	36	15	5

By Grants from County Council:

	£	s.	d.			
Term's Grant ..	293	9	2			
Technical	83	12	9			

	£	s.	d.	£	s.	d.
				377	1	11
Bursar Grant under Clause 5 of						
Scheme	15	10	0			
				392	11	11
Pupils' Fees	174	6	8			
Books		12	4			
				174	19	0
Student Teachers. County Scholars						
Prospective Bursars Fees				54	13	4
Board of Education Grant				296	0	0
Rent of School House				35	0	0
				989	19	8
Balance due to Treasurer 31/3/12 ..				295	10	0

	£	s.	d.
	£1,285	9	8

Footnote in pencil £ s. d.	£	s.	d.
Balance due to Treasurer	£295	10	0
less Credit Balance	23	10	0
	£262	0	0

	£	s.	d.	£	s.	d.
To						
Maintenance Allowance	3	9	6			
Repairs and Improvements	19	9	9			
Repayments of Principal and Interest						
on Loan	175	7	0			
Salaries of School Staff	634	15	1			
Salary of Clerk	17	10	0			
Health Insurance	2	8	6			
Apparatus Consumable	52	14	11			
Administration	17	15	6			
Maintenance of Schools	103	14	6			
Value of Scholarships, Free Places ..	143	11	0			
				1,182	0	3
Balance 31/3/15				290	2	4
				1,472	2	7

Note (in red ink)

	£	s.	d.	£	s.	d.
Bank Balance ..	351	7	8			
Add Credit April 1st ..		10	0			
				351	17	8
Less cheques outstanding				61	8	2
				290	9	6

Maintenance Account 1914-15

	£	s.	d.	£	s.	d.
By						
Balance 31/3/14				144	18	6
Share of General Fund	365	3	5			
Grants from Board of Education ..	300	0	0			
Grants from County Council ..	95	10	3			
Half Service of Loan	22	11	9			
Sales from Cookery Classes ..	9	16	3			
School Fees	293	3	6			
County Council Student Teachers'						
Fees	58	15	4			
Special Grant County Council ..	146	13	7			
Head Master's Rent	35	0	0			
Amount disallowed and repaid by						
H.M.	10	0				
				1,327	4	1
				£1,472	2	7

Due to Clerk on Petty				
Cash account ..	13/9			
In Clerk's Hand Health				
Insurance	6/7			
Less Cash due to Clerk		7	2	
		290	2	4

To	£ s. d.	£ s. d.
Maintenance Allowance of Pupils ..	1 3 2	
Repayment of Principle and Interest		
on Loan	173 15 5	
		174 18 7
Maintenance of Schools		
Salaries	730 0 4	
Wages School Cleaner £29-11-5		
N. Insurance 10/3	30 1 8	
		760 2 0
Administration		
Salary of Clerk	20 0 0	
Printing and Advertising £19-13-10		
Audit Stamp £4-0-0	23 13 10	
Other expenses	17 7 9	
Health Insurance (Employer's) ..	3 3 0	
		64 4 7
Maintenance of Premises		
Rates, Taxes and Insurance ..	42 8 0	
Fuel and Light	27 4 2	
Upkeep of Grounds	13 15 0	
Repairs and Improvements ..	37 6 2	
Other Expenses including material	6 4 1	
		126 17 5
Books, Stationery and Apparatus ..		16 2 1
Cookery Requisites		14 10 11
Prize Distribution and Speech Day		9 0 1
Miscellaneous		13 0
Value of Scholarships and Free Places		167 4 0
		1,333 12 8
Balance		260 13 9
		1,594 6 5

Balance as Treasurer's Account ..	260 2 11	
In Clerk's Hands Petty £. s. d.		
Cash a/c 11 10		
In favour of Clerk's		
Stam a/c 1 0		
Nett Amount in Hand	10 10	
	260 13 9	

Maintenance Account 1915-16

By		£	s.	d.	£	s.	d.
Balance brought forward	.. ..				290	2	4
Share of General Fund	.. ..	333	18	0			
Board of Education Grant	.. ..	363	0	0			
Grants from County Council	..	121	14	8			
Service of Loan	.. .. ..	22	3	2			
Cookery Sales	.. .. ..	10	7	1			
School Fees ..	.. .. ..	347	7	10			
County Scholars. Student Teachers		70	13	4			
Rent of School House	.. ..	35	0	0			
					1,304	4	1

£1,594 6 5

Appendix C

A Summary of the New Scheme for Intermediate and Technical Education in Pembrokeshire, 1912

The Scheme for Pembroke, approved by His Majesty in Council on 14 May 1912, came into effect in August 1912. 'The provisions of the Scheme made under the Endowed Schools Acts 1869 to 1889, on 30 April 1894, as altered by a Scheme of the Board of Education of 15 July 1904, regulating the Pembrokeshire Intermediate and Technical Education Fund and Haverfordwest Grammar School, are hereby repealed, and the provisions of this Scheme substituted therefore . . . '.

The eight Parts of the Scheme comprised 93 Sections and there were four Schedules, as against 110 Sections and six Schedules in the 1894 Scheme. Although there were differences in wording here and there, the bulk of the two Schemes was the same. Some modifications should be noticed. The Board of Education had replaced the Charity Commission as the channel through which central funds were made available and to whom the County Council would be responsible. In Part II, concerned with 'Funds, Governing Bodies, etc.', it was stated that the County Council should continue to pay into a separate account (i.e. the General Fund), instead of to the County Governing Body, the product of a halfpenny rate, the Exchequer contribution, the Treasury Grant and, certain stated endowments as before. Already the functions of the County Governing Body had been transferred to the Education Committee, as defined, 'This Scheme shall have effect as if the powers of the County Council under it were powers transferred to the Council by the Scheme made by the Council under Section 17 of the Education Act 1902, approved by the Board of Education on 24 September 1903; and accordingly any reference in this Scheme to the County Council or to a meeting thereof, shall where the power exercisable by the Council is delegated to the Education Committee of the Council, include a reference to that Committee or to a meeting thereof.'

The County School Districts listed in the Second Schedule, remained the same as before. So did the provision for the administration of District Funds. The County Schools already established retained their character—dual schools at Pembroke Dock, Tenby, Narberth, and Milford Haven; mixed schools at Fishguard and

364

St. David's and a girls' school at Haverfordwest (Tasker's). The provisions of the Scheme affected Haverfordwest Grammar School only as mentioned in certain clauses.

Part III contained Transitory Provisions 'Until the expiration of three months from the coming into operation of this Scheme, or such further period as may be sanctioned in writing by the Board of Education, the present School Managers of the Districts under the Scheme of 30 April 1894 shall remain unaltered and shall retain such powers as will enable them to administer their respective Districts in the meantime under this scheme, but on . . . . such expiration they shall become discharged from their Office by virtue of this Scheme and the administration of the Foundation shall pass to the School Governors.'

The Clerk of the existing School Managers of each District was to summon the first meeting of the School Governors; if he failed to do this for three months after the expiry of the old Scheme, a meeting could be summoned after that date by any two School Governors. The existing Head Masters and Head Mistresses, if willing, were to continue in office for the same stipend and the interests of holders of Scholarships, Bursaries and Exhibitions were to be safeguarded.

Part IV was concerned with the Governing Bodies—the qualifications of the Governors, the keeping of Books of Account and Minute Books—the qualification of the Governors, the keeping of Books of Account and Minute Books. All accounts were to be made out and certified; copies were to be sent to the Board of Education; copies were to be displayed for public inspection after due notice and after being audited by an auditor appointed by the County Council. There were provisions for consultation between Governors and the County Council, for the vesting of property, for dealing with additional endowments and various matters relating to property. Within the limits of the Scheme the Governors, subject to any statute regulating the conduct of business by the L.E.A., had the power to make rules for the management of their trust and the conduct of business, including the summoning of meetings, the deposit of money at a proper bank, the custody of documents and the appointment during their pleasure of a Clerk or any necessary officers at rates of remuneration approved by the Board of Education. Governors were to keep in repair and insure against fire all the buildings in their trust. Terms of office of School Governors were stated. The term of office of those appointed by the County Council were stated. The term of office of those appointed by the County Council was to expire on the date of the appointment of their successors. The other Representative Governors and the Co-optative Governors were to be appointed each for a term of three years, reckoned in the case of Representative Governors as from January 1st next after the date of the appointment. In the case of one filling a casual vacancy, he was to hold office for the unexpired term of the one he replaced. There were rules for the appointment of additional Governors, for Declarations upon taking up office, and for the filling of vacancies. Ordinary Meetings were to be held at least twice a year, provision being made for the summoning of Special Meetings. The Chairman was to be appointed annually at the first Ordinary Meeting. There would be a quorum when more than one third of the whole body were present. When there was no quorum the Meeting would be summoned as soon as convenient. In the Third Schedule the membership of the County School Governors was set out. In the case of Tenby: (1) the County Council—four (of whom at least one must be a woman); (2) the Town Council of the town from whom the District is named—two; (3) District Councillors representing parishes included in the School District—one; (4) Managers of Public Elementary Schools in the District—one; (6) Co-optative—three (of which at least one must be a woman). The total of twelve was two less than under the 1894 Scheme, which at first had included sub-scribers of £5 and over. Under the new Scheme District Councils were represented instead of the Guardians of the Poor. The County Council representation had increased by one.

In Part V the 'Functions of the County Councils' included the important task of distributing finance: (1) For the purpose of allotment of the Treasury Grant the County Council was to apportion the County Rate between the schools and set out such apportionment in a Schedule for the approval of the Board of Education. (2) Subject to certain payments out of the income from the Tasker's Endowment, the County Council, at the beginning of each year, was to estimate the amount (being not more than one fifth part and not less than one tenth of the Income of the General Fund) which would be necessary for expenses incurred in the management of property and business, the examination and inspection of County Schools, travelling teachers of County Schools, County Exhibitions and contributions to the Pension

366

Fund, and then apply any balance of such sum in special grants to the most necessitous County Schools (including Cardigan and the Haverfordwest Grammar School). In addition the County Council was to pay out of the residue of the yearly income of the General Fund to the Governors of Haverfordwest Grammar School £100 and to the Governors of each County School (except Cardigan) the sum of £150, provided that, if on any grounds of inefficiency the Treasury Grant was reduced, the County Council could also deduct the sum payable under this clause. The sum received by the School Governors of each District, together with any sum received by them under the clause of this Scheme as to 'Application of ultimate residue' was to be applied by them in the maintenances of (1) the County School and (2) Exemptions and Maintenance Allowances in the County School. Under clause (48) there were provisions for yearly Inspection and Examination of all County Schools and Haverfordwest Grammar School by competent examiners unconnected with the schools, appointed by the C.W.B. 'or in such manner as the Board of Education in any year by Order direct for that year'. The County Council could contribute to the payment of travelling teachers and, if they thought fit, form a Pension Fund for 'Masters' (means Mistresses as well) in the County Schools. They also had sole power of appointment and dismissal of Head Masters.

Part VI, headed 'The County Schools'. As in the 1894 Scheme, the schools were defined and the buildings and accommodation described. Clause 54 was new: 'Subject to the provisions of this Scheme, a County School shall be so conducted as to allow of a grant being made in aid of it by the Treasury under the Welsh Act, and also by the Board of Education under their Regulations for Secondary Schools'. The clauses relating to the Head Master and Staff were similar to those in the original Scheme, and so were those concerned with Organisation and Curriculum, though under the heading 'General Instruction' the emphasis in one sentence should be noticed: 'So far as may be consistent with the working of the School, special attention shall be given to instruction in such branches of Natural Science as bear on the industries in the neighbourhood, including agriculture'. Conditions concerning admission were as before.

In Part VI, 'Free Places, Exhibitions, etc.' some changes should be noticed. In Clause (83) 'The Rules for Payments for each County

School shall provide for total or partial exemptions from payment of tuition fees or entrance fees'. Among other things they were to provide: (a) that in every school year total exemption from payment of tuition fees, to an extent of not less than five per cent of the pupils admitted to the school during the previous school year, was to be offered on admission to children who were and had not less than two years been in attendance at Public Elementary Schools. They could also provide (b) that any pupils who were exempted from payment of tuition fees, and who by reason of their proficiency were deserving of the distinction, should be called 'County Scholars'. According to Clause (84) Maintenance Allowances were to be awardable by the Governors to (a) pupils who had been exempt from fees or (b) had for not less than two years been in an elementary school, and, in the opinion of the School Governors were in need of financial assistance to enable them to remain in the School. Maintenance Allowances each of a yearly value of not more than £10 would be payable at the discretion of the Governors to the parent of the pupil or towards travelling expenses or meals.

Clause (85) concerned County Exhibitions: (a) the County Council was to offer one or more Leaving Exhibitions to be called County Exhibitions tenable at any University or Training College. (b) Each Exhibition was to consist of either a single payment or series of payments extending over not more than four years, not exceeding in either case, a total value of £200, awardable to a pupil who had been for two years in a Pembrokeshire or Cardigan School. (c) Within the limits of the Scheme, the Exhibitions were to be freeely and openly competed for and were to be awarded for merit on the results of such examination and under such conditions as the County Council must determine. (d) No award was to be made if there was no duly qualified candidate.

Part VIII consisted of General Provisions.

Tenby—Proposed Grammar/Modern School (Bilateral) 20 June 1952

	2 FE mixed Sec. Gram. Sch. with 60 6th Form Pupils 5 yr. course. 6th Fm.		2 FE mixed Sec. Mod. School 4 year course	Full Scheme 2 FE Sec. Gram. 3 FE Sec. Mod.
No. of Pupils	300	60	360	720
Min. Teaching Area sq. ft. ...	14180	2880	17,028	
Places for Cost Purposes ..	360	72	372	804
Number of Form Units ..	10	2	11	
Halls	1—2000 sq. ft. 1— 900 sq. ft.		1—2,000 sq. ft. —	1—3,200 sq. ft. 1— 900 sq. ft.
Gymnasium	1—2,800 sq. ft.		1—2,800 sq. ft.	2—2,800 sq. ft.
	5,700 sq. ft.		4,800	9,700
Library	1— 960 sq. ft.		1— 960 sq. ft.	1— 960 sq. ft.
	960 sq. ft.		960 sq. ft.	960 sq. ft.
General Teaching				
Classrooms	2— 600 sq. ft. 7— 480 sq. ft.		5—600 sq. ft. 5—480 sq. ft.	7— 600 sq. ft. 12— 480 sq. ft.
Division Rooms	2— 300 sq. ft.		—	2— 300 sq. ft.
	5,160 sq. ft.		5,400 sq. ft.	10,560 sq. ft.
Practical Accommodation				
Science Labs.	4— 960 sq. ft.		1— 960 sq. ft.	5—960 sq. ft.
Art and Craft Room	1— 960 sq. ft.		1— 960 sq. ft.	2—960 sq. ft.
Wood/Metal Workshop ..	1— 850 sq. ft.		1— 850 sq. ft.	2—850 sq. ft.
Housecraft Room	1— 850 sq. ft.		1— 850 sq. ft.	2—850 sq. ft.
	6,500 sq. ft.		3,620 sq. ft.	10,160 sq. ft.

369

Total	22 spaces	17 spaces	38 spaces
Total Area	18,380 sq. ft.	14,780 sq. ft.	31,380 sq. ft.
No. of Teaching Spaces ..	—	15	32
No. of Form Bases	11	11	22
Dining Requirements			
(two sittings)	1,170 sq. ft.	1,120 sq. ft.	2,290 sq. ft.
65			
Nett Cost	432 places	372 places	804 places
	£240—£103,680	£240—£89,080	£240—£192,700

Continued:
Estimate of Cost

(a) *Full Scheme*

	£.	s.	d.
Nett Cost	192,760	0	0
Additional Cost including extra works on drainage, site levelling, etc.	19,276	0	0
Total Grand Cost	£212,036	0	0

(b) 1st *Instalment Secondary Grammar School*

	£.	s.	d.
	103,680	0	0
Additional Cost of providing in First Instalment the large Assembly Hall and Staff Rooms for full Scheme	10,000	0	0
Total Nett Cost	£113,680	0	0
Additional Cost	15,000	0	0
Total Grand Cost	£128,680	0	0

Provision of Dining Accommodation
It is proposed that the small Hall shall be used for Dining.
Site: Additional land adjoining existing Grammar School Playing Fields is to be acquired.
Secondary Modern School—accommodation is based on First Alternative Appendix to Circular 245.

WALTER BARRETT,
County Architect.

County Offices,
Haverfordwest.
20th June, 1952.

Analysis of Governors Estimates Year Ending 31st March 1950

	Actual Expenditure 1947-48	Estimated Expenditure 1948-49	Probable Expenditure 1948-49	Estimated Expenditure 1949-50
	£	£	£	£
Salaries of Teachers	6,037	6,700	6,500	6,800
Books, Stationery, etc.				
(Capitation Allowance) ..	490	450	450	600
Replacement of Furniture ..	243	200	200	220
Upkeep of Buildings and grounds	332	2,670	2670	450
Fuel and light	380	220	220	250
Wages of Caretaker and Lab. Boy	365	425	400	450
Cost of Cleaning Materials ..	8	50	50	50
Rates and Taxes	125	120	20	20
Clerk's Salary	10	—	—	—
Games	28	35	35	90
Printing, advertising, etc. ..	13	35	35	35
Audit Stamp Duty	—	35	—	—
State and other Insurances ..	24	15	15	15
New National Ins. Employer's Contributions	—	130	130	190
Employers' Superannuation Contributions	300	335	325	340
Cookery and special subjects..	95	100	100	100
Interviews, Telephones, Sundries	44	45	45	45
Clerical assistance (H.M.) ..	52	52	52	52
Total Estimated Payments ..	8,546	11,617	11,247	9,677
Total Estimated Receipts ..	—	—	—	—
Deficiency	8,546	11,617	11,247	9,707

Provision has been made by the County Architect for the following Capital Items:

		£
(a)	Two Classrooms	2,500
(b)	Heating Installation	1,500
(c)	Tarmac	1,000
		£5,000

Governors' Estimates for 1960-61

RESOLVED that the following Estimates be submitted for the approval of the Education Committee:

Head of Expenditure	*Estimate* 1960-61 £.
Salaries of Teachers ..	24,000
Salary of Clerical Assistant	198
Salary of Laboratory Assistants	42
Employer's Contributions:	
Teachers' Superannuation	1,425
National Insurance	475
Furniture	400
Books, Stationery, Equipment	1,604
Rents, Rates, Insurance	700
Upkeep of Buildings	800
Upkeep of Grounds:	
Allocation of County Grounds Staff	100
Other Expenditure	50
Fuel, Light, Cleaning:	
Wages of Caretakers and Cleaners	Defer
Fuel, Light, Water and Cleaning materials	900
Postage, Telephone, Carriage	75
Speech Day Expenses	70
School Magazine Grant	25
Travel of Teaching Staff	50
Examination Expenses	—
Miscellaneous..	10
Capital:	
Erection of New School ..	100,000

WYNFORD DAVIES
Clerk to the Governors.

Governors Estimates for 1963-64

RESOLVED to submit the following Estimates of Expenditure for 1963/64 to the Education Committee for approval:

Head of Expenditure	*Estimate* 1963/64 £
Employees:	
Teachers—Salaries	53,325
—National Insurance	971

—Superannuation	.. ..	3,150
Clerical Assistants—Salaries	.. ..	640
—National Insurance	.. ..	39
—Superannuation	.. ..	33
Laboratory Assistants—Salaries	.. .. ..	42
—National Insurance	.. ..	3
Caretakers and Cleaners—Wages	.. .. ..	3,565
—National Insurance	.. ..	260
Handyman—Wages	.. ..	620
—National Insurance	.. ..	29
Groundsmen—Wages	.. ..	630
—National Insurance	.. ..	30
Premises:		
Repair and Maintenance of Buildings	.. .. ..	400
Maintenance of Grounds	.. ..	620
Fuel, Light, Cleaning Materials and Water	.. ..	2,750
Furniture and Fittings	.. ..	300
Rents and Rates	.. ..	7,200
Supplies:		
Books, Stationery, Materials and Equipment	.. ..	3,739
Sports Equipment and Expenses	.. .. ..	365
Establishment Expenses:		
Postage, Telephone, Carriage	.. ..	120
Insurances	.. ..	90
Travel of Teaching Staff ..	.. ..	100
Miscellaneous:		
Speech Day	.. ..	80
School Magazine Grant ..	.. ..	25
Examination Expenses	.. ..	500
Miscellaneous	.. ..	50
		79,676

Head of Income

School Sales ..	.. ..	130
Rents, Lettings, etc. ..	.. ..	100
		230

WYNFORD DAVIES
Clerk to the Governors.

Appendix F

List of Former Greenhillians who Held the Office of Mayor of the Borough of Tenby

Name	*Year of Office*
Arrol Ewart Davies	1937-38
Sydney Herbert Hughes ...	1940-41
Maurice Charles Ormond ...	1950-51 and 1958-59
David Colwyn Williams ...	1963-64
Morgan Bowen Eastlake ...	1968-69
Thomas Gilroy Phillips ...	1969-70
Frederick C. Fry	1972-73
Iris Davies	1973-74 (584th and last Mayor of the Borough, until 31 March 1974).

BIBLIOGRAPHY

A. UNPUBLISHED SOURCES.

1. *Borough of Tenby Muniments*
   Order Book 1776-1835.
   Chamberlains' Vouchers 1725-1750.
   Minute Books 1881-1900.
   Charters and other documents now in Tenby Museum.
2. *Pembrokeshire County Council*
   Minutes of County Council from 24 January 1889 onwards.
   Draft Conveyance (Greenhill) 16 December 1895 (Legal Dept.)
   Conveyance (Greenhill) 18 August 1896 (Legal Dept.)
3. *Pembrokeshire Local Education Authority*
   Material deposited in Pembrokeshire County Record Office
   Minutes of the Managers (local Governors) of the Tenby County
   Intermediate School from 31 August 1894 onwards.
   Minutes of the Governors of Tenby Grammar School from 12 May 1948.
   onwards.
   Minutes of the Governors of Greenhill County Secondary School from
   12 October 1961.
   From County Offices
   Minutes of Pembrokeshire Education Committee 1904-1965.
4. *Pembrokeshire County Record Office*
   Account Books of Tenby County Intermediate School later Tenby
   Grammar School.
5. *From Greenhill County Secondary School, Tenby*
   (Through the Head Master, Mr. L. G. Hill, M.Ed., B.Sc.)
   Copy of Draft Mortgage for securing £935 and interest on Greenhill
   property 16 May 1896.
   Admission Registers from 1896 onwards.
   Staff Register under Rules 42 (Wales) 1909.
   Copies of Head Masters' Reports to the Governors.
   L.E.A. and Board of Education Circulars relating to Pupil Teachers,
   Probationers, Bursars and Student Teachers.
   Sundry items of correspondence.
   Copies of proposed Amendments to the Scheme for Intermediate and
   Technical Education in Pembrokeshire 1903, 1094. The Amended
   Scheme 1912.
6. *From Tenby Heywood Lane Infants School*
   (Through Head Mistress, Mrs. M. James)
   Excerpts from Registers 1856 onwards—transcribed by Dr. D. Rhys-
   Phillips.

7. *St. Mary's Church, Tenby*
   By courtesy of Rector and Churchwardens.
   Churchwardens' Accounts.
8. *Mr. and Mrs. Norman Bleines*
   Correspondence relating to William Husband and his family. Certificates
   and other data associated with his family.
9. *Reminiscences of Old Pupils*
   See Acknowledgments.
10. *From Welsh Office (Legal Division)*—Mr. J. H. Grainger.
   Copy of *Scheme for administration of the Funds Applicable to the Inter-
   mediate and Technical Education of the Inhabitants of the County of
   Pembroke* 1894.
   Copy of *Order of the Charity Commission 24 January 1899 concerning*
   raising of a Loan in respect of Tenby County Intermediate School.
11. *National Library of Wales*—through Mr. B. G. Owens.
   Copies of Central Welsh Board Reports on Tenby County Intermediate
   School from 1897 onwards.

B. PUBLISHED SOURCES

1. *Official Reports.*
   First Report of Commissioners appointed to inquire into the Municipal
   Corporations in England and Wales, 1834.
   *Reports of the Commissioners of Enquiry into the State of Education in
   Wales* 1847.
   *Report of the Committee Appointed to Inquire into the Condition of Inter-
   mediate and Higher Education in Wales* (Aberdare) 1881.
   Report of the Consultative Committee of the Board of Education—
   The Education of the Adolescent 1926.
   *Report of the Consultative Committee of the Board of Education on
   Secondary Education.* (The Spens Report) 1939.
2. *Acts of Parliament.*
   Municipal Corporations Act 1835
   Act for the Improvement of the Borough of Tenby, 1838.
   The Welsh Intermediate Education Act 1889.
   Board of Education Act 1899.
   Education Act 1902.
   Education Act 1918.
   Education Act 1936.
   Education Act 1944.
3. *From Tenby Museum Library.*
   Pigot & Co. National Commercial Directory (17 Basing Lane, London)
   1830, 1831, 1835, 1844.
   Sketches of Tenby and its Neighbourhood. An Historical and Descriptive
   Guide. Fanny Price Gwynne. 1846.

Guide to Tenby and Neighbourhood. Mary Anne Bourne. W. Spurrell. Carmarthen 1843.

The Tenby Guide, Comprehending Such Information Relating to the Town and its Vicinity. J. Voss. Swansea. 1810.

Etchings of Tenby. Charles Norris. 1812. John Booth, London.

An Account of Tenby. Charles Norris. 1818. W. Wilmot.

The Earls, Earldom and Castle of Pembroke. G. T. Clark, F.S.A. 1880. R. Mason. Tenby.

Pembroke Royal Dockyard and Neighbourhood. Historical Sketch. George Mason. Peter House. 1905.

John Morgan, M.A. (Narberth). Abel J. Jones. Gomerian Press. 1919.

Some Aspects of Tenby's History. Wilfred Harrison. *Pembrokeshire* Historian. 1966.

History of Carmarthenshire. (Vol. II). Edit. Sir John Lloyd.

The History of the Civil War (1642-49) *in Pembrokeshire and on its Borders.* A. L. Leach. Witherby. 1937.

Leaves from a Notebook and other articles on Tenby and neighbourhood, written by Arthur L. Leach for *The Tenby and County News* and the *Tenby Observer* cut out and filed.

The Tenby Observer 1854, 1887, 1888, 1889, 1890, 1891, 1892, 1893, 1895, 1896, 1897, 1901, 1902, 1905-1911, 194 (several of these were consulted in the office of *The Tenby Observer.*

Tenby and County News 1893, 1894, 1895, 1896, 1910, 1911.

Dictionary of Welsh Biography.

The Church Book of St. Mary the Virgin, Tenby. Edward Laws. John Leach. Tenby. 1907.

Tenby Parish Church. W. Gwyn Thomas (3rd. Edit. 1967).

A Calendar of Public Records Relating to Pembrokeshire. Vol. III. *The Earldom of Pembroke and its Members.* Cymmrodorion Record Series No. 7. Edit. Henry Owen. 1918

I. *From Pembrokeshire County Library.*

Dictionary of National Biography.

Encyclopaedia Britannica.

English Philanthropy 1660-1960. David Owen. Harvard University Press. O.U.P. 1964.

Charity School Movement. M. G. Jones. C.U.P. 1938.

Correspondence and Minutes of the S.P.C.K. relating to Wales 1699-1740. Mary Clement. U.W.P. Cardiff. 1952.

The S.P.C.K. and Wales. Mary Clement. London. S.P.C.K. 1954.

Brief History of Education in Pembrokeshire. David Salmon.

Chiaroscuro. Augustus John. Jonathan Cape. 1952.

A Manual to the Intermediate Education (Wales) Act 1889. Thomas Ellis and Ellis and Ellis Griffith. I.E.A.M. 1889.

Census returns relating to the Tenby catchment area (schools) 1891, 1901, 1911, 1921, 1931, 1951, 1961.

5. *Other published sources.*

The Greenhillian. 1937-1964.

Early Victorian England 1830-1865. Edit. G. M. Young. O.U.P. 1934.

English History 1914-1945. A. J. P. Taylor. Oxford History England. Vol. 15. 1965.

King George V, His Life and Reign. Harold Nicolson. Constable, London. 1952.

England in the Twentieth Century 1914-63. David Thomson. Penguin Books 1964.

Education in England. W. Kenneth Richmond. Pelican 1945.

A History of English Education from 1760. H. C. Barnard. University of London Press 1961.

Four Hundred Years of English Education. W. H. G. Armitage. Cambridge University Press. 2nd Edn. 1970.

History of Education in Great Britain. S. J. Curtis. University Tutorial Press. 7th Edn. 1967.

An Atlas of Welsh History. William Rees. 3rd Edit. 1967.

Modern Wales. David Williams. John Murray. 1950.

An Illustrated History of Modern Britain, 1783-1964. D. Richards and J. W. Hunt. Longman's.

C. *Maps, Plans and Pictures in the Tenby Museum.*

An Exact Survey of Lands Belonging to Tenby. John Butcher. 1740.

Lands Belonging to the Corporation of Tenby Situate in the Parish of St. Mary's, Tenby 1811. Wm. Couling, Surveyor.

Plan of the Town of Tenby in the County of Pembroke showing the Property of the Corporation, 1811. Wm. Couling.

Tithe Map and Schedule. St. Mary's, Tenby. September 1841.

Map of the Town of Tenby from an Actual Survey. E. B. Hughes, Narberth, 1849.

Pembrokeshire Sheet XLI 11 1/1500 Ordnance Survey Office, Southampton 1890.

Elevations. Tenby County School. Pembrokeshire County Architect.

Topographical drawings and paintings from Charles Norris and John Norris onwards 19th and 20 centuries.

INDEX

Aberdare, Lord, 23
Aberystwyth: University College of Wales, 33, 86, 278-9
Acts of Parliament
Board of Education (1899), 120-1, Welsh Department established (1907), 174
Education Act-Balfour (1902), 121
Education Act (1936), 200-1
Education Act-Butler (1944), 289-293
Miscellaneous Provisions Act (1948), 294
Endowed Schools Act (1869), 23
Education Act-Fisher (1918), 187-8
Elementary Education Act-Forster (1870), 17
Improvement of the Borough of Tenby (1838), 5
Local Government Act (1888)-County Councils, 28
Municipal Corporations Act (1835), 5
Municipal Corporations Act (1882), 45
Local Taxation (Customs and Exise) (1890), 32
Physical Training and Recreation Act (1937), 201
Propagation of the Gospel in Wales (1650), 9
Teachers' Superannuation Act (1918), 191
Union of England and Wales (1536-42), 3
Welsh Intermediate Education Act (1889), 24-6
Technical Education Act (1889), 25
Adams, J. W. B. , First Head Master at Greenhill, 83-180
Adrian, A. D., 45
Aeronautics
Frost, William, 7
Alcock and Brown, 184
Cobham, Alan, 184
British Imperial Airways, 185
B.O.A.C., 185
Whittle, Sir Frank, 185
Wright, Orville and Wilbur, 180
Tymms, Sir Frederick, 111-112
Albert, Prince Consort, 6
Allen, Mrs. Bird, 16
Allen, C. F. Egerton, 7, 41-3, 50 passim
Allen, G. H., 28-9
Anthony, Evan, 342
Armada, Spanish, 3

379

Baird, John Logie, 185
Barrett, Col. Walter, 342
Board of Education, 120 passim
Boyle, Sir Edward, 340-1
Bristol, 2, 4
Britain, Festival of (1951), 288
British Empire, 174-5
British and Foreign School Society, 17
Broadcasting, B.B.C., 185
Bruce, the Hon. W. W. (Board of Education), 29, 31, 46 passim
Burnham Scales, 189-91, 295
Butler, R. A. , 289

Camden, William, 2
Cardiff: University College of South Wales and Monmouthshire 3,
        100, 104, 192
Cardigan, Intermediate School and District, 33, 39, 40
Central Welsh Board (1896), 27, 40-1. Examinations and Inspections, 95
        passim
Charity Commission, 23, 26, 29, 30, 32 passim
Charles I, 3
Charles II, 4
Churchill, Winston, 110, 287
Cinematograph, 185
Civil War (1642-8,) 4
Colleges, Training, 192; Emergency Training, 294-5
Cromwell, Oliver 4

Davies, David (of Llandinam), 5
Davies, Capt. E. T. Director of Education for Pembrokeshire (1919-27),
        183 passim
Davies, Thomas, Assistant Director for Pembrokeshire (1920-51),
        County Librarian (1924-51), 183 passim
Davies, Wynford, Assistant Director for Pembrokeshire (1951-7),
        Director (1957-74); continued reorganisation, 299 passim
Dinbych, 1
Disestablishment of Welsh Church, 6, 181
Donnelly, Desmond, M.P. for Pembrokeshire, 342
Dyfed, Kingdom of, 1

Eccles, Sir David, Minister of Education, 297
Education, Ministry of, 290
Edward III, 2
Edward, Prince of Wales (Edward VII), 85; Edward VII, 174
Edwards, Owen M., Chief Inspector of Board of Education (Welsh
        Department), 174

Einstein, Albert, 184,
Elizabeth I, 3, 13
Elizabeth II, Coronation (1953), 288
Ellis, Thomas, 24
Examinations: School Certificate standardised (1917), 193-5; Free
    Place and Special Place Examinations, 198-200; Ordinary
    Level and Advanced Level, 295; Certificate of Secondary
    Education, 296-8

Fishguard
    French Invasion 1797, 4
    Intermediate School and District (1894 Scheme), 33, 39, 40;
    County Secondary School and District (1947), Development Plan,
        305-8
Fisher, H.A.L., 185-191
Ford, Henry, 184

Geddes, Sir Eric, economies, 189, 191
George, Lloyd, 174
George, Prince Regent (George IV), 4
George V, 174
George VI, 287
George, W. Davies (Deputy Clerk of the Peace), 30-40 passim
Gibson, Graham C., third Head Master of Greenhill (1942-1963),
    239, 288-349
Giraldus Cambrensis, 2, 3
Gladstone, W. E., 23
Goward, Henry (Principal of Private School at Greenhill), 20-22
Greenhill estate and private school, 20, 21. Intermediate, Grammar and
    County Secondary-see 'Schools'
Griffith, John Thomas, second Head Master at Greenhill (1911-42),
    20, 60, 179-181, 183, 215-285

Hadow, Sir Henry, 192; Reports 195-6 passim
Hallam, Canon H.J.B., Rector of Tenby, 342
Harries, Benjamin, Mayor of Tenby. Officially opened Tenby
    Intermediate School (1896), 87
Haverfordwest, 5; Grammar School, 18, 32; Tasker's School, 32;
    1894 Scheme, 39, 40. 1947 reorganisation plan, 305, 307-8
Henry IV, 2
Henry VII (see Henry Tudor)
Henry VIII, 1, 2
Hill, Llewelyn George, fourth Head Master of Greenhill, 349
Holcombe, the Rev. John, 9, 10, 13
Horton, General, 4
Husband, William, 66 passim

Ireland, Home Rule, 6. 181

James, H. E., Director of Education for Pembrokeshire (1904-19).
First Director under L. E. A. Administrative changes after Balfour Act, 122 passim, 183
James, the Rev. Lewis, 28-90
Jones, D. T., Director of Education for Pembrokeshire (1927-57).
Entrance Examination, 183, 198-200; reorganisation plans in the twenties and thirites, 200-203; re-organisation after 1944 Education Act, 301 passim

Kensington, Lord, 28

Leland, John, 1
Lewis, H. J., Assistant Director of Education (1904-20), 183
Lingen, R. R. Wheeler, Commissioner Blue Books 1847, 15
Llwyd, Humphrey, 3
Local Government Board, 45
Lords Commissioners of the Treasury, 45 passim

MacDonald, J. Ramsay, 195
Marconi, Marchese Gugliemo, 185
Marshall Plan for economic aid (1947), 288
Medical Science progress of, 184
Milford Haven, 6; Intermediate School and District (1894 Scheme), 33, 39, 40; Central School opened (1931), 197; 1947 Development Plan, 305, 307, 308
Ministry of Education, 290, 303 passim
Morgan, Capt. D. Hughes (Sir), 181
Morgan, Capt. Edmund, 59
Morris, Lewis, 23, (Sir) 87-8, 136
Morris, William (Lord Nuffield), 184
Mundella, A. J. , 23-4

Napoleon III, 6
Narberth Intermediate School and District (1894 Scheme), 33, 39, 40; 1947 Development Plan, 305, 307
Nash, John, 4
National Health Service, 287
National Insurance Act, 181
Nationalisation, 287-8
National Library of Wales: Foundation Stone laid by George V and Queen Mary 1911, 181
Nelson, Horatio (Lord), 4
Norris, Charles, 4

Salisbury, Lord, 23-4

Schools in the Tenby area:

Board, 18; Charity, 9-11, 14; Council, 197; Grammar, 10, 11, 14; Infants, 16; National, 15, 18, 120, 197; Private, 18-22; Puritan (Commonwealth), 9, Sunday, 16, 17; Wesleyan, 17.

Intermediate (Greenhill): negotiations to secure site for school and funds, 41-65; first School Govenors (Managers), 65; Greenhill estate and purchase of premises, 59-70; problems down to Official Opening, 71-85; Official Opening, 85-90.

Adams period: staff and curriculum, 84, 95, 151-9; accommodation and equipment, 92-4; social background, examinations, careers, cross-section of pupils, 94-118, 165-172; recognition as a Secondary School, 123-5; Pupil Teachers, 130-1; first extension (1905), 134-7; second extension (1908), 139-40; financial difficulties, 141-9; out-of school activities, 160-5; Prize Days, 136, 139 170, 172.

Griffith period: salaries 189-91, 138; financial problems, 215-17, 220-2; new County Scheme (1912), 218-19 with Appendix; Governors under new Scheme 219-20; World War I 222-8; curriculum 237-8; Staff, examinations, reminiscences; number of pupils and population of catchment area in Griffith period, 238-9; description of school premises, 241-5; Author's reminiscences, 245 passim; internal and external examinations, 256-8; out-of school activities, School Magazine, purchase of school field, Library, 258-70; World War II, Staff and wartime service, evacuees, 243-275; careers of Old Pupils, 277-282; retirement of J. T. Griffith, 282-5.

Gibson period: changes in school organisation, 312; school war efforts, 313; school became a Voluntary Controlled Grammar School (1947), 314; new constitution for Governors and first Governors' meeting, 314-5; changes in curriculum and staffing, 316; refurnishing and new equipment, 317; Savings Groups and charity collections, 318; catchment area increase in population and number of pupils, 318; raising of school leaving age to 15, 318; pressure on accommodation, especially on science laboratory, 319-20; extension to premises, 320; Jubilee celebrations and Jubilee number of School Magazine, 321-2; Roll of Honour and Decorations, 322; War Memorial unveiled, 323; extension of out-of school activities-P.E., Drama, Music. A.T.C., and Duke of Edinburgh's Award Scheme, Eisteddfodau etc., 324-336; Prize Days, school courses and examination successes, 324-339; effect of Authority's Reorganisation Scheme upon Contributory Schools, 306; events down to Official Opening of new school, 306-342; organisation of new school as Grammar-Modern, 343-347; death of G. C. Gibson, 345; sample careers of Old Pupils, 347.

Science and Art Department, South Kensington, 27, 120.

SUBSCRIPTIONS

Financial contributions from the following sponsors towards the production costs of this book are gratefully acknowledged.

Miranda M. Braund, the author's daughter, and her late husband, William D. Braund, of Toronto (to cover the cost of illustrations)

Greenhill County Secondary School

Dyfed County Council (Welsh Church Fund)

Tenby Museum

Friends of Tenby

Frank B. Mason & Co. Tenby

Lowless & Lowless, Solicitors of Tenby

E. G. Evans, Tenby

Peggy Regemortel, Tenby

George Ace Limited, Tenby

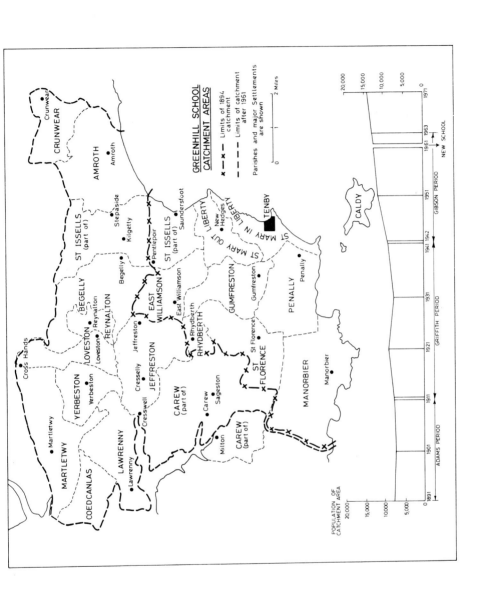

GREENHILL SCHOOL
CATCHMENT AREAS

×—×—× Limits of 1894 catchment

—●—●— Limits of catchment after 1951

Parishes and major settlements are shown

0   1   2 Miles

CRUNWEAR

Crunwear ●

AMROTH

Amroth ●

ST ISSELLS (part of)

Stepaside ●

Kilgetty ●

Saundersfoot ●

LIBERTY

New Hedges

ST MARY IN LIBERTY

ST MARY OUT LIBERTY

TENBY

BEGELLY

Begelly ●

Pentlepoir ●

ST ISSELLS (part of)

REYNALTON

Reynalton ●

EAST WILLIAMSON

East Williamson ●

GUMFRESTON

Gumfreston ●

PENALLY

Penally ●

LOVESTON

Loveston ●

Cross Hands ●

VERBESTON

Verbeston ●

JEFFRESTON

Jeffreston ●

Cresselly ●

RHYDBERTH

Rhydberth ●

St Florence ●

ST FLORENCE

MARTLETWY

Martletwy ●

LAWRENNY

Lawrenny ●

CAREW (part of)

Cresswell ●

Carew ●

Sageston ●

Milton ●

CAREW (part of)

MANORBIER

Manorbier ●

COEDCANLAS

CALDY

POPULATION OF CATCHMENT AREA

20,000

15,000

10,000

5,000

0

1891   1901   1911   1921   1931   1941 1942   1951   1961 1963   1971

ADAMS PERIOD   GRIFFITH PERIOD   GIBSON PERIOD   NEW SCHOOL

20,000

15,000

10,000

5,000

0

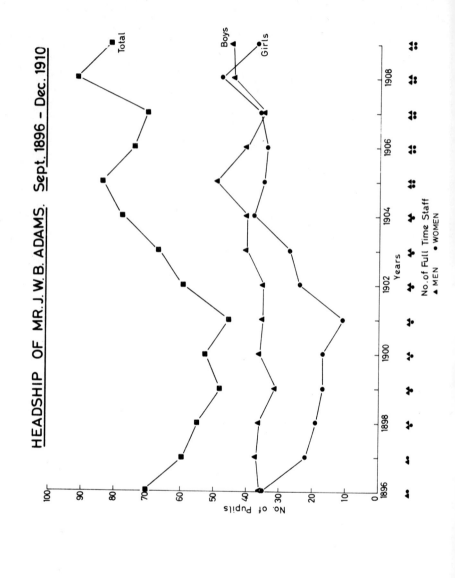

HEADSHIP OF MR. J.W.B. ADAMS. Sept. 1896 – Dec. 1910

Total

Boys

Girls

No. of Pupils

100
90
80
70
60
50
40
30
20
10
0

1896   1898   1900   1902   1904   1906   1908

Years

No. of Full Time Staff

▲ MEN   ● WOMEN

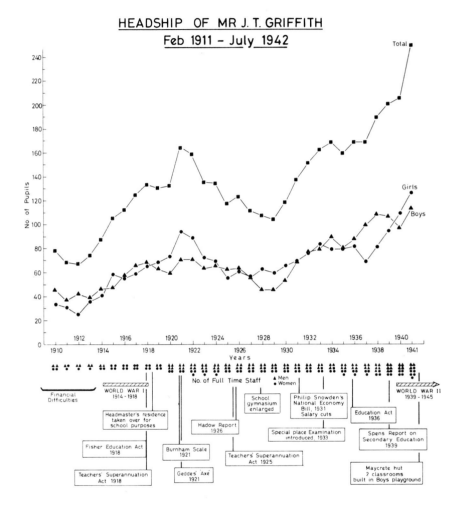

HEADSHIP OF MR J. T. GRIFFITH
Feb 1911 – July 1942

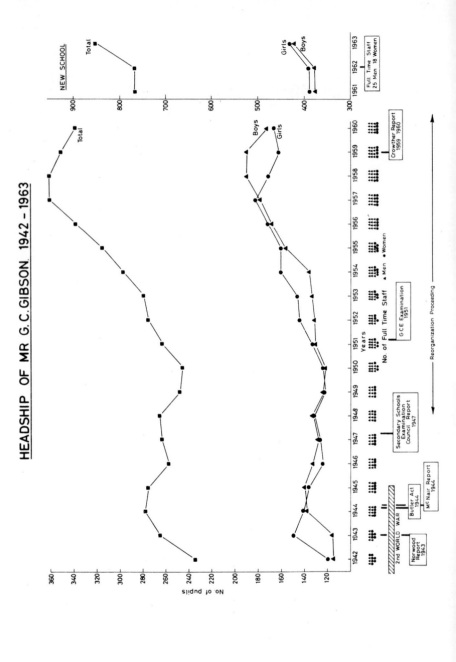

HEADSHIP OF MR G.C.GIBSON 1942 – 1963